Automobile Year book of

MODELS

2

1983 EDITA

Publisher: Jean-Rodolphe Piccard
Editor-in-chief: Alain van den Abeele
Editor (English language edition): Ian Norris
Assistant editor: Simon Fear
Contributing editors: Jean-François Balieu, Yves de Vooght, Jean-Daniel Favrod-Coune, Jacques Sauvan
Contributing photographers: Eric de Ville, Horst Neuffer
Layout: Max Thommen
Production: Charles Riesen

Correspondents: Eduardo Azpilicueta (Spain), Victor Davey (Hong Kong), Dennis Doty (USA), Ed Force (USA), Yoshiya Fujimatsu (Japan), Bryan Garfield-Jones (United Kingdom), Junichiro Hiramatsu (Japan), Frantisek Hronik (Czechoslovakia), Clive Rigby (Hong Kong), Jean-Michel Roulet (France), Aldo Zana (Italy), Henri Zwicky (Switzerland)

Contents

THE AUTOMOBILE YEAR BOOK OF MODELS is published in French under the title L'ANNÉE AUTOMOBILE DES MODÈLES RÉDUITS

Published by EDITA SA
10, rue du Valentin
CH-1000 Lausanne 9
Tel. (021) 20 56 31 Telex CH 26 296

ISBN 2-88001-139-6
Printed in Switzerland

A year of ups and downs

1982 has not been a growth year for model car enthusiasts. Certainly there have been new models — some of a very high standard — and some of the big manufacturers have seen their production figures rise, but as a general rule the mood has been one of pessimism. The euphoria of a couple of years ago is past; gloom is the over-riding feeling now.

It has been an eventful period, the fourteen months since April 1981 when we learned that Dinky Toys had been bought by American food giants General Mills of Minneapolis. General Mills took over a large part of the old Airfix empire on its bankruptcy, among their purchases being Dinky Toys, Meccano, and Airfix, three of the best-known names in the British toy industry. A few months later it was the turn of the *Le Jouet Français* group to go to the wall, leaving the Solido brand to go to Majorette and Humbrol to take over Heller.

A little later on we learnt that General Mills had no plans to re-launch Dinky Toys for at least two or three years and that Majorette was planning to move Solido down market to line up with their own distribution, which is essentially through supermarkets. The three models in the *Age d'Or* series introduced in 1982 did little to calm the worries of collectors for this classic marque's future.

Following these shocks there was relative calm on the mass-production front, with Corgi, Gama, Brumm, Matchbox, Polistil, Heller, Esci, Burago and Eligor coming up with some satisfying models and giving cause to think hopeful thoughts for the future of the handful of European manufacturers.

Then, just as work on this edition of the *Automobile Year Book of Models* (*AYBM*) was coming to an end, at mid-year, another bombshell dropped with the news that Matchbox — which had just celebrated the 25th anniversary of its Yesteryear series and was regarded as one of the leaders of the British model and toy industry — had been put into liquidation after its bank had decided not to renew its line of credit. The reasons for the troubles of Matchbox were twofold — ageing manufacturing plant and the difficulties of operating in the North American market.

Matchbox USA represented 55 percent of the group, but competition in the States is so fierce, particularly from Mattel, that Matchbox was forced to sell its products at prices whose profit margins were insufficient to cover the increase in raw material costs in Britain, where the models were being made. In addition to this problem, Matchbox had also attempted to give itself a stronger foothold in the USA by its purchase in 1979 of the American kit-makers AMT. It was a well known name, with an extensive range, but the purchase was an ill-advised one it seems, for AMT's moulds were ageing, as was its range of models and much of its production machinery. Coupled with the low quality of the plastic it used, these factors made the American firm less than a good investment, and its contribution to the parent company's profits was much less than had been expected. It was a hard blow to withstand. Matchbox's first real difficulties made themselves felt at the end of 1979. Ready cash was lacking, but it was needed merely to continue production. Unfortunately, the need for money co-incided with a period when British interest rates were at their highest for years. From this point on, the company was in trouble and became more and more dependent on the support of the Midland Bank, which was finally forced to set Matchbox on the road to liquidation. All this was in spite of a severe programme of economy measures which included a reduction in the number of employees from some seven thousand to four thousand all told.

Paradoxically, the company's European sales were healthy, including those in the United Kingdom. Equally paradoxically, the Midland Bank had been supporting Matchbox's new model development programme with the cash which was needed to plan for the future, a fact that should ensure that by the time these words appear Matchbox Toys (which was the name adopted by the re-structured company in July 1982) will have been sold to a British or American multinational. If that company is one from outside the toy industry — from the realms of food or finance, for instance — the business may be able to continue along its established lines. If the take-over is by another toy company, however, we must expect a break-up of the Matchbox empire and its ranges with all the negative effects that this must bring in its wake for our hobby.

The production problems Matchbox had are put in perspective when one realizes that no less than seventeen factories in the London area were involved in the production of Matchbox toys. An axle from here, a casting for a grille there, the whole posing a considerable logistics problem to the company's production planners. The manner in which they overcame it is a great credit to them. Another problem which faced Matchbox was the fact that its production facilities, new and up-to-the-minute in the sixties, were growing older and more out-dated as the years went by.

The specialist craftsmen

Productivity and efficiency were two words which were ringing in the ears of the small specialist constructors during the period covered by our annual review, for they too were feeling the cold wind of crisis. There was a flood of ideas from Italy, which showed itself in a proliferation of small brands, the majority of which confined their limited sales to the country itself, despite the quality of their productions. In spite of this, the general feeling was not encouraging. There were new manufacturers, full of enthusiasm, but the market was stagnating, with money both rare and expensive — a fact to which any number of specialist manufacturers can attest. For the collector, the problem was the same, and most cut back on their purchases as a result of continuing price increases.

It is painful to report, but it must be said that the boom for the specialist craftsmen is over, and sales figures are ample evidence of the unpleasant truth.

The pioneers of the breed were Jacques Simonet (1969), John Day (1971), Paddy Stanley (1971) and Barry Lester (1972). Francesco Di Stasio, Brian Harvey and Mike Richardson were quick to follow the movement, but the real growth in specialist manufacturers took place in the period between 1975 and 1978. At the end of that year there were more than 80 companies engaged in the manufacture of 1:43 kits in white metal or resin, mainly in Britain, France, Germany and Italy. A very small proportion of them were producing in respectable quantities of more than a thousand for each model, and the rest were engaged in supplying a very restricted market rarely totalling more than five hundred — and in some cases as low as one hundred — models per production.

A score or so of firms of varying sizes joined this number between 1979 and 1981, but a slimming-down process is now in progress. So far, more than 45 brands have disappeared from our original lists, which ignored those with extremely limited production. Among those which have disappeared are John Day, Circuit, Hobby Tecnica, Motorkits, MRE, Rampini, and A.P. Stanley. The newcomers are not filling up the gaps left by those that fall by the wayside, and there is no evidence that more companies will not fail in the face of the continuing climate of financial stringency, which is of course a disappointing prospect for the model car fan, particularly one specializing in limited production models. In order to track down these rare models he will have to become even more of an explorer and treasure-hunter, relying on subscriptions to magazines which themselves are often of a very limited lifespan and a network of correspondent enthusiasts in other parts of the world.

What are the serious possibilities for the specialist collector in 1983? Currently, the list of active manufacturers comprises the following firms: Abingdon Classics, AMR with the X and BAM-X ranges, Bosica, Brooklin Models, C-scale, Classic Cars with its subsiduaries GPM, Modsport and Dannini, FDS, Grand Tourisme, Hi-Fi, Idea 3, Ma Collection, Merri Kits, Mikansue and Mikansue Competition, Mini Racing, Plumbies and Plumbies Inter, Precision Miniatures, Manou Le Mans, Somerville, Tenariv, and Western Models. Twenty-eight brands which have a more or less regular production of worthwhile 1:43 models and which are distributed internationally to a greater or lesser degree. How many will still be here in June 1983? Of the group, only Western Models has achieved a semi-industrial status that seems to ensure its future.

It is obvious that the production volume of these specialist companies prevents them from carrying out the same type of commercial activity as the larger manufacturers, but they still have an important role to play, particularly in France, Italy, Germany and Great Britain. In the United States, however, Gene Parrill's Precision Miniatures and the Auto Buff brand, taken over by Automotive Miniatures selling under the Oakland Models label, are trying hard to make this kind of model better known. In Japan, Newcom and Cam are producing vehicles that are remarkable for the amount of detail crammed into a 1:43 model. Only craftsmen like Bosica and Brianza in Italy or Mike Stephens and John Hall in Britain, together with André-Marie Ruf in France, can produce models to similar standards. It should be mentioned at this juncture that the latest productions from Bosica, such as the Ferrari 375 MM Panamericana, are real masterpieces of detail, as is the Mercedes-Benz W 165 Grand Prix car produced by Mike Stephens' Western Models in 1:24.

The past twelve months have seen the specialist manufacturers confirming their split into three different camps. The first is composed of those manufacturing white metal kits at a relatively low price, such as FDS, Mikansue, Classic Cars, C-Scale, Tron, Idea 3, and Tenariv; the second group provides better quality, more detailed and more expensive models in built-up or kit form. Typical of these are Western Models, CAR, Bosica, and Somerville. The third segment is composed of those manufacturers whose irregular production is of super-detailed resin models, supplied fully finished at prices which reflect the high degree of handwork involved. Examples of these companies are Ma Collection, ABC, Eco-Design, Styling Models, Fadini, Progetto K, Etruria Models and Smart. From these hotbeds of craftsmanship come models which are elevating the art of automobile modelling to the same level as that of the finest railway models.

The industry

But Europe is home to much more than just specialists, and the period between June 1981 and June 1982 saw firms like Brumm and Eligor join the leading group which already comprised Burago, making progress in every scale, Polistil, Matchbox, Corgi Toys, and the slightly smaller trio of Gama, Conrad and Rio.

As far as plastic kits are concerned, Europe has nothing to fear from the rest of the world, with companies like Heller, Esci and Italeri producing collectors' items that will stand comparison with the best that America and Japan can offer. The case of Airfix is a little different from the point of automobile models because the company is now a part of the American General Mills group, whose toy division, Fundimensions, includes MPC, and a certain degree of cross-fertilization is therefore to be expected.

In Japan, Tamiya continues its unchallenged leadership of an industry whose production has fallen, together with that of the rest of the world, by anything from 15 to 20 percent. There has been an increasing trend among the Japanese manufacturers towards a stronger domestic flavour in their ranges, with more Japanese saloon cars and fewer European racing cars being modelled. It is a trend which will no doubt continue, fuelled by the antipathy towards Formula 1 which motor sport's politicians have engendered, thus damaging the reputation of the Formula and reducing public interest in it. The increased interest in the World Championship of Makes and endurance racing could see model makers turning towards this field of competition and producing models of Porsche 956s and Ford C 100s in place of the less interesting F1 cars. Such is the way the wheel of public taste turns.

But let us take a more detailed view of the way things were between June 1981 and June 1982 in two particular, and very different markets: Britain, with Bryan Garfield-Jones, and the United States, with Ed Force.

Britain: reasons for satisfaction

In Britain, the state of the toy industry through the year was an accurate reflection of the condition of British industry in general. The big manufacturers were feeling the pressure of imports, particularly from the far east, while the specialist manufacturers, selling to the top segment of the market, had difficulty in keeping up with demand. The interesting thing is that the orders came mainly from abroad; Western Models, Brooklin Models and Grand Prix Models (Classic Cars etc.) all reported this trend in their comments on the year.

The outlook was not so rosy for the big manufacturers, whose target market is a much younger — five to ten years of age — group of toy buyers (or recipients of presents) who are spoilt for choice. Their tastes demand brightly coloured models, with a preponderance of items based on the TV series which are the staple diet of the British child. There is little to attract the collector in such productions.

In the past, twenty-five or so years ago, boys played with model cars until they were ten or twelve years old before passing on to building kits and from there to the joys of a bicycle, motorcycle, or even an old car. Today, the six- or seven-year-old has an immense choice open to him, including electronic games, active sports, radio and records, and TV games — the list is almost without end. For those whose memory stretches so far, the difference between the toy store of today and the toy shop of twenty-five years ago is very striking; the space given over to model cars is one of the most remarkable differences.

What does the future hold for Britain? It must be admitted that the good old days are past, never to return. The day of the gadget is upon us, even in the field of miniatures; opening doors, low-friction wheels, the sounds of engines and sirens, remote control — we have come a long way from the Dinky Toys of yesteryear, with their attendant accessories of road signs, petrol pumps and road layouts.

Children still appreciate the qualities of a good model, but the industry has its own problems. For two years now it has been short of money as a result of the general recession and so it hesitates to invest and innovate, preferring to stick with the tried and true products which have shown themselves to be money-makers. And yet there is a place in the British market for a firm in the Brumm mould, as the relative success of the specialists has shown. They have made advances in their technique as a result of experience with their moulding techniques and their choice of materials; trial and error has made the business more art than science, but the results are satisfactory and on the whole today's models are much improved over those of ten years ago. We pay more for these improved products, but we get models which look well in the showcase and which the toy industry would never be able to produce.

On balance, an overall view of the year from June to June is an encouraging one, and there is satisfaction to be found with the progress made in Great Britain in view of the general economic conditions — apart, of course, from the failure of Matchbox at the end of June. But even this event may not be as bad as it seems, and we must wait to see whether it actually means a halt to the company's activities or merely another reorganization.

In general, the British can be satisfied, for there are some excellent specialized shops, a good mail-order network selling the products of the specialist manufacturers, a toy industry that is stronger than it was twenty-five years ago despite the unhealthy economic climate, and swapmeets which have grown from an almost unknown phenomenon ten years ago to weekly events. It has to be said that things are not going too badly.

The USA: survival and hope

What has happened in the United States this year? Not a lot! The economic situation has not helped, with the value of the dollar declining and the costs of models increasing — a state of affairs that has naturally led to a decrease in sales of those models that are available on the market. The brands that have ceased production, like Solido and Dinky Toys, are disappearing at a frightening rate from the few shops that stocked them, but there are many marques that never reach America except through the good offices of such dealers as Jim Wieland, who scour the world in order to obtain them. The net result is a small quantity disseminated among a limited clientèle. Another problem in the United States is that although some brands are imported, only a part of the range is available. Thus of the 150 Tomica models produced in Japan, only 72 are to be found in America — and then only one version of each model is available.

The typical American retailer buys his stocks from a typical American wholesaler, with a view to selling the maximum number of toys in a supermarket without any consideration for the collector, who finds himself on the margins. The supermarkets sell to their customers and don't want any hassles. Why should they bother if they don't have a particular model from Tomica in Japan, Zylmex or Playart from Hong Kong, or even Corgi Junior in the UK? They are in the business of selling toys to kids and their parents, who serve themselves from the rack next to the underwear counter. Most customers don't even know that any other models exist, so why should the traders bother?

Then, of course, there's the case of Lesney. For years, the company has offered its "75" range, and like collectors all over the world Americans knew that if they applied themselves and hunted around a bit — in fact a lot, because they had to cover a great deal of country — they could get hold of the complete range. Now, as sales fall for a variety of reasons, Lesney has made an effort to cater for the Amercian market by selling its 75 series in packaging specially produced to suit American taste. The models are those which, according to the latest market research, will most appeal to American children, who want only spectacular, gimmick-laden models, or those based on their favourite TV series or science-fiction film. However, these are not the models that appeal to the collector, despite the fact that Matchbox is by far the most popular range with the enthusiast, and a growing number of collectors are losing heart because of the increasing number of models they have to buy to keep their collections complete. They are obliged to buy models that do not interest them or to start a new collection — something that is not always to their taste.

This has led to an increase in interest in the so-called junk models, models which for the most part have their origins in Hong Kong and which sell for a dollar each. The quality may not be what we have come to expect, but they do have a certain charm, and can provide some unexpected pleasure from their haphazard style, which shows itself in such ways as a 1914 Vauxhall marked

"1941", a truck carrying the old Majorette emblem and labelled simply "Majorette Truck", and a copy of the Matchbox "Hairy Hustler" bearing the single word "Hairy"!

There are swapmeets, which have grown in size, but which consist mainly of the same people offering the same stock to the same collectors, and one can do little else but shake one's head on confronting the painfully familiar contents of the tables again and again. The situation gets worse as more and more collectors become participants in the hope of getting together some extra money to spend on their own collections, thus creating even more competition for the few new pieces which do appear. USA swapmeets are reaching a situation where more and more of the models are bought by collector/dealers who are discovering that their stock is almost identical to that of all their fellows and that consequently nothing moves.

In spite of all this, the hobby has continued to grow in America, and to attract growing numbers of collectors. Swapmeets are being held in new areas, which ensures a steady, if slow, trickle of new material. The main swapmeets are held in the Northeast, the Midwest, and California, which remains a priveleged place for collectors.

Among the big manufacturers, Kenner, the most co-operative and friendly, launched their Fast 111s (Fast Ones) this year, but they are more in the line of childrens' toys in the tradition of Mattel's Hot Wheels than accurate miniatures. Fortunately, the Hot Wheels series includes some very good models of real vehicles — even if the wheels do look somewhat out of place on something like a pre-war Cadillac limousine, for example. But at least the big manufacturers, catering for the mass market, are healthy enough. What of the others? What brand has done more to expand the market than Auto Buff, offering something new to the real amateurs? And yet there are rumours of financial problems for the young company. Last year there were queries as to whether Lionel would take over Dinky Toys, but now we hear that Lionel itself is in big trouble. Despite all this, the hobby is surviving and collections grow gradually, even if Americans do not always find everything they want and complain how badly the world treats them.

A healthy press is a healthy hobby

Yes, the hobby is surviving, and *AYBM* is here as the proof. There is no need to express pessimism: in fact, the opposite is the case. It has to be said that model cars, like any form of collection, need their journals to inform and link collectors round the world.

As examples of these journals, we can cite France's *Argus de la Miniature*, *Ma Collection* in Switzerland, *Model Car Journal* and *Scale Auto Enthusiast* in the USA, and *Collector's Gazette*, *Four Small Wheels*, *Modeller's World* and the new *Model Auto Review* in Great Britain. Monthlies and quarterly magazines from many countries reflect the vitality and interest of a thriving pastime. Similarly, such books as this one, together with such publications as New Cavendish Books, *Hornby Companion Series*, Haynes Publishing's book on Scalextric, the guides to Corgi Toys and Tootsietoys from Motorbooks International and the *Die-cast Models Easy Reference Evaluator* from Railway City of Ipswich Publications bear witness to the constant interest in the field of model cars.

And then there are the catalogues. They form a vital part of the hobby, almost the cement which holds it together. The productions of Märklin, Dinky Toys — both English and French, Solido, and Tekno belong to the past, but are still actively sought. They set a standard, however, which today's publications set out to match or surpass. From Brumm, Matchbox, Polistil, Rio, Burago, Siku, Western Models, Eligor, Majorette, Airfix, Revell, Tamiya, Italeri, Esci, Heller, Wiking and the rest come our contemporary references, the collectors' pieces of tomorrow. They follow a tradition which reaches back to before 1940, a tradition of continuing interest and pleasure. In addition, there are the catalogues issued by specialist suppliers such as *TSSK* from the Tron brothers from Loano in Italy and the *World Model Car Book* issued by the Lang brothers of Aachen in Germany. These catalogues are valuable reference works for those searching for information on a difficult subject.

Finally there are the various columns concerning model car topics that appear in motoring magazines throughout the world. They try to give news of new developments and products, to inform their readers, and occasionally to guide them. Each has its regular readers and contributes to the general well-being of the hobby.

It can be said that in spite of everything which may go against it, the hobby is in excellent health, and thriving.

An intruder in the non-smoking section causes a major turnout of the mixed-scale Fire Service! From top to bottom, the appliances are a Chubb Pathfinder (Corgi 1118), Citroën 'Traction Avant' 1948 (Eligor 1038, 1:43), Daimler-Benz turntable ladder (Wiking, HO), 1930 Citroën C4 (Solido 4403, 1:43), Magirus crane (Wiking 630, HO), 1928 Renault KZ (Eligor 1049, 1:43), Pinzgauer (Roco 1303, HO), Munga jeep (Roco 1300, HO), 1926 Citroën 5CV (Eligor 1056, 1:43) and Unimog (Roco 1304, HO). ▷

Airport Fire Service
Emergency Unit
5

NEW MODELS

on 4 wheels or more

It hardly seems like it, but a year has passed since our last edition, and once again it is time to take a look at the new models which the world's manufacturers, large and small, have introduced in the period since our last review.
The months between June 1981 and June 1982 brought some pleasant surprises and some moments of disquiet about the future of our hobby. It is obvious that the world economic crisis has had an appreciable effect on the model car world, and the flow of new models has slowed in the same manner as have production and sales figures.
Thus it is that we start this review in an unfavourable climate. Compared to that of last year, this review is more selective, since we have decided to concentrate on those models which have a real appeal for the enthusiast. It is a difficult task, made more difficult by the problems which beset the distribution of many models. Late availability of new models and the complete lack of availability in certain countries are just two of the setbacks which the collector faces.
The selective nature of this review naturally poses some problems in that it is of course influenced by the authors' tastes and interests. However, let us hope that it will be of value not only in that it gives notice that such and such a model has been produced, but also in that the few lines of description will avoid disappointment for those collectors who must buy without seeing the model. As more and more prototypes are modelled by more than one manufacturer it is worthwhile to compare the products of one firm with another — as it is valuable to compare with the same model which might have been produced elsewhere in the past.
Our annual catalogue is above all an overview of a total production, selecting that which seems to us to be classic and interesting. It is a production which we hope will permit model car collectors to draw even more pleasure from a hobby which shows every sign of growth — despite the less than encouraging atmosphere in which we find ourselves.

JUNE 1981

It is a well known fact that collectors do not take holidays, and every keen enthusiast knows before he leaves for a trip just what he will be looking for once he reaches his destination. How often has a trip abroad produced something special for the collection in terms of a version or colour which is not available at home, or a model never seen before. Before departure it's necessary to have the right addresses and a list of what to look for on arrival. Whatever happens, there is no rest in the hunt — even if constriction of the pocket-book limits one's buying power to the extent that some agonizing decisions have to be made as to what can be brought home.
Let us start off this first month of the holiday season with the models which were making their first appearances on British model shop shelves. *Mikansue* produced a 1:43 white metal kit of the 1943 Morris Minor. Yes, the date is correct — 1943 — the kit portrays the prototype of the car which provided the motoring backbone of Britain in the years which followed the war. The model needs a degree of preparation before assembly, but building is simple and the finished model is an attractive one. In his *Mikansue Competition* range, Mike Richardson introduced the Lister Jaguar which raced at Le Mans in 1963. This is one for the Le Mans fans — and there are enough of them. Mike Richardson produces a third range of models, called *Grand Tourisme*, and this

was joined by a Jaguar XK150. A true GT car sure enough, but the model leaves one a little unsatisfied.
Another white metal kit manufacturer, *C-Scale*, specializes in the models that others have ignored. Their 1961 Porsche Formula 1 car is a case in point. It is a good 1:43 kit which brings back memories of the time when Porsche fielded a factory F1 team of Bonnier and Gurney, plus the tall privateer from Holland, Karel Godin de Beaufort, in his orange car.
Grand Prix Models' *Classic Cars* range, under the direction of Brian Harvey, was increased by the addition of a Ford GT40 Mk II in its Daytona 1965 form. This was the first of what was to become a whole gaggle of GT40s from the Watling Street firm, all of which were to the same high standards.
In OO scale, *DG Models* introduced a 1930 Austin Seven Swallow Saloon, a simple kit which is none the less full of charm and character. *K & B*, a new name on the scene, announced a 1:43 kit of a 1964 Atkinson tractor unit. An unusual model that will appeal to commercial vehicle fans.
The popular *Corgi* and *Lesney* marques had not been idle either. Corgi issued a Peugeot 505 STI, a Chevrolet Caprice stock car, a BMW M1 racer, and a fine Ford Transit breakdown truck, all in 1:36. Although essentially toys, they are of excellent quality. Lesney's contribution was a Chevrolet stock car and a Ferrari 308 GTB in the 1-75 series and a Dodge truck in the SuperKings series at 1:35.
Finally, we come to *Western Models*, who introduced the 1955 Le Mans-winning D Type Jaguar. Available as a kit or in built-up form in 1:43, it is a particularly fine model.
Now to Japan to discover — not an easy task — the Bugatti Atlanta type 57S from *Rotarex* in 1:43. This exceptional model is made of resin for the bodywork and white metal for the accessories. Bugatti fans will love this one, but since it is produced in a limited edition of only 200 examples, not many will be able to afford it — still, where there's a will, there's a way!
The new models from the mass producers are more affordable, however. In *Tomy's Dandy* range there is a Hino fire escape in 1:43, a Nissan diesel "Pepsi" truck and trailer in 1:60, a Hino "Vanline" tractor and semi (1:60) and 1:43 VW Beetles carrying Ford and Rolls Royce — sacrilege! — noses. In the *Tomica* range there was a new four-wheel-drive Toyota Hilux truck in 1:62.
From Italy, *Brumm* is rapidly assuming the mantle of a classic model manufacturer. While fans were waiting for new cars from the marque, their appetites were whetted with a selection of driver figures, whose modern all-enveloping helmets made them more suited to contemporary cars than the kind of machine in which Brumm specializes. Although there is an air of toy about them, the figures come with an excellent sheet of decals that contain some seventy well known trademarks and emblems such as Ferrari, NART, Michelin, and national flags.
FDS remains the most active of the smaller craftsmen, as can be seen from the month's introductions in 1:43: a 1964 Ferrari 512 F1 car, a 1947 Fiat 1100S Mille Miglia Coupé, a 1961 Ferrari 250 GT Tour de France car, and a Ferrari 308 GTB in the colours of Olio Fiat as it appeared in the Costa Smeralda rally in 1980. It is evident that Francesco Di Stasio's main interests remain Ferraris and Formula 1.
The real excitement from Italy this month came from a new name, *Bosica*, who had alreaday produced a very detailed Alfa Romeo 1750. They followed up this 1:43 masterpiece with a same-scale white metal Ferrari 375 MM, which has everything. The bonnet opens to reveal a fully detailed engine, and the doors open on a completely equipped interior. The underside is as detailed as the upper surfaces, and the tyres have grooves of unbelievable fineness. It qualifies as one of the top models of this first crop of the season. Alongside it, one can place the series of four Porsche 911s produced by *André-Marie Ruf* in his *X* range. They are all

Grand prix models offers the Ford GT 40 in several versions in its 1:43 Classic Car range; this one is the 1969 Le Mans winner.

cars which have taken part in the Le Mans 24 Hour race, as was his other new introduction, one of the three Maserati type 151s entered by Briggs Cunningham in 1962. The models have photo-etched windscreen wipers, chromed accessories, and white metal construction.
From the USA came the Duesenberg SJ Speedster with Weyman body modelled by *Precision Miniatures*. Gene Parrill's company also offered an 'Andial' Porsche Targa which will appeal to the Porsche 911 collectors.
Finally, to Germany, where *Gama* introduced a very nice Audi Coupé in 1:43, featuring opening doors, bonnet, and boot (or hood and trunk for American readers). The grille, rear lamps and spoiler are all well reproduced, as is the interior detail, showing that European industry is still turning out fine models. An encouraging start to our new year.

Promotional models are popular in Germany, and luckily for us they also find their way onto the open market. Shown here are Conrad's VW Polo C, VW Scirocco GLI, Audi Coupé GT 5S, and VW Santana GL, all in 1:43, facing up to NZG's Mercedes 380 SEC in 1:35.

Bugattis in 1:43 from Brumm (the 1921 Brescia in British and French versions, refs 40 and 39) and Eligor (excellent miniatures of the 35B, here in French and Swiss colours, ref. 1025).

All those beautiful old adverts: a collectors' theme well supplied by Eligor and Lesney. From Eligor come 500 kg and 5 CV Citroëns and Opel Laubfroschs, among others (left: refs 1027, 1058, 1057, 1060 and 1064). Lesney favours the 1912 Ford T, 1927 Talbot and 1927 Ford A (page right: refs Y12, Y5, Y21 and Y3).

A rhapsody in blue: Western Models' 1981 Lotus Esprit Essex Turbo (WP 104K) and Solido's 1980 Renault 5 Turbo "Tour de Corse" (1023) and BMW M1 "Air Press" (1031). All in 1:43.

BIRD'S
CUSTARD POWDER
THE ORIGINAL & ONLY GENUINE
Alfred Bird & Sons.

NESTLÉ'S
MILK
The Richest in Cream
MOTOR "BP" SPIRIT
"BP"
2603
BRITISH PETROLEUM
COMPANY LTD

USA plastic kits

The market for plastic kits in the USA is considered "soft" at present. One would like to think the reason for this is the lack of exciting kits coming from the manufacturers, but that is not the case; excellent and exciting kits of general interest are being released. The real problem with a soft market may well be that people can't actually find the models they are interested in, and the hobbyist may not even know that his model is available. Here is where companies should take the lead and promote an active advertising program in the model car magazines. Ads and reviews generate interest in a kit, and if hobbyists don't see the kit on the shelves, they can ask for it. Hopefully the hobby shop will then be able to get the kit from the wholesaler, though all too often the shop can't supply it and a sale is lost.

Mail order may well be the key to obtaining the kits you're interested in. Buying mail order is not as much fun as going to your local hobby shop or discount store, but it's better than not being able to obtain the kit you want. Getting models out to the buying public is one of the biggest problems facing the manufacturers.

Another problem brought to light by reading the 1982 manufacturers' catalogs is the lack of models of older cars. In looking over all the catalogs, the oldest (new tooling) car is a 1969 GTO. Thankfully, there are some reissues of older cars, but even these are few. Street rods are hot now, customs are making a strong comeback and showroom stock-built models are more popular today than ever. Except for Lindberg and Jo-Han, all the model companies will have 1982 Firebirds and Camaros (scales from 1:32 to 1:8) in their line. They may be beautiful cars, but a little more variety would have been appreciated. Still, the companies have to go with the product they think will sell, and when it comes to the 1982 Firebird and Camaro, they are likely right. But can modelers support so many versions?

Finally, before the reviews of the year in plastic kits from the USA, a correction needs to be made. In our first volume of *AYBM* (1982) it was stated Jo-Han was out of business. Thankfully, that is not so. They haven't done much new tooling recently, but are into a great reissue program — and that is nothing but good news for the kit builders. And still more good news: they are also reissuing many of the promotionals they produced for the auto companies over the years. Unfortunately, USAirfix (not a part of Airfix toward the end) is gone and you have likely heard Airfix tooling was sold to Fundimensions (parent firm of MPC). MPC will be releasing much of the Airfix tooling, so that is good news for hobbyists this side of the pond. With that bit of gossip out of the way, let us proceed to the June 1981 releases.

AMT released two versions of the 1:25 Toyota 4 × 4 pickup in snap form. The stock one comes with a raft (2513) while the other has a camper cap and Fire Chief decals (2512). Well detailed and rugged enough for use as a toy, they're nice models a little plating would have helped. Reissued by AMT was the 1977 Ford Ranger F-350 Pickup (4611). Molded in light blue, and based on the annual kit, this model is a very well detailed and attractive truck in 1:25 scale.

Monogram released two new versions of their 1:20 models: the Jeep CJ-7 (2405) in Off Road trim, and the 1980 Corvette (2406) as a custom. In the series of 1:32 big rig snap trucks, Monogram added the Peterbilt Cabover (1208) and Kenworth Aerodyne Cabover (1209). The Aerodyne is one large, impressive truck and Monogram has captured it well. The Peterbilt also has the longer cab, popular with family truckers. As with all snap kits, a bit of paint detailing goes a long way to turn an impressive out-of-the-box model into a showpiece. Beautiful kits.

Hardly had the new Pontiac Firebird hit the showrooms before kits of it reached the model shop shelves in both standard and modified forms. This convertible from Revell is a 1:32 "no cement needed" kit.

MPC's 1:16 scale 1981 Firebird gets a few new parts in the Turbo Blackbird version (3083). A beautiful model when finished, the early releases need the hood shaved a bit near the windshield to get the hood to lift completely. You should also cut the seat hinges down near the transmission hump. This will allow the doors to close completely. This version comes with honeycomb wheels and is very impressive when completed.

Thunders Truck (0442) is MPC's 1981 Dodge pickup, but with parts for Truck Pulling competition; giant wheels and tires, blower and headers through the hood. The Outcast (0812) is a reissue of the "Firetruck" of the 60s, an interesting model in its own right, and there are also a great many parts for any street rod model. The 1981 Dodge D-50 pickup gets the off-road treatment in the Freedom Rider (0855) release; excellent wheels. In 1:20 is the Saber Vette (3751), a custom version of a 1981 Corvette. These custom releases should be appreciated by those who don't like the stock models, but even those who do could take these releases with their different-color moldings, add the stock parts, and have two different models of the 1981 Corvette. MPC's 1:32 snap series gets another version of the Jeep CJ in the Golden Eagle (3226). For the racing-car buff, MPC has reissued two very interesting models, the 1:25 scale Ford Mark IV (0561) and the 1:20 McLaren MK8d (0571) with decals for Denny Hulme and Bruce McLaren. Neither kit has been available for a while so both will be greatly appreciated by the racecar fans. And in the Dukes of Hazzard series Cooter's Tow Truck (0441) has been added; it's a 1972 Chevy.

MPC's experiment with 1:16 construction toy kits aimed at the youngster seems to have flopped. Out of production after less than a year, these kits deserved a better fate. Details were quite good and the models were interesting. Called Action Snaps, these four models were released earlier in a series called Construct-A-Truck. Unfortunately, they didn't make the grade then, either. Too bad.

Revell's releases were headed by the 1:25 snap truck of the Ford Ranger Styleside pickup (6413). Some of the parts are on the delicate side, so assemble with care; some parts just have to be glued. Detailing is excellent and makes for a most exciting model of this 4 × 4 truck. The rally version of the BMW 320i (7313) also has excellent detail; plated wheels would have been nice. When properly detailed, these chromeless kits do look pretty good. In the area of sets comes the Chevy Scottsdale 10 pickup and the Sandman Dune Buggy (with trailer) to make an interesting set (7404) in 1:25. The Sandman is a snap model and at the price of kits today, sets make for great value. Testor brought out a 1:20 Peterbilt Conventional (926) in snap form. It's quite impressive in this large scale.

European and Japanese plastic kits

June was the month of the utilitarian vehicle with the introduction of nine trucks, cross country vehicles and other jeeps.
Aoshima and Bandai, the only manufacturers who turned their attention to the touring car during the month, came out with almost identical models. Aoshima introduced a Toyota Soarer 2800 GT Extra and Bandai produced the basic model without the Extra. However, for the modeller these cars are quite different — Aoshima's car having 35 parts and Bandai's no fewer than 150. The former is a so-called modified car — the Japanese equivalent of the American term customized — with a special steering wheel, full CB (citizen band) radio gear, bucket seats, fins, extra wide wheels and lowered suspension.
Aoshima's car is in 1:24 scale, but Bandai chose 1:20 for its original version of the same machine. Bandai's is a much more detailed model, having four times as many parts as Aoshima's. The detail is reflected in the Japanese price — 1200 Yen as against 500 Yen. These two models, which complement Nichimo's 97-part, 1:24 scale Toyota 2000 GT, mark the beginning of a new era in Japanese plastic modelling. Gone are the days of total dedication to the super sports car like the Lamborghini Countach or Porsches of every variety. Today, Japanese model manufacturers follow more closely the series production makes of their national constructors. Four-wheel-drive is also making its appearence with Nichimo introducing four 1:20 scale models of what they call "comical jeeps" based on the Mitsubishi jeep, the Suzuki Jimmy, the AMC Jeep CJ-7 and the Toyota Landcruiser. These models, which range from 69 to 81 parts, are moulded in white, red, yellow and midnight blue and sell for 800 Yen in Japan. The quality of the moulding is good, and so are the general finish and decorations. Note that these jeeps are driven by an electric motor which does not detract too much from the end product.
In Europe, or more exactly in Italy, Italeri chose two trucks — both of them versions of the Volvo F 12 — the Standard and the Globetrotter. Although neither model has a single chromed part, they are well executed on the whole. Unfortunately the Globetrotter does not have the same markings as the one shown on the box. The transfers are not the traditional water type, but stickers which you should take care to put in soapy water first to make positioning easier. It's worth noting that there's a choice of 13 different number plates. The markings on the Volvo F 12 do correspond to those on the box. With their 230 or so parts, these models are generally satisfactory, and Italeri has been inspired to produce a container trailer with two axles for the two rigs. It is a very well made model, 50 cm (11.5 inches) long and weighing 1200 g (2.5 lbs) for a total of 120 parts. Sadly, once again, there is a difference between the picture on the box and the model inside, especially so far as the markings and the back door of the trailer are concerned. Moreover, the painting instructions are quite inadequate.

JULY

New model of the month is the 1936/37 Auto Union Type C 16-cylinder racer from *Casadio*. Long awaited, the model is not disappointing; a beautiful kit which will leave nobody unhappy. A difficult kit to build, without a doubt, but one which will give great satisfaction to its builders. To increase their satisfaction, we have a detailed article on the kit and its building techniques elsewhere in our annual.
Good as it is, the Auto Union still does not overshadow some of the products of the specialist 1:43 white metal manufacturers. One which immediately comes to mind is the Ferrari P4 from the Italian company, *CAR*. Once again, this is a model in which the bodywork can be removed to reveal a well detailed chassis and engine. Another Italian firm, *Artigiana*, beat Brumm to the post with their model of the "Auto Avio Construzioni", which is better known as the first car built by Ferrari, the type 815, made up from Fiat components. The 1:43 kit is in resin, and difficult to find outside Italy. Most people will wait for the Brumm version!
Bugatti fans will be looking out for the Bugatti Royale in its Esders roadster version from *Western Models*. Regrettably, the moulding quality is not up to Western's previous high standards, and the finished model is preferable to the kit version. The 1936 four and a quarter litre Bentley with Mulliner coachwork is better, but still not up to standard where moulding quality is concerned. While we are in England, let us mention *Lesney*'s introduction of a BMW M1 and a Rover 3500 in its 1-75 series. Other new models from the company were a Massey Ferguson tractor in the King Size range and a Mercedes 540K of 1937 vintage in the Yesteryear series. From *Classic Cars* came another GT40, this time the Mk II that won at Le Mans in 1966. There is plenty of work in this kit, but the results are worth it, and it is a car that was not previously available.

There is no record of the actual colour of the Bugatti Royale which M. Armand Esders ordered with the stipulation that since he would not be driving at night, no headlamps were required. The lines of the Western Models version of the car are accurate, but contemporary black and white photographs show that whatever colours the car was painted, they were not *those chosen by Western!*

An excellently detailed chassis and engine bay revealed beneath a lift-off body; the 1:43 white metal Ferrari P4 from CAR in Italy.

Stopped in front of the local pub are two gentlemen's speedy roadsters of the thirties. The first is Western Models' 1:43 SS 1 (WMS 35); behind it is an SS 100 (Solido 4002, 1:43).

The Duchess goes to the shops — in a 20/25 Rolls Royce with side-mounted spare wheel (Eligor 1030, 1:43).

What kind of woman goes alone to the cinema in a Mulliner-bodied 1936 Bentley? A little imagination, a few models like this 1:43 Western Models production, some 1:72 scale buildings as background, and a cast of 1:43 figurines enabled us to create a variety of scenarios. The buildings are from the Superquick range from Model Express Ltd, 331, Old St, London EC1V 9LE, and the figurines from Omen Miniatures of 22, Shelley Road, Horsham, West Sussex RH12 2JH, England.

If ever there were a couple of manufacturers adding fuel to the fiery argument about whether today's toys are tomorrow's collector's pieces, they are Italy's Polistil and Burago. On the top row we have, from the left, a Lamborghini Countach 400 in 1:23 from Polistil, a Martini Lancia Monte Carlo Turbo in 1:25 from the same company, a Group 5 Ford Capri racer from rivals Burago in 1:25, and a Ferrari Mondial 8 in 1:25 from Polistil. Below them is the new range of 1:43 models from Burago, comprising two versions each of the Lancia Stratos, Lancia Beta Monte Carlo, and Porsche 935. Transkits are already available to improve their accuracy.

In France, *Solido* was in its death throes prior to rising again in another life. The last true Solido was a real — and justified — success. It was the Renault 5 Turbo rally car, and it underlined the sadness which collectors felt at the financial problems of this classic French manufacturer. The Renault's lines were perfect, the interior was correct, even the wheels were accurate. There was only one quibble with the excellent Cartograf decals, and that was with the spelling of the word *championnat* on the rally plates, which reproduced those carried by Bruno Saby's car on the 1980 Tour de Corse. The miniature plates lack a letter N, but quibbles like this cannot spoil such a fine model. Another Solido model, not new, but more widely distributed than before, was the "Green Line" London bus, a companion to the more familiar red version and also with a detailed Cartograf decal sheet.

It was only a matter of time before the Le Mans-winning "Jules"-sponsored Porsche 936 driven by Jackie Ickx and Derek Bell appeared in model form, and it was the French specialist firm of *Mini Racing* which got there first, with a car that shows little variation from the equivalent 1980 model. Introduced at the same time was a nice de Cadenet in the colours of Belga, as raced by Alain de Cadenet and the Martin brothers.

After their Renault KZ Coupé de Ville, *Eligor* offered a Renault KZ Coupé Chauffeur. At first glance there seems to be little difference, but in fact the zamac body has been well modified. A cane finish decal and tiny carriage lamps give the model a charm all its own.

The fight between scales continued unabated, and evidence of the battle came from Italy, where *Polistil* introduced a Mercedes W 196 in 1:16. The model, moulded in zamac, has a number of interesting features, including operating steering, removable engine cover with a detailed 8-cylinder power unit in a tubular chassis, spoked wheels, and a detailed instrument panel. The competition between Polistil and Burago continued to push both of the antagonists to new heights. Polistil now manufactures to a number of scales and in a number of ranges, and the SN series was augmented by six newcomers the collecter should be aware of: a Porsche 924 Turbo (not a great success), a Ferrari Mondial 8, a Lamborghini Countach S and Miura, a Renault 5 Turbo, and a Rover 2600. The range is to a scale of 1:41, and is completed by models of the Lancia Monte Carlo, Alfetta, BMW M1, Ferrari Daytona, and Jaguar XK E. It's a pity about the oddball scale and trouser-button wheels.

Burago had not been guilty of sitting on their laurels, and their 1:43 series hit the market like a bombshell. The first six, despite their toy-like style, are well worthy of the collector's attention. There are two versions each of the Lancia Stratos, Porsche 935 TT and Lancia Beta Monte Carlo, and they are notable for well painted zamac bodies, plastic chassis, and a realistic interior. It has to pointed out that the Porsche and Lancia lack steering wheels, and all the models have standard-issue wheels on plastic axles, but at the price Burago charge, they are all bargains. We can expect a multitude of variations on these basic themes in the future, and Burago can only be congratulated.

And what of *FDS*? The Neapolitan specialist has come up with a boatload of new models: a 1981 Arrows A3, a 1981 Alfa Romeo 179C, a 1981 Tyrrell 010, and a 1963 Ferrari 330 LMB — as we said before, Ferraris and Formula 1!

At the end of the month, the long-awaited new models from *Brumm* made their appearance, underlining the important place the firm has now taken in the contemporary modelling scene. The new additions were versions of the Type 13 Brescia Bugatti, in black and Bugatti blue, and the first Ferrari, the Auto Avio Construzioni, in black. Bodies and chassis are in zamac, the lines are right, the details correct, and the value for the money is fantastic.

To finish off this month, let us turn to another Italian model, the Ferrari 275 GTB from *Progetto K*. The body is in polyester resin, there is a detailed interior,

Testor kits are almost unknown outside the USA, and the numerous European fans of fire-fighting vehicles will therefore have difficulty in finding this Chevy Scottsdale 4 × 4 fire control vehicle in the livery of the U.S. Forest Service.

spoked wheels, and some fine detailing. All in all, an attractive model for the rich collector.

USA plastic kits

AMT's reissue of the Cobra Roadster (4182) was welcome news. The last issue (four years out of production) was already selling for the incredible sum of 30 dollars. Reissued in the baseball superstar Reggie Jackson Series, the Cobra is still pretty much the same as originally issued in the 60s. Other models in the series are the 1963 Avanti (4181, rather hard to build, but impressive when completed), a 1959 Corvette (4183) — it's really a 1960 version, the only difference is in the seat pattern — which is almost as easy to build as a snap kit, and a 1932 Ford Roadster (4180). Four excellent 1:25 kits. AMT also reissued non-stock versions of the 1969 Mercury Cougar (4169) and 1976 Nova (4168) in the Street Machines series. Nice kits for those who don't care if they don't get all the parts to build a stock model.
Monogram's lone release for this month included a nice surprise. Their beautifully done (as modelers have come to expect from Monogram) 1981 Trans Am (2407) in 1:20 came with decals to make the Pace Car for the Daytona 500; minus the lights for the roof. The white body with red interior makes for quite a striking model with minimal detailing needed.
MPC released a 1:25 custom version of the 1981 El Camino, added a camper cap and called it "Branding Iron" (0854). Also reissued was a 1:25 near stock version of the 1957 Corvette given the title Velvet Vette (3717).
If you like snap pickups, you'll love Revell's 1:32 VW (6009) with Honda ATC. Detailing is very good and, with a minimum of parts, assembly should be simple. There are almost as many Jeep models as there are Firebirds and with its soft-top up, Revell's 1:32 snap version of the Renegade (6014) is a little different. In 1:25, the Ford 6-Wheeler Pickup (6414) shares many parts with the June release Ford Pickup, but the bed has outsized fenders to accommodate the two extra tires in the rear. The Blacktop Cowboy Corvette (6227) is a well done custom snap in 1:25 scale.
Testor's 1:20 snap series got three additions this month with a Chevy 4×4 Pickup with "Firefighter" accessories (927), a Chevy Blazer "Medivac" (928), and a 4×4 Chevy Van with "Coast Guard" markings (929).

European and Japanese plastic kits

No holidays for the Japanese this month; Aoshima, Nichimo, Otaki and Tamiya put seven new models on the market. Aoshima came out with a turbo version of the Toyota Soarer 2000 VR in 1:24 scale. This model, which is very close to June's 2800 GT Extra, also has 35 parts, is moulded in red and white and costs the same.
The customized cars also seem to have impressed Nichimo's designers because they introduced three models in July: a Mitsubishi Galant GTO 2000 GSR, a Nissan Violet Turbo and a Nissan Skyline 2000 GT-R — three highly aggressive machines in 1:24 scale with between 64 and 76 parts each. These constitute the next step for the modeller after Aoshima's Toyota Soarer, for example. It must be mentioned that Otaki's Toyota Corolla 27 Levin 1600, which comes in either green or orange, is the successor to a 1972 model. Before leaving Japan let us not forget Tamiya's Datsun Bluebird SSS-S Turbo in 1:24 scale. Japan's leading manufacturer of scale model cars and motorbikes has come out with the novel idea of matching a production car with a scooter, in this case the 50 cc Yamaha Towny. These Tamiya models are naturally in line with tradition, although they are simply made and aimed at the less experienced modeller and not the enthusiast who takes on 1:12 scale cars or 1:6 scale bikes. However Tamiya's range is wide enough to meet all requirements.
On to France where Heller has produced its version of the supercharged Bentley of Le Mans fame. "What, another one?" I hear you cry. You're right. It follows the 1:12 scale Airfix (the finest), the 1:32 scale version brought out some years ago by a Japanese manufacturer, and so on. Heller's 1:24 scale model comprises 123 parts. Moulding is good and the details are satisfactory. The two-piece engine cowling doesn't really open but can be removed. The painting is a major job, but Heller's instructions are always very full and there should be no difficulties.

AUGUST

Although it was, as ever, the height of the holiday season, the specialist manufacturers seemed not to know it, and the flow of new models and kits continued unabated. In England *Mikansue* announced a 1938 Triumph Dolomite roadster and *Classic Car Models* continued their theme of GT 40s with a road-going version, available, like its full-size counterpart, with left- or right-hand drive according to the customer's wishes. *Dannini Models*, another outpost of the Brian Harvey empire, introduced a Ferrari 750 Monza as a white metal kit in 1:43. This is a car that the pioneer of white metal, John Day, once produced in model form. Of particular interest to model railway enthusiasts, but also attractive to the car collector, are the *Dave Gilbert* OO models. Three new ones this month — a 1931 Morris two-seater tourer, a 1930 Model A Ford van and a 1934 Austin LL taxi. They are easy to make and very attractive, particularly the taxi.
Among the big manufacturers, *Lesney* introduced a Mercedes truck and timber trailer in their King Size series, and *Britains*, the agricultural model specialists, announced a Magirus-Deutz truck in flat-truck and livestock-transporter versions. The model has a tipping cab which displays the internal detail.
In Germany, *Gama* brought out two versions of the VW Passat, a saloon and a station wagon. Good models at a realistic price that make the passing of Dinky Toys, Solido and Tekno even more painful for the collector on a budget.
Putting such unhappy thoughts aside, we turn to the latest products from *Western Models*. They had tuned to Italy for two of their new models, a Ferrari 312 T4 and an Alfa Romeo 8C 2900 B Spyder. The Formula 1 car is well enough known, but the Alfa is a model of special interest. Mike Stephens, the boss of Western Models (see *AYBM 1*), had chosen to reproduce the car now belonging to Lord Doune, a Scot who owns and runs one of Britain's best motor museums; the car has a body by Touring of Milan. This model marked a return to Western's former high moulding standards, and is equally attractive as a kit or as a finished model. To maintain an English flavour in his range, Mike Stephens also modelled a 1933 Rolls Royce Phantom Continental — an extremely nice production.
If the British were building models of Italian cars, there was no reason why the Italians should not build models of English vehicles — and that is just what *Polistil* did. The firm's Jaguar E-type convertible in 1:16 — a scale which allows for plenty of detail — includes operating

steering, a detailed interior, and an optional top.

From France came two new Formula 1 cars from *Tenariv*, a Parisian specialist firm that has made this type of car its speciality. The Alfa Romeo 179C is better than its FDS counterpart both in terms of the realism of its lines and the quality of its moulding. The Renault RE 20 in the form seen first at Long Beach 1981 is not so well moulded by comparison.

The calm of the holiday season was broken somewhat for collectors by the news that *Matchbox* were to issue a selection of limited-edition vans in their Yesteryear series. To celebrate the 25th anniversary of the *marque*, Lesney announced plans to produce a van on the basis of their Ford Model T that would carry the inscription "25 years Models of Yesteryear — 1956-1981". It also became known that this van would be followed by a BP tanker on the same chassis and a "Nestlé's" van on the Talbot chassis. Although these models, and a wooden-bodied station wagon, were not due for release before October, the chase was already on for many collectors.

In the meantime the flow of new models from the Japanese factories continued. New additions to *Yonezawa's Diapet* series were a Mitsubishi Galant, a Toyota Soarer 2800 GT, a Nissan Leopard 280 X, and a Datsun Fairlady 280 Z with hard top, all the same 1:40 scale. *Tomy's Dandy* range was expanded with the addition of a 1:43 Toyota Land Cruiser and a new version of the excellent 1:43 London bus. Still in its traditional red finish, it now bore the inscription "Scotland Bagpipe", a phrase so meaningless as to bring complaints from both Scotsmen and London Transport enthusiasts. It no doubt goes down well in Japan, however. Previous inscriptions on the bus have been "Haig" (as in whisky), "Round London Sightseeing Tour", and the equally Japanenglish "London Toransport". How one appreciates the perfection of Solido's comprehensive decal set for their buses...

USA plastic kits

This month the 1:43 Street Magic reissues started coming from AMT. Some of these models have not been available in ten years, so they should be welcome. As far as detail is concerned, they are the best 1:43 plastic kits ever made. Unfortunately, AMT made this a budget series and eliminated the plated parts. That detracts a lot; I would rather have paid more and had the plated parts. Still, excellent models. This month's offerings are the 1968 Firebird (2105), 1969 Camaro (2104, first time for these kits in over ten years), 1967 Corvette Custom (2101), 1957 Chevy (2102), 1969 Mustang (2103), and 1969 Chevelle (2106). Also reissued this month is the 1:25 GMC Astro 95 cabover (6133). This kit comes with the popular airfoil (not shown on the box). I like the fact these AMT big rig trucks are still molded in white — it's so much easier to paint them. The cab on this kit is very well detailed; maybe you should add a light to the interior to show it all off.

Lindberg's contribution to kitdom this month is a reissue of a futuristic sports car renamed the Monte Carlo Racer (6555M). With many working features, even if you don't like the styling, this kit will supply a good number of parts for other projects.

If you think a 1:25 truck is big, you haven't seen Monogram's 1:16 big rig series. What 1:8 is to cars, 1:16 is to trucks. Monogram's latest is the Kenworth W-900 Conventional (2501). Top detail to a massive scale in a model 20 inches (50.8 cm) long. Much fine detail work on the tooling makes this kit worth a little extra effort in detailing. There are many plated parts, some bright chrome, some aluminum dull. In 1:24 is the Land Rover (2279). A rather plain car (no plated parts), Monogram has captured it well. All the doors are molded separately so hinging these would be a simple detailing feature. Also in 1:24 is the Chevy LUV (2280) in the four-wheel-drive High Rollers series, with very high ground clearance. In 1:32, Monogram combined several of its big rig models into sets. One with "Eskimo Pie" decals is a Peterbilt Conventional and Reefer Van (1302), and the Kenworth W-900 Aerodyne Conventional and 40' Van have Sea Land decals (1303). The different decals in these sets make them desirable, even if you have the single releases. Well detailed snap kits, interesting trucks.

MPC's 1982 annual releases started this month with the Omni 024 (0815), Mustang (0816), Jeep (0856), El Camino (0857), Dodge D-50 (0858) and the Corvette (3718), all in 1:25. Because the real cars were changed so little, the models followed suit. New annual releases are exciting, and the Cavalier (0813) was no exception. Best news for the month though were the 1:16 scale 427 Cobra (3082) and 1:12 Christie Fire Engine (2002) in the Masterpiece Collection series. The Cobra had been eagerly awaited and we were not disappointed. MPC not only provided the expected opening hood, but also opened the doors and trunk. This kit builds fairly well, though early releases had a bit of a problem with the windshield, which has now been corrected. With two sets of wheels, two engine options and soft-top up, this is a great kit of a great car. Quality is also the same for the Christie, with its choice of fire-station decals, and a built model is truly impressive. Not for the novice, these Masterpiece kits are aimed at the adult builder. Parts are plated in "brass" and chrome, and there are a lot.

An old fire engine — now there's a nice change from the Firebirds and Camaros! This MPC kit reproduces in 1:12 a Christie steam pump of 1911. With over 300 pieces, it is strictly for the experienced modeller, who will no doubt notice the chrome and brass plated parts are a little heavy and that mould marks are just a little too numerous.

Revell released a 1:25 Escort Turbo Street Machine (7316), a tasteful custom, and two 1:32 snap kits; a VW Pickup Street Custom (6011) and a Safari Jeep (6016).

European and Japanese plastic kits

The end of the holidays was in sight and the manufacturers jockied for position. No fewer than 13 new 1:24 scale models came from the Land of the Rising Sun, and they were made by Fujimi, Nichimo, Crown, LS and Tamiya. From Fujimi, apart from three versions of the Nissan Leopard (TR-X American 280 X, 280 X SF-L hot rod and TR-X American hot rod), came the Isuzu Piazza XE. It's a very pretty car in silver and was designed by the prominent Italian coachbuilder, Giugiaro, of Ital Design. Shown first as a prototype in the 1979 Geneva Motor Show, this car came on the Japanese market in June 1981 powered by a two-litre engine with single or twin overhead camshafts developing 120 bhp and 135 bhp respectively. It was therefore a worthy performance by Fujimi to bring out a scale model just two months after the real car appeared on the roads.

Nichimo offered four big-booted, hot rod models with impressively wide wheel arches and spoilers everywhere. They are all in 1:24 scale, consist of between 63 and 71 parts and cost 600 Yen in Japan. Crown introduced a Honda Z GS and a Mitsubishi Minicar GSS in 1:20 scale, while LS, which specializes in replica pistols, continued its car collection with a Toyota Soarer 2000 VR Turbo in 1:20 scale. We're beginning to see doubles appearing with this car, and if things go on at this rate, we might find ourselves in the same situation as at Nuremberg in 1978 where no fewer than 15 versions of the Lamborghini Countach were discovered. On the other hand it is just this sort of event that stimulates competition and results in progress in model-car production.

Tamiya, which had not forgotten 1:24 scale — far from it — announced two new models: a Nissan Leopard with a Honda Tact 50 scooter, and yet another Toyota Soarer 2000 VR Turbo, this one matched with an 80 cc Yamaha Beluga.

SEPTEMBER

Let us start with a model so near to perfection that it has become almost unobtainable since its appearance. It is the Ferrari 250 GT produced in Japan by *Kojima Newcon*, a specialist brand which produces models in built-up or kit form. The 1:43 models are extremely expensive by the time they leave Japan, and only a few collectors will be able to afford them. However, when you see the quality of this model, on the rare occasions when it is to be found outside the Land of the Rising Sun, it is no surprise that it will also no doubt be bought by many who *cannot* afford it! In terms of quality, it is reminiscent of a Fulgurex model railway engine... enough said.

Back to reality however, with a German car from a German company, *Gama*, whose name is a guarantee of high quality. The car is the new Opel Ascona, reproduced in 1:43 and available in two or three box versions, just like the real thing. Gama worked from the factory's own drawings when preparing this model.

Apart from this, the scene was quiet, indicative of either the holiday spirit — or the start of an economic down-turn.

Among the few new introductions, one of the best was from *Ugo Fadini*, the Italian craftsman, who announced two versions of Mickey Thompson's 'Challenger One' land speed record car, in polyester resin, and to a faithful 1:43. The first version of Challenger One was equipped with four 6.7-litre Pontiac V8s and made an unsuccessful attempt on the record in 1959 at the famous Utah salt flats. Thompson could only better the existing record in one direction, so he returned to his workshop and fitted four GM diesels with Roots-type superchargers. They produced 3000 horsepower, but gave up the ghost after only one run. Fadini's models, supplied completely finished and decorated, are nothing short of perfect in their reproduction of the lines of the originals. We have come to expect high quality from this maker, and these models maintain the standards.

Another brand with an excellent image is that of *Brooklin Models*. The English firm has produced a 1931 Hudson Greater 8 roadster, whose boat-tail body and white sidewall tyres are particularly well reproduced. John Hall has worked well on this one, with a model and paint job which live up to the reputation he has made for himself.

Among the more industrial firms, *Lesney* introduced a Peugeot 305 in its Super-Kings series and a Ford Model A "Woody" in the Yesteryear range. The latter is a good model, if a little let down by its plastic-looking woodwork. Another newcomer to the Yesteryear range was a Ford T van with "Smith's Crisps" decals. This model was originally produced as a promotional for the makers of the crisps (potato chips for American readers), and there were a number of stories of collectors who had spent a fortune on buying crisps so that they could qualify for what they thought would be a very limited edition. Now that the model is to be released

Simply superb — if you can ever find one and afford to pay for it outside Japan — Kojima's Ferrari 250 GT in 1:43, sold under the Newcon label.

to the general public, one wonders what the reaction of those who paid large sums for the originals will be. For their sake let us hope that there is some small detail which will distinguish their models from the latest ones.

Just as collectors were coming to the end of the month and feeling that it had not been too expensive, *Eligor* brought out their new models to tempt them into opening their wallets again. There was a Renault NN of 1927 with a closed hood and a bonnet which could be removed to display a detailed engine, a Mercedes saloon which now appeared with "Kaiserhof Hotel" on its flanks and baggage on its roof, and a 1928 Renault KZ fire truck. On the commercial side, there was a 5CV Citroën van in Michelin colours complete with the figure of "M. Bibendum" on the roof, as well as a Citroën 500 kg van in the same livery. Whilst on the subject of Eligor Citroën 500 kg vans, collectors may like to know that the rarest of these are those bearing the André Citroën, Franz Carl Weber, and Autotint liveries.

Last newcomer of the month was from *Western Models*, whose SS 1 Jaguar is one of their best products to date. The essence of realism, it is a classic, with smooth flowing lines that capture the spirit of the original perfectly. Another classic was the Ferrari Testa Rossa in the *Burago Diamonds* series of 1:18 cars. The Testa Rossa will be a must for collectors in years to come, with good mould quality, movable parts, and fine detail. After the Bugatti and the Mercedes, this 1958 Ferrari worthily upholds the high standards of the Diamonds range.

USA plastic kits

One of the year's most exciting releases finally arrived from AMT. Announced over a year before, the 1:25 scale 1968 Camaro (4173) was in the shops! The wait was well worth it. Even though AMT had a 1968 Camaro in their annual releases, this version was designed with totally new tooling. Proportion is ex-

A symphony in silver-grey brings together a group of Mercedes models in front of a selection of pictures of the real thing. On the right, three Brumm 1:43 miniatures of varying quality: the 1964 W 196 (R 74), the 1937 W 125 (R 70) and the 1938 Vanderbilt Cup W 125 (R 71).

Polistil was another firm to produce the W 196, this time in 1:16, but the model is more of a toy than an accurate replica, as the contemporary photographs show. Cursor's version of the same car in 1:43 was originally produced as a promotional for Mercedes Benz, and is accurate right down to the tartan seats.

After tractor-pulling, the next American sport just had to be truck racing, and of course the kit manufacturers are right up with the trend. This 1:25 International Conventional comes from Ertl, long-time commercial vehicle specialists.

Planned to tie in with the Burt Reynolds film "The Cannonball Run", only three of these models actually got away from the start-line. The Chevrolet Malibu Grand National racer, Lamborghini Countach and Ambulance reached the stores, but the Airfix-tooled Aston Martin was never marketed.

American kit manufacturers do not always draw on the products of their domestic industry when choosing cars to model. These two 1:25 models of European cars from Revell supply the proof. The Escort XR-3 is strictly stock, but the Porsche 928 is a heavily modified Targa version by Germany's b&b styling studio.

Now that it has been replaced, the old Chevrolet Camaro will no doubt soon achieve the status of a classic car. Revell chose to help the legend along with this 1:25 Snapkit of a Z-28 in black with red trim.

cellent and there are a minimum of parts, so construction receives only two dots on AMT's "Skill Level" (an excellent method to tell how difficult a kit is to build). A special order blank for Scale Auto Enthusiast was also enclosed in early runs of this kit offering this fine magazine at a hard-to-beat price. The model companies finally seemed to be listening; other "Muscle Car" era kits were to come. AMT also reissued their Logging Trailer (6605) this month, complete with load of logs or a girder.

Ertl's International Race Truck (8039) was their first plastic truck kit in a while. This Conventional includes all the extra goodies needed to take a truck for a trip around the race track. Interesting kit.

Further MPC 1982 annuals were released this month. With no years on the boxes, they hardly seem like annuals any more, but available are the 1982 Chevy Pickup (0444), Dodge Van (0445) and Ford Bronco (0446) in 1:25 and the 1:20 Corvette (3757). This was also the month for the Cannonball Run kits. Unfortunately, the Aston Martin DB5 (Airfix tooling) was never released. The rest were, though, and of these the Chevelle Stock Car Racer (0681) seems the best received (it's easily modified into a true NASCAR racer); others are the Dodge Emergency Van (0447) and a Lamborghini (0682). Molded black, the Lamborghini looks good, but lacks engine detail. In 1:32 came the Fast 111s series. Based on the Kenner die cast models of the same name, the big feature here is the individual license plates. Pretty much aimed at the kids, the four models had two releases each, molded in different colors. The Jet Vette was the best and is a nearly stock 1981 Corvette (custom wheels); the Dirt Digger is a nice dune buggy model. These are snap models.

The USA received the European version of the Ford Escort XR-3 (7317) in 1:25 from Revell. I am really fond of these small cars (great custom potential if you so desire) and the European version looks great. I also like the decals for the seats; a great way to get a pattern on them without paint. Also released this month was a custom Ford Courier (7231; not my personal styling favorite) and a Firebird Street Custom (7230; which was, except for the whale tail spoiler). Also out were another version of the 1:16 scale custom Corvette, Turbo Vette (6603) and a 1:25 snap Chevy Blazer "Mudslinger" (6217), Ford Flairside Pickup (6414), Z-28 Camaro (6221), and the "Malibu Grand Prix Racing Team" (6412) with a Virage racer and Toyota pickup which makes a very interesting set.

In 1:32 scale, snaps (with garages) from Lindberg included four excellent reissues of their simple but well detailed annual models of several years ago. Available again are a 1974 El Camino (387), 1974 Mercedes Benz 450SL (388), 1975 Monte Carlo (389), and 280Z Datsun (390). Also reissued are their series of construction vehicles; a 1:40 Dump Truck (1244), 1:40 Loader (1225), and 1:60 Road Scraper (1226).

European and Japanese plastic kits

So far as production was concerned, Japan held the inside track with unceasing output, 1:24 scale being the most popular. Nichimo alone generously brought out seven new models. Nissan was decidedly the most favoured with

1:24 scale models of the Fairlady, Skyline, Violet and Laurel as well as the 168-part Skyline 2000 GT Turbo in 1:20 scale, also in hot rod versions. There was an interesting new model from Mitsuwa of a Japanese truck: a Fuso K-FV 214 JR cab which deserves a mention even though it lacks the impressive looks of the American rigs. The offering from LS is the 1:20 scale Nissan Leopard Turbo.
From France comes a welcome surprise with the 1950 Talbot-Lago Record. Its 110 parts in 1:24 scale need a lot of work, especially the painting. Indeed, the body is full of mould marks and the bonnet is brown, quite different from the original which was all blue, like French racing cars have always been. The moulding on the whole is good, and the wire wheels are probably the best example today of plastic work in this scale. The dashboard is cast in one piece with the windscreen and is therefore transparent. The painting instructions are very precise, allowing a perfectly respectable finished product. Heller supplies two transfers for the main dials and the others have to be painted. The chromed parts are fine but they are too firmly attached to the stalks and this detracts from the finish. The tyres are no more than adequate. Let us add that the rim of the windscreen should be chromed; it will have to be painted or covered with aluminium foil, Bare-Metal or a similar product. Heller can be congratulated for producing a very fine model, one of its best, of a fascinating car which can be seen at the Rochetaillée museum near Lyon. Apart from the Talbot-Lago, Heller's other September offering was a 1:43 scale R 5 Turbo of 30 parts in a Tour of Italy version.

A pleasing kit of the 1950 Talbot Lago Record from Heller in 1:24 — the wire wheels are particularly good. Heller have also produced a 1:12 version of the Renault RE 20/23. Formula 1 fans have the choice of three kits of this car, from Heller, Tamiya and Protar. The choice is between French simplicity, Japanese complexity, or extreme precision from Italy.

OCTOBER

Once again, it was the British specialist firms who set the pace this month. *Western Models* continued its breathtaking rhythm with a new Formula 1 car, the Marlboro McLaren MP4 which took John Watson to victory in the 1981 British Grand Prix, accompanied by a Lotus Essex Esprit Turbo.
Dave Gilbert also maintains a regular flow of new models, and the latest additions to his range of OO gauge white metal kits were a 1925 Austin van, a 1934 MG Tickford, and an MG PA 4-seat Tourer of the same year.
Auto-Replicas, Barry Lester's company, announced a Chevrolet Bel Air in hardtop and convertible forms. It has to be said that this is not a good replica, and it is disappointing to see the way in which the quality of the products of this company has fallen, particularly in view of the fact that in the past they have produced some very good 1:43 kits.
Lesney's Talbot van in the colours of Nestlé's Milk finally hit the shops and collectors were not disappointed with the attractive pale blue, grey and black colour scheme with high-quality decals in dark blue and white. The model will have a strong appeal to collectors as well as aunts looking for attractive presents for nephews. The Yesteryear Talbot van was introduced in 1979, and just for the record, the versions which preceded this model bore the colours of Lipton's Tea (firstly with the Royal crest and latterly with the City Road London address), Chocolat Menier, and Taystee Old Fashioned Enriched Bread.
Continental European collectors were busily engaged in working out how to get hold of the 25th anniversary version of the Yesteryear Ford van, which had gone on sale in Britain. Finished in pale green with a grey roof and dark green chassis, it carries attractive silver lining and lettering to celebrate the marque's Silver Jubilee. Even the box is white and silver instead of buff and gold. In short, a must for collectors.
Still in Great Britain, there was a new model from *Scale Racing Cars*, a small specialist manufacturer whose philosophy is to work slowly, but to produce models of great accuracy and very good detail. The new model is of the Marlboro-sponsored BRM P 160 B with which Jean-Pierre Beltoise won the rain-soaked Monaco Grand Prix in 1972. It is well up to the standards of previous models from the company.
The same comments which we have made about the BRM and its makers are also applicable to the Italian firm of *Hi-Fi*, which produced models of the 1966 and

Scale Racing Car's 1972 BRM P 160 B; a British model that nears the peak of 1:43 scale accuracy.

One of the most realistic models of the year is this 1:43 Lada Niva 4×4 exported from the USSR by Saratov. Features include opening doors, coil-spring suspension, individually moulded headlamps and working steering.

1967 Brabham-Repcos that enabled Jack Brabham and Denny Hulme to take the World Championship in those two years. These are another two cars which John Day produced in his time — which was, let us not forget, almost ten years ago... almost a generation of collectors. Previous Hi-Fi productions have been an Osella FA Formula 1 car of 1980 and a 1964 Ferrari 158 Formula 1 car in NART colours.
From *Brumm* came some new variations on existing themes. The Ferrari 815 Mille Miglia car in black was joined by a road version in red, and the 1937 Fiat 508C Millecento appeared as a fire brigade car and a very nicely finished replica of a Milan taxi, in the dark green and black colours used in that city until comparatively recent years.
The new *Burago* model was of the Zakspeed Ford Capri Turbo and is up to the standards we have come to expect from this company. In 1:24, the car has opening doors, bonnet and hatchback, operating steering, and an interior which is fully furnished with a bucket seat, roll-bar and detailed instrument panel. The engine is fully detailed too — what more could you ask?
Turning to a country that has not so far appeared in our review, Russia, we find the new model from *Saratov*, the Lada

If the success of the real car is anything to go by, there will soon be as many kits of the 1982 Pontiac Firebird Trans Am as there were of its illustrious predecessor. Monogram offer this perfect reproduction in 1:24 with chrome parts, a detailed engine, vinyl tyres and a wealth of fascia panel detail.

Even if you are only interested in production vehicles, do not neglect this 1:24 Monogram Street Vette. In fact the kit contains all the parts necessary to build a stock 1957 Corvette apart from the wheels and tyres, which are modern. Paint it in contemporary colours and you will have an excellent model of what Chevrolet love to tell us is ''America's only sports car''.

The 1971 Plymouth 'Cuda two-door was a real muscle car, with horsepower to spare. The 6.9-litre V8 developed 425 hp and returned an average fuel consumption of around 10 miles to the gallon. Monogram's 1:24 kit only consumes cement and paint.

Monogram's metal-bodied kits went out of production this year, but the 1956 Thunderbird continues to be produced in plastic, alongside the 1953 Corvette and the MG TC. However, the Jaguar XK 120, the Duesenburg Boatail Speedster and the Packard Dual Cowl Phaeton have disappeared from the range.

The fact that Monogram have chosen to model a 1969 Pontiac GTO Judge in 1:24 for 1982 introduction shows how popular taste is turning back towards the old breed of muscle cars.

This Turbo Vette is not something you will be able to see at your friendly neighbourhood Chevvy dealership. It comes from the Revell styling department rather than that of GM, and exists only as a 1:16 cementless construction kit. Detroit would not be ashamed of it, however; it shows nicely restrained taste.

The colourful box of this Ertl Volvo N-10 in 1:25 does not deceive its buyers. The kit combines over 150 metal and plastic parts to produce a highly-detailed model with steerable front wheels, full engine and interior equipment, and a full set of decals. Everything needed to create a very satisfying model.

Niva four-wheel-drive vehicle. This is a truly beautiful little model in 1:43, with a chassis and body in zamac and an interior in black plastic. The doors open, there are separate front and rear lamps, the exterior mirrors are chromed, the steering works, the suspension is faithfully reproduced with four coil springs — in brief, this model is an example of just what can be done with a mass-produced 1:43 model car and qualifies as one of the models of the year.

October turned out to be a very good month, for it also saw the introduction of a new version of the 1955 Mercedes W 196 Formula 1 car. This one came from the German company *Cursor* who originally supplied it to Mercedes as a promotional model — a sure measure of its accuracy and quality. Every detail is there, the line is right, the tyres are supple, the wheels have spokes — even the tartan seat-covers are reproduced. A model of extremely high quality at an affordable price.

The month ended with an exciting news item: *FDS* was to collaborate with *Bosica* to produce a model of the 1981 Ferrari 126K Formula 1 car. Rumour hinted at superdetailing, and collectors were all agog to see what the marriage would bring forth.

USA plastic kits

AMT issued four more of their 1:43 snap kits, again without plated parts: the 1969 Torino (2107), custom 1967 Camaro (2108), custom 1967 Barracuda (2109), and 1969 AMX (2110). Even without the chrome, these are still excellent kits worth picking up. Also released was a 1:25 custom version of the 1968 Camaro (4166) in the Street Machines series. This version came with hole in the hood for the velocity stacks, and custom wheels. Also in the Street Machines series is the 1:25 1973 Mustang Mach I (6167), a reissue of an annual that was modified into a Trans Am type racer. In 1:25 snap kit is the 1980 style Camaro Z-28; the Cheverra Z-28 with a stock trunk lid.

Truck modelers received an early Christmas present from Ertl in the form of a new and not previously announced truck — and a foreign one at that. It was also a bit different in that the frame rails (but not cross members), axles and fifth wheel were in die cast metal, for strength. The 1:25 Volvo N-10 (8037) is a beautiful truck and the Ertl team have outdone themselves in transfering it to plastic (and metal). I especially like the two-piece gas tanks (differently done) and pretty much flash-free metal parts. A true must for truck modelers. Early releases had an 8 x 10 inch color photo of the real truck included in the kit.

Lindberg reissued some more of their 1:32 annuals (snaps), added some gaudy parts and called them Stock Cars; racing variety. Available are the 1975 Grand Am (391), 1973 Barracuda (392), 1975 Grand Prix (393), and 1975 Buick Century (394). No stock wheels, but these are otherwise excellent models.

Monogram released four 1:32 snap kits in the "Hot Wheels" series: the "Hot Bird" Trans Am (1039), Turbo Mustang (1038), Bronco 4-Wheeler (1041), and "Corvette Sting Ray" (1040). Also in 1:32, but glue kits, are the Ford EXP (pleasant surprise, the Escort was the an-

Monogram make kits in both 1:24 and 1:32, but it is difficult to tell the difference from a photograph, for the same attention is paid to both, with accurate lines, chromed parts, and vinyl tyres. From the left, top, they are: Ford Turbo Mustang (1:32), 1968 Pontiac GTO (1:32), 1970 Mustang Mach 1 (1:32), Corvette Sting Ray (1:32), Chevy Malibu Police Car (1:32), 1970 Chevy Malibu Modified (1:24), BMW 635 CSi Group II racer (1:24), Chevy Citation "X" (1:24), and 1969 Z-28 Camaro (1:32). All the 1:32 scale models are no-glue kits.

nounced model, 2005), 1969 Nova (2006) and 1969 Charger (2007). Unlike most 1:32 models these kits come with not only plated parts, but also engine and vinyl tires. About the only thing these excellent models lack set against their 1:24 relatives is the number of parts. Just looking at the pictures, there is no way to tell the scale. Even if you are not into 1:32, these models are not to be passed up.

European and Japanese plastic kits

This month's major new product came from France: Heller's 1:12 version of the Renault RE 20/RE 23 Formula 1. It appeared a year later than Tamiya's model and failed to attain the unbeleivable quality of the Japanese product. In spite of this, it has all the makings of an interesting model, not least because it is supplied with two cockpits: the RE 20 with outside rear-view mirrors in which René Arnoux won the 1980 South African Grand Prix, and the RE 23 with built-in mirrors which Jean-Pierre Jabouille drove to victory in the Austrian Grand Prix of the same year. Consisting of some 200 well moulded pieces, this model marks a distinct step in Heller's progress from the Ligier JS 11, which was too short, too chubby and fitted with unattractive, plastic tyres. Moulded in yellow, grey and chrome, the Renault requires, like all Heller models, a major paint job. However, again like all Heller models, the blueprint includes perfect painting instructions. Moreover the box cover provides all the colour references for the best possible result. The number of parts means that Heller's Renault is a simpler assembly job than Tamiya's 370-part version. The detailing is therefore more modest and so is the overall result. This model will suit better the modeller with less experience than the person who takes up the Tamiya challenge. Heller deserves strong criticism for insisting on providing its large-scale models with fixed suspension and rigid springs. To be frank, it's a serious and unexpected deficiency on the part of a manufacturer which otherwise does good work. The front wheels cannot be turned from the steering wheel and the two half axles of the back wheels are fixed. Of course simplification, whether intentional or not, pays, especially as Heller's Renault RE 20/RE 23 is as expensive as Tamiya's. At least, unlike the Ligier, it is provided with soft rubber tyres; some recompense.
In the Far East, Nichimo expanded its jeep collection with four slightly modified versions of its June offerings. Nagano launched a 1:20 scale, motorized Nissan Fairlady 280 ZX Turbo in black with an aluminium bonnet. It's the Targa version with two small removable hoods above each front seat. This model has beautiful lines and magnificent star wheels. Tamiya continued its 1:24 scale collection with a Nissan Leopard and a Toyota Celica XX 2800 GT, each with its now inevitable scooter — a Honda Tact 50 for the Nissan and a Yamaha Beluga for the Toyota. These scooters are riding the crest of a fashion in Japan, and some specialists predict that the craze will soon reach Europe. Wait and see!

We can only hope the Newcon Mercedes 300 SLR Coupe will be distributed a little more widely than previous offerings from the unchallengeable producers of Japan's best models.

NOVEMBER

The months of November and December are two of the best of the year for collectors. As the wintry weather worsens outside, we are warm and comfortable at home, building, painting, sorting. It is at this time that the hobby takes on its most satisfying form, made even more satisfying if there are swapmeets and shows to visit, with the opportunities to find bargains and pick up snippets of information about new introductions. Readers in more temperate climes and south of the Equator must forgive this strictly European outlook on the seasons, but the basic premise is the same the world over, and the search for information about our hobby continues to reveal new sources in a manner which suggests that we shall never be able to keep in contact with all of them.
For instance, the lines to Japan from Europe and America are often somewhat tenuous, so we tend to sieze on news like that which came from *Newcon* this month. This high quality manufacturer made its name with the 1958 Ferrari 250 GT Berlinetta, and ever since, collectors have been looking for news of newcomers from the same stable.
Now the news was out, and Newcon had announced a Mercedes 300 SLR Coupé that should be well worth waiting for. At the same time, Newcon announced its intention to produce a fine selection of classic cars — the Lotus Elite first, followed by a racing Cobra 289, a Ford GT Mk II, a Ferrari 250 GT Spyder California, a Lotus Elan, and a 1956 Ford Thunderbird. While we wait, we can save up the money, for Newcon models are not cheap!
Those lucky enough to have a line of supply from Japan will no doubt also collect the models from *CAM*, who announced a Ferrari 275 GTB/4 to follow their Nissan Skyline 2000 GT.
More affordable and easier to find than the specialist marques from Japan are *Yonezawa's Diapet* models. Notable among their new productions are an Isuzu Piazza, a Toyota New Celica XX 2800 GT, and a Nissan New Skyline 2000 Turbo. They are all in 1:40.
Sakura announced some models made from the moulds the company acquired when Grip Zechin of the Edai group went bankrupt. The cars are a Jaguar XJ Sedan and three Formula 1 cars, the Brabham BT 45B, Renault RS 01, and March 761B.
Tomy's Dandy range sticks to a fairly uniform 1:43 and specializes in variations on a theme. Newcomers to the range are the Rolls Royce Phantom in a new colour scheme, a new "Candy" livery for the

A work of art: this 1937 Mercedes W125 Grand Prix car in 1:24 would surely satisfy even the most demanding modeller. Western's models are getting even better.

The forward-control Volvo F-12 is a tractor unit which is well known on European highways and is beginning to make an appearance in the United States. Italeri chose it as the first model in their new range of trucks in 1:24.

It is unusual for an American kit manufacturer to choose European trucks as a subject for its models, but Revell, with branches in Germany, Great Britain and Japan, has a more international outlook than many others in line with its widespread distribution network. This Mercedes-Benz 1628s in 1:25 makes a welcome addition to their range.

Six wheels out of an eighteen-wheeler combination. The massive hood, the smokestacks, the chrome, the colours — this Peterbilt Conventional 'Midnight Express' in 1:25 from AMT typifies the style of independent truckers right across the USA.

Monogram's series of 1:32 scale truck kits designed to be assembled without cement continues to grow, and this Mack R with a standard cab is one of the latest additions. The quality of 'no-glue' kits, even in this scale, continues to improve, and this model, with its wealth of chrome parts and fine detail, is a very good example of the state of the art.

Japanese production covers a variety of vehicles and countries, and this selection is typical. Tomica have followed current Japanese fashion and introduced a number of leisure-oriented vehicles in 1:43, like the Nissan van with a roof-mounted go-kart and the cyclists' Mini Cooper. They are in the Dandy range. The same manufacturer, but a different scale, 1:60, for the Mazda RX-7 which is well modelled in competition trim. Specialized models from Japan are also made to a very high standard, as the Ferrari 275 GTB 4 (right) from CAM shows. The model is in 1:43 and comes as a kit or in built-up form. Below are three more well made models from Tomica: a Ford cattle truck in 1:95 and two saloons, a Nissan Bluebird SSS in 1:43 and a Renault 5 Turbo in 1:58.

Citroën delivery van, and roof-racks carrying bicycles or a go-kart for the Mini Cooper.

Back in Europe, it is again *Mikansue* which kicks off the report from Britain's specialist craftsmen. Their new one was a 1935 Voisin Aerodyne saloon, and comparisons with the model produced by the French specialist Gérard Dehinden will naturally be made. The material is not the same — white metal rather than resin — and British collectors will be glad to have Mike Richardson's version, which is not bad at all.

C-Scale continued with a 1958 Ferrari Testa Rossa which was not all that new. More interesting were the latest 1:43 offerings from *Dave Gilbert*, a 1936 Reliant three-wheeler and a 1925 Austin van.

The real knock-out of the month came from *Western Models* with their 1:24-scale 1937 Mercedes 5.6-litre W125 Grand Prix. The only possible reaction to it is sheer amazement at its perfection. Available as a kit or fully finished it is truly a work of art, showing the continual progress of Mike Stephens' expertise and skill. It has spoked wheels, suspension, a detailed engine — and oh, how it is detailed — a scrupulously accurate tubular chassis, accurately formed tyres in soft plastic... in short, it has everything, and the lover of high quality models will find a place for it alongside Western's Maserati 250F in the best showcase. As if this was not enough, the company also announced a 1955 Le Mans Aston Martin in 1:43, a model which will overshadow the one produced in John Day's old "V de C" range.

And this wasn't all, for *Wills Finecast*, one of the oldest British manufacturers, launched a superkit of an MC TC Midget in 1:24. A realistic model, but one which will require some skill in assembling its more than one hundred parts. Coming back to earth, *Matchbox* released a BP tanker on the 1912 Ford Model T chassis in the Yesteryear series. A charming model which will tempt many, not least because of its relatively low price.

Classic Cars chose this month to release its model of the 1957 Le Mans-winning Ecurie Ecosse D-Type Jaguar. It is a 1:43 white metal kit which will find many fans. Following their trend of the past few months, the company also brought out a couple more Ford GT 40s, this time the 1968 and 1969 Le Mans winners. November was proving to be a very good month, for other newcomers were the 1956 Carrera Panamerica Ferrari from *Bosica* and the 1981 Ferrari 126 K1 Formula 1 car made by the same craftsman for *FDS*. Congatulations are in order for Signor Bosica, who has managed to get almost as much detail into 1:43 cars as one is used to finding in one of Western's 1:24 productions. The Panamerica Ferrari has opening doors and bonnet which reveal a complete interior and an engine which even has plug leads — all this and spoked wheels too! The Formula 1 car also has a detailed engine and chassis and a cockpit which is absolutely true to life.

Overleaf: Keep on Truckin! Left, from the top — An Atlas skip truck on a MAN Diesel chassis (Conrad 3155, 1:50), Ford tractor with Michelin container trailer (Corgi 1108), Daimler Benz gas transporter (Conrad 3024), Ford Cargo and trailer (NZG 227, 1:50) and Magirus tipper (Conrad 3040). On the right, again from the top, Ford Guinness tanker (Corgi 1169), MAN Diesel Haniel tanker (Conrad 3122), MAN Diesel Total tanker (Conrad 3026) and Elba-Scheele drainage pump on a Magirus Deutz chassis (Conrad 3281).

MICHELIN
MICHELIN
GRIESHEIM

GUINNESS
Energieversorgt mit HANIEL
TOTAL
Würze
der
Natur
ELBA-Scheele

Francesco De Stasio is one of the most prolific of the Italian craftsmen, but that doesn't mean his models — like this 1951 Lancia B 20 Carrera Panamericana — suffer in quality.

All these goodies are revealed by means of detachable bodywork. The two cars are real gems, and put the rest of the FDS introductions — a 1963 Le Mans Ferrari 330 LMB, a 1981 McLaren MP 4, and a 1951 Lancia Aurelia B 20 Carrera Panamericana race car — in the shade.
The *Tron* brothers turned their attention to the Ferrari Daytona as re-bodied by Michelotti for NART in the 1975 Le Mans race and a couple of BB 512 models entered by the European University and Crockfords in the 1980 event. Made in collaboration with AMR, the models therefore have excellent references.
As a final flourish to this month's new issue list, let us look at the superb Hudson Hornet from *Precision Miniatures* in America. Gene Parrill has excelled himself with this one, with detailed decals for the dashboard, chromed parts, and whitewall tyres. There are two versions — a touring car and a 1952 NASCAR racer.

USA plastic kits

November was truck month for AMT who reissued their 1:25 Autocar Dump Truck (8403). This is a large (I mean *large*) truck model, one needing four sheets of instructions and getting four dots on the Skill Level. Definitely one of the better detailed AMT truck kits. I also like the cab design; it looks like an older truck and I have always wanted a 30s big rig truck model (and a reissue of the Bulldog Macks from Monogram). Speaking of Macks, these are the subject of the latest AMT 1:32 snap trucks. Two versions are offered, a Conventional Super-Liner (6804) and a wrecker with Holmes Twin-Boom units (6803). Snap kits are getting better all the time and should not be overlooked by the veteran enthusiast. There is a challenge to a snap kit if you want to take it.
Monogram has done cost-conscious modelers a favor by releasing a 1970 Boss Mustang (2282); annual releases of this car go for 30 dollars and up. Muscle Cars are definitely coming on strong. Monogram really has done a job on this Mustang and it looks great. I appreciated the small mounting lugs for the interior and glass, and the decals for the engine compartment; more companies should supply under-hood decals. Those who like only stock models might pass by Monogram's 1:24 scale '57 Street Vette (2283), but inside the box are all the stock parts. A black molded body, paint the cove silver, and you have one fantastic looking model. Also released is the 1970 Malibu (2284) in a non-stock version. Monogram is to be congratulated for keeping the stock versions in the line when they reissue their non-stock variations. Thanks, Monogram.

The Tron brothers brought out their 1:43 scale 1980 Ferrari 512 BB "Cockfords" Le Mans in collaboration with AMR; now there's a reference for you.

European and Japanese plastic kits

This month's production of 17 new models foreshadowed the imminence of Christmas. Heller, recovering strongly from its troubles earlier in the year, brought out kit number 724 in 1:24 scale: a 1932 Renault Vivastella PG 7, one of the luxury cars that came out of the Régie's factories at the time. Powered by an in-line, six-cylinder engine, it developed 57 bhp at 2700 rpm. Heller's model consists of about 100 pieces moulded in black, beige, chrome and transparent plastic, as well as proper rubber tyres. It is a well produced model having a magnificent steering wheel with spokes of astonishing delicacy, and perfectly satisfactory moulding, especially of the leaf springs. Many more retaining lugs are provided than on previous models, and these are precious assembly aids. Nevertheless there are some black marks: the chrome is a bit heavy, the side windows are cast in one piece with the door interiors, giving rise to painting difficulties, and the radiator is chromed all over, whereas only the frame and the mascot should be. These points are compensated for by an excellent imitation of the canvas hood, and fine coachwork with well moulded details. On the whole, Heller has made a happy choice with a good-looking model.
Three new models came from the Esci stable, two of them Renault R 5 Alpines. The first was the road version with admirable Pirelli P7 tyres. The other Alpine, a model in Gitanes colours of the car Ragnotti/Andrié drove to second place behind Darniche's Stratos in the 1979 Tour de France, provokes two reactions: admiration and a howl of laughter. Admiration first: Esci has produced slicks marked Dunlop on one side and Goodyear on the other — a fantastic idea. Now for the laughs: the transfers, marvels of the kind that only Cartograph can make, come in a single version — Michelin. That apart, these two models are satisfactory, although some extra details, notably in the engine, wouldn't do any harm. We have to point out that the blue of the racing version is too light and the moulding needs a lot of trimming. Finally, Esci's third new model was the Bandama Rally version of the five-litre, 450 SLC Mercedes which is featured elsewhere in this book.
In Japan, Nichimo had still not exhausted the possibilities of the jeep theme and brought out four more, bringing the total to 12. Otaki, on the other hand, offered two motorized Nissans: a Gloria 200 Custom Deluxe and a Cedric, also 200, just as Custom and no less Deluxe. They differ only in their radiator grilles and other minor details. A final mention for the 1:24 scale Porsche 928 S from Gunze Sangyo — a model not entirely similar to the car it is meant to reproduce. It is too short overall and its front is too square.

DECEMBER

Let's start with the latest products from the small German specialists *Tin Wizzard*, who make Porsches, no doubt because Porsches sell well, and no-one will complain when the models are interesting and well chosen, as is the case with the various versions of the 924 which ran at Le Mans in 1981. The models were of the Kremer GTR and the "Boss"-sponsored Carrera GT (the prototype of the 944). Tin Wizzard are also Bugatti specialists, and their new offerings were a Figoni-bodied Type 46 cabriolet, a Type 49 with a Gangloff cabriolet body, and a Type 50 cabriolet. A Type 44 Fiacre Coupé is in preparation.
The most important event from the collector's point of view in this last month of the year was the arrival of two new models from the resuscitated *Solido* company. They followed the pattern of the "Age d'Or" series; a Citroën 1000 kg van of 1930 vintage bearing two different bodies, one a Paris fire engine, and the other a bus carrying the name "Palace Hotel" on its flanks. The appearance of the two newcomers gave hope to Solido fans who had been hit hard by the

numerous problems the firm had suffered. The company continues to exist, but there is no way to replace the Vazeilles family. Some day, someone will write the story of how companies like Bassett-Lowke, Hornby-Meccano and Solido were adversely affected by the loss of the men who founded and nurtured them. We hope we shall never have to have the same thoughts about Reno Tatarletti's firm, *Brumm*. So far, all seems fine with the company, who show no signs of slowing down the flood of new models. Italian collectors are lucky, because they were the first to receive the new models which celebrated the year's end. They were the 1954/55 Mercedes W 196 Grand Prix car, the 1911 "Blitzen Benz" record car, the 1948 Talbot Lago F1 car, the 1937 8-cylinder Grand Prix Maserati, the 1955 Lancia D 50 8-cylinder, and the 1931 Alfa Romeo 2300-8 in Tourer and 1932 Mille Miglia form. Brumm enthusiasts in other countries must wait their turn according to distributors whims, but one model which did become generally available was the *Matchbox* Silver Jubilee Ford T van in the Yesteryear series. Despite earlier stories of limited production and rarity, the model is being produced in normal numbers and distributed through the regular channels, so as it turns out everyone will be able to get their hands on an example.

It seems these days that every month brings a fresh crop of large-scale models, and December was no exception. *Polistil* announced a Morgan Plus 8 Roadster which fell flat, despite being accurate. It was probably too accurate, in fact, because it was a model of a contemporary race-prepared model with a roll-bar and metallic blue paint-job. Collectors are of the opinion that *all* Morgans are green, and no other colour will attract them. If Polistil make it look suitably vintage, it will sell, even in 1:16.

Norev came to our notice with the introduction of a 1:43 Mercedes 280 "S"-class saloon. It's a well known fact that before any collector puts a Norev on his shelf he has to change the wheels, but it is also well known that their lines are accurate for the most part and the cars which they choose to model are usually not available elsewhere. This is the case with the Mercedes, and although the all-in-one grille and headlight assembly detract from the realism of the model, the overall effect is good, and the car will merit its display space.

There has been a proliferation of models from Brumm in the past twelve months, and these two are among the additions to the company's range of competition cars. They are both examples of the Dino 246 Ferrari Formula 1 car; on the left the 1958 version (R 69) and on the right the 1957 car (R 68). Being critical, the inlet trumpets for the V6 engine are too big and should be offset rather than parallel, the Ferrari badges are too big, and why black wheels?

Somerville produces 1:43 white metal kits at a steady rhythm and of some original subjects. This is the Fordson van.

A selection of small models shows what quality can be crammed into a space of two or three inches. Clockwise, starting at the top, they are a Peugeot 305 STI from Siku, a Rolls Royce featured in the "Cannonball Run" film (Ertl, 1:64), a Dino 246 GT from the same film (Ertl, 1:64), two from the "Dukes of Hazzard" TV series, Boss Hogg's Cadillac and the "General Lee" Dodge Charger (both Ertl, 1:64), and three European saloons from Norev's Minijet series — an Alfa 6, a Volvo 264, and a Mercedes 280 SE. Finally comes a Chevy Pro Stocker from Matchbox's 75 range.

The past twelve months have seen a glut of Renault 5 Turbos and Alpines — as you might expect for a car that looks good, that has made such a mark on motor sport in its many different, brightly coloured versions and has featured so strongly in the motoring press. A good selling proposition, then; one that Burago, with a 1:24 version, didn't overlook.

Esci modified its touring Alpine kit to produce a competition version. It has the same high-quality moulding, precise decals and attention to detail as the Italian firm's other 1:24 productions.

Who better than the French firm Heller to bring out an R5 Turbo? It was an addition to the 1:43 range, and will stand comparison with productions from the specialist makers, including the Solido-based conversion kits.

Almost a complete history of Ferrari in miniature. ▷ Above, the latest 126 CK turbocharged Formula 1 car, a jewel-like creation in 1:43 by Bosica, who has become the new master craftsman of Italian modelling; in the center, the 375 MM which competed in the 1953 Panamericana race, also in 1:43 by Bosica and blessed with such features as opening doors and engine cover, and on its right, the first car made by Enzo Ferrari, the 815 of 1940, modelled in 1:43 by Brumm and leaving something to be desired in terms of accuracy. Right, a model to make every collector dream — a 1958 Ferrari 250 Testa Rossa in 1:10 scale and bearing the mark of Michele Conti in every intricate detail.

27
MICHELIN
RICCI
26

Brooklin Models sells its 1:43 miniatures ready built and concentrates on American classic cars, such as this 1956 Ford Thunderbird hardtop.

Coming back to the craftsmen, we must again note a veritable crop of new models from *FDS*. There is no lack of energy in this outfit, and they offer a 1981 Theodore Formula 1, an Ensign F1 car of the same year, and a Mercedes race transporter as used by the works Martini Porsche team in 1978. An excellent reproduction, but one hesitates to think of the price!

The British *Somerville* brand is known for the quality of its kits and built-up models in 1:43, which come at regular intervals and have the merit of being not too expensive. The firm's new production is of a little known, but very acceptable, variation on a well known British car of the immediate post-war years. It is the Ford Anglia in a Tourer version, produced in Australia in 1949. An interesting model, turned into a good quality kit which offers the choice of finishing the model with the top up or down.

Another brand which is establishing a reputation for quality is that of *Brooklin Models*. John Hall followed up his 1956 Ford T-bird hardtop with a 1940 Cadillac V-16 convertible with a Fisher body. The original car could not exactly have been called handsome, but the model — supplied in finished form, as are all Brooklin productions — succeeds in looking semi-attractive, a tribute to the skill of the Brooklin staff.

USA plastic kits

An unusually busy month of December starts with AMT's Datsun 280 ZX Turbo (4165) in 1:25. Though not a car with much chrome on it, AMT listened to those chromeless gripes and have included plated parts in this kit. They also wanted to go a little farther than normal, and it shows; just take a look at all the separate parts in the engine compartment. This is a well done kit of excellent detail and proportion.

A prolific month for Monogram started with several 1:32 snap kits. Lacking only plated parts and rubber-like tires, these kits are so well done and of such interesting vehicles (for the most part) they will surely find a home with many who either don't like snap kits, or even 1:32 kits in general. Reissues are a third version of the Ford Bronco (1034) with a tarp over the rear, which makes for a really different model, while the Jeep CJ (1033) gets a top. For new toolings there is plenty to get really excited about, like the 1969 Camaro Z-28 (1032), the four-door Chevy Malibu Police Car (1031), the 1970 Mustang (1030), and the 1969 GTO (1029). These really should have had plated parts; they don't but are still beautiful kits. Not a lot of parts to them, easy assembly for fast building, but with enough detail to keep you busy for as long as you want. Interesting kits, then, but that's not all. In 1:24 comes a 1955 Ford Pickup with decals for Stroh's Beer, a Detroit legend — beer kegs, of course, included (2285, StrohMobile). In racing trim is the BMW 635 Csi (2287) and Citation "X" (2288). New addition to the High Rollers series is the Ford Bronco (2286), again following the theme of large tires and all wheel drive.

The 1:32 snaps dominated Revell's December program with items like the Toyota Bluehawk Camper (6002), Datsun King Cab Streamliner (6006, similar to the regular King Cab released the year before, very nice and a fresh change of pace from the regular pickup models), VW Pickup with Mini Racer (6012 — the Mini Racer is a go kart), Jeep CJ Laredo (6015) with enclosed cab, and two kits based on the TV show "Code Red"; a Chevy Nova "Fire Chief's Car" (6030), and a Chevy Emergency Van (6029). There is also a "Code Red" chopper in this series. Moving to 1:25 snap kits we find three based on the popular TV show CHiPs. The Camaro Z-28 "Chase Car" (6228) is very interesting, as is the "Ponch" Firebird (6226); lacking a few trim pieces to be totally stock, both are still quality kits. The last model in this series is "Jon's Chevy 4 × 4 Pickup" (6424). All in all, a rather snappy month for Revell.

European and Japanese plastic kits

Christmas at last! And with it came 19 new models — not all quite new, but a good selection of series fillers, some doubles and still more custom-builts, mainly from the Japanese. Therefore we will give priority to the only non-Japanese model — the Mercedes 230 G Cross Country from Esci in 1:24 scale. Esci put all its money on simplicity, not to say extreme simplification, to the extent that the engine has been omitted altogether. An opening bonnet is therefore unnecessary. The model consists of some 70 parts and a guide with first-class painting instructions. The model can be built with its back doors either open or closed, the plastic being already cut on the inside. The excellent imitation of the cloth seat covers and the spare wheel cover is worthy of mention.

Let us pass over to the Land of the Rising Sun where we find an Isuzu Piazza from Bandai in 1:20 scale. The popularity of this model continues to grow; it consists of about 150 parts. There was something of a surprise from Fujimi with an American car, and a highly prized model to boot, being none other than a Camaro

Two names well known in the Detroit area, Ford and Stroh's, come together in this Monogram model of a 1955 Ford pickup customized into one of the world's smartest beer delivery vehicles. The scale is 1:24, as it is for the high-rise Ford Bronco 4 × 4. Below are two more off-road vehicles, also from Monogram, as is the Bronco. The Chevy LUV has the currently fashionable style of a little girl wearing her mother's shoes, but the Jeep CJ 7 has a pleasantly standard look about it.

Tamiya's American army Ford M151A2 is sure to become popular with diorama builders and those who like to produce modifications based on production models. The Mutt is the latest addition to Tamiya's 1:35 range of Military Miniatures, which continue to be top sellers across the world.

Top right: Tamiya and Italeri have produced the world-famous Land Rover in 1:35, but Monogram have added it to their 1:24 range in civil version. Most modellers will no doubt prefer to make it in a more realistic colour scheme, but the outsize tyres give it a boulevard poser's aspect whatever the colour. It would be interesting to know how a driver is supposed to see over the hood-mounted spare. A good aspect of the kit from the modeller's viewpoint is that the doors are separate parts and can be mounted in open or shut positions.

As this Ford Flareside Night Rider in 1:25 by Revell shows, cementless construction does not necessarily mean a lack of detail. Certainly there is a need for care in construction and the expenditure of a little extra time, but at the prices charged for such kits it is worth the effort.

Good value: kits which build more than one model are rare nowadays, so this 1:25 Chevrolet Scottsdale 40 with a beach buggy on a trailer will prove popular with cost-conscious modellers.

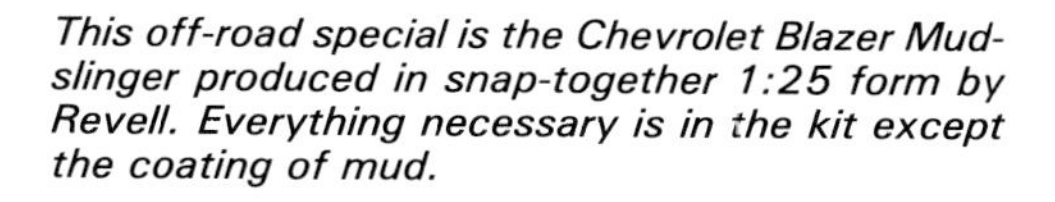

This off-road special is the Chevrolet Blazer Mudslinger produced in snap-together 1:25 form by Revell. Everything necessary is in the kit except the coating of mud.

Z 28 Turbo — hot rod, of course. It is in 1:24, as were Fujimi's two other models, notably the Toyota Celica XX 2800 GT which doubles Tamiya's version. There were also a couple of commercials in 1:24 scale: a Toyota Town Ace and a Datsun Vanette SGX.

JANUARY 1982

For the collector, January is a month to look both back and forwards, like the god Janus himself. Looking back, you can check on the gaps in the collection which remain to be filled from past production and, looking forward, you can look through the catalogues that traditionally appear at this time of the year to set out everything that will be tempting you in future months.

1982 promises to be an interesting year as a result of the efforts of three big producers — Brumm, Eligor, and Matchbox — if their published programmes are anything to go by. Brumm announced plans to introduce an incredible number of new models in their Revival range, Eligor envisaged no less than 36 new models, and Matchbox proposed to add a number of models to their range, with the additions to the Yesteryear series being of the most interest.

And all that is without counting the Japanese manufacturers — strangely silent this January — and other companies such as Burago, Polistil and Corgi.

First model to come up for inspection in this new year was one which had in fact made its first appearance in certain quarters towards the end of December — the Mercedes-Benz SSKL in Mille Miglia form from *Solido*. Based on the Age d'Or model, it has been "racerized" by the addition of red-painted wings, a running-board, a tool-box and competition numbers. Majorette, who have taken over Solido's operations, intend to put the existing moulds to good use, and this is one example. We await others.

Still in France, the Paris-based specialist *BAM-X* introduced a new version of the Audi Quattro rally car. André-Marie Ruf is the man behind the production of the model, which represents the car driven to victory in the San Remo Rally by French wonder-girl Michèle Mouton. It's a good choice, and the model is more attractive than the original one produced by the firm.

André-Marie Ruf also produces his own kits under the *X* label, and his two latest productions are the Ferrari 512BB entered by the European University at Le Mans in 1981 — not to be confused with the similar 1980 car co-produced by AMR and the Tron brothers in Italy — and the "Moby Dick" Porsche 935 driven by Moretti at Le Mans in 1981 under the Mo-Mo colours. The quality is up to standard, with clean moulding, turned wheels, photo-etched wipers and impeccable decals, but one would prefer to see the French craftsman working on more important cars rather than wasting his time on limited-interest models like these. This artist — to use the term in its strictest sense, for he is — needs to be creative; to feel shapes and interpret them as a form of self-expression. Every model which leaves his hands bears the mark of his individuality and is born of his need to give form to his material — in short, to create.

Following an oval course are these four 1:43 models from Ertl of contemporary Indianapolis cars. They are not exactly accurate, particularly in terms of their decals, and this fault is made more noticeable when they are compared with the pictures of the real cars that feature so strongly on the boxes.

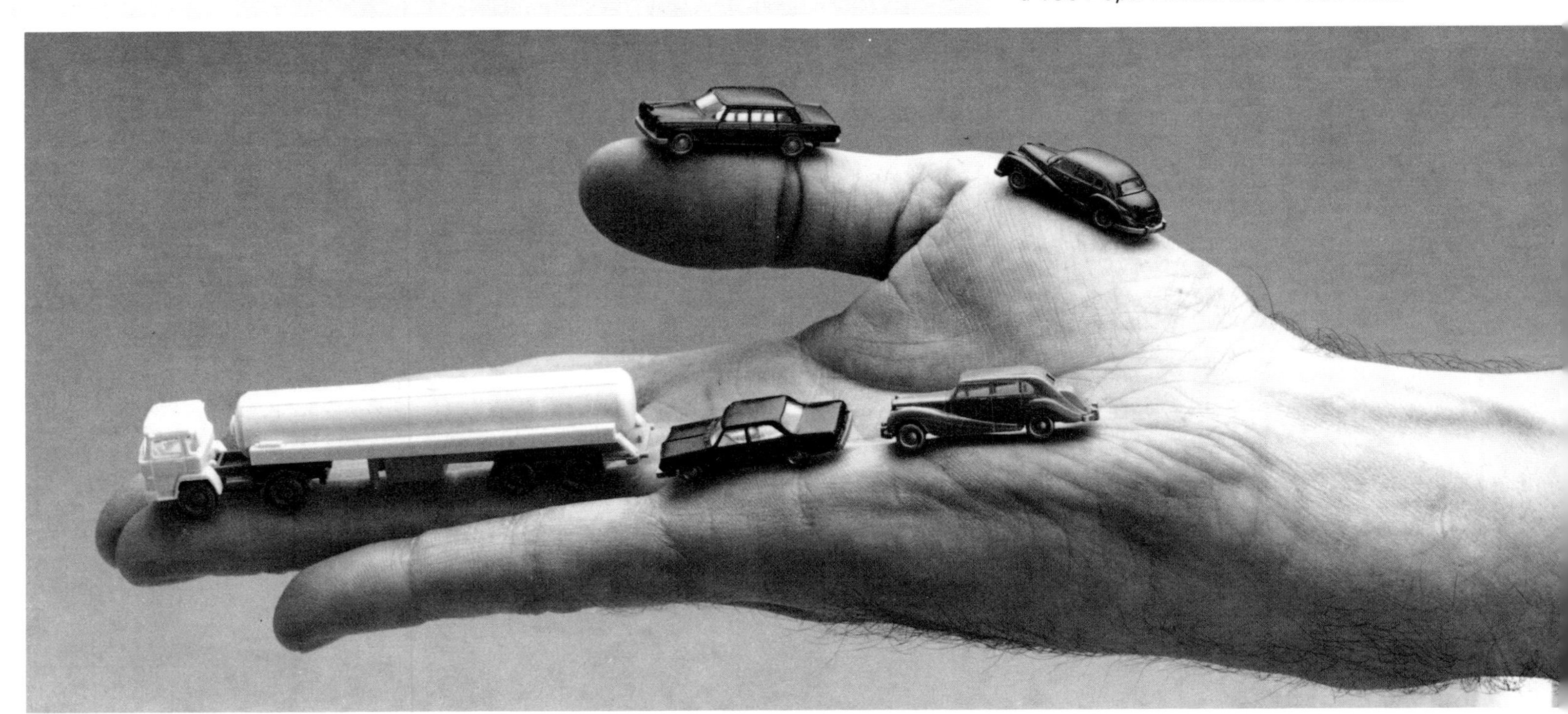

Limited space and the excellence of the models are making many collectors turn to 1:160 scale. This handful comes from Wiking, and comprises a Magirus tanker, a Mercedes 600, a BMW 501, a 1964 Opel Admiral and a 1951 Rolls.

A passionate personality, André-Marie Ruf needs time to work, and when he is rushed he does not give the best of himself because of the pressure of his many commissions. Perhaps one day he will have the time, free of day-to-day pressures, to work in freedom and to produce models in a variety of scales, reproducing only cars which appeal to him.
In another world, that of the industrial producers, *Burago* announced its first 1:24 model of an American car, the Ford Mustang Cobra. Doors, bonnet and hatchback all open, and the steering operates. The model has all the features which we have come to expect — and get — from the company.
In Germany, *NZG* have produced a superb promotional for Mercedes-Benz in the shape of a Mercedes 500 SEC in 1:36. This is a real top-of-the-range model of a top-of-the-range car, equipped with all that one expects from such a reproduction; opening doors, bonnet and boot, a detailed interior, and such fine detail as door handles, trim strips on the sides, headlamps and rear lamps, and a multitude of chromed parts. Truly a quality production, up to Mercedes standards.
Because January is a little short on actual new introductions, let us take a look at the programmes the manufacturers made public at this time. *Eligor* promises a Bugatti Type 35B racer as well as two new vans, a Ford V8 and an Opel Laubfrosch. You can imagine what possibilities these will open up in the realm of publicity versions for the Franco-Swiss manufacturer!
Brumm has plans for a flood of new productions which will enchant collectors. According to the advance information, there is going to be a 1930 Le Mans Bentley, a Vanwall, a Jaguar XK 120, a D-type Auto Union, a Tropfenwagen, a Bugatti Type 57S Atlantic, a Testa Rossa Ferrari…
From *Matchbox* comes news of proposed additions to the range which are also exciting prospects. 1982 will see the appearance of a new Peterbilt tractor and trailer in the livery of Euro-Express, while the tanker version will become available in the colours of Chemco. The Yesteryear series will have a 1922 AEC bus, a 1930 Ford Model A van with Oxo decals, the Talbot van in the colours of Chivers and Sons Ltd, and a new version of the Ford T van carrying signwriting for Bird's Custard Powder. Collectors of publicity vehicles will need to buy new showcases to house their Matchboxes and Eligors.

USA plastic kits

For those hungering for models of the new and beautiful Firebirds and Camaros, January was *the* month. Monogram had announced their 1:32 scale 1982 Camaro Z-28 (2004) and 1:24 Firebird Trans Am (2281) as being available earlier. Unfortunately, GM was late in releasing the real cars (just like when the 1970 Camaro and Firebird were launched) and Monogram had to delay their releases as well. The Camaro is along the lines of the December releases with full engine, plated parts and vinyl-like tires. Detailing you just don't expect (until now) from a 1:32 kit — beautiful! The Trans Am (Monogram is the only company allowed to use the name) is all the Camaro is and more. I especially like the way the rear window attaches from the outside, and the dash could be blown up to twice its size and still not need extra detailing. GM has produced a very pleasing design with these cars, but dare I say it — I like the custom potential; customs are coming back.
This was also the month for MPC's annual kits of not only the 1982 Firebird and Camaro, but also the Ford EXP; all in 1:25. It is hard to compare the two Firebird kits as each have their points. Monogram's version is much longer (a large 1:24; or is MPC's a small 1:25?) and has the edge in engine compartment detail, though MPC gives you two engine options, and two hoods. What it really boils down to is: if you prefer 1:25 you will buy the MPC Firebird (0808), if you like 1:24, Monogram will be your choice. If you are smart, you will buy both as each has a lot to offer the builder. MPC's kit comes with two sets of wheels, roll cage and steerable wheels. The Camaro (0814) comes with two engine options, turbocharged or fuel injected. Also in the kit are IMSA type fender add-ons and two sets of wheels. Few parts seem to be shared with the Firebird; MPC likely figured both kits would be so popular two complete molds would be needed to keep up with demand — and they may be right. Turning to the EXP (0818) the story is similar, though there are no steerable wheels. The interior is multi-piece which makes it a little harder to assemble, but allows more detail than would otherwise be possible. There are two engine options in the EXP kit as well. MPC seems to be giving more-detailed painting instructions than they did in the past. Three kits that should not be missed.
In the reissue department MPC has made Firebird fans happy. Yes, they did drop the 1969 White Lightning version, but they replaced it with a 1969 Firebird convertible (0822). The convertible is available in kit form for the first time, though in 1969 it was available as a promotional. It's a welcome release, not completely stock, but lacking only the wheels to be so; and that is close enough for most of us. Included are two engines to really make this a wanted kit. The 1973 Cougar (0803) was also reissued. This is the first time it has been available since its annual release in 1973 and, like the Firebird, it lacks only wheels to be completely stock. Last on the list from MPC comes their Turbobird (0819), a custom version of the 1981 Firebird annual. Very well done with beautiful (non-stock) wheels. It is nice to see the 1981 Firebird still included in the lineup.

Not every model Ferrari gets stamped Made in Italy; this beautifully executed 375 California Sport in 1:43 comes from Record in France.

This is the Sunbeam that Major Henry Segrave pushed up to 245 km/h (152 mph) in March 1926. Aurore Models produced it in 1:43 for the record-car enthusiasts — and there are certainly plenty of those around.

European and Japanese plastic kits

The model car industry is like tourism — you notice how quiet it becomes in January. The only offerings were seven models left over from the end of year festivities, and all of them straight from Japan. LS dug into its Nissan range to come up with what it calls a "New Skyline 2000 Turbo" in 1:20 with either white or red livery. Nichimo served up its Toyota Town Ace in three sauces all based on the leisure vehicle: Extra, Custom and even Super-Custom. There are enough ingredients to excite the palate of even the most jaded gourmet: wide aluminium wheels, lateral exhausts on the Custom and Super-Custom, sliding roof, chromed luggage rack, side ladder, and even a rear-view mirror — rear right to see where the wheel is when you reverse. Ever seen anything like it? All in 1:24 scale.
From Tamiya came the Nissan Skyline 2000 RS (I'm sure I've seen one somewhere before…) with its scooter, a Suzuki Gemma 50, to launch the 1982 collection. As always it's in 1:24 scale, and as always it's aimed at the young modeller.

Different eras, different continents, and mildly differing scales between 1:36 and 1:43 from three of the top mass producers. From top to bottom, Ford Thunderbird (Corgi 801), Mercedes 300SL (Corgi 802), Ford Cobra Mustang (Corgi 370), Alfa 6 (Norev Jet Car 888), Peugot 305 (Matchbox Superking K-84), VW Golf (Matchbox Superking K-86), Mercedes 280 SE (Norev Jet Car 890), Renault Fuego (Norev Jet Car 891), Plymouth Taxi (Matchbox Superking K-79) and Volvo 264 (Norev Jet Car 886).

Classic models from classic manufacturers (both full size and miniature). Starting from the top, Rio's 1928 Bugatti Royale (ref. 74, 1:43) and 1904 Fiat 60 hp 'berlina' (ref. 75). Solido's Mille Miglia SSKL Mercedes (ref. 4004, 1:43) and Citroën C4 hotel taxi (ref. 4005). At the bottom, Matchbox's 1937 Mercedes 540K roadster (Y-20) in the Models of Yesteryear series.

More and more collectors are turning to HO scale ▷ vehicles, which some say give the maximum detail in the minimum space. The products from Wiking, Herpa and Roco shown here go a long way to bear that opinion out. Lack of space prevents us from giving details of all of them, but especially noteworthy among this crop of new models are the giant Setra S228 DT Kässbohrer touring coach from Herpa, the Wiking model of the Berlin double-decker bus, and the tiny Jeep CJ-7 Golden Eagles from Roco.

IPEC
IVECO SERVICE
IVECO SERVICE
norfrig
Bayerns grosse Frische
Franken Brunnen
Bayerns grosse Frische
Franken Brunnen
DANISH
Tiefkühlkost
Tiefkühlkost
RINGEL
Tiefkühlkost
Tiefkühlkost
RINGEL

Mercedes-Benz
union
M·A·N

Grand Prix Models has launched out into series-production cars and called the resulting new line Classic 43. This is the 1:43 prototype, in bronze, of the Jaguar Mk 2 Saloon.

How Formula 1 fans can recreate an air of the paddock — the Ferrari team's Fiat transporter from FDS and the Ferrari 126 C2 from Hi Fi Models. Two 1:43 Italian productions.

Western Models did a perfect job on the streamlining of the MG EX record car. Older collectors will no doubt remember the Dinky Toys version.

Two 1:43 GT classics from Tenariv: ninth at Le Mans 1963, the E-type Jaguar of Grossman/Cunningham and, seventh at Le Mans 1965, the Ford Cobra Daytona of Sears/Thompson.

FEBRUARY

While we were waiting to see if all the new year's promises would be held, February set off on the right foot with the latest newcomers from Japan. *CAM* introduced a Ferrari 275 GTB/4 as a kit or a built-up model. This is a model which is just beautiful, because it is, like some other Japanese models, on a par with the best miniature railway engines. It is well made, carefully thought out, and correct in its lines; the spoked wheels and the interior and exterior details are true to life. If all vehicle models were like this one, collectors would stop feeling like the poor relations of the modelling fraternity. Unfortunately, the price is restrictive; at 19,500 Yen (look up the exchange rate in your newspaper, but sit down before you do the conversion!) it is beyond the reach of many pockets. It is impossible for the average collector to acquire many models at this sort of price — but then on the other hand, a little splurge every now and then never hurt anybody...

Another notable introduction from Japan was a "Turbo Gift Set" from *Yonezawa*, containing four cars fitted with Japan's latest status symbol, a turbocharger. They are the Nissan Bluebird SSS, Mitsubishi Galant, Nissan Leopard and Toyota Soarer. The Japanese have rediscovered the gift set, and Tomica Dandy also have some in their range. It brings back memories of the sixties, when the European manufacturers, free of international competition, let their creative spirit run free.

The month saw Brian Harvey trying to pump a little life into the specialist world, which was in decline as a result of the economic situation. The father of such ranges as Classic Cars, GPM Racing, Dannini Modelli, Modsport, and the rarest of all, the Edgar Jessop series, launched *Classic 43*. Production numbers are limited and the models are supplied assembled and painted, so the series should be interesting. The first introduction is a Jaguar Mark II saloon with right- or left-hand drive to choice. A Ferrari Mondial 8 is promised as the second in the range.

At *Mikansue*, the speciality is forgotten English cars, and the month's introductions are a 1934 Riley Monaco of good workmanship, a 1961 Rover 100 saloon which is not so good from the point of view of mould quality, and which will need a fair amount of file-work before assembly, and a 1954 Riley RME 1.2-litre saloon.

In the *Mikansue Competition* range the aims are the same, and the new addition was a 1954 Kieft Coventry Climax-engined Le Mans car. Plans were also announced for an ERA G-Type Formula II car of the type driven by Stirling Moss in 1952.

Western Models returned to the limelight with two interesting models, the MG EX135 record car driven by the famous "Goldie" Gardner in 1939 and a Rolls Royce Phantom I of 1927 vintage, an apt means of celebrating the 75th anniversary of the Silver Ghost. The MG is well known to older collectors from the model produced by Dinky Toys that was a staple of their range in the fifties. There is no comparison with the Western production however, which is a collector's piece rather that a simple toy. Available in kit or assembled form, it captures the lines of the original to perfection.

In France, *Tenariv* introduced an Arrows A3 in the colours of Beta and Ragno as it raced in the South African Grand Prix in 1981, and a 1965 Cobra Daytona Le Mans car, made more interesting by the provision of two decal sets allowing it to be built as either a Carroll Shelby or Alan Mann car.

Italy's *FDS* never misses a monthly introduction. This time it was a Ferrari 340MM as driven by Marzotto in the 1954 Mille Miglia and the Ensign 180 B 15 as driven by Marc Surer in the 1981 Brazilian Grand Prix. A good white metal kit with no surprises. Another FDS introduction is a Marlboro McLaren MP 4 Formula 1 car as raced in 1981. The model duplicates the one produced by Western Models, but the respective local markets are strong enough to support the two.

Brumm continued its advance with new publicity versions of its little Fiat 500 van. The new names were Gillette and Stipel, and they followed the Post Office and Fire Brigade versions. The charming little Brescia Bugatti was made available in French (blue) and English (black) versions. Also becoming available was the 1933 Type 59 Bugatti and its rather curious sister, the "Biposto" two-seater. The single-seater version has finely-spoked wheels, while the other has the Bugatti alloy type. The first model is very close to reality, and is to be found in Paul Kestler's book, *Bugatti, Evolution of a Style* (Edita, 1975), as a colour illustration on page 126. The veracity of the two-seater is less certain however — but that does not detract from its qualities as a model!

USA plastic kits

Revell's 1982 Firebird (7215) starts this month off, and it's a beauty! Differing from other versions, the Revell model comes with clear roof hatches, steerable wheels, up or retracted headlight options and even a rear window wiper. This kit has a lot going for it in a crowded field. Also from Revell is a VW Cabriolet (7243); detailing is excellent and the model can be built with the top up or down. With its famous chassis, this kit is also a prime candidate for many VW-based conversions — a must for VW fans. The Ford EXP (7318) comes with T-Top options and a turbocharged engine. Another idea I like is the decals for the seat patterns for added realism; nice. The final 1:25 kit from Revell is the Datsun King Cab 4 x 4 Pickup (7361). Engraving is especially well done here, and the King Cab feature makes for a different type of pickup.

European and Japanese plastic kits

Italeri has opted for both the classic and the long haul vehicle. The first model introduced this month by the Italian manufacturer is a fine American car from the thirties. It's a Chrysler Imperial Phaeton copied from the renowned Harrah's collection, a virtually inexhaustible source for manufacturers of scale-model classic vehicles who can study at leisure the admirably restored cars. This 1933 model in 1:24 scale is of one of the first cars from the drawing board of a major coach-builder (Le Baron in this case) to have been built in series production. Its European rather than American-style coachwork hides a 6307 cc, eight-cylinder engine under an enormous bonnet. It developed 135 bhp to propel the two-ton (2218 kg) vehicle at more than 80 mph (130 km/h). The model consists of some 120 parts in black, beige, brown and chrome. It's an interesting model but far from being fault-free. The least that can be said about the tyres, for example, is that they contribute nothing to the looks of the car. Not much more than a mediocre result can be expected from two bits of plastic that have to be cemented together, especially as the removal of traces of glue is at the risk of rubbing out the tyre tread. The steering wheel is chromed, which is not accurate because cars in the thirties were generally fitted with ebonite steering wheels. The frame of the glass partition is too heavy, and the entire bodywork needs to be repainted. Fortunately the painting instructions are adequate. The dashboard has been reduced to the minimum. But not all the points are negative; the chrome work is good and it's an interesting basic model for those who don't mind a lot of work. The 1:24 scale gives it a place in a collection.

The other Italeri offering for the month was a Scania 142 H rig, also in 1:24 scale, which matches the realism of other heavy duty vehicles from the Italian manufacturer. As always, there are about 250 well moulded parts. Some parts have suffered from plastic shrinkage during the cooling process, notably the leaf springs. The chassis and engine are well executed but the plans are totally lacking in painting instructions. The modeller is left to his imagination, unless of course his local trucking company runs a Scania. The cab tilts to reveal the engine, but the doors are fixed. A bonus point is the good quality of the various cooling grilles. The transfers are by Cartograph, which says enough about their quality; the dashboard instruments are especially well done. This model, like the others in the series, comes with nine different number plates. In short, it's a fine piece of work.

Apart from a special Esci-sponsored version of the Fiat 131 Abarth Rally, Esci introduced the West German fire service version of the Mercedes 230 G. This is a nice development of December's Cross Country Mercedes with all the fire fighting accoutrements.

MARCH

This month *Corgi* unveiled its future plans, which show a growing number of models in 1:36, such as the "Datasport" racing Metro, the Ferrari 308 GTS from the "Magnum" TV series, a Golf Turbo competition car, a Porsche 924 Turbo, a rally-preparled Mercedes 240, a Ford Capri S racer, a Jaguar XJS-HE, a Ford Cobra Mustang, a 1957 Ford Thunderbird, and a 1954 Mercedes 300SL, the two latter models being especially attractive.

The collector had little enough time to digest this news before the two Italian

Italeri have put as much care into their truck models as they did into the military kits which made their excellent reputation. The latest addition to their range of European trucks is this Scania T-142H, modelled, like its predecessors, in 1:24. One small complaint is that the tyres are in rigid plastic rather than rubber or vinyl.

A new series of contemporary Formula 1 cars in 1:24 from Burago includes the Ferrari 126 K Turbo (left) and the Alfa Romeo 179 (right). They were later joined by a Renault RE 30, and the Italian manufacturer has done well to produce such good quality at a realistic price. They may be toys, but they are collectable toys.

CHEMCO

WATNEYS

euro-express

Left: Following Texaco, Shell and Exxon versions, Matchbox has produced this tanker in Chemco trim. It carries the reference number K-16 in the SuperKings series.

Below left: A new base model for Eligor, the thirties' Ford V8 van, was an excellent choice on the Franco-Swiss firm's part and allowed a number of 1:43 versions — closed van, pickup and cattle truck (1059) — with beautiful period liveries, such as the Cross & Blackwell (1078), Watneys (1067), Ford Motor Company (1070) and Guiness (1076) delivery trucks.

Bottom left: The latest Matchbox SuperKings Peterbilt, ref. K-31, which has previously borne Christian Salvesen, Langnese and Pepsi decals.

Below: In the same series, Matchbox's Ford Continental, this time in Polara trim. Previous versions were "Continental" and "Santa Fe".

Collector's nightmare — the 1981 Ferrari BB "European University" has been brought out in 1:43 by FDS (shown here), by Tron and by BAM-X. And here's the rub: the decals for all three versions come from the same place!

giants, *Burago* and *Polistil*, let their plans be known. The battle between the two is a hard one and they put their all into every model, whatever its scale.
Burago showed the new addition to its *Diamonds* range, a 1932 Alfa Romeo 2300 Spider. Seeing the advance model at the toy fairs gave rise to the question as to whether we ought to collect the Diamonds series, confident that they will be the classic collector's models of twenty or thirty years hence. Purists will say that they cannot be real classics because they have plastic parts. Plastic, they say, is not a noble material like metal, wood, or sheet metal. Plastic, they say, will deform with the ravages of time — ah, old, old quarrels!
The rest of the Burago programme had some interesting new models in 1:24, such as an Audi Quattro, a "Calberson" Renault 5 Turbo rally car, a Ford Mustang, a Mercury Capri RS, and a new series of Formula 1 cars under the title *New Line*. The first models in this range are a Ferrari 126K, Alfa 179, and a Renault RE 30 — obviously, the Grandee

AMT celebrated the 75th anniversary of the New York to Paris race with this 1:25 model of the winning Thomas Flyer. Detail work is excellent, and only the American flag carried by the original (now in the Harrah Museum in Reno) is missing.

constructors are appreciated in Italy! As for 1:43, the plans call for a Range Rover, a BMW M 1, a Ferrari 512 BB, a Mercedes 450 SC, and a Fiat Ritmo (Strada in Britain and the U.S.) Abarth.
Polistil refused to give up an inch of territory in the battle and fought back with today's buzz-word in models as in full size cars — Turbo. There is a Ferrari 208 GTB turbo and a Porsche 928 turbo in the *TS* series and, in the *SN* series, Formula 1 cars, turbocharged and otherwise, come to the fore with a Ferrari 126 CK, Alfa 179, Renault RE 30 and Ligier JS 17. The SN range is generally to a scale of between 1:22 and 1:26, but there are a number of new additions, such as the Renault Fuego, a Mercedes 450 SC rally car, an Opel Ascona, a Talbot Sunbeam rally car, a Toyota Celica GT and a Ford rally Escort which are all in 1:43!
Mattel burst back on the scene with a range which will be welcomed by enthusiasts. Their series of 1:25 Formula 1 cars is very good, despite some strange colour schemes and lettering such as a green "Dallah" Williams, and a blue "Pemex" Brabham. Fortunately, these are counterbalanced by realistic models of the Williams FW07B, Ferrari 126 CK, Arrows A2, Ligier JS 17 and Alfa Romeo 179.
Why are we presenting these details of future releases at this time, rather than following our monthly releases format? Mainly because *AYBM* is an international publication, and the arrival dates of models vary from country to country. In addition, every enthusiast likes to get hold of information concerning new models as soon as possible, a fact which explains the interest which the model manufacturers pay to their catalogues, and the pains which they go to in order to have them distributed as widely as possible. Catalogues are — and always have been — the model manufacturer's most potent selling tool.
But what about the real new releases at the beginning of European spring? Well, there was a Renault Fuego in 1:43 from *Norev* in their *Jet-Cars* series. Norev are a company who do some good things in a quiet way, making no great noise, but turning out nice models which find many fans. This one has finely reproduced lines and good detail apart from the windscreen wipers, which are too big.
More off-beat was an Excalibur by *Majorette* in 1:40. This is a model which will go down with those who like models of unusual cars. The reproduction is realistic, and it's not every day you can find an Excalibur to add to your display.
Solido dusted off the Renault TN 6H bus and turned it out in red and cream, the colours of "Les Transports en Commun de la Région Lyonnaise", the municipal transport undertaking of Lyons. It looks nice, but did Lyons ever use this typically Parisian mode of transport? A fine model, nevertheless.
There was a new surprise from *Tenariv* of Paris, who introduced a 1:43 white metal kit of the Aston Martin DBS V8 convertible. The kit features chromed parts, soft tyres, and assembly by means of screws.
Francesco Di Stasio kept his monthly rendezvous in the guise of *FDS*. His tireless workshops offered Nelson Piquet's Championship-winning Brabham BT 49C, a Ferrari 308 GTB in Tour de France guise (that's four wheels, not two), and three Ferrari 512 BBs. This is the third time we have come across this car in these pages. Following the path blazed by Tron and BAM-X, FDS offers the cars entered at Le Mans in 1980 and 1981 by the "European University". The third car is the 1981 Bellancauto entry. Just to underline that *déjà vu* feeling, the decals are all from the same source!
Truck fans will be happy to see the Scania 142M normal-control tractor and trailer from *Tekno*. Coming after the 142H conventional, this unit and three-axle trailer with Scania signwriting is absolutely superb. In 1:50, it has opening doors, full interior detail, a grille which lifts to reveal a detailed engine, windshield wipers, steps up to the cab, a sun-visor and nicely moulded air intakes. A superb model which will provide competition for the Ford Cargo, voted Truck of the Year, and modelled in 1:50 by *NZG*. The quality is as high as the Dutch product, and the features as numerous: a spoiler under the front bumper, a wind-deflector on the cab roof, windshield wipers, rear-view mirrors — even the window surrounds are faithfully reproduced to make it an impeccable production.

USA plastic kits

For the 75th anniversary of the 1908 New York/Paris race, AMT reissued the winning Thomas Flyer (4101) in 1:25. A well detailed kit, impressive when built and missing only the U.S. flag. The Datsun 280 ZX (4176) released in December got the Street Machine treatment and the 1972 Chevelle (4177) received some retooling to make it easier to build; it can still be built stock and is molded in sea blue, beautiful! AMT also reissued the first of their excellent 1:43 big rig trucks this month. Available are the Peterbilt 359 (7106), Peterbilt Wrecker (7107) and Freuhauf 40' Reefer trailer (7108) with Pepsi decals. Beautiful little models. In 1:25 came a Peterbilt 359 called "Midnight Express" (6134), a most impressive offering of an old favorite.
Monogram dropped their metal-bodied 1:24 kits this year, but reissued the 1956 Thunderbird (2289), MG-TC (2290) and

1953 Corvette (2291) in plastic. Also released was the 1:20 scale 1982 Corvette Collectors Edition (2408) with decals included for the special painted panels of the real car. Very nice.
Lindberg brought out a series of modern snap kits in 1:24 that look excellent when built; the 1980 versions of the Corvette (6501), Mustang (6504), Camaro (6502) and Firebird (6503) are excellent additions to their line. From Revell came 1:25 versions of the Porsche 911 Twin Turbo (6214) and a Camaro convertible (6225) as snap kits, and a Mustang convertible (7324) 80s style and custom Bronco (7334) in glue form. MPC produced a Maverick-based street racer called "Warhorse" (0831) and a custom called "Demon Vette" (3719; basically the old Turbo Shark) in 1:25. In HO scale, Con-Cor released the old Revell 1961 Chrysler cars (6019; 7-car set). March was a very good month for reissues.

European and Japanese plastic kits

This is the so-called quiet month of the Nuremberg International Toy fair. Quiet so far as production is concerned, but rather busy for manufacturers' representatives who have a frantic week in this beautiful medieval town in the east of the German Federal Republic. The only model to have come out in March was Revell's Ford Bronco Custom — a 1:25 scale, plastic kit.
But while nothing much was happening in the way of European production, the Japanese were going full speed ahead. Nichimo brought out no less than eight models, and yet again they were variations on well known themes, this time Nissan (Fairlady, Skyline and Silvia), Toyota (Celica, Corona and Sprinter), Mitsubishi (Lancer) and Mazda (Cosmo R6). These kits are to a new scale of 1:28 in contrast to Nichimo's normal 1:20 and 1:24 ranges; with between 33 and 38 parts each, they seem to be designed for beginners. From Tamiya came a Renault 5 Turbo in 1:24, a very nice model to be followed in mid-summer 1982 by a rally version.

APRIL

This was the month when the 1932 Alfa Romeo 2300 Spider from *Burago* arrived in the shops. Reduced to 1:8 scale, Vittorio Jano's masterpiece had zamac bodywork, plastic wings and spoked wheels. The four-part bonnet opened and folded neatly and fitted well. The twin overhead camshaft supercharged engine and the transmission were faithfully reproduced, as was the dash panel. The gear lever and the handbrake were movable and the steering wheel controlled the front wheels. Could this really be only a toy? The answer was yes if you looked at the cockpit and the seats, no if you looked at the care which had gone into the creation of the whole.
In the other ranges, two Formula 1 cars were already on sale, the Ferrari 126 CK and the Alfa Romeo 179, as well as the Mercury Capri RS Turbo. Scale for all these is 1:24.
Germany's VW Audi Group have a very good relationship with the *Conrad* company, and after having produced the Passat and Scirocco models for VW, Conrad now introduced the Santana and Polo built with full VAG co-operation from factory plans. The resulting 1:43 replicas are worthy of anybody's showcase, with opening doors, bonnets and boots, detailed interiors, realistic wheels, chrome, and nicely fitted components — the engines are in there too, so what more could one ask?
Gama's new release is the BMW 528i in 1:43. Although it is not a true promotional, it will do a good job of promoting the Munich marque with its realism and a list of features that matches the Conrads'. It is evident that the Germans put as much care into their model cars as they do with their full-sized counterparts.
And so to the first batch of new models from *Eligor*. *En masse* they line up as follows: 1926 Citroën 5CV van in new colours of Bally and Nicolas, 1934 Ford V8 van in Guinness livery, 1934 Citroën 500kg van with Miror colours, and a 1928 Renault KZ Paris taxi. The Ford V8 van will bear closer scrutiny, for it is the only really new model in the batch from Jacques Greilsamer's Franco-Swiss company. Painted in blue with the Guinness brand name on its flanks, it is an attractive model. More important from the purist's viewpoint is that the moulding is of excellent quality, the chrome is good, and that the many parts are finely finished, to such an extent that the "V8" inscription is clearly legible on the grille.
The fact that the decals are from Cartograf is sufficient to show their quality — their work for a number of specialists has earned the Italian decal specialists an enviable reputation.
Jacques Greilsamer shows every intention of spreading his company's influence over a wide sector of the market and is working hard toward that end. We await his Bugatti Type 35 with anticipation.
From France comes news of a new specialist, *Techni France*. A new entry in the field in this period of financial uncertainty is a welcome event, and much to be commended. Simply to start the business is a sign of courage, but to choose such unusual subjects for the first essay rather than tried and tested sellers is truly brave. Techni France has chosen to produce 1:43 replicas of two Citroën Rosalie record cars; the Citroën Rosalie I and II dates from 1931 and the Rosalie IV from 1934. The models are in resin, and are supplied fully assembled and painted on a wooden base with details of the original car. Citroën fans and lovers of record cars alike will be interested in these models. The third product from the company will be a streamlined Auto Union record car. We must await its arrival to see if it maintains the standards set by the first two.
Time for our monthly dose from *FDS*, and this month it was almost the same prescription as before — a Ferrari 126 CK as raced in the South African GP of 1981. The base is identical to that of the one used in the company's co-production with Bosica, and there is little in the way of modification; the price is pretty high for a re-hash.
Brumm launched a second version of the Blitzen Benz record car, as driven by the great Barney Oldfield in America in 1910. The base is the same, but the differences are marked. There is a white paint finish, a gold-coloured nose, side exhaust, "Blitzen Benz" decals, and black German eagle coat of arms. The most important thing is that they should be authentic: referring to Cyril Posthumus' book on the Land Speed Record, practically the bible on this subject, we find a picture on page 76 showing the car almost as modelled, except that it has black wheel-spokes and no driver's name on the tail. A further photograph, on page 43, does show the driver's name, but the car's name is "Lightning" Benz rather than "Blitzen" and there is no eagle crest. This picture was no doubt taken during the car's period as a track racer in Oldfield's hands.
The thing about Brumm is that the moment you look away, they come out with new models! This was the case with a very nice little Lancia Aprilia, which serves as a basis for the traditional Brumm variants of methane and gas-driven versions together with a Mille Miglia version. A specially noteworthy aspect of this model is the wheels, which look absolutely right and are beautifully finished. All this, and we still haven't seen the gaggle of single-seaters which are promised for the coming months!

USA plastic kits

AMT's five reissues this month were the 1:43 Jaguar XK-E (2111) and 1969 Corvette (2112; again, the plated parts were left out of these well detailed kits), a near stock 1977 Ford Mustang II (4179) and a racing version of the VW Scirocco (4153) in 1:25, and the Kenworth Aerodyne 108 COE (6807) in 1:32 snap.
Monogram is on a real "muscle car" kick

Time for an overview of this year's Tomy models and a pause to regret that the 1:43 Tomica Dandy range is not available in some countries, despite the Japanese manufacturer's size. Above, the Mitsubishi Canter in tipper and refuse truck form (D-20 and D-19); left, a Toyota Land Cruiser with snowmobile (L-14) and VW Beetle with cycles (L-11); below, also from the Leisure series, a Nissan Caravan with kart (L-13) and bikes (L-12).

Tomy's chief rival, Yonezawa, uses a wide range of scales for its Diapet range. The Neoplan Skyliner bus is in 1:60 (above, ref. B-41), but the Isuzu Piazza is in 1:40 (right, G-4) as are the cars in Gift Set S-6 — a Toyota Soarer, Nissan Leopard, Nissan Bluebird and Mitsubishi Galant.

No hurdle is too great for Italian specialist Vincenzo Bosica. The proof: this 1929 Alfa Romeo 1750 GS in 1:43, also available in kit form. The bonnet lifts to reveal an unbelievably detailed engine, and the doors open and close.

and this month saw the appearance of the much anticipated 1971 "Hemi 'Cuda" (2292), 1970 GTX Plymouth (2293) and 1969 Pontiac GTO "Judge" (2294) in 1:24. These cars were nearly the last for the muscle car era as insurance rates and government regulations helped kill of the breed. The stock kits are once again in the modern "Monogram Tradition," meaning it would be hard to think of ways to improve them. The company is paying more attention to detail than they ever have done in the past, and that is saying something; engraving of the deep-set dials in the GTO's dash is excellent and you can hardly see them. What is also significant about these releases is that all were once available from other companies (Jo-Han with a GTX and MPC with a GTO and Barracuda). That Monogram would not only release these particular cars but release them in stock form is important. I see this as a future trend as muscle cars are popular with both modelers and real car collectors. Monogram also brought out a beautiful 1:32 snap version of the Mack R Series Conventional (1210) with much plating and excellent detail.

Ertl's 1:32 International Eagle (8050) was the start of a new snap series and, unlike most snap truck kits, this model has a detailed engine. Revell released a 1982 Camaro (7216) to complement the Firebird, a Porsche 928 (7218; b&b conversion), reissues of the 1927 Ford T Touring (7238) and 1934 Ford Chopped Top Coupe (7239), along with a personal favorite (and a new model), the Vanagon VW Van (7328), all in 1:25.

Scale Craft imports many great kits from Japan into the USA and this month saw the arrival of the VW Super Beetle in both convertible (SC2416) and sedan (SC2417) versions, a Scirocco GTI Sedan (SC2418) and the De Tomaso "Pantera" (SC2520), all in 1:24.

Full marks to Belgian specialist firm Playtoy for their 1:43 reproduction of the Mazda RX 7 that Tom Wakinsaw and Pierre Dieudonné drove to victory in the 1981 Francorchamps 24-hour race.

European and Japanese plastic kits

While the charming Michèle Mouton was thumbing her nose at the heavyweights of the world rally championship from behind the wheel of her Audi Quattro, Esci launched two versions of this astonishing car. There's no chance that they will win any rally, even in the imagination of the modeller, for these cars, like the Mercedes 230 G replica, are engineless. Perhaps it was to console the modeller — or even to make his mouth water — that the Italian kit maker included an exploded drawing of the Audi's turbocharged power unit in the assembly plans. However, having to build a car with the prestige of the Audi Quattro out of 59 parts and four tyres sounds like provocation. But without malice or exaggeration, we can qualify the model as interesting, especially as it is the first Quattro replica in 1:24 scale. Furthermore, Esci says the model is aimed at children aged 10 and over. Success is assured among the young, especially as a Quattro Rally accompanies the road version. It is not a replica of the most renowned machine, being a model of the car in which Hannu Mikkola and Arne Hertz had an argument with a wall during the 1981 Monte Carlo Rally. But the interesting aspect is that this Quattro was the first example of this revolutionary car to participate in the Monte Carlo. It gets the same criticisms that apply to the series version, except that the transfers in red, grey and black are excellent. I also appreciated the rally version's speedometer (the figures are readable in both models) with its three indicated speeds — 80 km/h, 140 km/h and 200 km/h. Evidently, Quattro drivers have a limited choice as to how fast they go, and it is easy to guess Michèle Mouton's choice. Esci once again tantalizingly provided an exploded drawing of the engine, but this time they reversed the picture so that you need a mirror to read the graphist's signature. Criticism is easy, you may say — fine: let's give Esci its due for a model which despite everything should turn out to be very pretty.

In Japan, Nichimo's list of nearly indistinguishable variations had three new entries in the form of a Nissan Laurel, Toyota Celica and Nissan Skyline in 1:24, and along the same lines came a 1:24 Mazda RX 3 with the Savanna moniker. Bearing in mind the width of the tyres and the ground clearance, it's hard to imagine driving such a car into the tropics... LS released a 1977 Nissan 330 Cedric 2800 E "Brougham" as a 75-part 1:20 kit, and Tamiya released its long-awaited army Ford Mutt M151A2 jeep in 1:35, the now traditional military model scale.

MAY

And so to the end of year fireworks. Well, the end of *our* year at any rate, for we can stay no longer than the beginning of June if *AYBM* is to be in your hands before Christmas. There is a crowd of new introductions this month, so let's get going. We'll start with *Brumm*, who were particularly productive as the Italian summer approached. The 1948 Talbot Lago Grand Prix car, the 1937 Maserati 8-cylinder Grand Prix racer, the 1956 Lancia Ferrari D50, the 1931 Alfa Romeo 2300 8C and its 1932 Mille Miglia version all made their first appearances. They are to the usual high Brumm quality, and the company's *Revival* range is rapidly becoming a classic collection on its own. We are already up to reference number 78, and the 1982 catalogue finishes with number 110, and so we are tempted to wonder whether Reno Tatarletti will have exhausted his programme by the end of the next seven months. The summer and the Christmas period are the best selling periods, and therefore the time to bring out the new models, so we can be sure that Signor Tatarletti has a few up his sleeve for later in the year — for instance, there is the Bugatti 57S, the Maserati 250F, the Ferrari Testa Rossa, the Vanwall, the 1930 Le Mans Bentley... There is plenty yet to come from our friend at Brumm.

Eligor introduced its 1927 Bugatti 35B, and a very fine model it is. Available in six colours, blue, red, black, green, yellow and black, it is to an accurate 1:43 and is beautifully detailed. Undoubtedly, it will be a must for many collectors. If M. Greilsamer can turn out a few models like this every year, his success is assured.

The Bugatti was supported by a flotilla of publicity vehicles, of which the most important, to our eyes, was the Opel Laubfrosch van, which constitutes another completely new model and will certainly serve as the basis for a whole new family of colourful liveries. To keep you up to date, the newest Eligor commercials are as follows: 1925 Opel Laubfrosch in Hag, Continental, Opel Service, and Ovomaltine liveries (the Swiss influence is strong here); the 1933 Ford V8 open pickup (metal body); the same Ford V8 as a closed pickup (wooden body) in Watney's and Texaco colours; and the 1934 Ford V8 van with Ford Service, Chocolat Lindt, Castrol, Mobiloil, Crosse &. Blackwell, Longines, Stephens Inks, and Sir Alan Cobham liveries. Not forgetting the 1926 Citroën 5CV in the colours of the Loiret fire brigade and the 1948 11CV bearing the badges of the Ariège brigade.

While on the subject of fire appliances, let us refer to the introduction of some new models in 1:43 by *Conrad* in their popular series of fire-fighting vehicles. Notable among them is a superb Gräf & Stift, and they are all bound to appeal to the many fire engine enthusiasts.

From *Matchbox* came the Peterbilt tractor and refrigerated trailer of the Super-Kings range in a new colour scheme, that of Euro Express. The outfit is in blue, with a line of red, orange and yellow running horizontally from the grille to the rear doors. This collection of Peterbilts is gradually growing, with the following versions already available: Iglo Langnese, Christian Salvesen, Burger King, Coca Cola, Pepsi Cola, and Gervais Ice Cream. The same is also true of the Ford LTS articulated tanker, which will from now on be available in the colours of Chemco.

Looking through the lists of the specialist manufacturers, one gains the impression that this is the year of the Testa Rossa. Ferrari-lovers will rejoice, but even non-specialists will appreciate the qualities of this model from Precision Miniatures in the USA. In 1:43, it comes in four different versions and is available as a kit or in fully finished form.

Previous liveries have been Texaco (with red or metallic red cab), Shell, Total, Aral and Exxon, and the vehicle has also been produced in military guise. It is amazing how Matchbox can turn out a multiplicity of different versions without us ever really noticing.

The Bird's Custard Powder version of the Yesteryear Model T van also became available this month, and turned out to be clad in a coat of many colours, with a dark blue body, a yellow roof, red spoked wheels with white sidewall tyres, and red and white lettering. This is another model which has appeared in a number of different liveries. Since it was introduced in 1979, they have been Colmans Mustard, Coca Cola, Suze, Smith's Potato Crisps (in two different versions, with single or double designs on the rear doors), BP (with tank body), and now in Bird's colours.

In the specialist field one sees signs of opportunism on the part of *Meri Kits* from Italy, who have re-launched the Lotus 49 Grand Prix car and its derivatives. This was an idea which John Day first tried in

Rotarex, a Japanese specialist firm, reproduced the 1937 Bugatti T 57 S in 1:43 with extreme care. Note the spoked wheels, brake drums and ventilation grills on the bonnet.

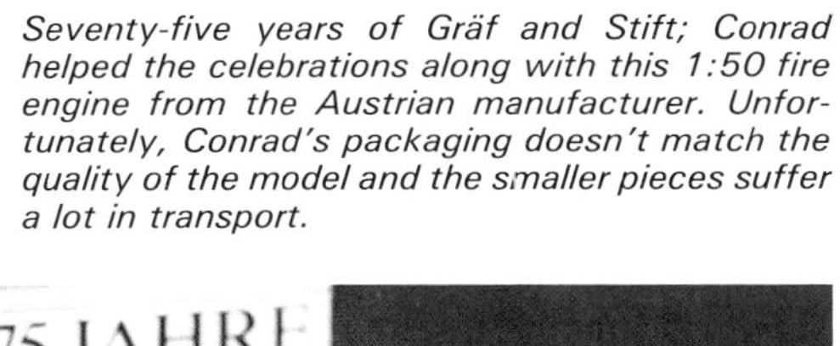

Seventy-five years of Gräf and Stift; Conrad helped the celebrations along with this 1:50 fire engine from the Austrian manufacturer. Unfortunately, Conrad's packaging doesn't match the quality of the model and the smaller pieces suffer a lot in transport.

975161MI

the early seventies. Meri Kits have dusted it off with the collaboration of Vincenzo Bosica, the new maestro of the Italian model-making world. The possibilities are enormous, and we have the choice of four Grand Prix winners — Clark's victorious car from the 1967 South African GP, still in green and gold Team Lotus colours; the Walker-Durlacher Racing Team car in which Jo Siffert won the 1968 British GP, midnight blue with a white band around the nose; Graham Hill's 1968 Monaco winner in Gold Leaf Team Lotus colours with a wing-cum-engine cover; and finally the Gold Leaf car in which Graham Hill won in South Africa in 1968, bearing high-set front and rear wings. The Italian kit is a real beauty, finely detailed, and with over 70 pieces, which is a fair number for a 1:43 kit in white metal. Maybe too many? Certainly the assembly of the suspension and engine assemblies from a multitude of small parts is not easy, but fortunately there is a comprehensive instruction book which explains things well — although it still needs a great deal of patience to assemble the front suspension. The John Day kit was much easier!

A month without something from *FDS*? Of course not — there is a 1957 Ferrari MM as driven by Taruffi and a 1981 Theodore TY 01 Formula 1 car as driven by Patrick Tambay.

Last of the year is *Western Models*' Chrysler Imperial Le Baron Phaeton. A really classy model — whitewall tyres, raised hood (since it's an American car, that should be top), bonnet mascot (and that should be hood ornament), and rear view mirrors fixed to the side-mounted spare wheels (no problems there!). A beautiful creation, a real millionnaire's dream in 1:43.

Now that's styling: the Corvette John Greenwood and John Adam took to Watkins Glen in 1975 with its hood paint running from deep red to pale yellow. A 1:43 model in polyester resin from Eco Design, an Italian specialist marque.

USA plastic kits

This was a most exciting month. For the HO big rig truck fans Lindberg brought out the first four of a new range; two different cabs (GMC Astro 95 and Ford CL-9000) and three different trailers will make up the first series. These impressive models are selling well, so there may be a lot more of them from Lindberg in the future; excellent news if you like HO trucks as much as I do. Monogram's lone release for the month was a 1:32 snap Union Oil tanker trailer (1211) that makes a nice addition to this line. Jo-Han reissued two 1:25 models that should be popular — the 1963 Plymouth hardtop (C-5263) and 1968 Cadillac convertible (C-5368) are very hard kits to find on the collectors market. Detailing is what you'd expect from Jo-Han: excellent. AMT's reissue of the 1:25 scale 1970 Chevy Blazer (4631) is called "Chevy Bandit," and the 1929 Ford A Roadster (4156) is back for what I am sure will be a popular run; the Model A is an old tool, but a good one.

MPC had been busy and came out with a 1978 Firebird (0820) as a custom "War Eagle" version, as well as a rather far out street racing version of the 1981 Camaro called "Thunder Z" (0821), two 1982 Charger-based funny cars called "Nitro Charger" (0829) and "Prime Time" (0828), another version of the Datsun dragster pickup called "Lil Hustler" (0859), and a 1969 Barracuda called "The Avenger" (0860; not totally stock, but close to it), all in 1:25; and in 1:16 there were reissues of the 1957 Corvette (3085; truly impressive kit when built, though the side trim on the right side doesn't line up exactly — not enough to hurt the model though) and the 1978 Corvette (3087).

This month also saw 1:32 versions of the Camaro and Firebird from Revell (6017 and 6018; snap form). There *is* no end to the versions of these two beautiful cars! Turning to 1:25 big rig trucks, Revell have a Mercedes Benz 1628 cabover with roof spoiler (7409) and the Globetrotter version of the Volvo F12 cabover (7407). Non-American big rigs are sure injecting new blood into the domestic lines of most USA companies — about time.

Ma Collection is a series of Swiss-made superkits. Michel Sordet, who runs the operation, goes in for vintage classics, as witness these 1:43 models of the 1936 Renault Nerva Grand Sport.

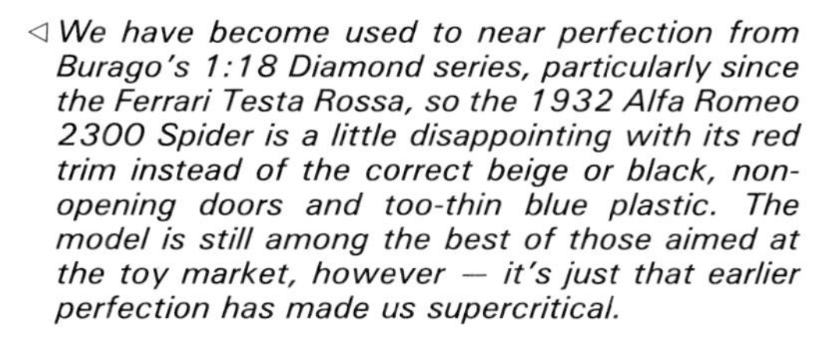

◁ *We have become used to near perfection from Burago's 1:18 Diamond series, particularly since the Ferrari Testa Rossa, so the 1932 Alfa Romeo 2300 Spider is a little disappointing with its red trim instead of the correct beige or black, non-opening doors and too-thin blue plastic. The model is still among the best of those aimed at the toy market, however — it's just that earlier perfection has made us supercritical.*

Even in 1:24 scale, the Renault 5 Turbo looks purposeful, crouched on its wide rims and ready to put up a good time on any stage. Nor did Tamiya's designers keep full-blooded rallying enthusiasts waiting for long — a Monte Carlo 1981 version was announced in June 1982.

Congratulations to Nichimo on adding this Toyota 2000 GT to its catalogue. One of the rare Japanese sports models of the sixties, the car was powered by a 2-litre overhead-cam six. The body showed a coming together of oriental and western influences.

The American fashion for muscle cars has made the passage to Japan, and this Mitsubishi Galant GTO 2000 GSR in 1:24 by Nichimo is typical of the trend.

RVs — recreational vehicles — are another fad imported to Japan from the US. The basic vans are smaller than their American counterparts so the degree of customization is by necessity more restrained. This Toyota Twin Ace Custom has been faithfully reproduced by Nichimo.

Only three or four years ago the catalogues of the Japanese kit manufacturers were full of exotica such as the Lamborghini Countach, Porsche 935, Ferrari BB512 and Lancia Stratos. Today the scene has changed and it is the products of the Japanese motor industry which hold the stage. The models are available in standard or modified form almost as soon as the real car makes its debut on the motor show stand. Tamiya were the first to bring out the Honda City R — and the Motocompo minibike which goes in the back.

Japanese kits not only reflect national production, but the makers are not afraid to produce different versions of the same car. Thus Tamiya offer the Nissan Skyline 2000 GT Turbo, 2000 RS and 2000 GT Turbo Hardtop. Supporting Japan's two-wheel industry as well, Tamiya offer a model scooter with each car.

Revell has entered the model truck market with a range of 1:25 kits which offer a great deal, such as opening cab doors and steerable front wheels. This "Black Magic" Peterbilt Conventional is typical of the range in its fine detailing and colourful decoration. The kits seem to have every feature needed to make them winners in the markets of the world.

From Scale Craft there were five "packages for the U.S." in 1:24. For those interested in the exotic, there's the "Dome-O" Sports Coupe (SC2413), a 1981 style Camaro (SC2412) which makes an interesting version of this modern classic styled Z-28, along with a Z-28 Turbo Custom (SC2419) set for street racing. For real race car fans, Scale Craft have versions of the "Black" Porsche 935-78 Twin Turbo (SC2414; 1978 Le Mans "Special") and the beautiful BMW M1 "Procar" racer (SC2415). It's nice seeing these interesting imported kits having a place on the shelves of the better stocked hobby shops.

Any way you look at it, these last twelve months were filled with excellent and wanted plastic kits from all the model companies. I don't think there has ever been a better year for true variety since I began building. Still, the companies are slow to climb on the muscle car bandwagon, and at the 1982 hobby industry trade shows there was a noticeable lack of older cars being modeled. As for antique cars, only the Thomas Flyer could be seen. Custom cars are again becoming very popular (many are starting to show up at model car contests, and they are tastefully styled and excellent models in all respects), while street rods are more popular than ever. These are areas the companies should be looking at but, with few exceptions, are not. For all that, the outlook is far from gloomy, and as the companies realize there is a world market for plastic car kits, the hobby will continue to grow. Good years are ahead.

European and Japanese plastic kits

In spring my fancy turns to thoughts of building Protar's Renault RE-23 in 1:12 scale. And once more this reminds me of Tarquinio Provini's spirited defence of his model at Nuremberg. "It's an exact copy of the real car measured and photographed during four days at the 1980 Imola Grand Prix trials and is therefore identical to the original, down to the smallest details... and not based on rough snapshots." End of quote. This is what appears on the box cover — a direct attack against Heller and Tamiya. Mr Provini moreover took pains to point out to us that his model was "much more comprehensive and realistic that those of the competition," failing to add, perhaps that a Formula 1 car changes after each race, at least in certain details. Let us at least acknowledge that even though we have yet to complete the model, the Protar is rich in unimagined details. It consists of an incredible number of parts — more than 1000 according to Protar — with extremely comprehensive cabling; serrated, rubber belts driving the camshafts, water and oil pumps, and an impressive number of screws, heralding the arrival in September of a metal model in line with the new Protar philosophy. The whole thing boils down to 97 assembly stages outlined in a 32-page instruction book. There's enough for at least 100 hours work provided you follow the painting instructions to the letter, or even add to them. The moulding of this Renault is a great step forward in progress from the previous models, and Protar has done wonders in casting the engine block, sump and gearbox in a single piece without central adhesion — you won't believe your eyes.

The various plastic parts are moulded in yellow, white, grey, chrome and in an amazing steel grey for the suspension arms, wheel hubs and other pieces. More interesting details: the cooling air intakes for the rear disc brakes are cast in one piece, the skirts are sprung (like those on the 312 T 4) and Provini has taken detailing to the extreme of simulating the jubilee clips on some of the air and oil hoses. Also worth pointing out are the adjustable safety harnesses, which can be clicked into place, the tyres, which can be pumped up using any syringe, the moving back aerofoil, and more. This model, as Tarquinio Provini himself admits, "is a little more expensive than those of the competition, but the price, we are sure, is fully justified." Needless to say, it's a model for the highly experienced builder.

We are fully aware that Tarquinio Provini is a winner. One doesn't become world motorcycle champion, as he did in 1957 and 1958, without putting one's heart into it. His pursuit of originality and new solutions, whether for his cars or his bikes, is unrelenting, even though he sometimes goes a little far and ignores the odd detail here and there. However, I cannot help liking Tarquinio Provini, who with enormous will overcame the handicap he has suffered since his serious motorcycle crash during the Isle of Man TT on 16 September 1966.

Italy apart, this month's news came from Japan. The Nuremberg show two months before had attracted the modelling world's jet set and, if you're on the lookout for new model subjects, Nuremberg is a good place to be... might this just have helped the 20 new models in 1:20 and 1:24 on their path to production? One of them was truly outstanding: the De Tomaso Pantera GTS in 1:24 from Marui. It's always nice to see initiative, especially when the model is as good as this one. Otherwise, excepting only Fujimi's 1:24 Chevrolet Camaro Z-28 Special, May's offerings were based on series — or pseudo-series — domestic production. It's no longer just a question of duplicates here; for the Nissan Skylines of this month alone, we're talking about septuplicates... To us it seems excessive, but who are we to query the manufacturers' supply and demand equations? The Honda City (in quadruplicate) and, right behind it, the Suzuki Cervo are two others on a road signposted success. Incidentally, statisticians may care to note that this month, the last in our year, saw new kits from ten different Japanese makers, from Aoshima to Tamiya.

NEW MODELS

on 2 or 3 wheels

The motorcycle shows of the end of 1981 and the beginning of 1982 provided a firm — and welcome — denial of what was said in these pages last year concerning progress in the world of two wheels. In fact, the styling and technology of the motorcycle has been on the move since the end of 1980 and is now in top gear. The appearance of turbochargers on machines which are already not short of power, the styling of such machines as the Suzuki Katana, the magnificent architecture of a water-cooled V4 with twin overhead cams and four valves per cylinder — everything points to the way in which manufacturers are fighting to attract a clientèle which has such a wide choice. Germany has followed the Japanese lead, and the styling of the latest BMWs leaves them with nothing to be ashamed of when compared to oriental counterparts. Italy, a little more conservative perhaps, still stays ahead in terms of frame design and the outstanding road manners of its products.

If the smaller car manufacturers continue to disappear like soap bubbles, two-wheel craftsmen continue to multiply, a fact which ensures a continuous supply of new models and which has not gone unnoticed by model manufacturers.

There are those who say that the motorcycle kit no longer enjoys the popularity which it did some years ago, but this is a song we have heard before, and it does not ring true. Does the fault lie with importers, who believe either not enough or not at all in the motorcycle market? It is a difficult question to answer. Every year the production of models is bigger, better designed, and better finished. Can it be that manufacturers like Tamiya, Nichimo, Fujimi, Heller and Protar among others continue purely out of a masochistic pleasure in making models just for glory? It seems unlikely, particularly when one considers that even the lowest quality models of today are satisfactory and that the best leave one almost speechless. The motorcycle kit is certainly not dead, and its full-size counterpart is going through a golden era. Thus, by the law of probability, there is likely to be an increased interest in bike models — the more motorcycles there are, the more motorcyclists there are, and in consequence a larger number of potential buyers for kits of the full-size machine which they spend their days riding.

From the smallest to the largest

Production of motorcycle models in the year under review has followed two directions. First, it has reflected the growing Japanese interest in scooters, and this trend has been particularly noticeable in the field of kits. The Yamaha Beluga, Suzuki Gemma 50 and Honda Tact are only three of the small-capacity newcomers that have been modelled from a flood of such machines, which may or may not repeat their Japanese sales success in Europe. On the other hand there has been a noticeable increase in the number of models of large capacity machines, which again echoes the sales policy of the factories — although Japanese modellers have no chance to see the biggest of them in real life because of a law which bans anything over 400 cc from the overcrowded Japanese roads. Still, this does not stop them from enjoying the beauty of a Honda CB 1100R or a 1340 cc Harley Davidson in their model showcase. This limitation is the reason for the number of customized, choppered, and turbocharged versions of 400 cc machines from Japanese sources, in such a variety that every fan can find something to suit his fancy.

The Japanese are not the only ones to have successfully exploited their market. Take the example of Heller, which has successfully overcome the problems which beset it last year to come up with some very high quality 1:8 kits. America is working hard to tread water in the current economic storms and is only just succeeding, while Italy has one of the most enthusiastic manufacturers in Protar, which shows that enthusiasm in its choice of models, its dynamism, and its faith in the hobby. It's also good to see Esci back with civilian versions of military models that have been in existence for some time. Let us hope that others will follow. One last word concerning this review of the year: many of the models here are described only briefly, because we have not been able to obtain full details, enabling us to comment properly, from a few manufacturers. To those manufacturers that took the time to help us, our thanks — the photographs in these pages are a reflection of their co-operation.

New models from Japan

As usual in the past few years, the Land of the Rising Sun has sent us a flood of new models. There is a newcomer in the form of Tsukuda with some metal models, but the established producers stick to the well worn path of Harley, Honda, Yamaha, Kawasaki and Suzuki. There is an abundance of scales, from 1:6 to 1:16,

Last year's flood of Harley-Davidsons has been ▷ replaced by a flood of Yamaha's water-cooled sportsters, the RZ and RD 350 and 250. Here is Nichimo's RZ 250 in 1:10.

Although we should be used to them by now, there is still something about a 1:6 Tamiya kit that leaves one breathless! This is the Honda CB 750 F, an interesting new introduction which blazes a trail for more modern versions of this four-cylinder classic.

The second version of Tamiya's Kawasaki 1300 is this 'Touring' model. The kit contains 500 parts and builds up into a replica more than 40 cm (15.75 ins) long. At the risk of being labelled as nit-pickers, we would like to have seen real springs for the suspension of the upper rear carrying box.

One of the two models in 1:12 introduced by Revell. This 'Heavy Harley' chopper will prove ideal for modelling beginners.

Like many of its contemporaries, ▷ Nichimo has covered all the angles; here is the 350 to complete the pair of RZ Yamahas, and there are 1:10 replicas of both the 250 and 350 RD as well. None of them are up to the standards of the 1:12 kits from Tamiya.

YAMAHA
RZ 250

YAMAHA
RZ 350

and an abundance of novelties — so many in fact, that one begins to wonder how the manufacturers continue to survive in such a crowded market, which grows by some 40 models a year. Let us just accept it as proof that competition is good for business and set off on our trip from Aoshima to Yodel. The only omission is Nitto, whose single new introduction of the year is a Honda CB 750F — developed in America of all places — and covered in detail in a kit review elsewhere in this annual.

Aoshima

One-twelfth is the preferred scale at Aoshima, which offers three new kits, all available in both standard and so-called Special forms. First are two scooters of the type that is enjoying such success in Japan: a Yamaha Beluga 80 and a Suzuki Gemma 50, each comprising some 50 parts, moulded in styrol in red and white. The Special versions are made up of around 65 parts and are moulded in red and white for the Beluga and blue and white for the Gemma. They are relatively inexpensive models which will probably be more popular in their home market than in other countries.

The third of the kits will be of more interest to European and American modellers, representing a Suzuki GSX 400F. The standard version has 90 pieces and is in red and silver. The Special, comprising 100 parts, comes in red and purple, a combination not the most visually pleasing we have ever seen. The choice of 1:12 scale is a good one, giving adequate detail while being compact.

Finally, a note of pleasure which we cannot hide colours our mention of four little

The Honda Gold Wing Special — or is it a GL 1100 Interstate? — from Fujimi is a very fine model in 1:15.

beauties in 1:16, reproductions of machines to be found in the Harrah collection in Reno, Nevada. They are a 1918 Harley Davidson, a 1924 Ace, a 1912 Henderson, and a 1914 Militaire, the last three being equipped with magnificent in-line four-cylinder engines. These models have led a complicated life, starting off in anonymity, surfacing in the Entex range, and now coming up again with Aoshima. No distribution plans are known, but it is to be hoped that they will make an appearance worldwide.

Fujimi

Fujimi are undertaking a policy which is already commonplace with many of their contemporaries — that of taking a basic model and serving it up in a number of different sauces. Thus, although they announce seven new 1:15 models, they are all in fact varieties of the popular Yamaha water-cooled two-strokes and the flat-four Honda. The first is the Yamaha RD 250LC, equipped with a handlebar cowling and another cowling covering the lower part of the engine, in standard colours. Next comes an RZ 250, a more sporting version, without cowlings but with a sports exhaust system incorporating chromed silencers (mufflers), a more squared-off tank profile, and a red paint-job with special decorative trim. Then there is a Custom RZ and an RZ 350 which we have not yet had the pleasure of seeing. The Honda comes in three versions — a Gold Wing Special, a GL 1100, and a GL 1100 Interstate.

Imai

More scooters from Imai, in 1:12. A Honda Tact "Full Back" and a Yamaha Pasetta. There are some forty parts moulded in red for each model and their prices will break nobody's bank.

Nagano

Although Nagano's Honda CB 750 (or 900) F2 Bol d'Or is a good model, its quality does not approach that of the Tamiya, which remains the uncontested master of the Japanese manufacturers. However, its 1:8 scale, not so common among motorcycle kits, should ensure it a good distribution. The moulding is acceptable and the colours of the plastic are very good, but it fails to match other Japanese models — particularly large scale ones — by having fixed suspension and rear shock-absorber/spring units moulded in one piece. This is unforgivable, especially when one remembers that Tamiya use a real spring in the rear suspension of their Suzuki RGB 500 in 1:12 scale. In spite of this failing, it is still a good model offering some 200 parts at an economic price and would make an ideal stepping-stone for the modeller moving from a 1:8 Revell model to a Tamiya, Union or Yodel.

Nichimo

Yamaha's RZ series has also inspired Nichimo, whose 250 and 350 in 1:10 contain 117 and 120 parts respectively.

Tamiya

Tamiya's skill has always been to be one step ahead of the market or to react to changes in taste with dazzling speed. The Japanese market leaders were the first to produce kits of motorcycles in large scale (1:6), and only Protar, with an impressive

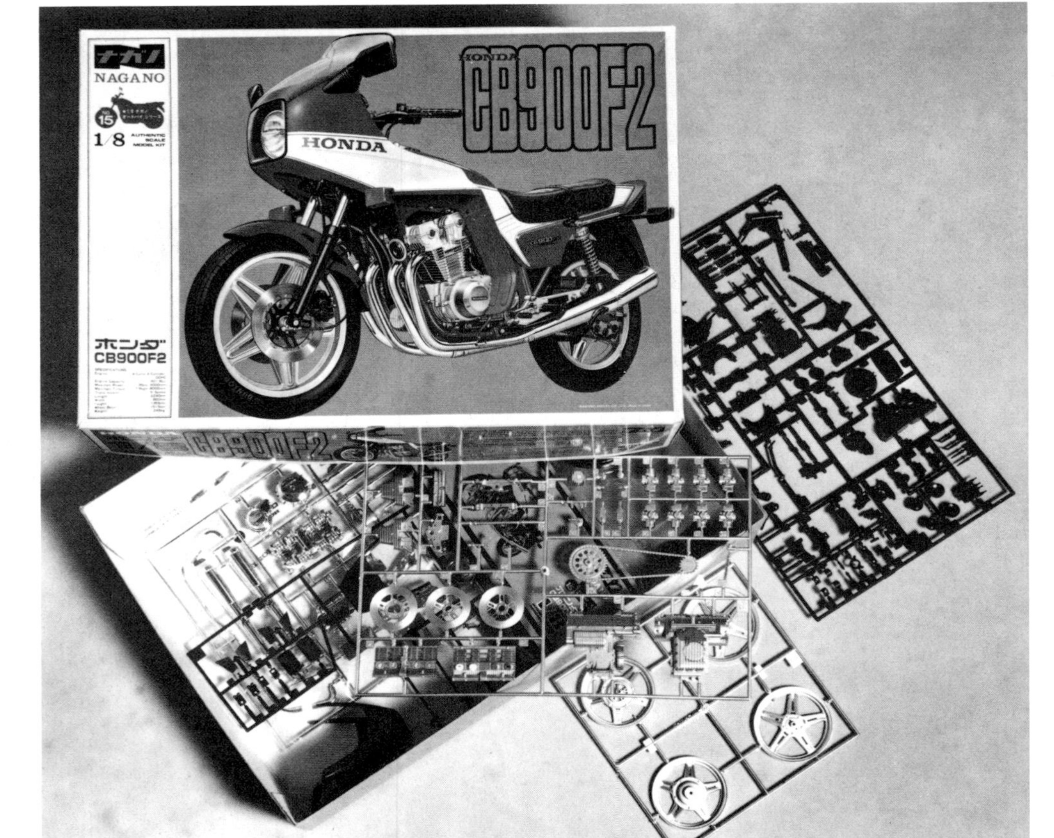

A monster that has inspired many a Japanese manufacturer: the Honda CB 900 F2. Nagano's version, in 1:8, isn't among the very best, especially as far as moulding is concerned. But the scale and the price still make it attractive.

Available in 1:6 or 1:12 (these are 1:12), ▷ Tamiya's Honda CB 750 F can be finished in a choice of black, grey, or red, and is supplied with three decal sets to match.

HONDA
HONDA
CB750-F

Moto Guzzi California featuring a high degree of internal detail, has tried to follow that lead. But models in 1:6 scale eat up display space and realizing the way public taste was going, Tamiya turned into one of the leaders in the field of 1:12 motorcycle models in less than a year, following the lead it has established in 1:12 cars. The firm has not, however, abandoned the biggies, and issued two new models in December 1981 and May 1982. The big push has nonetheless been on the 1:12 front, and in 12 months Tamiya has announced no less than 12 little beauties, comprising the Yamaha YZR500, Suzuki RGB 500 in factory (Barry Sheene) and Team Gallina (Marco Lucchinelli) versions, road-going RZ 250 and 350 Yamahas, a Yamaha Beluga scooter, and three versions of the now-legendary Honda fours, a CB 750F, a CB 900 Bol d'Or, and a splendid CB 110R which will also be produced in 1:6 scale in the near future. It should be noted that neither the Team Gallina Suzuki nor the CB 1100R appear in the 1982 Tamiya catalogue. The two new big-scale kits are a Honda CB 750F and a Kawasaki KZ 1300B Touring, and they completely live up to Tamiya's high reputation for perfection. The Kawasaki Touring is a real gem, nearly 17 inches (40 cm) long and beating the record for the highest number of parts for a Tamiya solo motorcycle with over 500, a number only exceeded by the truly exceptional Harley Davidson Classic Sidecar.

The smaller 1:12 models do not disappoint either, even though their assembly is not, contrary to what one might think, simpler than that of the large models. On the contrary, the painting process is difficult and the process of cementing the parts needs care and accuracy. One can count on painting one of these little models taking up two thirds of the total time expended on its building — apart from the Beluga, which is much simpler than the others — and the 80 to 100 part kits will need around 12 hours work each. Moulding quality is, as usual, superb, particularly in the area of fine detailing. Cleaning up the parts will take longer than with a 1:6 kit because of their smaller size, and it must also be remembered that mould marks and careless application of cement are more noticeable on a smaller scale model. Nevertheless, a carefully assembled 1:12 Tamiya will make a welcome addition to any showcase.

Mention must be made of the cables, which are of too great a diameter, but this is a fault which is forgotten when one inspects the tyres, whose detailed pattern — and smell — are just like the real thing.

We should mention at this point another item not included in the 1982 catalogue of the Shizuoka-based manufacturer, a Harley Davidson Classic "Black Flash", ref. BS-0615S. The S is for Special because the model was only produced in strictly limited numbers. It is the only Tamiya motorcycle kit to carry a photograph on the box top rather than a painting by Mr Tamiya, one of the sons of Y. Tamiya, the company's founder. The collector who gets hold of one of these kits will be a lucky one. The same comment applies to an all-chrome Honda Gorilla 50 cc which appears nowhere in the company's publicity material and which was also produced in strictly limited numbers. Both of these models cannot help but become sought-after and valuable collectors' pieces.

Finally, Tamiya has set the woods on fire with the announcement of a Suzuki GSX 1100S Katana, which will be an early introduction in both scales. The company's New Year's greeting card for 1982 shows the machine ridden by a fearsome samurai in full regalia and ready to set off to do battle with whatever enemies might present themselves. Although there was advance warning of the arrival of the Katana, there was no such advance information about a new addition to the 1:12 range at mid-year. It is a very fine Honda CR 250R motocross machine carrying the reference number 1411. It has a real spring for the cantilever rear suspension and meets all the usual Tamiya quality standards. It will no doubt prove to be a big hit with the many motocross fans, who have been a little neglected of late.

Tsukuda

One has fond memories of the meritorious efforts of the British company that introduced a couple of 1:8 motorcycles in white metal a few years ago under the name Big Six Classic Replicas. The models were of the AJS 7R 350 and a Matchless G 50, and the attempt was not exactly crowned with success; the kits were not well finished, difficult to assemble, and the models tended to collapse soon after construction if they were not supported by a form of scaffolding which was as clumsy and cumbersome as it was unlovely.

Now a Japanese constructor, Tsukuda, has taken up the torch with a single model — of a Yamaha RZ 250, of course — which is claimed to be the forerunner of a 1:12 range which will comprise an RZ 350, a Suzuki GSX 1100 Katana, and then a Honda CX 500 Turbo. Made in "compound tin metal" according to the manufacturers, they will be of interest to experienced modellers who have exhausted the possibilities of plastic kits and yearn for something more challenging. The descriptive leaflet we received even speaks of the Katana in terms of white metal "for every detail of this superbly equipped machine." We shall see.

Union

The Harley Davidson family from Union continues to increase, with two very similar choppers, an FXB-80 Sturgis and an FXS-80 Lowrider. In fact the only difference between the two lies in their colour and some very fine details.

There are new offspring for the Honda four-cylinder clan too, with a CB 750F, a 900 F2 Bol d'Or, and a CB 1100R. A "New CBX" is a derivation of the "Europe Type" version of the six-cylinder we have already seen. The 1982 model has a touring style fairing and panniers and a new tank and saddle unit. Finally, there is a Kawasaki Z 400 FX equipped with a turbo, which will make a nice companion for the Z1-R Turbo introduced last year.

Yodel

Only one new model from Yodel, and in fact it is a modification rather than a totally new kit, being a Honda CBX in road racing guise. It is in 1:8 and comprises some 230 parts, including fully operating suspension. Finish is in the best Japanese tradition, and Yodel are, in fact, the strongest competitors for Tamiya, although differing scales avoid a direct confrontation between the two marques.

New Models from Italy

Esci

No real newcomers from the Italian manufacturer, but some interesting adaptations of existing models, for at Nuremberg Esci showed civilian models of the Harley Davidson WLA 45, Triumph 3H 350, and BMW R-75 Sidecar that are already well known in their military guise. There are not many changes to the kits apart from those necessary to de-militarize them. The kits are by no means new, but they are of sufficient quality to bear comparison with any other 1:9 scale motorcycles.

Polistil

Although they are toys rather than real scale models, Polistil's 1:15 motorcycles have the merits of being well built and solid. The company introduced four new models during the year, and showed that the Harley vogue is not finished by making them four different "Hawgs": a Café Racer, a Sportster 1000, and two Classics, one with, and one without, sidecar. They are models which are equally at home in the toy drawer or in the showcase alongside equivalently-priced productions but they do not really bear comparison with a Japanese construction kit. However, this should not be construed as a criticism, for they are aimed at a totally different market.

Protar

Tarquinio Provini never fails to amaze us with his competitiveness — which took him to two world motorcycle championships, in the 125 cc class in 1957 and the 250 class in 1958 — and his charm. Working with facilities which are much less than those of a Japanese manufacturer, he still succeeds in astonishing us each year with his inventiveness, his dynamism, and the innovative ideas he introduces into his productions. They may not always be the ideal solution, but they are the fruit of faith and determination. Provini was the first with metal frames and suspensions for 1:9 models, and the first with interior detail (sadly discontinued now, but understandably so, since its appeal was mainly only to those who wanted to build cutaways). He now has a range which covers 41 models in 1:9, including four which are labelled as *prossima novita*, or coming shortly. One of these, the Anton Mang Kawasaki 250/350, was expected to be available before the end of summer 1982. We are still waiting, with an impatience which borders on masochism, for the AJS 7R 350, the Gilera blown 4-cylinder 500, the 1939 Benelli 250, and the Guzzi

What an excellent idea of Esci's to bring out a civilian version of the Triumph 3H-350 cc, which up until now has only been available in military trim. A fine kit which remains every bit as good as most of the newer productions.

The second member of the modern Honda four-cylinder family to be modelled by Tamiya in 1:12 is the CB 900 F2 'Bol d'Or'. Also promised is a CB 1100 R — a mouth-watering prospect! ▷

This series of Japanese scooters in 1:24 is made up of models which come as an additional feature in certain Tamiya kits of contemporary Japanese cars. An amusing marketing ploy.

Tamiya offer two versions of the Suzuki RGB 500: this one (above) is the Team Gallina version ridden to the 1981 World Championship by Marco Lucchinelli.

Reacting quickly to public demand, the Tamiya range of motorcycles in 1:12 now contains six models, despite only having been launched in mid-1981. The first one was Kenny Roberts' 500 cc Yamaha Grand Prix bike.

A dozen patient hours of work after opening the box of Tamiya's 1:12 Suzuki RGB 500, and this is the result. Painstaking work with paints and brushes brings its own reward in satisfaction from a model a mere 14 cm (6.7 ins) long. ▷

HONDA
HONDA

SUZUKI

3-cylinder 500, a group of classics which were announced as *prossima novita* some years ago...

For 1982, Promini offers us a 125 cc Minarelli, Kenny Roberts' Yamaha 500, and Lucchinelli's Suzuki RG 500. The former has the now-traditional metal frame and suspension while the two Japanese machines are all plastic and, apart from their colour schemes, identical to the earlier models bearing the reference numbers 169 and 163. They cost approximately half as much as the metal-framed kits, and they enable collectors to build up a comprehensive collection at moderate cost, a policy which Provini introduced some years ago and on which he is to be congratulated. Less welcome is the quality of the moulding, which is still a bit hit and miss and requires a fair amount of file-work, enjoyable for some, but not for all. As a matter of interest, mention must be made of the introduction of a bicycle, a replica of that with which Gino Bartali won the Tour de France in 1938. It is noteworthy for the way in which the wheels have been reproduced and for the fineness of the metal frame tubing.

The Minarelli introduces for the first time in a Protar kit new steel nuts and screws that are much stronger than those previously supplied. It is a development regular Protar builders will welcome, as they will also welcome the quality of the wire mesh thath makes up the Minarelli's radiator and makes its contribution to what is a very fine kit.

New Models from the USA

The American market is far from being as prolific as that of Japan. The only new models from Ertl are the three machines which *Esci* has introduced in civilian versions and which the American firm has issued under its own label. The same is true of *Monogram*, whose Yamaha XS11, Honda CBX, Kawasaki Z-1R Turbo, and Kawasaki Z 400FX in 1:15 were all produced in Japan by *Union* and figured in that company's catalogue last year.

Revell

Three new kits from Revell, starting with a Harley Davidson 1200 Electra-Glide of the California Highway Patrol, a variation on a well-known theme in 1:8 and a fitting companion for last year's Kawasaki 1000 "Chips" police bike. The kit boasts "many chrome parts", but in fact there are too many, including such components as the cylinders, valve-covers, sumps, and the gearbox, none of which should be chromed. The only remedy is to set to with paint brushes and aluminium paint or to spray the offending parts with a coat of matt varnish such as Humbrol's Number 49. All the other parts are black, meaning that there is a fair amount of painting to be done, particularly on the mudgards and fuel tank sides, which should be white. The decals provided are limited, covering a sheet a mere $1^{1}/4$ by $2^{1}/2$ inches and comprising a speedometer, two "Electra-Glide" badges, a couple of California Police stars, and a representation of the switches on the tank-mounted dash panel. A final source of regret is the non-functioning suspension system.

Together with this Harley are two 1:12 machines; a Heavy Harley Chopper and a Kawasaki 1000 LTD. The first boasts frame, rear mudguard, tank, gearbox, and the chain, chainguard and sprockets assembly moulded in a rather doubtful orange plastic while the rest of the ensemble is chromed. The wheels have spokes which, if scaled up, would be at least half an inch in diameter. Only the real rubber tyres salvage a trace of honour for the makers.

The Kawasaki 1000 LTD is the American-style little brother of the Z 1000 introduced in 1981. The chrome is better, but the rest leaves much to be desired, especially the tyres, which are of plastic, moulded in two parts, and need to be cemented in place. Even if these two models are satisfactory for younger modellers, one still feels that Revell really ought to visit some of their Japanese contemporaries, in search of inspiration.

The Kawasaki KZ-1000 LTD is a new model from Revell in 1:12 which shows that the American company has quite a way to go before it can begin to seriously challenge the supremacy of its Japanese competitors.

New Models from France

Heller

One-eighth remains Heller's favourite scale for motorcycles, and the company offers two new versions of the Kawasaki 1000, the Z and the LTD Chopper, and two new BMW 1000s, the R 100S and the R 100T. Although they were announced last year, and mentioned in our first edition, they did not appear until this year as a result of the difficulties which Heller met with in 1981, so this is the first opportunity we have had of commenting on them in detail.

The manufacturing quality is typical Heller, that is to say very good, but there are some little criticisms, such as the fact that the suspensions do not work — as they should on a model of this scale. The base colours are generally good and the moulding quality, while not commanding the same enthusiasm as that of a good Japanese factory, is perfectly satisfactory. There are too many moulding marks from the injection process, particularly on the aluminium wheels of the BMWs, which require very careful sanding if they are to be eradicated. This remark is not so applicable to the Kawasaki, whose wheels are much more simple by comparison with those of the BMW. This European-style chopper is nevertheless supplied with an American-style exhaust, which bends outward at the rear, whereas the machine as sold in Europe has flared pipes. A small detail maybe, but one which is made all the more noticeable because the box il-

Polistil's family of 1:15 models is growing, and here are three new Harley-Davidsons from it. From the left, a Cafe Racer, Classic Sidecar, and Sportster 1000.

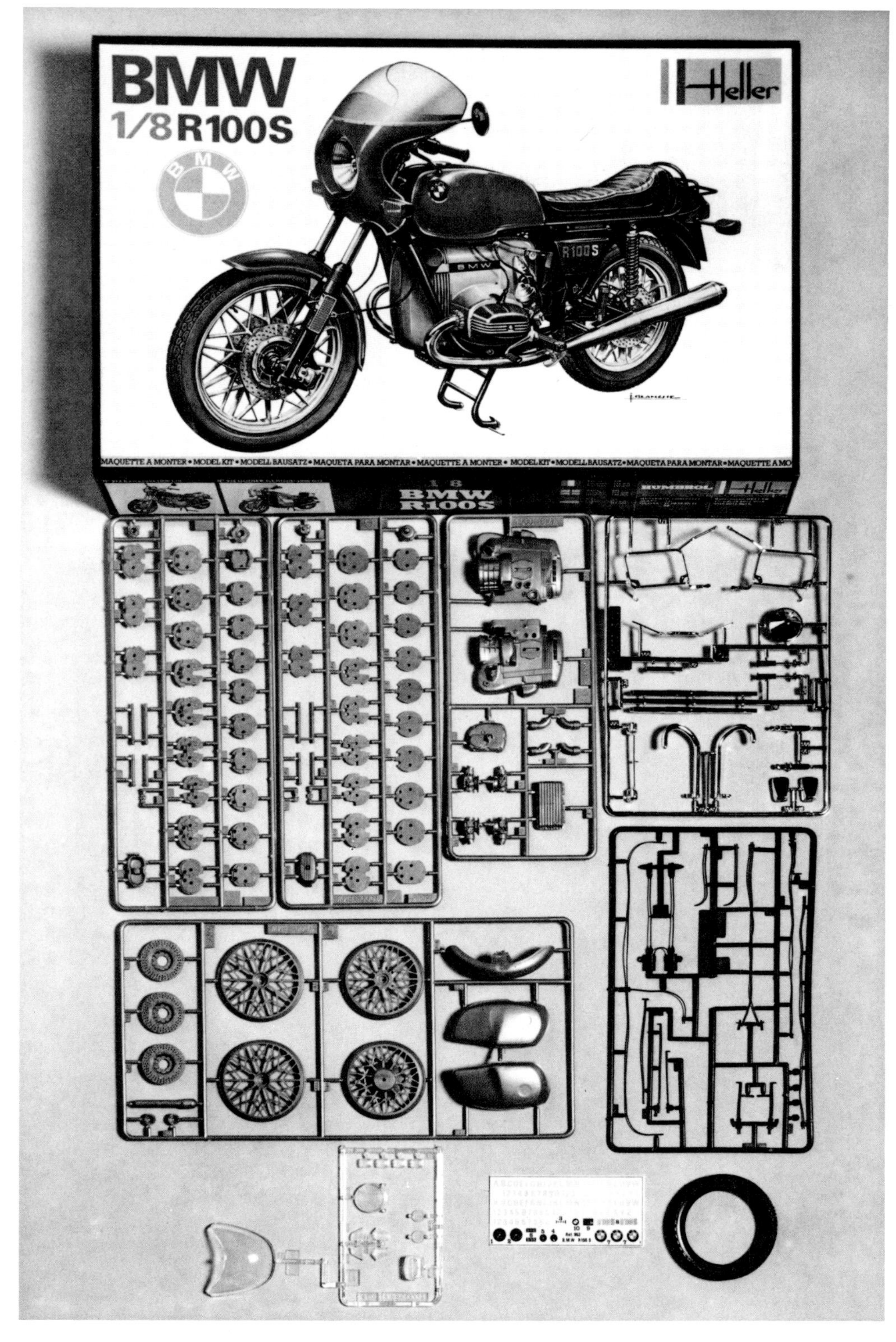

Heller's BMW R100S features cylinder blocks that are built up cooling fin by cooling fin, an admirable innovation for the firm (Protar were the first to do it). Non-functioning suspension lets down badly an otherwise excellent model.

lustration shows the bike with long exhaust pipes like those of the Z 1000, together with engine crash-bars carrying spotlamps which are to be found nowhere in the kit.

The BMW R 100S, which follows the 100 RS and the 100 RT that appeared in 1981, is free of these criticisms, apart from its fixed suspension. The cylinders, containing no less than 24 parts each, are specially noteworthy. Although this multiplicity of variations on a single model may seem a little too much, it does enable practically every owner to make a model of his very own machine.

New Models from Great Britain

Matchbox

Following last year's Vincent "Black Shadow", Matchbox has released a 1:12 scale BMW R 100 RS of similar quality. The plastic moulding is satisfactory throughout, and even very good on some parts, notably the front forks. Chrome plating — as excellent as ever, hard wearing and very shiny — covers all the parts that are not yellow or black, which means that in places resort will have to be had to clear, matt varnish or aluminium paint as indicated on the instructions. Neither the wheel rims nor the engine block — and not even the cylinder heads and rear suspension — are chromed.

The parts-holding runners are very thick and solid, so transport damage should be minimal. The instructions are lucid and the drawings large, so that the kit would present little difficulty to the young or inexperienced modeller. Painting details are precise and given in no less than seven languages, and there are alternative sets of decals.

The kit gets three dots on Matchbox's own skill-level rating (four being the most difficult), which promises (and delivers) an interesting model. Although with only one or two motorcycle kits a year Matchbox couldn't be called prolific, most of these kits are of a high, if not yet Japanese, standard.

Oh dear, another insurance claim! What looks like the aftermath of a nasty accident is in fact a 1957 Triumph 5T Speed Twin in 1:43 by Omen Miniatures. The ten-piece kit is made of pewter and is available for home construction or ready-made in either painted or polished bare-metal form. One for all the British traditionalists — of any nationality.

ON THE WORKBENCH

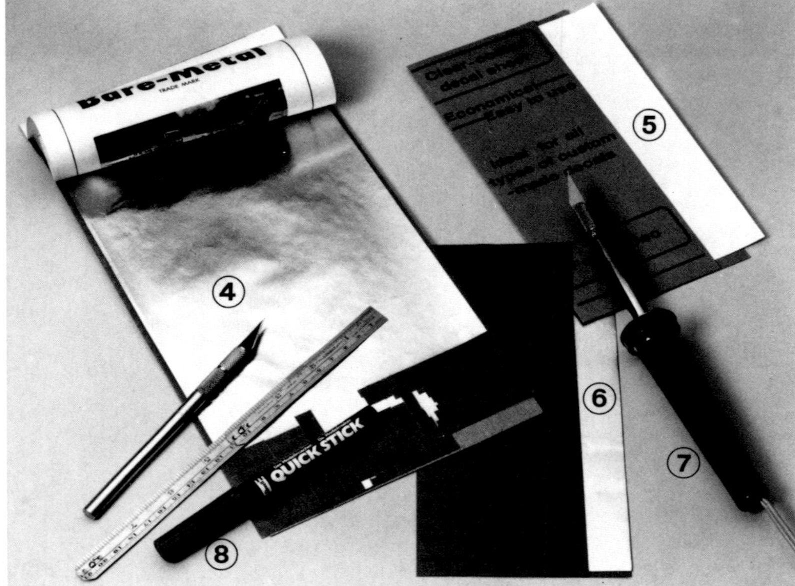

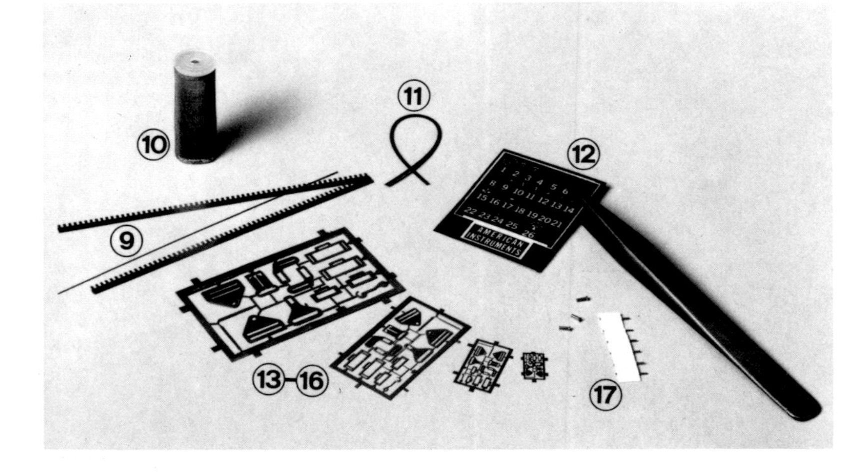

The finest metal or plastic kit is of little value if you don't have the tools, products and accessories to build, paint and detail it as necessary. Finding these necessities is the problem. In the USA, to a certain extent in Britain, and definitely in Japan, there is no lack of them, and modellers in these countries are privileged. Elsewhere, enthusiasts see national legislation depriving them of certain paints and glues because it is too difficult for local importers to bother with handling them, and model shop proprietors who cannot be bothered to procure the few products which can be obtained. In spite of this lack of interest on the part of certain segments of the trade, new products do keep coming along, and this short article is designed to present some of them to our readers.

Up to now, the only way to touch up chrome parts or to give a chrome coat to an entire part was to resort to the silver paint pot, an unsatisfactory method, or to struggle with a film coating which was difficult to apply to compound curves. Pactra have come up with a new 73 gram aerosol (1) which gives a finish equivalent to manufacturers' plating. Tamiya have launched their new range of acrylic paints (2) comprising 10 gloss finishes, 45 matt colours, thinner, and a coating which renders the gloss colours matt or semi-matt, in glass jars containing 23 ml. The paints flow well, have excellent covering power, good resistance to finger marks, and good drying properties. Take care to de-grease the surface to be painted thoroughly, use laquers only on top of the acrylic finish, and you will achieve good results. Tamiya have also introduced a series of 12 Paint Markers (3) in traditional glossy and matt finishes which have the advantage that the point may be sharpened to paint fine detail. A gentle pumping action fills the marker with just enough paint for fine work. The colours, including metallics, are superb.

We have referred to Bare-Metal foil in previous kit reviews, and this extremely thin metallized foil coating (4) gives miraculous results when carefully applied. It is made by Bare-Metal Foil Co., 19419 Ingram, Livonia MI 48152, USA, to whom orders should be sent, since very few model shops stock it — even in the USA. The same kind of product, but not so fine, is Formaskin (6), available in chrome, aluminium and silver, and available from Croydon Impex, 10, Stoneyfield Road, Old Coulsden, Surrey CR3 2HJ, England. The same company also supplies Formadec (5), a clear sheet which enables the modeller to paint his own decals.

Well known in the USA but new to Europe is the X-Acto Hot Knife (7) which operates on a 220 volt supply and can be used to cut out doors, bonnets, grilles, and any other form of opening in plastic. Revell has introduced some new products to the European market, including the Quick Stick (8), a glue pen suitable for polystyrene. It is a good idea, but the point has a tendency to lose its rigidity and the cement evaporates. From Badger comes a useful accessory for the airbrush user, a paint filter (10), which prevents the jet from getting clogged by too-large particles.

Model car specialists are not the only source for useful items, a fact which is proved by the example of the range of Waldron Model Products. This company, located at 1358 Stephen Way, San José, CA 95129, USA (with an outlet in Croydon in England), is a specialist in model aircraft accessories, but car builders will be interested in the continuous hinge (9), 1:32 oxygen hose — intended for use in cockpits but invaluable for a number of engine applications (11), 1:24 cockpit instruments (12), photo-etched safety harness buckles realized in great detail in 1:8, 1:12, 1:16, 1:20, 1:24 and 1:43 (13-16) and miniature swivels and sockets with associated tubing (17) which can be used to create moving suspensions, steering systems, hinges and even 1:43 scale intake trumpets.

NEW MODELS LIST

This list of models put on sale between June 1981 and May 1982 inclusive was drawn up on the basis of information supplied by our various local correspondents. Manufacturers are listed in alphabetical order; dates in parentheses following the model descriptions indicate production date of the real vehicle, and are themselves followed, where necessary, by further details such as the particular version modelled. The column to the right of the scales describes the type of model using the following abbreviations:

Ready-built model in unspecified metal	=	MM	KM	=	Kit in unspecified metal
Ready-built model in plastic	=	MP	KP	=	Kit in plastic
Ready-built model in resin	=	MR	KR	=	Kit in resin
Ready-built model in white metal	=	MW	KW	=	Kit in white metal
Ready-built model in zamak	=	MZ	SP	=	No-glue kit in plastic

Country of origin is indicated at the first entry of each manufacturer's name using the international country codes summarized on page 148. Manufacturers' reference numbers are given except where not quoted in publicity material or catalogues.

Model	Scale	Type	Manufacturer
Lancia Fulvia HF Monte Carlo (1972)	1:43	KR	**AMC Menna (I)** AMC 1
Chevrolet Corvette (1967)—custom / *hors série*	1:43	KP	**AMT (USA)** 2101—Street Magic series
Chevrolet Bel Air (1957)	1:43	KP	AMT 2102—Street Magic series
Ford Mustang (1969)	1:43	KP	AMT 2103—Street Magic series
Chevrolet Camaro (1969)	1:43	KP	AMT 2104—Street Magic series
Pontiac Firebird (1968)	1:43	KP	AMT 2105—Street Magic series
Chevrolet Chevelle (1969)	1:43	KP	AMT 2106—Street Magic series
Ford Torino (1969)	1:43	KP	AMT 2107—Street Magic series
Chevrolet Camaro (1967)—custom / *hors série*	1:43	KP	AMT 2108—Street Magic series
Plymouth Barracuda (1967)—"Custom 'Cuda" / *hors série*	1:43	KP	AMT 2109—Street Magic series
AMC AMX (1969)	1:43	KP	AMT 2110—Street Magic series
Jaguar XK-E	1:43	KP	AMT 2111—Street Magic series
Chevrolet Corvette (1967)	1:43	KP	AMT 2112—Street Magic series
Chevrolet Camaro Z-28 (1981)	1:25	SP	AMT 2308
Toyota 4×4 pickup (1981)—"Fire Chief" with camper cap / *avec camper*	1:25	SP	AMT 2512
Toyota 4×4 pickup (1981)	1:25	SP	AMT 2513
Thomas Flyer (1908)—New York to Paris winner / *vainqueur New York-Paris*	1:25	KP	AMT 4101
VW Scirocco (1978)—racing version / *compétition*	1:25	KP	AMT 4153
Ford Model A roadster (1929)	1:25	KP	AMT 4156
Datsun 280 ZX Turbo (1981)	1:25	KP	AMT 4165
Chevrolet Camaro (1968)—non-stock / *hors série*	1:25	KP	AMT 4166—Street Machine series
Ford Mustang (1973)—non-stock / *hors série*	1:25	KP	AMT 4167—Street Machine series
Chevrolet Nova (1976)—non-stock / *hors série.*	1:25	KP	AMT 4168—Street Machine series
Mercury Cougar RX-7 (1969)—non-stock / *hors série*	1:25	KP	AMT 4169—Street Machine series
Chevrolet Camaro Z-28 (1968)	1:25	KP	AMT 4173
Datsun 280 ZX (1981)	1:25	KP	AMT 4176—Street Machine series
Chevrolet Chevelle (1972)	1:25	KP	AMT 4177—Street Machine series
Ford Mustang II (1977)	1:25	KP	AMT 4179
Ford "Roadster" (1932)	1:25	KP	AMT 4180—Reggie Jackson series
Studebaker Avanti (1963)	1:25	KP	AMT 4181—Reggie Jackson series
Ford Cobra roadster (1964)	1:25	KP	AMT 4182—Reggie Jackson series
Chevrolet Corvette (1959)	1:25	KP	AMT 4183—Reggie Jackson series
Ford F-350 Ranger pickup (1977)	1:25	KP	AMT 4611
Chevrolet Blazer 4×4 (1970)—"Chevy Bandit"	1:25	KP	AMT 4631
GMC Astro 95—cabover truck / *cabine avancée*	1:25	KP	AMT 6133
Peterbilt—conventional / *cabine normale*	1:25	KP	AMT 6134
Peerless—log trailer with load / *transport de bois avec chargement*	1:25	KP	AMT 6605
Mack—wrecker with Holmes twin booms / *dépanneuse avec double grue Holmes*	1:32	SP	AMT 6803
Mack Superliner—conventional / *cabine normale*	1:32	SP	AMT 6804
Kenworth Aerodyne—cabover / *cabine avancée*	1:32	KP	AMT 6807
Peterbilt 359—conventional / *cabine normale*	1:43	KP	AMT 7106
Peterbilt 359—wercker with Holmes 750 twin booms / *dépanneuse avec double grue Holmes 750*	1:43	KP	AMT 7107
Fruehauf—reefer van "Pepsi" / *fourgon réfrigérateur «Pepsi»*	1:43	KP	AMT 7108
Autocar—dump truck / *dumper.*	1:25	KP	AMT 8403
Ferrari BB 512 (1980)	1:43	MR	**Annecy Miniatures (F)** —Le Mans, numbers 47, 74, 76 and 77 / *Le Mans, voitures 47, 74, 76, 77*
Latil-Laffly—fire engine / *fourgon incendie normalisé*	1:50	MR	Annecy Miniatures
Ford SAF—fire engine / *fourgon I.N.*	1:50	MR	Annecy Miniatures
Citroën PSS—fire engine / *fourgon I.N.*	1:50	MR	Annecy Miniatures
Toyota Soarer 2800 GT Extra	1:24	KP	**Aoshima (J)** 6G-001-500
Toyota Soarer 2000 VR Turbo	1:24	KP	Aoshima 6G-002-500
Nissan Cedric 330 2000 SGL-E	1:24	KP	Aoshima 3G-27-800
Toyota Celica XX 2800 GT	1:24	KP	Aoshima 6G-004-600
Nissan Skyline 2000 GT Turbo	1:24	KP	Aoshima 3G-28-800 Japanese model / *version Japon*
* Yamaha Beluga 80	1:12	KP	Aoshima MS-01-400
* Yamaha Beluga 80 (Special)	1:12	KP	Aoshima MS-02-500
* Suzuki Gemma 50	1:12	KP	Aoshima MS-03-400
* Suzuki Gemma 50 (Special)	1:12	KP	Aoshima MS-04-500
* Suzuki GSX 400F	1:12	KP	Aoshima G6-010-800
* Suzuki GSX 400F (Special)	1:12	KP	Aoshima G6-020-800
Honda City	1:24	KP	Aoshima G5-01-600

Nissan Skyline HT 2000 GT-X	1:24	KP	Aoshima 3G-31-800
* Honda Stream Special	1:12	KP	Aoshima MS-08-600
Nissan Skyline 2000 GT-X—4 door / *4 portes*	1:24	KP	Aoshima 3G-36-900
Nissan Skyline 2000 GT Turbo—4-door / *4 portes*	1:24	KP	Aoshima 3G-33-900 Japanese model / *version Japon*
Nissan Skyline HT 2000 GT Turbo	1:24	KP	Aoshima 3G-38-900 Japanese model / *version Japon*
Honda City-R	1:24	KP	**Arii (J)** AR132A-600
Honda City Pro T	1:24	KP	Arii AR132C-600
Chevrolet Bel-Air—hardtop or convertible / *hardtop ou décapotable*	1:43	KW	**Auto Replicas (GB)**—
Ferrari 250 GT Pininfarina—competition model / *modèle de compétition*	1:43	MR	**Bal Car (I)** BC 1
Audi Quattro (1981)—Monte Carlo Rally / *rallye Monte Carlo*	1:43	MW	**BAM-X (F)** —
Audi Quattro (1981)—San Remo Rally / *rally San Remo*	1:43	KM	BAM-X
BMW M1—Group 5 / *groupe 5*	1:43	KM	**BAM (F)** —Solido-based kit, "VSD-LOÏS" / *trankit base Solido, «VSD-LOÏS»*
Renault 5 Turbo	1:43	KM	BAM —Solido-based kit / *transkit base Solido*
Toyota Soarer 2800 GT	1:20	KP	**Bandai (J)** 35269
Isuzu Piazza	1:20	KP	Bandai 35278
Datsun 2000 SGX—vanette coach / *minibus*	1:24	KP	Bandai 35219
Toyota Town Ace Grand Extra—wagon / *break*	1:24	KP	Bandai 35220
Isuzu Fargo LS—wagon / *break*	1:24	KP	Bandai 35221
Berliet Dauphine (1939)	1:43	KR	**Belle-Epoque (F)** —based on Peugeot 402 / *sur base Peugeot 402*
Ferrari 375 MM (1953)	1:43	MM	**Bosica (I)** 2—Carrera Panamericana 1953, also KM / *version Carrera Panamericana 1953, aussi KM*
Magirus-Deutz—flat truck / *camion à pont plat*	—	MM	**Britains (GB)**—
Magirus-Deutz—timber truck and trailer / *camion transport bois et remorque*	—	MM	Britains—
Bugatti Brescia (1921)—"England" type / *type Angleterre*	1:43	MM	**Brumm (I)** R 39
Bugatti Brescia (1921)—"France" type / *type France*	1:43	MM	Brumm R 40
AVO (Ferrari) 815 (1940)	1:43	MM	Brumm R 66
AVO (Ferrari) 815—Mille Miglia 1940	1:43	MM	Brumm R 67
Fiat 500 B—PT van / *fourgon P & T.*	1:43	MM	Brumm R 45
Fiat 500 B "Stipel"—telephone service van / *fourgon service téléphone*	1:43	MM	Brumm R 46 yellow ladder on roof / *avec échelle*
Ferrari 246 Dino (1958)	1:43	MM	Brumm R 68
Ferrari 246 Dino (1958)—Phil Hill, Italian GP / *Phil Hill, GP d'Italie*	1:43	MM	Brumm R 69 chrome wheels and exhaust / *jantes et échappements chromés*
Mercedes-Benz W 125 (1937)	1:43	MM	Brumm R 70
Mercedes-Benz W 125 (1938)—Vanderbilt Cup	1:43	MM	Brumm R 71
Mercedes-Benz W 196 (1955)—short wheelbase / *châssis court*	1:43	MM	Brumm R 72
Blitzen Benz (1911)	1:43	MM	Brumm R 73 stub exhausts / *échappements courts*
Fiat 500 B "Gillette"—van / *fourgon*	1:43	MM	Brumm R 79
Fiat 500 C "Pompieri"—fire dept. van / *fourgon pompiers*	1:43	MM	Brumm R 70 yellow ladder on roof / *avec échelle*
Blitzen Benz (1911) Indianapolis	1:43	MM	Brumm R 81 copper radiator, long exhausts, Barney Oldfield / *radiateur cuivré, échappements longs, voiture de Barney Oldfield*
Bugatti Brescia (1921)—Bugatti team / *écurie Bugatti*	1:43	MM	Brumm R 82 copper tank, black wheels / *radiateur cuivré, roues noires*
Talbot Lago 4,5 l (1948)—4.5 l. Grand Prix	1:43	MM	Brumm R 74
Maserati 8 CT F (1939) Indianapolis	1:43	MM	Brumm R 75
Lancia-Ferrari V8 (1956) Grand Prix	1:43	MM	Brumm R 76
Alfa Romeo 8 C 2300 spyder Touring (1931)	1:43	MM	Brumm R 77
Alfa Romeo 8 C 2300 spyder Touring—Mille Miglia 1931	1:43	MM	Brumm R 78
Lancia Stratos "Michel Vaillant"	1:24	MM	**B Burago (I)** 0154
Ford Capri—Group 5 / *groupe 5*	1:24	MM	B Burago 0181
BMW M1 "Grösser Beer"	1:24	KM	B Burago 5169 with plastic parts / *avec pièces en plastique*
Ford Mustang	1:24	MM	B Burago 0182
Lamborghini Cheetah—Forest fire appliance / *pompiers*	1:24	MM	B Burago 0186 new series / *nouvelle série*
Renault 14 "Ecurie Renault servizio corse"	1:24	MM	B Burago 0192
Alfa Romeo Giulietta "Jolly Club"—Group 2 rally car / *groupe 2 rallye*	1:24	MM	B Burago 5164
Lancia Stratos "VDS"	1:43	MM	B Burago 4108 new series / *nouvelle série*
Porsche 935 "Vaillant"	1:43	MM	B Burago 4142 new series / *nouvelle série*
Lancia Stratos "Pirelli"	1:43	MM	B Burago 4166 new series / *nouvelle série*
Lancia Beta Montecarlo "Martini"	1:43	MM	B Burago 4170 new series / *nouvelle série*
Lancia Beta Montecarlo "Alitalia"	1:43	MM	B Burago 4172 new series / *nouvelle série*
Porsche 935 "Momo"	1:43	MM	B Burago 4184 new series / *nouvelle série*
Renault 4 "Routes du Monde"	1:24	MM	B Burago 0191
Ferrari 126 CK—Formula 1 / *Formule 1*	1:24	MM	B Burago 6101 new Grand Prix series / *nouvelle série Grand Prix*
Alfa Romeo 179 turbo—Formula 1 / *Formule 1*	1:24	MM	B Burago 6102 new Grand Prix series / *nouvelle série Grand Prix*
Opel Ascona 400 "Publimmo"	1:24	KM	B Burago 5153 1981 Monte Carlo Rally, with plastic parts / *Monte Carlo 1981, avec pièces en plastique*
Alfa Romeo 2300 B Touring (1932)	1:18	MM	B Burago 3008 Diamonds series / *série Diamonds*
Ford Mercury Capri RS	1:24	MM	B Burago 0183
Lamborghini Cheetah "Explorer"	1:24	MM	B Burago 0187 new series / *nouvelle série*
Fiat Ritmo "Naranjto"	1:24	MM	B Burago 0200 Football World Cup, Spain 1982 / *Championnat du monde defootball, Espagne 1982*
Ford Capri Zakspeed—Group 5 / *groupe 5*	1:24	KM	B Burago 5181 with plastic parts / *avec pièces en plastique*
Renault R5 Turbo	1:24	MM	B Burago 0160
Land Rover—long wheelbase station wagon / *station-wagon châssis long*	1:24	MM	B Burago 0167
Ford Mustang Indy	1:24	MM	B Burago 5182
Ferrari Testa Rossa "Ecurie belge" Le Mans	1:18	KM	B Burago 7007 with plastic parts / *avec pièces en plastique*
Ferrari 250 GT SWB	1:43	KW	**CAM (J)** F-001—also MW / *aussi MW*
Honda S600—coupé	1:43	MW	CAM 003a

Honda S600—convertible / *cabriolet*	1:43	MW	CAM 003b
Ferrari 275 GTB 4	1:43	KW	CAM F-002—also MW / *aussi MW*
Ferrari 330 P3/4 (1967)	1:43	KM	**CAR (I)** 02—team Filippinetti / *écurie Filippinetti*
Panhard Dyna X 4 CV (1950)	1:43	KW	**CJM (F)** —
Chrysler (1961)	1:72	KP	**Con-Cor (USA)** 6019—set containing / *boîte contenant:* Imperial hardtop, Valiant station wagon, Plymouth station wagon, Dodge Dart sedan, Dodge Lancer sedan, Chrysler Newport convertible / *décapotable*, Dodge Polara hardtop—1961 Revell molds / *moules Revell 1961*
VW Passat GLS	1:43	MZ	**Conrad (D)** 1010
VW Passat LS Variant	1:43	MZ	Conrad 1011
Audi GT 5S—coupé	1:43	MZ	Conrad 1012
VW Scirocco GLI	1:43	MZ	Conrad 1013
VW Polo C	1:43	MZ	Conrad 1014
VW Santana GL	1:43	MZ	Conrad 1015
MAN "Atlas"—bucket truck / *multibenne*	1:50	MZ	Conrad—
Mercedes "Atlas"—bucket truck / *multibenne*	1:50	MZ	Conrad—
Magirus "Atlas"—bucket truck / *multibenne*	1:50	MZ	Conrad—
Mercedes—milk truck / *porteur laitier*	1:50	MZ	Conrad—
Steyr 91—fire rescue van / *fourgon sauvetage pompiers*	1:50	MZ	Conrad—
Mercedes—gas truck / *transport gaz*	1:50	MZ	Conrad—
MAN—platform truck / *plateau à ridelles*	1:50	MZ	Conrad—
Peugeot 500 STI	1:36	MM	**Corgi (GB)** C373
Chevrolet Caprice—stock racer / *voiture course stock car*	1:36	MM	Corgi C341
Ford Transit—wrecker / *dépanneuse*	1:36	MM	Corgi C1140
BMW M1—racing / *course*	1:36	MM	Corgi C308
Rover 3500 "Triplex"	1:36	MM	Corgi C340
Jeep—and van "Corgi Pony Club" / *avec van chevaux «Corgi Pony Club»*	1:36	MM	Corgi C29
Chubb Pathfinder—airport fire engine / *engin pompiers aéroport*	—	MM	Corgi 1118
Ford—artic. "Michelin" / *semi-remorque «Michelin»*	—	MM	Corgi 1109
Honda Prelude—with glider / *avec planeur*	1:36	MM	Corgi C12
Ford Thunderbird	1:36	MM	Corgi C801
Ford Cobra Mustang	1:36	MM	Corgi C370
Mercedes-Benz 300 SL	1:36	MM	Corgi C802
Ford Transit—milk van / *fourgon laitier*	1:36	MM	Corgi C405
Ford—artic. "Guiness" / *semi-remorque «Guiness»*	—	MM	Corgi 1169
Jeep—with 2 drag bikes / *avec motos dragsters*	1:36	MM	Corgi C10
Honda Z GS	1:20	KP	**Crown (J)** C563-600
Mitsubishi Minica GSS	1:20	KP	Crown C565-600
Porsche F1 (1961)	1:43	KW	**C-Scale (GB)** 026
Ferrari Testa Rossa 250 (1957)	1:43	KW	C-Scale 027
Mercedes W 196 (1955)	1:43	MZ	**Cursor (D)** 12
Citroën 15 CV—"Tour de France" 1954	1:43	KM	**Decalkit (F)** —Solido-based kit / *transkit base Solido, Yvette Horner*
Porsche 908/81 (1981)	1:43	KM	Decalkit —Solido-based kit / *transkit base Solido, "Techno Car-Klein"*
Ferrari 380 P3 spyder (1966)	1:43	KM	**Dallari (I)** DA 2—Nürburgring
Ferrari 750 Monza	1:43	KW	**Dannini Modelli (GB)** DN 10
Aston Martin DB4	1:43	KW	Dannini Modelli 22
Austin Swallow Saloon (1930)	1:76	KW	**DG Models (GB)** 0012
Morris Tourer (1931)—2-seater / *2 places*	1:76	KW	DG Models 0013
Ford A (1930)—van / *camionnette*	1:76	KW	DG Models 0014
Austin LL (1934)—taxi	1:76	KW	DG Models 0015
Austin (1925)—van / *camionnette*	1:76	KW	DG Models 0018
MG Tickford Coupé (1934)	1:76	KW	DG Models 0019
MG PA Tourer (1934)—4-seater / *4 places*	1:76	KW	DG Models 0020
Reliant (1936)—3-wheeled van / *camionnette 3 roues*	1:43	KW	DG Models —
Austin (1925)—van / *camionnette*	1:43	KW	DG Models —
Austin (1930)—ambulance	1:76	KW	DG Models —
Austin (1934)—5cwt van / *camionnette*	1:43	KW	DG Models also MW / *aussi MW*
MG PB (1934)—2-seater sports / *2 places sport*	1:76	KW	DG Models 0022
Renault R8 Gordini	1:43	KW	**DM Modèles (F)** —
Alpine Renault 1600	1:43	KM	DM Modèles —Solido-based kit / *transkit base Alpine 1600 Solido*
Messerschmitt KR 200	1:43	KW	**Duesentrieb (D)** 1
Ferrari 350 Can Am (1967)	1:43	MR	**Eco-Design (I)** 10
Renault KZ (1928)—coupé de ville	1:43	MZ	**Eligor (CH)** 1041 A
Renault NN KZ (1928)—taxi	1:43	MZ	Eligor 1042
Mercedes-Benz "Nürburg" (1931)—hotel taxi / *taxi d'hôtel*	1:43	MZ	Eligor 1044
Talbot Pacific (1930)—hotel taxi / *«Hôtel de France»*	1:43	MZ	Eligor 1052
Citroën Traction Avant—Paris taxi / *taxi parisien*	1:43	MZ	Eligor 1053
Citroën Rosalie (1934)—Paris taxi / *taxi parisien*	1:43	MZ	Eligor 1035
Citroën 5 CV (1926)—"Michelin" van / *camionnette «Michelin»*	1:43	MZ	Eligor 1054
Renault KZ (1928)—fire dept. / *premiers secours pompiers*	1:43	MZ	Eligor 1049
Citroën 500 kg (1934)—"Vache qui rit" van / *camionnette «Vache qui rit»*	1:43	MZ	Eligor 1009
Citroën 5 CV (1926)—"Lu-Lu" van / *camionnette «Lu-Lu»*	1:43	MZ	Eligor 1013
Citroën 500 kg (1934)—"Dubonnet" van / *camionnette «Dubonnet»*	1:43	MZ	Eligor 1007
Sunbeam Tiger	1:43	MW	**ENCO (GB)**—
Volvo N 10—conventional / *cabine normale*	1:25	KP	**Ertl (USA)** 8037—some metal parts / *qq. pièces métal*
International 4300 Eagle—conventional "Race Truck" / *cabine normale compétition*	1:25	KP	Ertl 8038
International Eagle—cabover / *cabine avancée*	1:32	SP	Ertl 8050
*Honda XL 125S	1:12	KP	Ertl 8098—Imai molds / *moules Imai*
*Yamaha TY 125	1:12	KP	Ertl 8099—Imai molds / *moules Imai*
Porsche RSR-934 Turbo	1:24	KP	Ertl 8260—USA import, made by Esci (3001) / *modèle Esci (3001) importé aux USA*

Model	Scale	Type	Maker / Reference
BMW 320—Citicorp/Junior Team / *Ecurie Citicorp/Junior*	1:24	KP	Ertl 8261—Esci 3002
BMW M1—Marlboro Procar	1:24	KP	Ertl 8262—Esci 3011
Lancia Beta Monte Carlo Gr. 5	1:24	KP	Ertl 8263—Esci 3017
*BMW R-75—with sidecar / *avec sidecar*	1:9	KP	Ertl 8290—Esci 7001
*Harley-Davidson WLA-45	1:9	KP	Ertl 8291—Esci 7002
*Triumph 3-HW	1:9	KP	Ertl 8292—Esci 7004
Indy Winners Set / *ensemble vainqueurs Indianapolis*	1:43	MM	**Ertl (USA)** 1555 Cars of / *voitures de* Mears, Unser, Alsup, Andretti
Mercedes-Benz 350 SE	1:43	MM	Ertl 1545
BMW M1	1:43	MM	Ertl 1546
VW "Beetle" / *Coccinelle*	1:43	MM	Ertl 1547
Porsche 924	1:43	MM	Ertl 1548
VW Rabbit / *Golf*	1:43	MM	Ertl 1549
BMW 733	1:43	MM	Ertl 1550
International Classic	1:43	MM	Ertl 1560 Set of 6 previously mentioned cars / *ensemble des 6 voitures précédentes*
"Dukes of Hazzard" gift set / *ensemble «Dukes of Hazzard»*	1:64	MM	Ertl 1570 General Lee stock car, Jeep, 2 Police cars / *Dodge Charger «General Lee», Jeep, 2 voitures de police*
Blues Brothers' Bluesmobile / *Dodge (1974)*	1:64	MM	Ertl 1580
Ford T (1914)—delivery van / *fourgon de livraison*	1:25	MM	Ertl 1640 "Country Time"
Ford Bronco	1:25	MM	Ertl 1681
Ford (1932)—roadster	1:25	MM	Ertl 1682
Chevrolet Corvette (1963)	1:25	MM	Ertl 1782
Ford Mustang (1965)	1:25	MM	Ertl 1783
Stock Car Set / *ensemble stock car*	1:64	MM	Ertl 1785 Pickup truck, stock car and trailer / *pickup, voiture stock car et remorque*
Dodge Charger (1970) "General Lee"	1:25	MM	Ertl 1791
GMC—semi-trailer truck / *semi-remorque*	1:87	MM	Ertl 1906 "Smokey and the Bandit"
Two-Truck Set / *ensemble à 2 camions*	1:87	MM	Ertl 1907 "Pepsi-Cola" semi, "Exxon" tanker semi and 2 cabs (any 2 of the 4 below / *semi-remorque «Pepsi-Cola», citerne «Exxon» et 2 tracteurs parmi les 4 ci-dessous*
Truck Cabs / *tracteurs*	1:87	MM	Ertl 1910 GMC, Kenworth, Mack, Peterbilt
Cadillac "Boss Hog"	1:64	MM	Ertl 1561
"Dukes of Hazzard" Set / *ensemble «Dukes of Hazzard»*	1:64	MM	Ertl 1572 Cadillac "Boss Hog", Dodge Charger "General Lee"
Chevrolet—stock car	1:43	MM	Ertl 1719 Richard Petty, "STP"
Chevrolet—stock car	1:43	MM	Ertl 1720 Darrell Waltrip, "Mountain Dew"
Chevrolet—stock car	1:43	MM	Ertl 1721 Harry Gant, "Skoal Bandit"
GMC Fleetside—pickup	1:43	MM	Ertl 1722 "Fallguy"
Chevrolet Bel-Air (1957)—hardtop	1:25	MM	Ertl 1800
Chevrolet Camaro (1982)	1:25	MM	Ertl 1801
Ford EXP (1982)	1:64	MM	Ertl 1825
Pontiac Firebird (1982)	1:25	MM	Ertl 1826
Richard Petty stock car	1:25	MM	Ertl 1827 "STP"
Cale Yarborough stock car	1:25	MM	Ertl 1828 "Valvoline"
GMC Fleetside—pickup	1:64	MM	Ertl 1875 "Fallguy"
Indy Winners Set / *ensemble vainqueurs Indianapolis*	1:43	MM	Ertl 1555 New variations, cars of Unser, Mears, Alsup, Garza / *nouvelles variantes, voitures de Unser, Mears, Alsup, Garza*
Datsun 280 ZX Turbo	1:64	MM	Ertl 1888
Ford Mustang (1964)	1:64	MM	Ertl 1889
Jaguar XJ 10	1:64	MM	Ertl 1898
Ferrari Dino 246 GT	1:64	MM	Ertl 1909
Porsche 930 Turbo	1:64	MM	Ertl 1908
Super Stockers / *ensemble voitures stock car*	1:64	MM	Ertl 1912 Petty, Yarborough, Waltrip, Rudd cars / *voitures de Petty, Yarborough, Waltrip et Rudd*
Renault 5—rally "Gitanes" / *rallye «Gitanes»*	1:24	KP	**Esci (I)** 3016
Renault 5 Alpine	1:24	KP	Esci 3019
Mercedes 450 SLC 5.0—Bandama Rally / *rallye Bandama*	1:24	KP	Esci 3018
Mercedes-Benz 230 G—off-road / *tout-terrain*	1:24	KP	Esci 3022
Fiat 131 Abarth—rally / *rallye*	1:24	KP	Esci 3031
Audi Quattro (1981)—Monte Carlo Rally / *rallye de Monte Carlo*	1:24	KP	Esci 3026
Audi Quattro—road version / *version routière*	1:24	KP	Esci 3024
Mercedes-Benz 230 G—off-road fire dept. / *tout-terrain pompiers.*	1:24	KP	Esci 3023
Mercedes-Benz 230 G (1981)—off-road Paris-Dakar rally / *tout-terrain rallye Paris-Dakar*	1:24	KP	Esci 3025
Darl'Mat (1939)—record, 2 l. / *record 2 l*	1:43	MR	**Esdo (F)** —also KR / *aussi KR*
BMW 2002 Touring	1:43	KM	Esdo —Solido-based kit / *transkit base Solido*
Renault Jura—wagon / *break*	1:43	KM	Esdo —Eligor-based kit / *transkit base Eligor*
Ferrari Dino 296 500 Miglia Monza (1958), Luigi Musso	1:43	MR	**Etruria Model (I)** EM 4
Ferrari 375 Thinwall Special	1:43	MR	Etruria Model EM 5—Silverstone 1952
Alfa Romeo 1900 SS (1953)	1:43	MR	**Excalibur (I)**—3 versions, all built-up, made by Carlo Brianza for Paolo Rampini / *3 versions, toutes montées par Carlo Brianza pour Paolo Rampini*
Porsche 917 K Zeltweg 1969	1:43	MR	**Faster 43 (I)** 02
Porsche 917 K "Wrangler" Zeltweg 1969	1:43	MR	Faster 43 03
Talbot Ligier JS 17 (1981)	1:43	KM	Faster 43 03
Fiat—Ferrari autocarrier (1980) / *transporteur écurie Ferrari (1980)*	1:43	KM	**FDS (I)** 1001
Daimler-Benz—Porsche autocarrier (1976) / *transporteur écurie Porsche (1976)*	1:43	KM	FDS 1002
Ferrari 512 (1964)—Formula 1 / *Formule 1*	1:43	KM	FDS 97—Mexican GP version / *version GP du Mexique*
Tyrrel 010 (1981)	1:43	KM	FDS 100
McLaren MP4 (1981)	1:43	KM	FDS 101
Lancia Aurelia B20 (1951)	1:43	KM	FDS 102—Carrera Panamericana 1951
Theodore TY 01 "Rombo" (1981)	1:43	KM	FDS 103—San Marino GP 1981
Ferrari 315 MM (1957)	1:43	KM	FDS 104
Osella FA 013 (1981)	1:43	KM	FDS 105
Ensign MN 180 B (1981)	1:43	KM	FDS 107—Marc Surer's car / *voiture Marc Surer*
Fittipaldi F.8 (1981) "Pastamatic"	1:43	KM	FDS —Imola 1981

Model	Scale		Manufacturer / No.
Ferrari 126 CK (1981)	1:43	KM	FDS 702—prototype by Bosica / *prototype fait par Bosica*
Brabham BT 49 C (1981)	1:43	KM	FDS 108
Ferrari 340 MM (1953)	1:43	KM	FDS 106
Ferrari 512 BB "European University"	1:43	KM	FDS 611—Le Mans 1980
Ferrari 512 BB "Bellaucauto"	1:43	KM	FDS 613—Le Mans 1981
Ferrari 512 BB "European University"	1:43	KM	FDS 612—Le Mans 1981
Ferrari 126 CK (1982)	1:43	KM	FDS 703—South African GP '82 / *GP Afrique du Sud 82*
Nissan Leopard TR-X—American 280 X / *280 X USA*	1:24	KP	**Fujimi (J)** SM-49
Nissan Leopard 280 X SF-L—hotrod	1:24	KP	Fujimi SM-50
Nissan Leopard TR-X—American 280 X, hotrod / *280 X USA, hotrod*	1:24	KP	Fujimi SM-51
Isuzu Piazza XE	1:24	KP	Fujimi SM-54
Isuzu Piazza XE—body-down type / *surbaissé*	1:24	KP	Fujimi SM-52
Nissan Cedric 430 Turbo—body-down type / *surbaissé*	1:24	KP	Fujimi SM-53
Toyota Celica XX 2800 GT	1:24	KP	Fujimi SM-57
Nissan Skyline 2000 GT-X—body-down type / *surbaissé*	1:24	KP	Fujimi SM-56
Chevrolet Camaro V8 Turbo—hotrod	1:24	KP	Fujimi SM-60
* Yamaha RZ 250	1:15	KP	Fujimi SB-8
* Yamaha RD 250 LC	1:15	KP	Fujimi SB-9
* Yamaha RZ 250—custom / *hors série*	1:15	KP	Fujimi SB-11
* Honda Gold Wing Special	1:15	KP	Fujimi SB-7
* Honda GL 1100 Interstate	1:15	KP	Fujimi SB-5
* Yamaha RZ 350	1:15	KP	Fujimi SB-10
* Honda GL 1100	1:15	KP	Fujimi SB-6
Chevrolet Camaro Z-28 Special	1:24	KP	Fujimi SM-70
Opel Ascona 1.6 LS	1:43	MZ	**Gama (D)** 1140
Opel Ascona 1.6 SR coupé	1:43	MZ	Gama 1141
BMW M1 "BASF"	1:43	MZ	Gama 1146
Audi GT 5S coupé	1:43	MZ	Gama 1148
BMW 528 i	1:43	MZ	Gama 1149
VW Passat GLS	1:43	MZ	Gama 1153
VW Passat GLS "Notarzt"	1:43	MZ	Gama 1153 P
VW Passat LS Variant	1:43	MZ	Gama 1154
BMW 528 i "Polizei"	1:43	MZ	Gama 1155
BMW 528 i "Notarzt"	1:43	MZ	Gama 1156
VW Scirocco GLI	1:43	MZ	Gama 1157
Opel Ascona 1.6 LS—fire chief / *pompiers*	1:43	MZ	Gama 1172
Mercedes 230 G—breakdown van / *dépanneuse*	1:43	MZ	Gama 1405
Mercedes 300 TD break	1:26	MZ	Gama
Ford GT Mk II A (1965)—Daytona	1:43	KW	**Grand Prix Models (GB)** 94 Classic Kits
Ford GT 40 (1966)—Le Mans winner / *vainqueur Le Mans.*	1:43	KW	Grand Prix Models 95 Classic Kits
Ford GT 40—road car / *version routière*	1:43	KW	Grand Prix Models 96 Classic Kits
Ford Escort Gr. 2 (1980) Zakspeed	1:43	KW	Grand Prix Models 8008 Racing Kits
Jaguar D (1957)—Le Mans	1:43	KW	Grand Prix Models 101 Classic Kits
Ford GT 40 Gulf (1968)—Le Mans	1:43	KW	Grand Prix Models 98 Classic Kits
Ford GT 40 Gulf (1969)—Le Mans	1:43	KW	Grand Prix Models 99 Classic Kits
Ford Escort RS1700 Turbo Proto	1:43	KW	Grand Prix Models 8102 Racing Kits
Triumph TR7 V8—RAC Rally / *Rallye RAC*	1:43	KW	Grand Prix Models 8016 Racing Kits
Ford GT 40 P—Targa Florio	1:43	KW	Grand Prix Models 97 Classic Kits
Ford Escort Gr. 4 (1981) Rothmans	1:43	KW	Grand Prix Models 8104 Racing Kits
Audi Quattro (1981)—RAC Rally winner / *vainqueur Rallye RAC*	1:43	KW	Grand Prix Models 8105 Racing Kits
Jaguar Mk II Saloon	1:43	KW	Grand Prix Models 1000/1001 Classic 43
Porsche 928 S	1:24	KP	**Gunze (J)**—G-212
Bentley (1930)—4.5 l. supercharged Le Mans / *4,5 l. à compresseur Le Mans.*	1:24	KP	**Heller (F)** 722
Talbot Lago Record (1950/51)—convertible / *cabriolet*	1:24	KP	Heller 711
Renault 5 Turbo—"Giro d'Italia"	1:43	KP	Heller 173
Renault RE 20/23—Formula 1 / *Formule 1*	1:12	KP	Heller 791
Renault Vivastella PG7 (1930)—convertible / *cabriolet*	1:24	KP	Heller 724
*Kawasaki 1000 LTD	1:8	KP	Heller 973 US version of 1000 Z 1 R / *version USA de la 1000 Z 1 R*
Peugeot 403	1:43	KP	Heller
Citroën 2 CV (1948)	1:43	KP	Heller
Lancia Beta Turbo	1:43	KP	Heller '81 Le Mans / *Le Mans 1981*
*BMW 100 RS	1:8	KP	Heller
Porsche Carrera 930 T	1:87	MP	**Herpa (D)** 2014
Porsche 928 S	1:87	MP	Herpa 2025
Ford Mustang Cobra	1:87	MP	Herpa 2029
Opel Kadett Caravan	1:87	MP	Herpa 2030
Opel Ascona	1:87	MP	Herpa 2032
Opel Ascona SR	1:87	MP	Herpa 2033
Opel Ascona—coupé	1:87	MP	Herpa 2034
Opel Ascona SR—coupé	1:87	MP	Herpa 2035
Opel Ascona SR—metallic paint / *métallisé*	1:87	MP	Herpa 3033
Opel Ascona—coupé, metallic paint / *coupé, métallisé*	1:87	MP	Herpa 3035
Ford Capri S—metallic paint / *métallisé*	1:87	MP	Herpa 3505
BMW 528 i Alpina	1:87	MP	Herpa 3515
Ford Capri—rally / *rallye*	1:87	MP	Herpa 3550
BMW M1 "Motorsport"	1:87	MP	Herpa 3551
Porsche 930 T "Martini"	1:87	MP	Herpa 3552
BMW 323 i "Warsteiner"	1:87	MP	Herpa 3553
BMW 635 CSi "Jägermeister"	1:87	MP	Herpa 3554
Audi 100 Avant—taxi	1:87	MP	Herpa 4004
Ford Transit "Teile Service"	1:87	MP	Herpa 4030
VW—fire fighting van / *bus pompiers*	1:87	MP	Herpa 4032
VW—"THW" van / *fourgon «THW»*	1:87	MP	Herpa 4035
VW—"Underberg" van / *fourgon «Underberg»*	1:87	MP	Herpa 4036
Opel Record—police	1:87	MP	Herpa 4040
Ford Capri—police	1:87	MP	Herpa 4048
BMW 528 i "ELW"	1:87	MP	Herpa 4062
Opel Record Caravan "Feuerwehr"—fire fighting vehicle / *break pompiers*	1:87	MP	Herpa 4064
Opel Kadett—fire fighting vehicle / *break pompiers*	1:87	MP	Herpa 4066
Range Rover "THW"	1:87	MP	Herpa 4067
Mercedes-Benz 207D—bus	1:87	MP	Herpa 4070
Mercedes-Benz 508D—van / *camionnette*	1:87	MP	Herpa 4080

Model	Scale	Type	Manufacturer / Ref.
Volvo F10—dumper / *camion benne*	1:87	MP	Herpa 800502
Volvo—tanker semitrailer "NMW" / *semi-remorque citerne «NMW»*	1:87	MP	Herpa 801204
Ford Transcontinental—container trailer / *container*	1:87	MP	Herpa 805220
Daimler-Benz—tanker trailer "Talke" / *semi-remorque citerne «Talke»*	1:87	MP	Herpa 806206
Daimler-Benz—removal van "Deutsche Möbelspedition / *déménageuse «Deutsche Möbelspedition»*	1:87	MP	Herpa 806390
Volvo Globetrotter—semitrailer "Norfrig" / *semi-remorque «Norfrig»*	1:87	MP	Herpa 807232
Magirus Deutz "Dachser Spedition"	1:87	MP	Herpa 808292
Unic—with trailer "Iveco Service" / *avec remorque «Iveco Service»*	1:87	MP	Herpa 810420
Daimler-Benz 2238—semitrailer "Panalpina" / *semi-remorque «Panalpina»*	1:87	MP	Herpa 811270
Daimler-Benz—canvas top delivery truck "Kieserling" / *camion expédition bâché «Kieserling»*	1:87	MP	Herpa 811285
Daimler-Benz—with trailer "Franken Brunner" / *avec remorque «Franken Brunner»*	1:87	MP	Herpa 811327
Daimler-Benz 2238—with trailer "Ringel" / *avec remorque «Ringel»*	1:87	MP	Herpa 811442
Magirus—tanker trailer "Aral" / *semi-remorque citerne «Aral»*	1:87	MP	Herpa 813371
Mercedes-Benz LP 813—dumper / *camion benne.*	1:87	MP	Herpa 814293
Mercedes-Benz—canvas top truck / *camion bâché*	1:87	MP	Herpa 814294
Saurer OM "Iveco"	1:87	MP	Herpa 815390
Setra S 228 DT—double-decker bus / *bus 2 étages*	1:87	MP	Herpa 830461
Setra S 228 DT—double-decker bus "Univers" / *bus 2 étages «Univers»*	1:87	MP	Herpa 830462
MAN Sü 240—Munich bus / *bus ville de Munich*	1:87	MP	Herpa 831470
MAN Sü 240—"Daimler-Benz" bus / *bus «Daimler-Benz»*	1:87	MP	Herpa 831471
Kenworth—platform semitrailer / *semi-remorque plateau*	1:87	MP	Herpa 850500
GMC—tanker semitrailer "Exxon" / *semi-remorque citerne «Exxon»*	1:87	MP	Herpa 851208
GMC General—semitrailer "Pepsi Cola" / *semi-remorque «Pepsi Cola»*	1:87	MP	Herpa 851227
Chevy Bison "Pabst Beer"	1:87	MP	Herpa 852228
Chevy Bison—platform semitrailer / *semi-remorque à ridelles*	1:87	MP	Herpa 852227
Ackerman—with Fruehauf "Hungaro-Camion" trailer / *avec remorque Fruehauf «Hungaro-Camion»*	1:87	MP	Herpa 912321
Kenworth—tanker semitrailer "Union 76" / *semi-remorque citerne «Union 76»*	1:87	MP	Herpa 950209
GMC—dumper / *camion benne*	1:87	MP	Herpa 951504
White Freightliner "Red Baron Air Racing Team"	1:87	MP	Herpa 953232
Freightliner—tanker "Gulf" / *citerne «Gulf»*	1:87	MP	Herpa 954214
White—dumper / *camion benne*	1:87	MP	Herpa 955503
Osella F1 (1980)	1:43	KM	**Hi Fi (I)** HF 8
Brabham BT 16 (1966)	1:43	KM	Hi Fi HF 9
Ferrari 126 CK (1981) Long Beach	1:43	KM	Hi Fi HF 10
Ferrari 126 CK (1981) Monte Carlo	1:43	KM	Hi Fi HF 10b
Ferrari 308 GTB Gr.5 Turbo	1:43	KM	Hi Fi HF 14
Renault RE 30 B Kyalami (1982)	1:43	KM	Hi Fi HF 16
Leyland-Metz (1932)—fire engine / *pompiers*	1:76	KW	**Highway Models (GB)**—
Citroën 2 CV (1938)—prototype	1:43	KW	**Idem (F)** —
* Honda TACT	1:12	KP	**Imai (J)** B-1059
* Yamaha Pasetta	1:12	KP	Imai B-1081
Mazda 323	1:24	KP	Imai B-1140
Honda City-R	1:20	KP	Imai B-1116
Suzuki Cervo SS40	1:20	KP	Imai B-1112
Suzuki Alto SS80	1:20	KP	Imai B-1113
Subaru Rex Combi	1:20	KP	Imai B-1114
Daihatsu Cuore	1:20	KP	Imai B-1115
* Honda CB 750 F Bol d'Or 2	1:12	KP	Imai B-1103
Volvo F-12—tractor / *tracteur*	1:24	KP	**Italeri (I)** 751
Volvo F-12 Globetrotter—tractor / *tracteur*	1:24	KP	Italeri 752
Container trailer / *semi-remorque container.*	1:24	KP	Italeri 754
Scania T-142H—tractor / *tracteur.*	1:24	KP	Italeri 753
Chrysler Imperial (1934)—phaeton, Le Baron body / *phaéton, carrosserie Le Baron*	1:24	KP	Italeri 704
Scania R 142H—tractor / *tracteur.*	1:24	KP	Italeri 755
MAN Formula 6—tractor / *tracteur*	1:24	KP	Italeri 756
Morris (1930)—van "Cooksey Wines" / *fourgonnette «Cooksey Wines»*	1:43	KW	**JEM (GB)**—
Morris (1930)—van "Boots The Chemist" / *fourgonnette «Boots The Chemist»*	1:43	KW	JEM—available only from Grand Prix Models / *disponible seulement auprès GPM*
Plymouth Fury hardtop (1963)—custom and stock / *de série et hors série*	1:25	KP	**Jo-Han (USA)** C-5263
Cadillac DeVille (1968)—convertible, custom and stock / *décapotable, de série et hors série*	1:25	KP	Jo-Han C-5368
Atkinson (1964)—truck / *camion*	1:43	KW	**K & B (GB)**—
DAF—semitrailer / *semi-remorque*	1:87	MP	**Kibri (D)** 10019 also KP 10018 / *aussi KP 10018*
DAF—bulk semitrailer / *semi-remorque silo*	1:87	MP	Kibri 10037 also KP 10036 / *aussi KP 10036*
Mercedes—concrete mixer truck / *malaxeur*	1:87	MP	Kibri 10039 also KP 10038 / *aussi KP 10038*
DAF—tanker semitrailer / *semi-remorque citerne*	1:87	MP	Kibri 10077 also KP 10076 / *aussi KP 10076*
Tractor / *tracteur* "Kaelble"—with mobilhome / *avec mobilhome*	1:87	MP	Kibri 10112
Faun—tractor with trailer / *tracteur avec remorque pour transports lourds.*	1:87	MP	Kibri 10121 also KP 10120 / *aussi KP 10120*
Mercedes—refrigerated semitrailer / *semi-remorque frigorifique*	1:87	MP	Kibri 10151 also KP 10150 / *aussi KP 10150*
DAF—refrigerated semitrailer / *semi-remorque frigorifique*	1:87	MP	Kibri 10161 also KP 10160 / *aussi KP 10160*
Mercedes—semitrailer van / *semi-remorque fourgon*	1:87	MP	Kibri 10171 also KP 10170 / *aussi KP 10170*
GAZ-AA (1932)—truck / *camion*	1:43	MM	**Leningrad (SU)**
Chevy Stock Car	—	MM	**Lesney (GB)** MB-34 1-75 Series
Ferrari 308 GTB	—	MM	Lesney MB-70 1-75 Series
Dodge—van / *fourgonnette*	1:35	MM	Lesney K-11 SuperKings
BMW M1	—	MM	Lesney MB-52 1-75 Series
Rover 3500	—	MM	Lesney MB-8 1-75 Series
Massey Ferguson—tractor / *tracteur agricole*	—	MM	Lesney K-87 King Size Series
Mercedes—timber truck / *camion transport de bois*	—	MM	Lesney K-43 King Size Series
Peugeot 305	—	MM	Lesney K-84 King Size Series
Ford A "Woody" wagon / *fourgon carrosserie en bois*	—	MM	Lesney Y-21 Yesteryear Series
Talbot—"Nestlé's Milk" van / *camionnette «Nestlé's Milk»*	—	MM	Lesney Y-5 Yesteryear Series
Ford T—"25 years of Models of Yesteryear" van / *fourgonnette 25e anniversaire*	—	MM	Lesney Y-12 Yesteryear Series
* Harley-Davidson Police	—	MM	Lesney K-83 SuperKings Series
Ford T—BP petrol tanker / *camionnette-citerne BP*	—	MM	Lesney Y-3 Yesteryear Series

Model	Scale	Material	Manufacturer / reference
Mercury Cougar (1971)—convertible / *décapotable*	1:32	SP	**Lindberg (USA)** 141
Ford Mustang (1971)—convertible / *décapotable*	1:32	SP	Lindberg 142
Ford Thunderbird (1971)	1:32	SP	Lindberg 143
Chevrolet Corvette (1971)—convertible / *décapotable*	1:32	SP	Lindberg 144
AMC Gremlin (1971)	1:32	SP	Lindberg 145
Ford Torino (1971)—convertible / *décapotable*	1:32	SP	Lindberg 146
Chevrolet El Camino pickup (1974)—with garage / *avec garage*	1:32	SP	Lindberg 387
Mercedes-Benz 450 SL (1974)—with garage / *avec garage*	1:32	SP	Lindberg 388
Chevrolet Monte Carlo (1975)—with garage / *avec garage*	1:32	SP	Lindberg 389
Datsun 280 Z—with garage / *avec garage*	1:32	SP	Lindberg 390
Pontiac Grand Am (1975)—stock car / *version stock car*	1:32	SP	Lindberg 391
Plymouth Barracuda (1973)—stock car / *version stock car*	1:32	SP	Lindberg 392
Pontiac Grand Prix (1975)—stock car / *version stock car*	1:32	SP	Lindberg 393
Buick Century (1975)—stock car / *version stock car*	1:32	SP	Lindberg 394
"Monte Carlo Racer"—futuristic / *voiture de course futuriste*	1:12	KP	Lindberg 655M
GMC Astro 95—cabover with box trailer / *cabine avancée avec semi-remorque*	1:87	SP	Lindberg 1045
GMC Astro 95—cabover with canvas covered trailer / *cabine avancée avec semi-remorque bâchée*	1:87	SP	Lindberg 1046
Ford CL-9000—cabover with box trailer / *cabine avancée avec semi-remorque*	1:87	SP	Lindberg 1047
Ford CL-9000—cabover with car carrier / *cabine avancée avec transporteur d'autos*	1:87	SP	Lindberg 1048
Dump truck / *dumper*	1:40	SP	Lindberg 1224—Heavy Wheelers series
Front loader / *chargeur*	1:40	SP	Lindberg 1225—Heavy Wheelers series
Super scraper / *scraper*	1:60	SP	Lindberg 1226—Heavy Wheelers series
Porsche Carrera	1:24	SP	Lindberg 6040
Cobra Daytona coupé (1964)	1:24	SP	Lindberg 6041
Jaguar D-type (1956)—Le Mans	1:24	SP	Lindberg 6042
Chevrolet Corvette (1980)—"Turbo Vette" / *hors série*	1:24	SP	Lindberg 6501
Chevrolet Camaro (1980)—"Custom Camaro" / *hors série*	1:24	SP	Lindberg 6502
Pontiac Firebird Trans Am (1980)	1:24	SP	Lindberg 6503
Ford Mustang Cobra (1980)—custom / *hors série*	1:24	SP	Lindberg 6504
Toyota Soarer 2000 VR Turbo	1:20	KP	**LS (J)** C1212
Nissan Leopard Turbo	1:20	KP	LS C1213
Nissan Skyline 2000 GT-X—4 door / *4 portes*	1:24	KP	LS C552
Nissan Skyline 2000 GT-X	1:24	KP	LS C553
Nissan Skyline 2000 GT-X—stunt car / *cascadeurs*	1:24	KP	LS C808
Nissan Skyline 2000 GT-X	1:24	KP	LS C809
Toyota Celica XX	1:20	KP	LS C1214 red / *rouge*
Toyota Celica XX	1:20	KP	LS C1215 white / *blanche*
Nissan New Skyline 2000 GT Turbo	1:20	KP	LS C1216 red / *rouge*
Nissan New Skyline 2000 GT Turbo	1:20	KP	LS C1217 white / *blanche*
Nissan 330 Cedric 2800 E (1977)—4 door brougham / *4 portes brougham*	1:20	KP	LS C1219
Nissan Gloria 330 2800 E—4 door hardtop / *4 portes hardtop*	1:20	KP	LS C1220
Suzuki Cervo CX-G	1:20	KP	LS C700 white / *blanche*
Suzuki Cervo CX-G	1:20	KP	LS C701 red / *rouge*
Renault 5 Turbo	1:60	MZ	**Majorette (F)** 255
Oldsmobile—4-door / *4 portes*	1:66	MZ	Majorette 253
Excalibur SS	1:40	MZ	Majorette 3020
Toyota Jeep—wagon / *break*	1:65	MZ	Majorette 277
Mercedes 0303—bus	1:50	MZ	Majorette —plastic roof / *toit en plastique*
Ford—tractor and trailer / *tracteur semi-remorque*	1:100	MZ	Majorette 361—"Demeco" or "Roadway" / *«Demeco» ou «Roadway»*
US Van—*fourgon américain*	1:80	MZ	Majorette —"Canon"
Triumph TR7	1:60	MZ	Majorette —
Saab 900 Turbo	1:60	MZ	Majorette —
Excalibur—top up / *capotée*	1:40	MZ	Majorette —
Mercedes—forage truck / *fourragère*	1:100	MZ	Majorette —
Ford—van / *fourgon*	1:85	MZ	Majorette —"Canon"
GMC—with van trailer / *fourgon semi-remorque*	1:100	MZ	Majorette —"Roadway"and "Demeco" / *publicités «Roadway» et «Demeco»*
London bus / *bus londonien*	1:119	MZ	Majorette —"Visit London"
Mercedes—tarpaulin-covered truck / *bâché*	1:60	MZ	Majorette —formerly Tonergam Solido series 3000 / *ex Solido Tonergam série 3000*
Mercedes—refuse truck / *benne à ordures*	1:60	MZ	Majorette —formerly Tonergam Solido / *ex Solido Tonergam*
GMC—flat-bed truck / *semi-plateau*	1:60	MZ	Majorette —with 2 "Supertrans" containers / *avec 2 containers «Supertrans»*
Toyota—jeep and horse van / *jeep avec van*	1:40	MZ	Majorette —
Renault GBH	1:150	MZ	Majorette —formerly Berliet, five versions / *ex Berliet, 5 versions produites*
Mercedes—0303 bus / *bus 0303*	1:50	MZ	Majorette —"Transports Philibert—Lyon"
De Tomaso Pantera GTS	1:24	KP	**Marui (J)** MT-82-ZK1-800 black / *noire*
De Tomaso Pantera GTS	1:24	KP	Marui MT-82-ZK2-800 purple / *pourpre*
Audi 100 Raid	1:43	MM	**Mattel (I)** A 137 paper stickers, "Decal" series / *autocollants papier, série «Decal»*
BMW 730—stunt-car / *voiture cascadeurs*	1:43	MM	Mattel A 146 "Decal" series / *série «Decal»*
Opel Kadett Rally	1:43	MM	Mattel A 156 "Decal" series / *série «Decal»*
Renault 5 Rally	1:43	MM	Mattel A 157 "Decal" series / *série «Decal»*
Fiat Ritmo—racing / *version course*	1:43	MM	Mattel A 159 "Decal" series / *série «Decal»*
Alfa Romeo Giulietta—racing / *version course*	1:43	MM	Mattel A 160 "Decal" series / *série «Decal»*
Porsche 924—racing / *version course*	1:43	MM	Mattel A 161 "Decal" series / *série «Decal»*
Volvo 343—racing / *version course*	1:43	MM	Mattel A 162 "Decal" series / *série «Decal»*
Ford Granada—stunt car / *voiture cascadeurs*	1:43	MM	Mattel A 164 "Decal" series / *série «Decal»*
Fiat Panda—rally version / *version rallye*	1:43	MM	Mattel A 166 "Decal" series / *série «Decal»*
Lancia Delta—racing / *version course*	1:43	MM	Mattel A 167 "Decal" series / *série «Decal»*
Citroën Visa Raid	1:43	MM	Mattel A 174 "Decal" series / *série «Decal»*
BMW 320 Rally	1:43	MM	Mattel A 113 "Super" series / *série «Super»*
Opel Monza	1:43	MM	Mattel A 143 "Super" series / *série «Super»*
Fiat 131 Abarth Rally	1:43	MM	Mattel A 152 "Super" series / *série «Super»*
Porsche 924 Rally	1:43	MM	Mattel A 168 "Super" series / *série «Super»*
Alfa Romeo Giulietta—police	1:43	MM	Mattel A 136 "Super" series / *série «Super»*
Opel Kadett	1:43	MM	Mattel A 169 with surfboards, "Super" series / *avec planches surf, série «Super»*
Volvo 343 Rally	1:43	MM	Mattel A 170 "Super" series / *série «Super»*
Lancia Delta	1:43	MM	Mattel A 172 with surfboards, "Super" series / *avec planches surf, série «Super»*

Model	Scale	Type	Make / No. / Notes
Peugeot 305	1:43	MM	Mattel A 173 "Super" series / *série «Super»*
Williams FW 07B (1981)	1:25	MM	Mattel 6815
Ferrari 126 CK (1981)	1:25	MM	Mattel 6816
Alfa Romeo 179 (1981)	1:25	MM	Mattel 6817
Brabham BT "Parmalat" (1981)	1:25	MM	Mattel 6818
Arrows "Beta/Ragno" (1981)	1:25	MM	Mattel 6819
Williams FW 07B "Dallah" (1981)	1:25	MM	Mattel 6836 same as 6815 / *idem 6815*
Ferrari 126 CK muletto—training car / *mulet*	1:25	MM	Mattel 6837 same as 6816 / *idem 6816*
Brabham BT 49C "Pemex" (1981)	1:25	MM	Mattel 6839 same as 6818 / *idem 6818*
Alfa Romeo "80"	1:25	MM	Mattel 6838 same as 6817 / *idem 6817*
Talbot Ligier (1981)	1:25	MM	Mattel 6820
Arrows "Warsteiner" (1980)	1:25	MM	Mattel 6840 same as 6819 / *idem 6819*
Ligier "80"	1:25	MM	Mattel 6841 same as 6820 / *idem 6820*
Opel Kadett	1:25	MM	Mattel 6791 "Standard" series / *série «Standard»*
Audi Quattro	1:25	MM	Mattel 6813 "Standard" series / *série «Standard»*
Citroën Visa	1:25	MM	Mattel 6797 "Standard" series / *série «Standard»*
Audi Quattro Rally	1:25	MM	Mattel 6814 "Decal" series / *série «Decal»*
Opel Kadett Rally	1:25	MM	Mattel 6811 "Decal" series / *série «Decal»*
Porsche 928 Rally	1:25	MM	Mattel 6823 "Decal" series / *série «Decal»*
BMW 730 Raid	1:25	MM	Mattel 6832 "Decal" series / *série «Decal»*
Peugeot 305 Raid	1:25	MM	Mattel 6833 "Decal" series / *série «Decal»*
Fiat Panda	1:25	MM	Mattel 6785 "Decal" series / *série «Decal»*
Opel Monza Rally	1:25	MM	Mattel 6794 "Decal" series / *série «Decal»*
Audi 100 NASA	1:25	MM	Mattel 6830 "Super" series / *série «Super»*
Talbot Horizon Rally	1:25	MM	Mattel 6825 "Super" series / *série «Super»*
Cadillac Seville	—	MM	**Mattel (USA)** 1698 Hot Wheels
'35 Classic Caddy	—	MM	Mattel 3252 Hot Wheels, Cadillac (1935)
Ford—dump truck / *dumper*	—	MM	Mattel 3253 Hot Wheels
Datsun 200 SX	—	MM	Mattel 3255 Hot Wheels
Rapid Transit—single deck bus / *autobus*	—	MM	Mattel 3256 Hot Wheels
Jeep CJ-7	—	MM	Mattel 3259 Hot Wheels
Ford Fairmont	—	MM	Mattel 3254 Hot Wheels
Malibu Grand Prix	—	MM	Mattel 9037 Racing car / *voiture de course*
Voisin (1923)—Grand Prix ACF	1:43	MW	**MCM (F)** —
Auburn 851 Speedster	1:87	KW	**Metal 87 (D)** 707
BMW 507—roadster	1:87	KW	Metal 87 709
BMW 315—roadster	1:87	KW	Metal 87 710
Talbot Lago (1938)—Figoni & Falaschi coupé / *coupé Figoni & Falaschi*	1:87	KW	Metal 87 712
Hispano-Suiza H6 (1932)—convertible / *cabriolet*	1:87	KW	Metal 87 714
Cord 812 (1937)—convertible / *cabriolet*	1:87	KW	Metal 87 715
BMW 326 (1937)—sedan / *conduite intérieure*	1:87	KW	Metal 87 716
Maybach Zeppelin (1932)—convertible / *cabriolet*	1:87	KW	Metal 87 717
Porsche Carrera 2	1:87	KW	Metal 87 718
Sunbeam 1000 HP (1927)—record car / *record.*	1:87	KW	Metal 87 719
Horch 853 A—convertible / *cabriolet*	1:87	KW	Metal 87 720
Mercedes 300 SLR (1955)—Mille Miglia	1:87	KW	Metal 87 721
Mercedes 170 S—convertible / *cabriolet.*	1:87	KW	Metal 87 722
Porsche 356—convertible / *cabriolet*	1:87	KW	Metal 87 723
Bugatti T 50(1932)—coupé / *coupé*	1:87	KW	Metal 87 724
Volvo PV 544	1:87	KW	Metal 87 726
Morris Minor (1943)—prototype	1:43	KW	**Mikansue (GB)** 29
Lister Jaguar (1963)—Le Mans	1:43	KW	Mikansue 63 Mikansue Competition
Jaguar XK 150—coupé	1:43	KW	Mikansue 22 Grand Tourisme
Aston Martin DB2 (1950)—saloon	1:43	KW	Mikansue 23 Grand Tourisme
Triumph Dolomite (1938)—roadster	1:43	KW	Mikansue 30
Healey Westland—convertible / *décapotable*	1:43	KW	Mikansue 64
Voisin Aerodyne (1935)—saloon	1:43	KW	Mikansue 24 Grand Tourisme
Riley Monaco (1934)	1:43	KW	Mikansue 31
Rover 100 P4 (1960)	1:43	KW	Mikansue 32
ERA G-Type F2 (1952)	1:43	KW	Mikansue 66 Mikansue Competition
Jaguar XK 150—coupé	1:43	KW	**Minichamps (D)** 49
Triumph TR 3 A	1:43	KW	Minichamps 50
Porsche 911 S (1972)—"Stan Towes"	1:43	KW	Minichamps 51
Porsche 911 Targa (1965)	1:43	KW	Minichamps 52
Triumph TR 3	1:43	KW	Minichamps 55
Triumph TR 2	1:43	KW	Minichamps 56
Porsche 356 C—coupé	1:43	KW	Minichamps 57
Porsche 356 C—convertible / *cabriolet*	1:43	KW	Minichamps 58
Porsche 356 C—hardtop	1:43	KW	Minichamps 59
Porsche 356 Speedster—"K. Kuerzel"	1:43	KW	Minichamps 60
Porsche 911—convertible / *cabriolet*	1:43	KW	Minichamps 61 1981 Frankfurt Motor Show prototype / *prototype Salon de Francfort 1981*
Porsche 936 (1981)—"Jules"	1:43	KW	**Mini Racing (F)** —Le Mans 1981 or number 12 / *Le Mans 81 ou voiture 12*
De Cadenet (1981)—"Belga"	1:43	KW	Mini Racing —
Peugeot 505 STI	1:43	KM	Mini Racing —Norev-based kit / *transkit base Norev*
Peugeot 504—wagon / *break*	1:43	KM	Mini Racing —Solido-based kit / *transkit base Solido «Assistance»*
Citroën C6—bus / *autocar*	1:50	MR	**Minitrucks (F)** —Dubray-based model or kit / *kit ou modèle base Dubray*
Fuso K-FV 214 JR—tractor / *tracteur*	1:24	KP	**Mitsuwa (J)** 301 MT-2800 yellow / *jaune*
Fuso K-FV 214 JR—tractor / *tracteur*	1:24	KP	Mitsuwa 302 MT-2800 blue / *bleu*
Fuso V-10—dump truck / *dumper*	1:24	KP	Mitsuwa 311 MT-3800 green / *vert*
Fuso V-10—dump truck / *dumper*	1:24	KP	Mitsuwa 321 MT-3800 black / *noir*
Pontiac GTO (1969)	1:32	SP	**Monogram (USA)** 1029
Ford Mustang (1970)—fastback roof / *fastback*	1:32	SP	Monogram 1030
Chevrolet Malibu (1982)—four-door Police car / *quatre portes police*	1:32	SP	Monogram 1031
Chevrolet Camaro Z-28 hardtop (1969)	1:32	SP	Monogram 1032
AMC Jeep CJ-7—"Off Road Jeep"	1:32	SP	Monogram 1033

Ford Bronco—"Off Road Bronco"	1:32	SP	Monogram 1034
Ford Mustang (1980)—"Turbo Mustang" / *hors série*	1:32	SP	Monogram 1038—Hot Wheels series
Pontiac Blackbird (1978)—"Hot Bird" / *hors série*	1:32	SP	Monogram 1039—Hot Wheels series
Chevrolet Corvette (1978)—"Corvette Sting Ray"	1:32	SP	Monogram 1040—Hot Wheels series
Ford Bronco—"Bronco 4-Wheeler" / *hors série*	1:32	SP	Monogram 1041—Hot Wheels series
Peterbilt—cabover / *cabine avancée*	1:32	SP	Monogram 1208
Kenworth Aerodyne—cabover / *cabine avancée*	1:32	SP	Monogram 1209
Mack R Series—conventional / *cabine normale*	1:32	SP	Monogram 1210
Union Oil tanker trailer / *semi-remorque citerne «Union»*	1:32	SP	Monogram 1211
Peterbilt—cabover reefer van / *cabine avancée avec fourgon réfrigérateur*—"Eskimo Pie"	1:32	SP	Monogram 1302
Kenworth Aerodyne—conventional and 40' van / *cabine normale avec fourgon 12 m*—"Sea Land"	1:32	SP	Monogram 1303
Chevrolet Camaro Z-28 (1982)	1:32	KP	Monogram 2004
Ford EXP (1982)	1:32	KP	Monogram 2005—detailed engine / *détails moteur*
Chevrolet Nova (1969)	1:32	KP	Monogram 2006—detailed engine / *détails moteur*
Dodge Charger (1969)	1:32	KP	Monogram 2007—detailed engine / *détails moteur*
Land Rover	1:24	KP	Monogram 2279
Chevrolet Luv 4×4 pickup	1:24	KP	Monogram 2280—High Roller series
Pontiac Trans Am (1982)	1:24	KP	Monogram 2281
Ford Mustang (1970)—"Boss 429" / *hors série*	1:24	KP	Monogram 2282
Chevrolet Corvette (1957)—"Vette Street Machine" / *hors série*	1:24	KP	Monogram 2283
Chevrolet Malibu (1970)—non-stock / *hors série*	1:24	KP	Monogram 2284
Ford pickup (1955)—"Strohmobile" / *hors série*	1:24	KP	Monogram 2285
Ford Bronco	1:24	KP	Monogram 2286—High Roller series
BMW—Group 2 coupé / *coupé groupe 2*	1:24	KP	Monogram 2287
Chevrolet Citation (1981)—"X" racing version / *compétition «X»*	1:24	KP	Monogram 2288
Ford Thunderbird (1956)	1:24	KP	Monogram 2289—former KM / *anciennement KM*
MG-TC (1946)	1:24	KP	Monogram 2290—former KM / *anciennement KM*
Chevrolette Corvette (1953)	1:24	KP	Monogram 2291—former KM / *anciennement KM*
Plymouth Barracuda (1971)—"Hemi Cuda" / *hors série*	1:24	KP	Monogram 2292
Plymouth GTX (1970)	1:24	KP	Monogram 2293
Pontiac GTO Judge (1969)	1:24	KP	Monogram 2294
AMC Jeep CJ-7 (1980)—"Off Road Jeep CJ-7"	1:20	KP	Monogram 2405
Chevrolet Corvette (1980)—"Custom Corvette" / *hors série*	1:20	KP	Monogram 2406
Pontiac Trans Am (1981)	1:20	KP	Monogram 2407—Daytona 500 Pace Car
Chevrolet Corvette Collectors Edition (1982)	1:20	KP	Monogram 2408
*Yamaha XS Eleven	1:15	KP	Monogram 2409—parts molded in Japan / *pièces moulées au Japon*
*Honda CBX	1:15	KP	Monogram 2410—parts molded in Japan / *pièces moulées au Japon*
*Kawasaki Z1-R Turbo	1:15	KP	Monogram 2411—parts molded in Japan / *pièces moulées au Japon*
*Kawasaki Z400 FX	1:15	KP	Monogram 2412—parts molded in Japan / *pièces moulées au Japon*
Kenworth W-900—conventional / *cabine normale*	1:16	KP	Monogram 2501
Chevrolet pickup (1972)—"Cooter's Tow Truck"	1:25	KP	**MPC (USA)** 1-0441—Dukes of Hazzard series / *série TV*
Dodge pickup (1981)—"Thunders Truck" / *hors série*	1:25	KP	MPC 1-0442
Chevrolet pickup (1982)—"Ground Shaker" / *hors série*	1:25	KP	MPC 1-0444—annual kit / *modèle de l'année*
Dodge (1982)—van/fourgonnette—"Bad Company" / *hors série*	1:25	KP	MPC 1-0445—annual kit / *modèle de l'année*
Ford Bronco (1982)—"Dust Devil" / *hors série*	1:25	KP	MPC 1-0446—annual kit / *modèle de l'année*
Dodge (1981)—"Emergency Van" / *fourgon premier secours*	1:25	KP	MPC 1-0447—Cannonball Run series
Ford Mark IV—Le Mans winner / *vainqueur Le Mans*	1:25	KP	MPC 1-0561
McLaren MK8d—racer / *voiture de course*	1:20	KP	MPC 1-0571
Chevrolet Chevelle (1977)—"Malibu Grand National"	1:25	KP	MPC 1-0681—Cannonball Run series
Lamborghini Countach	1:25	KP	MPC 1-0682—Cannonball Run series
Pontiac Firebird Trans Am (1982)	1:25	KP	MPC 1-0808—annual kit / *modèle de l'année*
"Outcast"—street rod	1:25	KP	MPC 1-0812
Chevrolet Cavalier (1982)	1:25	KP	MPC 1-0813—annual kit / *modèle de l'année*
Chevrolet Camaro Z-28 (1982)	1:25	KP	MPC 1-0814—annual kit / *modèle de l'année*
Dodge Omni 024 (1982)—"Sidewinder" / *hors série*	1:25	KP	MPC 1-0815—annual kit / *modèle de l'année*
Ford Mustang Cobra (1982)—"Wild Breed" / *hors série*	1:25	KP	MPC 1-0816—annual kit / *modèle de l'année*
Ford EXP coupé (1982)	1:25	KP	MPC 1-0818—annual kit / *modèle de l'année*
Pontiac Firebird (1981)—"Turbo Bird" / *hors série*	1:25	KP	MPC 1-0819
Pontiac Firebird (1978)—"War Eagle" / *hors série*	1:25	KP	MPC 1-0820
Chevrolet Camaro (1981)—"Thunder-Z" / *hors série*	1:25	KP	MPC 1-0821
Pontiac Firebird (1969)—"Sundancer" / *hors série*	1:25	KP	MPC 1-0822
Dodge Charger (1982)—funny car / *dragster*—"Prime Time"	1:25	KP	MPC 1-0828
Dodge Charger (1982)—funny car / *dragster*—"Nitro Charger"	1:25	KP	MPC 1-0829
Mercury Cougar (1973)—"The Cat" / *hors série*	1:25	KP	MPC 1-0830
Ford Maverick—"War Horse" / *hors série*	1:25	KP	MPC 1-0831
Chevrolet El Camino pickup (1981)—"Branding Iron" / *hors série*	1:25	KP	MPC 1-0854
Dodge D-50 pickup (1981)—"Freedom Rider" / *hors série*	1:25	KP	MPC 1-0855
AMC Jeep CJ (1982)—"Swamp Rat" / *hors série*	1:25	KP	MPC 1-0856—annual kit / *modèle de l'année*
Chevrolet El Camino pickup (1982)—"Red Light Bandit" / *hors série*	1:25	KP	MPC 1-0857—annual kit / *modèle de l'année*
Dodge D-50 Ram pickup (1982)—"Evil Spirit" / *hors série*	1:25	KP	MPC 1-0858—annual kit / *modèle de l'année*
Datsun pickup—"Lil Hustler" drag racer / *dragster*	1:25	KP	MPC 1-0859
Plymouth Barracuda (1969)—"The Avenger" / *hors série*	1:25	KP	MPC 1-0860
Christie (1911)—American steam fire engine / *pompe-incendie à vapeur américaine*	1:12	KP	MPC 1-2002
Ford 427 Cobra roadster (1965)	1:16	KP	MPC 1-3082
Pontiac Firebird (1981)—"Turbo Blackbird" / *hors série*	1:16	KP	MPC 1-3083
Chevrolet Corvette (1957)	1:16	KP	MPC 1-3085
Chevrolet Corvette (1978)—custom coupe / *hors série*	1:16	KP	MPC 1-3087
AMC Jeep CJ Golden Eagle	1:32	SP	MPC 1-3226
"Piston Pusher"	1:32	SP	MPC 1-3401—also 1-3405, different color / *aussi 1-3405, autre teinte*—Fast 111s series
"Jet Vet"	1:32	SP	MPC 1-3402—also 1-3406, different color / *aussi 1-3406, autre teinte*—Fast 111s series
"Dirt Digger"	1:32	SP	MPC 1-3403—also 1-3407, different color / *aussi 1-3407, autre teinte*—Fast 111s series

"Evil Eye"	1:32	SP	MPC 1-3404—also 1-3408, different color / *aussi 1-3408, autre teinte*—Fast 111s series
Chevrolet pickup—"Smoke Detector" / *hors série*	1:16	SP	MPC 1-3501—Action Snap series
Chevrolet pickup—"Road 'Recker" / *hors série*	1:16	SP	MPC 1-3502—Action Snap series
Chevrolet pickup—"Haulin Hauler" / *hors série*	1:16	SP	MPC 1-3503—Action Snap series
Chevrolet pickup—"Pushin' Pickup" / *hors série*	1:16	SP	MPC 1-3504—Action Snap series
Chevrolet Corvette (1957)—"Velvet Vette" / *hors série*	1:25	KP	MPC 1-3717
Chevrolet Corvette (1982)—"Dragon Vette" / *hors série*	1:25	KP	MPC 1-3718—annual kit / *modèle de l'année*
Chevrolet Corvette—"Demon Vette" / *hors série*	1:25	KP	MPC 1-3719—previously / *anciennement* "Turbo Shark"
Chevrolet Corvette (1981)—"Sabre Vette" / *hors série*	1:20	KP	MPC 1-3751
Chevrolet Corvette (1982)—"Class Act" / *hors série*	1:20	KP	MPC 1-3752—annual kit / *modèle de l'année*
Jaguar E—3.8 l. coupé / *coupé 3,8 l.*	1:43	KR	**MRF (F)** —first series / *première série*
Citroën Cx—ambulance	1:43	KM	**MVI (F)** —Solido-based kit, high roof / *transkit base Solido, toit surélevé*
Jeep—with pump / *avec moto-pompe*	1:43	KM	MVI —Solido-based kit / *transkit base Solido, Jeep fermée*
Nissan Fairlady 280 ZX Turbo	1:20	KP	**Nagano (J)** 3007
Toyota Soarer 2800 GT Extra	1:20	KP	Nagano 3008
* Honda CB 900 F2	1:8	KP	Nagano 1015
Toyota 2000 GT	1:24	KP	**Nichimo (J)** HC-2407
Mitsubishi Jeep	1:20	KP	Nichimo SP-2409
Suzuki Jimny	1:20	KP	Nichimo SP-2410
AMC Jeep CJ-7	1:20	KP	Nichimo SP-2411
Toyota Land Cruiser	1:20	KP	Nichimo SP-2412
Mitsubishi Galant GTO 2000 GSR	1:24	KP	Nichimo SP-2423
Nissan Violet Turbo	1:24	KP	Nichimo SP-2425
Nissan Skyline 2000 GT-R	1:24	KP	Nichimo SP-2421
Mazda Savanna RX-7—hotrod	1:24	KP	Nichimo SP-2422
Nissan Fairlady 240 Z—hotrod	1:24	KP	Nichimo SP-2420
Toyota Celica 1600 GT—hotrod	1:24	KP	Nichimo SP-2419
Nissan Skyline 2000 GT-R—body-down type / *surbaissé*	1:24	KP	Nichimo SP-2414
Nissan Fairlady 240 ZG—body-down type / *surbaissé*	1:24	KP	Nichimo SP-2416
Mazda Savanna RX-3—body-down type / *surbaissé*	1:24	KP	Nichimo SP-2415
Nissan Skyline 2000 GT Turbo	1:20	KP	Nichimo MC-2048
Toyota Celica 1600 GT—body-down type / *surbaissé*	1:24	KP	Nichimo SP-2417
Nissan Violet Turbo—body-down type / *surbaissé*	1:24	KP	Nichimo SP-2418
Nissan Laurel 2000 SGX—hotrod	1:24	KP	Nichimo SP-2413
Nissan Laurel 2000 SGX—body-down type / *surbaissé*	1:24	KP	Nichimo SP-2424
Mitsubishi Jeep H-J58	1:20	KP	Nichimo MC-2049
Daihatsu Taft	1:20	KP	Nichimo MC-2054
Suzuki Jimny 8	1:20	KP	Nichimo MC-2051
Ford M 151 Mutt	1:20	KP	Nichimo MC-2055
AMC Jeep CJ-7 Golden Hawk	1:20	KP	Nichimo MC-2056
AMC Jeep CJ-5 Renegade	1:20	KP	Nichimo MC-2052
AMC Jeep CJ-7 Golden Eagle	1:20	KP	Nichimo MC-2053
Toyota Land Cruiser	1:20	KP	Nichimo MC-2050
Nissan Laurel 2000 SGX	1:20	KP	Nichimo MC-2057
Nissan Skyline 2000 GT-X	1:20	KP	Nichimo MC-2058
Toyota Celica XX	1:24	KP	Nichimo SP-2426
Nissan Skyline 2000 GT-R—stunt car / *cascadeurs*	1:20	KP	Nichimo MC-2060
Nissan Fairlady Z-L—stunt car / *cascadeurs*	1:20	KP	Nichimo MC-2059
Nissan Skyline 2000 GT Turbo—stunt car / *cascadeurs*	1:20	KP	Nichimo MC-2062 Japanese model / *modèle Japon*
Toyota Celica 1600 GT—stunt car / *cascadeurs*	1:20	KP	Nichimo MC-2061
Toyota Town Ace	1:24	KP	Nichimo SP-2427
Toyota Town Ace—custom / *hors série*	1:24	KP	Nichimo SP-2428
Toyota Town Ace—super custom / *hors série*	1:24	KP	Nichimo SP-2429
* Yamaha RZ 250	1:10	KP	Nichimo MC-1005
* Yamaha RZ 350	1:10	KP	Nichimo MC-1006
Nissan Fairlady 240 ZG	1:28	KP	Nichimo MH-2809
Nissan Skyline HT 2000 GT-X	1:28	KP	Nichimo MH-2810
Nissan Silvia LS-E	1:28	KP	Nichimo MH-2811
Mazda Cosmo RE Limited	1:28	KP	Nichimo MH-2812
Toyota Celica LB 2000 GT	1:28	KP	Nichimo MH-2813
Toyota Corona HT "000 GT"	1:28	KP	Nichimo MH-2814
Mitsubishi Lancer 1600 GSR	1:28	KP	Nichimo MH-2815
Toyota Sprinter Trueno	1:28	KP	Nichimo MH-2816
Nissan Laurel 2000 SG-X	1:24	KP	Nichimo SP-2413
Toyota Celica 1750 GT	1:24	KP	Nichimo SP-2417
Mazda RX-3	1:24	KP	Nichimo SP-2415
Nissan Skyline 2000 GT	1:24	KP	Nichimo SP-2414
Toyota Hilux 4WD / *4 roues motrices*	1:20	KP	Nichimo MC-2064
* Honda CB 750 F Turbo	1:8	KP	**Nitto (J)** 781
Nissan Skyline RS DOHC	1:24	KP	Nitto 950
Volvo 264—coupé	1:43	MZ	**Norev (F)** 886
Alfa Romeo 6	1:43	MZ	Norev 888
Mercedes 280 SE—4-door / *4 portes*	1:43	MZ	Norev 890
Renault Fuego	1:43	MZ	Norev 891
Talbot Solara	1:43	MZ	Norev 893
Volvo 264 Break	1:43	MZ	Norev 896
Renault 9	1:43	MZ	Norev 898
Renault 18—saloon / *berline*	1:43	MZ	Norev 881
Renault 9—saloon / *berline*	1:66	MZ	Norev 450
Renault 18—saloon / *berline*	1:66	MZ	Norev 422
Fiat Ritmo—convertible / *cabriolet*	1:43	MM	**Novel (I)**
Mercedes 500 SEC	1:36	MZ	**NZG (D)** 201
Ford Cargo	1:50	MZ	NZG 219
Mercedes-Benz 0.3500 (1949)—German post bus / *autocar postes allemandes*	1:40	MZ	NZG—
Ford Cargo—with trailer van / *fourgon avec remorque*	1:50	MZ	NZG—
Toyota Corolla 27 Levin 1600 (1972)	1:24	KP	**Otaki (J)** OT3-152-600 green / *verte*
Toyota Corolla 27 Levin 1600 (1972)	1:24	KP	Otaki OT3-153-600 orange / *orange*
Nissan Gloria 200 Custom Deluxe	1:24	KP	Otaki OT3-154-1000

Nissan Cedric 200 Custom Deluxe	1:24	KP	Otaki OT3-155-1000
Nissan Gloria 200—taxi	1:24	KP	Otaki OT3-156-1000 yellow / *jaune*
Nissan Gloria 200—taxi	1:24	KP	Otaki OT3-157-1000 white / *blanc*
Nissan Skyline RS	1:24	KP	Otaki OT3-160 white / *blanche*
Nissan Skyline Turbo	1:24	KP	Otaki OT3-161
Nissan Skyline RS	1:24	KP	Otaki OT3-162 silver / *argent*
Nissan Skyline Turbo	1:24	KP	Otaki—OT3-163 black / *noire*
Audi 100 Avant	1:25	MP	**Piko (DDR)** flywheel / *à volant d'entraînement*
Porsche 911 Targa Watkins Glen 1980	1:43	MR	**PIT (I)** also KR / *aussi KR*
Citroën 2 CV—racing / *course*	1:43	MR	**Plastic Models (F)** —
Citroën Traction (1950)—van / *fourgonnette*	1:43	MR	Plastic Models —
Citroën Traction (1950)—van / *fourgonnette*	1:43	MR	Plactic Models —"Carlsberg"
Citroën Traction (1950)—van / *fourgonnette*	1:43	MR	Plastic Models —"Shell"
BMW 501 (1956)	1:43	KW	**Plumbies (D)** 65
Mercedes 300 D (1958)—"Adenauer" limousine / *limousine type «Adenauer»*	1:43	KW	Plumbies 66
Horch 853 A (1939)—Erdmann roadster	1:43	KW	Plumbies 67
Mercedes "Tropfenwagen" (1923)	1:43	KW	Plumbies 68 Italian GP / *GP d'Italie*
Auto Union C (1937)	1:43	KW	Plumbies 69
Peugeot 402 (1936)—Andreau limousine / *limousine Andreau*	1:43	KW	**Plumbies Inter (D)** 22
Bugatti 57 S (1934)—Ventoux	1:43	KW	Plumbies Inter 23
Alfa Romeo 8C (1936)—Castagna	1:43	KW	Plumbies Inter 26
Bugatti 101 (1951)—convertible / *cabriolet*	1:43	KW	Plumbies Inter 27
Bugatti 49 (1934)—convertible by Gangloff / *cabriolet Gangloff*	1:43	KW	Plumbies Inter 28
Jaguar XK-E 4.2 l	1:43	MM	**Polistil (I)** E 2001 scale approx. 1:40 / *échelle plus proche de 1:40*
Ferrari 365 GTB / 4 Daytona	1:43	MM	Polistil E 2002 scale approx. 1:40 / *échelle plus proche de 1:40*
Porsche 928	1:43	MM	Polistil E 2003 scale approx. 1:40 / *échelle plus proche de 1:40*
Alfa Romeo Alfetta GTV 2000 "Turbodelta"	1:43	MM	Polistil E 2004 scale approx. 1:40 / *échelle plus proche de 1:40*
BMW M1 Procar	1:43	MM	Polistil E 2005 scale approx. 1:40 / *échelle plus proche de 1:40*
Lancia Beta Montecarlo "Martini"	1:43	MM	Polistil E 2006 scale approx. 1:40 / *échelle plus proche de 1:40*
Mercedes W196 Grand Prix	1:16	MM	Polistil TG 9 with plastic parts / *avec pièces en plastique*
Rover 2600	1:26	MM	Polistil SN 22
Ferrari 308 Mondial	1:26	MM	Polistil SN 09
Lamborghini Miura	1:22	MM	Polistil SN 11
Renault 5 Turbo	1:22	MM	Polistil SN 16
Opel Ascona 400	1:22	MM	Polistil SN 27
Morgan Plus 8—racing / *version course*	1:16	MM	Polistil TG 11 with plastic parts / *avec pièces en plastique*
Ford Escort RS	1:22	MM	Polistil SN 28
Alfa Romeo Giulietta "Polizia"	1:26	MM	Polistil SN 19
Alfa Romeo Giulietta "Carabinieri"	1:26	MM	Polistil SN 20
BMW 328 spyder	1:16	MM	Polistil TG 6 with plastic parts / *avec pièces en plastique*
Renault Fuego	1:22	MM	Polistil SN 17
Mercedes 450 SLC—rally / *rallye*	1:25	MM	Polistil SN 24
Sunbeam Talbot Lotus—rally / *rallye*	1:23	MM	Polistil SN 25
Toyota Celica GT	1:24	MM	Polistil SN 26
Lamborghini Countach	1:43	MM	Polistil E 2007 rally trim / *décorations rallye*
Mercedes 450 SLC—rally / *rallye*	1:43	MM	Polistil E 2008
Sunbeam Talbot Lotus—rally / *rallye*	1:43	MM	Polistil E 2009
Opel Ascona 400—rally / *rallye*	1:43	MM	Polistil E 2011
Toyota Celica GT	1:43	MM	Polistil E 2010 rally trim / *décorations rallye*
Ford Escort RS	1:43	MM	Polistil E 2012 rally trim / *décorations rallye*
Ferrari 308 GTB "biturbo"	1:16	MM	Polistil TS 1 new series / *nouvelle série*
Porsche 928—racing / *version course*	1:16	MM	Polistil TS 2 new series / *nouvelle série*
Ferrari 126 C turbo (1981)	1:22	MM	Polistil SN 51 new series / *nouvelle série*
Alfa Romeo 179 (1981)	1:24	MM	Polistil SN 52 new series / *nouvelle série*
Renault RE30 (1981)	1:24	MM	Polistil SN 54 new series / *nouvelle série*
Ligier Talbot JS17	1:24	MM	Polistil SN 53 new series / *nouvelle série*
*Harley-Davidson Cafe Racer	1:15	MM	Polistil MS 639
*Harley-Davidson Sportser 1000	1:15	MM	Polistil MS 640
*Harley-Davidson 1200 Electra Glide Classic—sidecar / *side-car*	1:15	MM	Polistil MS 642
Ferrari 275 GTB (1965) Targa Florio	1:43	MR	**Progetto K (I)** PK 12
Ferrari 275 GTB (1965) Le Mans	1:43	MR	Progetto K PK 12b yellow / *jaune*
Alfa Romeo Alfetta Gr. 2 (1974)	1:43	KR	Progetto K 1—333 Minuti Rally 1974 or San Martino Rally 1974 / *version rallye 333 Minuti 1974 ou rallye San Martino 1974*
Citroën DS 19 (1964) Acropolis Rally	1:43	KR	Progetto K 2
Renault Gordini Dauphine (1962) Tour de Corse	1:43	KR	Progetto K 3
Renault RE-23 (1981)—Formula One / *Formule 1*	1:12	KP	**Protar (I)** —
Renault RE-23 (1981)—Formula One / *Formule 1*	1:12	KW	Protar — with some plastic parts / *avec pièces en plastique*
*Minarelli 125 (1979)	1:9	KP	Protar 165—some die-cast parts / *avec pièces métal*
*Kawasaki 250/350 (1980/1981)	1:9	KP	Protar — Randy Momola version / *version de Randy Mamola*
Matra M620 (1965)—BRM engined / *moteur BRM*	1:43	KW	**Quiralu (F)** —Le Mans number 41, 42 or 43 / *Le Mans voiture 41, 42 ou 43*
Ferrari 308 GTB "Entremont"	1:43	MR	**Record (F)** —also KR / *aussi KR*
Opel Ascona 400	1:43	MR	Record —also KR, Claar's car / *aussi KR, voiture de Claar*
Porsche 924 GTS "Eminence-Almeiras"	1:43	MR	Record —also KR / *aussi KR*
Toyota 4×4 pickup	1:32	SP	**Revell (D)** 6001 same as US release / *idem Revell USA*
Datsun King Cab pickup	1:32	SP	Revell 6004 same as US release / *idem Revell USA*

Model	Scale		Reference
Datsun King Cab camper	1:32	SP	Revell 6006 same as US release / *idem Revell USA*
Toyota SR5 pickup	1:32	SP	Revell 6008 same as US release / *idem Revell USA*
VW Golf pickup—wiht Honda ACT / *avec Honda ACT*	1:32	SP	Revell 6009 same as US release / *idem Revell USA*
VW Golf pickup—with mini racer / *avec kart*	1:32	SP	Revell 6012 same as US release / *idem Revell USA*
Jeep CJ Renegade	1:32	SP	Revell 6014 same as US release / *idem Revell USA*
Jeep CJ Laredo	1:32	SP	Revell 6015 same as US release / *idem Revell USA*
Pontiac Formula Firebird—convertible / *cabriolet*	1:25	SP	Revell 6222 same as US release / *idem Revell USA*
BMW 320i—rally / *rallye*	1:25	KP	Revell 7213 same as US release / *idem Revell USA*
Pontiac Firebird (1982)	1:25	KP	Revell 7215 same as US release / *idem Revell USA*
Chevrolet Camaro Z-28 (1982)	1:25	KP	Revell 7216 same as US release / *idem Revell USA*
Porsche 928 b+b	1:25	KP	Revell 7218 same as US release / *idem Revell USA*
VW—convertible / *cabriolet*	1:25	KP	Revell 7219 same as US Revell 7243 / *idem Revell USA 7243*
Ford Escort Turbo	1:25	KP	Revell 7316 same as US release / *idem Revell USA*
Ford Escort XR-3	1:25	KP	Revell 7317 same as US release / *idem Revell USA*
Triumph TR-3 (1959)	1:24	KP	Revell 7326
VW camper Westfalia "Joker 2"	1:25	KP	Revell 7329
Datsun King Cab	1:25	KP	Revell 7331 same as US release / *idem Revell USA*
VW—van / *mini bus*	1:25	KP	Revell 7347
Opel Coupé (1909)	1:28	KP	Revell 7351 Union tools / *moules Union*
Renault (1911)—2-seater / *2 places*	1:28	KP	Revell 7352 Union tools / *moules Union*
Stanley (1907)	1:28	KP	Revell 7353 Union tools / *moules Union*
Ford T (1911)	1:28	KP	Revell 7354 Union tools / *moules Union*
Bentley (1930)—Blower / *à compresseur*	1:24	KP	Revell 7361 Union tools / *moules Union*
Alfa Romeo Grand Sport	1:24	KP	Revell 7362 Union tools / *moules Union*
Rolls-Royce Silver Ghost (1906)	1:16	KP	Revell 7492 Gakken-Entex tools / *moules Gakken-Entex*
Ford A (1931)—delivery van / *camionnette de livraison*	1:16	KP	Revell 7493 Gakken-Entex tools / *moules Gakken-Entex*
Cadillac V16 (1933)	1:16	KP	Revell 7494 Gakken-Entex tools / *moules Gakken-Entex*
Mercedes SS (1928)—convertible / *cabriolet*	1:16	KP	Revell 7495 Gakken-Entex tools / *moules Gakken-Entex*
Volvo F1217 Globetrotter	1:25	KP	Revell 7407 same as US release / *idem Revell USA*
Mercedes-Benz 1628s	1:25	KP	Revell 7409 same as US release / *idem Revell USA*
Container trailer / *remorque container*	1:25	KP	Revell 7416
Volvo F1217 (7405) with container trailer / *Volvo F1217 (7405) avec remorque container*	1:25	KP	Revell 7417
*Harley-Davidson Low Rider	1:12	KP	Revell 7907 Japanese tools / *moules japonais*
*Harley-Davidson Electra Glide	1:12	KP	Revell 7908 Japanese tools / *moules japonais*
*Harley-Davidson Electra Classic	1:12	KP	Revell 7909 Japanese tools / *moules japonais*
Toyota pickup—"Bluehawk Camper" / *camper*	1:32	SP	**Revell (USA)** 6002
Datsun King Cab pickup	1:32	SP	Revell 6005
VW pickup—with / *avec* *Honda ATC	1:32	SP	Revell 6009
VW pickup—"Street Custom" / *hors série*	1:32	SP	Revell 6011
VW pickup—with Mini Racer / *avec kart*	1:32	SP	Revell 6012
AMC Jeep Renegade CJ	1:32	SP	Revell 6014
AMC Jeep Laredo CJ	1:32	SP	Revell 6015
AMC Jeep Safari	1:32	SP	Revell 6016
Pontiac Firebird (1982)	1:32	SP	Revell 6017
Chevrolet Camaro Z-28 (1982)	1:32	SP	Revell 6018
Chevrolet—emergency van / *fourgon premier secours*	1:32	SP	Revell 6029—"Code Red" series
Chevrolet Nova—Chief's car / *chef des pompiers*	1:32	SP	Revell 6030—"Code Red" series
Porsche 911—"Twin Turbo" / *hors série*	1:25	SP	Revell 6214
Chevrolet Blazer 4×4 (1979)—"Mudslinger" / *hors serie*	1:25	SP	Revell 6217
Chevrolet Camaro Z-28	1:25	SP	Revell 6221
Chevrolet Camaro Z-28—convertible / *décapotable*	1:25	SP	Revell 6225
Pontiac Firebird—"Ponch's Firebird" / *hors série*	1:25	SP	Revell 6226—"CHiPs" series
Chevrolet Corvette (1978)—"Blacktop Cowboy" / *hors série*	1:25	SP	Revell 6227
Chevrolet Camaro—"Chase Car" / *hors série*	1:25	SP	Revell 6228—"CHiPs" series
Toyota 4×4 pickup—"Malibu Grand Prix Race Team"—with Virage racer / *avec voiture de course Virage*	1:25	SP	Revell 6412
Ford Styleside 4×4 pickup	1:25	SP	Revell 6413
Ford Flairside 4×4 pickup—"Night Rider" / *hors série*	1:25	SP	Revell 6414
Ford 6-Wheeler pickup	1:25	SP	Revell 6415
Chevrolet 4×4 pickup—"Jon's Chevy" / *hors série*	1:25	SP	Revell 6421—"CHiPs" series
Chevrolet Corvette (1978)—"Corvette Turbo Hombre" / *hors série*	1:16	SP	Revell 6602
Chevrolet Corvette (1978)—"Turbo Vette" / *hors série*	1:16	SP	Revell 6603
BMW 320i Turbo—rally version / *version rallye*	1:25	KP	Revell 7213
Pontiac Firebird (1982)	1:25	KP	Revell 7215
Chevrolet Camaro Z-28 (1982)	1:25	KP	Revell 7216
Porsche 928—b&b Targa body / *carrosserie Targa b&b*	1:25	KP	Revell 7218
Pontiac Firebird—"Street Custom" / *hors série*	1:25	KP	Revell 7230
Ford Courier—"Rebel Courier"—custom / *hors série*	1:25	KP	Revell 7231
Ford Model T (1927)—"Touring Street Rod" / *hors série*	1:25	KP	Revell 7238
Ford coupé (1934)—chopped top / *toit abaissé*	1:25	KP	Revell 7239
VW cabriolet—with top down / *capote abaissée*	1:25	KP	Revell 7243
Ford Escorte (1981)—"Turbo Street Machine" / *hors série*	1:25	KP	Revell 7316
Ford Escort XR-3 (1981)	1:25	KP	Revell 7317
Ford EXP (1982)	1:25	KP	Revell 7318
Ford Mustang (1981)—convertible / *décapotable*	1:25	KP	Revell 7324

VW—"Magnum PI Vanagon" / *mini bus*	1:25	KP	Revell 7328
Datsun King Cab 4×4 pickup	1:25	KP	Revell 7331
Ford Bronco—custom / *hors série*	1:25	KP	Revell 7334
Chevrolet pickup—"Mr. Sandman" and dune buggy trailer / *avec buggy sur remorque*	1:25	KP	Revell 7404
Volvo Globetrotter—cabover / *cabine avancée*	1:25	KP	Revell 7407
Mercedes-Benz 1628s—cabover with roof spoiler / *cabine avancée avec spoiler de toit*	1:25	KP	Revell 7409
Porsche 928	1:16	KP	Revell 7484
*Kawasaki KZ-1000 LTD	1:12	KP	Revell 7801
*Kawasaki Cafe Racer	1:12	KP	Revell 7807
*Harley-Davidson—"Heavy Harley Street Chopper" / *chopper*	1:12	KP	Revell 7808
*Harley-Davidson 1200 Electra Glide—"California Highway Patrol Bike" / *police*	1:8	KP	Revell 7910
Auto Union (1937)—C-type record car / *type C record*	1:20	KM	**Revival (I)** 79101
Auto Union (1937)—C-type "Stromlinienwagen" Avus / *type C «Stromlinienwagen» Avus*	1:20	KM	Revival 79102
Bugatti Royale (1929)—Napoléon coupé / *coupé Napoléon*	1:43	MM	**Rio (I)** 74
Fiat 60 CV berlina (1905)—60 HP saloon / *berline*	1:43	MM	Rio 75
Nissan Cedric—sedan / *conduite int.*	1:43	MM	**Sakura (J)**—Sakura Pet
Jaguar XJ—sedan / *conduite int.*	1:43	MM	Sakura —Sakura Pet
Rolls-Royce Silver Wraith	1:43	MM	Sakura —Sakura Pet, new two-tone colors / *nouveaux coloris deux tons*
Brabham BT 45B—Formula 1 / *Formule 1*	1:43	MM	Sakura —Eidai Grip's molds / *moules Eidai Grip*
Renault RS 01—Formula 1 / *Formule 1*	1:43	MM	Sakura —Eidai Grip's molds / *moules Eidai Grip*
March 761 B—Formula 1 / *Formule 1*	1:43	MM	Sakura —Eidai Grip's molds / *moules Eidai Grip*
Nissan Cedric—van / *fourgonnette*	1:43	MM	Sakura —Sakura Pet
Toyota 4×4 Land Cruiser	1:35	MM	Sakura —Sakura Pet
Nissan Caravan—high roof / *toit surélevé*	1:50	MM	Sakura —Sakura Pet
Nissan Caravan—ambulance	1:50	MM	Sakura —Sakura Pet
Nissan Caravan—"Fire Chief" / *fourgon pompiers*	1:50	MM	Sakura —Sakura Pet
Nissan Caravan—police van / *fourgon police*	1:50	MM	Sakura —Sakura Pet
Nissan Caravan—kindergarten bus / *minibus école*	1:50	MM	Sakura —Sakura Pet
Japanese Police bus / *bus police japonaise*	1:70	MM	Sakura 4089
*Vespa Scooter	1:12	MM	Sakura 4004
*Suzuki Gemma 50	1:25	MM	Sakura —Mini Bike Series / *série mini motos*
*Yamaha Beluga 50	1:25	MM	Sakura —Mini Bike Series / *série mini motos*
Zil-117—limousine	1:43	MM	**Saratov (SU)**—black / *noire*
UAZ-469 4×4	1:43	MM	Saratov
GAZ-Volga—ambulance	1:43	MM	Saratov
GAZ-13-Volga "Escort"	1:43	MM	Saratov "Follow me" airport van / *voiture «Follow me» d'aéroport*
*Harley-Davidson FLT-80 "Tour Glide"	1:15	KP	**Scale Craft (USA)** SB-1—Fujimi tool / *moules Fujimi*
*Harley-Davidson FLH-80 Classic "75th Anniversary Edition"	1:15	KP	Scale Craft SB-2—Fujimi tool / *moules Fujimi*
*Harley-Davidson FLH-80 Elektra Glide	1:15	KP	Scale Craft SB-3—Fujimi tool / *moules Fujimi*
*Harley-Davidson FLH-80 "Police Special"	1:15	KP	Scale Craft SB-4—Fujimi tool / *moules Fujimi*
*Honda GL-1100 "Interstate"	1:15	KP	Scale Craft SB-5—Fujimi tool / *moules Fujimi*
*Honda GL-1100 Gold Wing	1:15	KP	Scale Craft SB-6—Fujimi tool / *moules Fujimi*
*Honda GL-1100 Gold Wing Special	1:15	KP	Scale Craft SB-7—Fujimi tool / *moules Fujimi*
Mazda RX-7—fancy version / *hors série*	1:24	KP	Scale Craft SC 2401—Fujimi tool / *moules Fujimi*
Mazda RX-7—exotic version / *hors série*	1:24	KP	Scale Craft SC 2402—Fujimi tool / *moules Fujimi*
Datsun 280ZX—fancy version / *hors série*	1:24	KP	Scale Craft SC 2403—Fujimi tool / *moules Fujimi*
Datsun 200-SX—fancy version / *hors série*	1:24	KP	Scale Craft SC 2405—Fujimi tool / *moules Fujimi*
Datsun 280ZX—exotic version / *hors série*	1:24	KP	Scale Craft SC 2406—Fujimi tool / *moules Fujimi*
Datsun 200-SX—exotic version / *hors série*	1:24	KP	Scale Craft SC 2408—Fujimi tool / *moules Fujimi*
Pontiac Firebird Trans Am (1981)	1:24	KP	Scale Craft SC 2409—Fujimi tool / *moules Fujimi*
Pontiac Firebird Trans Am Blackbird (1981)	1:24	KP	Scale Craft SC 2410—Fujimi tool / *moules Fujimi*
Pontiac Firebird "Super Trans Am"—dragster	1:24	KP	Scale Craft SC 2411—Fujimi tool / *moules Fujimi*
Chevrolet Camaro Z-28 (1981)—"Underground Camaro" / *hors série*	1:24	KP	Scale Craft SC 2412—Fujimi tool / *moules Fujimi*
Dome-O	1:24	KP	Scale Craft SC 2413—Fujimi tool / *moules Fujimi*
Porsche 935-78—twin turbo Group 5 racer / *double turbo Groupe 5*	1:24	KP	Scale Craft SC 2414—Fujimi tool / *moules Fujimi*
BMW M-1 Procar	1:24	KP	Scale Craft SC 2415—Fujimi tool / *moules Fujimi*
Volkswagen 1303 SE (1976)—convertible / *cabriolet*	1:24	KP	Scale Craft SC 2416—Imai tool / *moules Imai*
Volkswagen 1303 S (1976)—sedan / *berline*	1:24	KP	Scale Craft SC 2417—Imai tool / *moules Imai*
Volkswagen Scirocco STI—sedan / *berline*	1:24	KP	Scale Craft SC 2418—Imai tool / *moules Imai*
Chevrolet Camaro Z-28 Turbo (1981)—custom / *hors série*	1:24	KP	Scale Craft SC 2419—Fujimi tool / *moules Fujimi*
De Tomaso Pantera	1:24	KP	Scale Craft SC 2520—Imai tool / *moules Imai*
Lotus JPS (1977)—Peterson	1:43	KW	**Scale Racing Cars (GB)**—
Audi 200 5T	1:40	MZ	**Siku (D)** 1041
Mercedes 500 SE	1:40	MZ	Siku 1042
Mercedes 280 GE	1:40	MZ	Siku 1044
Opel Kadett SR	1:40	MZ	Siku 1047
Ford Escort GL	1:40	MZ	Siku 1048
VW—fire van / *camionnette pompiers*	1:40	MZ	Siku 1343
MAN—canvas top / *bâché*	1:40	MZ	Siku 1625
Range Rover—with surf board / *avec planche surf*	1:40	MZ	Siku 1626
MAN—"Siku Express" canvas top / *bâché «Siku Express»*	1:40	MZ	Siku 1919
Volvo—"Turbo Express" semitrailer / *semi-remorque «Turbo Express»*	1:40	MZ	Siku 3116
Mack—"Siku Transport Service" truck / *camion tous transports «Siku Transport Service»*	1:40	MZ	Siku 3117
Volvo—tanker trailer / *semi-remorque citerne*	1:40	MZ	Siku 3416
MAN—bus / *autobus*	1:40	MZ	Siku 3417
MAN—low-loader trailer with wheeled shovel / *remorque surbaissée avec pelle mécanique*	1:40	MZ	Siku 3716
Mack—wrecker with MAN truck / *dépanneuse avec camion MAN*	1:40	MZ	Siku 3717
Ferrari 250 GT Lusso Bertone (1961)	1:43	MR	**SMART (I)** 1
Renault 5 Turbo (1981)—Tour de Corse "Gitanes"	1:43	MZ	**Solido (F)** 1023
Mercedes SSKL (1931)—Mille Miglia	1:43	MZ	Solido 4004—new Age d'or series / *nouvelle série Age d'or*
AEC (1939)—London Double Decker bus "Green Line" / *bus londonien à impériale «Green Line»*	1:50	MZ	Solido 4443—based on red AEC London bus 4402 / *sur base bus AEC Londres rouge 4402*
Citroën C4—"Palace Hotel" taxi	1:43	MZ	Solido 4405—new Age d'or series / *nouvelle série Age d'or*

Citroën C4 (1930)—fire engine / *pompiers*	1:43	MZ	Solido 4403—new Age d'or series / *nouvelle série Age d'or*
Peugeot 505	1:43	MZ	Solido —formerly Cougar series / *série anciennement Cougar*
Renault—Lyon bus / *bus lyonnais*	1:54	MZ	Solido —repainted Paris bus TN6H / *bus parisien TN6H repeint*
Ford—5cwt van "A Design For A Butcher" / *fourgonnette «A Design For A Butcher»*	1:43	KW	**Somerville (GB)** 114 also MW / *aussi MW*
Ford—5cwt van "Colchester Tractors" / *fourgonnette «Colchester Tractors»*	1:43	KW	Somerville 115 also MW / *aussi MW*
Ford Anglia Tourer (1949)	1:43	KW	Somerville—also MW / *aussi MW*
Buick (1952)—Fire Chief / *chef pompiers*	1:43	MW	**STL (F)** —based on Dinky Toys France model / *base modèle Dinky Toys France*
Nissan Fairlady 280 ZX	1:80	MP	**Takara (J)** ML01—Silhouette, with Magic Motor / *motorisée*
Mazda Savanna RX-7	1:80	MP	Takara ML02—Silhouette, with Magic Motor / *motorisée*
Toyota Soarer 2800 GT	1:80	MP	Takara ML03—Silhouette, with Magic Motor / *motorisée*
Toyota Celica XX 2800 GT	1:80	MP	Takara ML04—Silhouette, with Magic Motor / *motorisée*
Nissan Bluebird SSS-S	1:24	KP	**Tamiya (J)** SS-2417 with / *avec* *Yamaha Towny
Nissan Leopard	1:24	KP	Tamiya SS-2418 with / *avec* scooter Honda Tact
Toyota Soarer Turbo 2000 VR	1:24	KP	Tamiya SS-2419 with / *avec* scooter Yamaha Beluga
Nissan Leopard TR-X Turbo	1:24	KP	Tamiya SS-2420 with / *avec* scooter Honda Tact
Toyota Celica XX 2800 GT	1:24	KP	Tamiya SS-2421 with / *avec* scooter Yamaha Beluga
Nissan Skyline 2000 Turbo GT-E.S	1:24	KP	Tamiya SS-2422 with / *avec* *Yamaha Towny
Nissan Skyline 2000 RS	1:24	KP	Tamiya SS-2423 with / *avec* scooter Suzuki Gemma
Renault 5 Turbo	1:24	KP	Tamiya SS-2424
Nissan Skyline Hardtop	1:24	KP	Tamiya SS-2425 with / *avec* scooter Honda Tact
Honda City	1:24	KP	Tamiya SS-2426 with / *avec* Honda Motocompo
Ford Mutt M151A2	1:35	KP	Tamiya MM-223
*Honda CB 750 F	1:6	KP	Tamiya BS-0620
*Kawasaki KZ 1300 B Touring	1:6	KP	Tamiya BS-0621
*Yamaha YZR 500	1:12	KP	Tamiya 1401
*Yamaha RZ 250	1:12	KP	Tamiya 1402
*Suzuki RGB 500	1:12	KP	Tamiya 1403
*Yamaha RZ 350	1:12	KP	Tamiya 1404
*Yamaha Beluga 80	1:12	KP	Tamiya 1405
*Honda CB 750 F	1:12	KP	Tamiya 1406
*Honda CB 900 F2 Bol d'Or	1:12	KP	Tamiya 1407
*Honda CB 1100 R	1:12	KP	Tamiya 1408
*Suzuki RGB 500 "Team Gallina"	1:12	KP	Tamiya 1409
*Honda Tact, Yamaha Beluga, Suzuki Gemma, Vespa 50 S	1:24	KP	Tamiya 1801
Citroën Rosalie (1931-1932)	1:43	MR	**Techni-France (F)** —
Citroën Rosalie iV (1933)	1:43	MR	Techni-France —
Renault 40 CV (1925)—record car / *record*	1:43	MR	Techni-France —
Talbot-Ligier JS 17	1:43	KW	**Tenariv (F)** —Laffite's number 26 / *voiture 26 de Laffite*
Jaguar XKE—3.8 l. / *3,8 l*	1:43	KW	Tenariv —convertible or coupé / *cabriolet ou coupé*
Peterbilt 359—conventional / *cabine normale*	1:20	SP	**Testor (USA)** 926
Chevrolet 4×4 pickup—"Firefighter" / *pompiers, incendie de forêt*	1:20	SP	Testor 927
Chevrolet Blazer (1980)—"Medivac" / *premier secours*	1:20	SP	Testor 928
Chevrolet 4×4 (1980)—US Coast Guard	1:20	SP	Testor 929
Porsche 944	1:43	KW	**Tin Wizard (D)** 104
Porsche 924 GTR "Boss"—Le Mans 1981	1:43	KW	Tin Wizard 205
Porsche 944 GTR "Boss"—Le Mans 1981	1:43	KW	Tin Wizard 206
Bugatti 49 (1930)—Gangloff convertible / *cabriolet Gangloff*	1:43	KW	Tin Wizard 302
Bugatti T 50—convertible / *cabriolet*	1:43	KW	Tin Wizard 303
Bugatti T 44—coupé Fiacre / *coupé Fiacre*	1:43	KW	Tin Wizard 304
Honda Accord—with surf boards / *avec planches surf*	1:45	MM	**Tomy (J)** DL-1—Tomica Dandy "Dandy Leisure Series" DL
Honda Accord—with pocket bikes / *avec mini motos*	1:45	MM	Tomy DL-2—Tomica Dandy "Dandy Leisure Series" DL
Nissan Skyline Turbo—with skis / *avec skis*	1:43	MM	Tomy DL-3—Tomica Dandy "Dandy Leisure Series" DL
Nissan Skyline Turbo—with surfboards / *avec planches surf*	1:43	MM	Tomy DL-4—Tomica Dandy "Dandy Leisure Series" DL
Mazda Savanna RX-7—with pocket bikes / *avec mini motos*	1:43	MM	Tomy DL-5—Tomica Dandy "Dandy Leisure Series" DL
Toyota Celica LB—with skis / *avec skis*	1:43	MM	Tomy DL-6—Tomica Dandy "Dandy Leisure Series" DL
Nissan Cedric—with surfboards / *avec planches surf*	1:43	MM	Tomy DL-7—Tomica Dandy "Dandy Leisure Series" DL
VW 1200—type RR, with surfboards / *type RR, avec planches surf*	1:43	MM	Tomy DF-28—Tomica Dandy
Rolls-Royce Phantom IV	1:43	MM	Tomy DF-6—Tomica Dandy, new color / *nouveau coloris*
Toyota Soarer 2800 GT	1:65	MM	Tomy 5—Tomica
London bus / *bus londonien*	1:43	MM	Tomy DF-19—Tomica Dandy, new decal "Welcome to London" / *nouveau décalque «Welcome to London»*
Toyota Land Cruiser 4×4	1:43	MM	Tomy D-13—Tomica Dandy
Nissan Caravan—high roof / *toit surélevé*	1:43	MM	Tomy D-23—Tomica Dandy
Toyota Hilux 4×4	1:62	MM	Tomy 61—Tomica
Komatsu—power shovel / *chargeur sur pneus*	1:122	MM	Tomy 9—Tomica
Hino—bus	1:116	MM	Tomy 41—Tomica

Nissan Diesel—tank lorry / *camion-citerne*	1:100	MM	Tomy 57—Tomica
Nissan Diesel—concrete mixer truck / *porte-malaxeur*	1:100	MM	Tomy 53—Tomica
Nissan Caball—panel truck / *fourgon*	1:68	MM	Tomy 67—Tomica
Citroën H—van / *fourgonnette*	1:43	MM	Tomy DF-14—Tomica, "Candy" decal / *décoration «Candy»*
Nissan Caravan—high-roof ambulance / *ambulance toit surélevé*	1:43	MM	Tomy D-12—Tomica Dandy
Nissan Caravan—high-roof police van / *fourgon police toit surélevé*	1:43	MM	Tomy D-1—Tomica Dandy
London bus / *bus londonien*	1:43	MM	Tomy DF-19—Tomica Dandy, new decal "Chessington Zoo" / *nouvelle décoration «Chessington Zoo»*
Mitsubishi Canter—refuse truck / *benne à ordures.*	1:43	MM	Tomy D-20—Tomica Dandy
Nissan Caravan—high roof, with pocket bikes / *toit surélevé, avec mini motos*	1:43	MM	Tomy L12—Tomica Dandy Leisure series
Nissan Caravan—high roof, with kart / *toit surélevé, avec kart.*	1:43	MM	Tomy L13—Tomica Dandy Leisure series
Toyota Land Cruiser 4×4—with snowmobile / *avec snowmobile*	1:43	MM	Tomy L14—Tomica Dandy Leisure series
Mitsubishi Jeep—with snowmobile on trailer / *avec snowmobile sur remorque*	1:43	MM	Tomy L15—Tomica Dandy Leisure series
Mitsubishi—kindergarten bus / *bus école*	1:84	MM	Tomy 60—Tomica
Mitsubishi Canter—street-sweeper / *balayeuse*	1:72	MM	Tomy 77—Tomica
Ford—cattle truck / *bétaillère.*	1:98	MM	Tomy F27—Tomica
*Suzuki Gemma 50	1:28	MM	Tomy 49—Tomica
"American West Coast"—gift set / *boîte-cadeau côte ouest Etats-Unis.*		MM	Tomy —with F42, F45, F64, F68 / *avec modèles Tomica F42, F45, F64 et F68*
"World Double Decker Bus Fair"—gift set / *boîte-cadeau autobus à impériale.*		MM	Tomy —with 15 models / *avec 15 modèles:* Tomica F15×6, F37×4, Long Tomica L8×2, L18×2, Dandy DF-19
"Zoo"—gift set / *boîte-cadeau jardin zoologique*		MM	Tomy —with 4 Tomicas / *avec 4 Tomica:* 39, 62, F15, F64
"Gasolin Station"—gift set / *boîte-cadeau station-service*		MM	Tomy —with 5 Tomicas / *avec 5 Tomica:* 2, 28, 67, 57, F43
"Land-Sea-Air"—gift set / *boîte-cadeau terre/mer/air*		MM	Tomy —with 8 Tomicas / *avec 8 Tomica:* 13, 19, 67, 84, 93, 98, F54, F68
"World Police Car"—gift set / *boîte-cadeau police*		MM	Tomy —with 8 Tomicas / *avec 8 Tomica:* 50, 58, F8, F9, F16, F44, F51, F70
"Vacation Set"—gift set / *boîte-cadeau vacances*		MM	Tomy —with 8 Tomicas / *avec 8 Tomica:* 2, 3, 4, 25, 34, 61, 78, F29
"Working Vehicles Set"—gift set / *boîte-cadeau travaux publics*		MM	Tomy —with 6 Tomicas / *avec 6 Tomica:* 3, 12, 14, 47, 57, 97, and / *et* Long Tomica L5
Renault 5 Turbo—Monte Carlo Rally / *Rallye Monte Carlo*	1:58	MM	Tomy F36—Tomica
Toyota Celica XX 2800 GT	1:62	MM	Tomy 33—Tomica
Toyota Celica XX 2800 GT	1:43	MM	Tomy D-4—Tomica Dandy
"Emergency Vehicles"—gift set / *boîte-cadeau véhicules d'urgences*		MM	Tomy —with 4 Tomicas / *avec 4 Tomica:* 29, 34, 36, 58
"Commercial Car Set"—gift set / *boîte-cadeau véhicules utilitaires et loisirs*		MM	Tomy —with 4 Tomicas / *avec 4 Tomica:* 3, 34, 38, 76
"Street Racer Set"—gift set / *boîte-cadeau voitures de sport*		MM	Tomy —with 4 Tomicas / *avec 4 Tomica:* 50, 58, 74, 86
Mitsubishi Canter—dump truck / *dumper*	1:43	MM	Tomy D-19—Tomica Dandy
London bus, open type / *bus londonien à impériale*	1:70	MM	Tomy L-17—Tomica Dandy "London Sightseeing Tour"
Isuzu High-Decker bus / *autobus à impériale*	1:60	MM	Tomy D-24A—Tomica Dandy "Hato Bus"
Isuzu High-Decker bus / *autobus à impériale*	1:60	MM	Tomy D-24B—Tomica Dandy "Toto Kanko"
Isuzu V12—truck with house trailer / *camion avec mobilhome*	1:100	MM	Tomy L-15—Long Tomica
Isuzu V12—truck with wing roof trailer / *camion avec caravane*	1:100	MM	Tomy L-16—Long Tomica
Porsche 939—"Kremer"	1:43	MZ	**Top 43 (F)** —former Solido 2 / *ex Solido 2*
BMW M1—"BASF"	1:43	KM	Top 43 —Solido-based kit / *transkit base Solido*
Renault 5 Turbo (1981)—Monte Carlo Rally / *Rallye Monte Carlo*	1:43	KM	Top 43 —Solido-based kit / *transkit base Solido*
Porsche 934	1:43	KM	Top 43 —Solido-based kit, Wittington team Daytona / *transkit base Solido, écurie Wittington Daytona*
Renault 20 "Paris-Dakar"	1:43	KM	Top 43 —transkit
Ferrari 512 BB NART Daytona 1979	1:43	KM	**Tron—AMR (I)** AT 07
Neoplan—bus	1:100	MM	**Tsukuda (J)**—made by Tomy, "Asakusa Ueno" decal / *fabriqué par Tomy, décoration «Asakusa Ueno»*
*Yamaha RZ 250	1:12	KM	Tsukuda 1—new "Metal collection motorcycles series / *nouvelle série motos en métal*
* Harley-Davidson FXS-80 "Lowrider" / *siège surbaissé*	1:15	KP	**Union (J)** MS-02 '79, '80 or '81 model / *modèle 79, 80, ou 81*
* Harley-Davidson FXB-80—"Sturgis"	1:15	KP	Union MS-03
* Honda CB 750 F Bol d'Or.	1:15	KP	Union MS-04 or CB 900 F2 / *ou CB 900 F2*
* Honda CBX—new model / *nouveau modèle*	1:15	KP	Union MS-05
* Kawasaki Z 400 FX Turbo	1:15	KP	Union 6
* Honda CB 1100 R	1:15	KP	Union MS-06
Fiat Fiorino	1:87	MP	**Walldorf-Praliné (D)** 87-140900
Fiat Fiorino	1:87	MP	Walldorf-Praliné 87-165009 "Alitalia", "Fiat Fiorino", "Gasthof Rangau"
Fiat 242—delivery van / *fourgon livraison*	1:87	MP	Walldorf-Praliné 87-141100
Fiat 242—delivery van / *fourgon livraison*	1:87	MP	Walldorf-Praliné 87-165011 "ABC-Florist Neuhann", "Ristorante Pizzeria Mario", "Deutsche Fiat"
Ferrari 312 T4	1:43	KW	**Western Models (GB)** also MW / *aussi MW*
SS1 (1934)—saloon	1:43	KW	Western Models 35 also MW / *aussi MW*
Rolls-Royce Phantom II (1927)—coupé	1:43	KW	Western Models 36 also MW / *aussi MW*
Alfa Romeo 8C 2900 B Spyder (1938)	1:43	KW	Western Models 33 also MW / *aussi MW*
Lotus Essex Esprit Turbo (1980)	1:43	KW	Western Models WP 104X also MW / *aussi MW*
Aston Martin DB3S (1955)	1:43	KW	Western Models 29 also MW / *aussi MW*
Mercedes-Benz W125—racing car / *voiture de course*	1:24	KW	Western Models—also MW / *aussi MW*
McLaren MP4 Marlboro (1981)	1:43	KW	Western Models WRK 30 also MW / *aussi MW*
Rolls-Royce Silver Spirit (1981)	1:43	KW	Western Models WP 105 aussi MW / *aussi MW*
Bentley Mulsanne (1981)	1:43	KW	Western Models WP 106 also MW / *aussi MW*

MG EX135 (1948)—Gardner's record car / *voiture de record de Gardner*	1:43	KW	Western Models WNS 38 also MW / *aussi MW*
Chrysler Imperial (1933)	1:43	KW	Western Models WMS 37 also MW / *aussi MW*
VW Jetta	1:90	MP	**Wiking (D)** 50
Mercedes-Benz 500 SE	1:90	MP	Wiking 157
Ford Taunus (1952)	1:90	MP	Wiking 200
Opel Caravan (1956)	1:90	MP	Wiking 77
Bedford Blitz—van / *camionnette combi*	1:90	MP	Wiking 355
Bedford Blitz—van / *fourgon*	1:90	MP	Wiking 356
VW LT 28—delivery van / *fourgonnette*	1:90	MP	Wiking 300
Mercedes-Benz 1017—delivery truck / *camion de livraison*	1:90	MP	Wiking 436
Mercedes-Benz—delivery truck / *camion de livraison*	1:90	MP	Wiking 435
MAN—canvas top with trailer / *bâché avec remorque*	1:90	MP	Wiking 424
Büssing 4500 V	1:90	MP	Wiking 476
Ford Transcontinental—"Meisterpreis" semitrailer / *semi-remorque «Meisterpreis»*	1:90	MP	Wiking 540
Scania LD 111—"Ipec" semitrailer / *semi-remorque «Ipec»*	1:90	MP	Wiking 546
Mercedes-Benz 1626—"Rama" semitrailer / *semi-remorque «Rama»*	1:90	MP	Wiking 542
MAN—semitrailer canvas top "MAN" / *semi-remorque bâché «MAN»*	1:90	MP	Wiking 535
Container "Fleisch-Export-Danish"	1:90	MP	Wiking 577
Mercedes-Benz—"Hoechst" tanker trailer / *semi-remorque citerne «Hoechst»*	1:90	MP	Wiking 825
Magirus KW 16—fire fighting truck crane / *camion grue pompiers*	1:90	MP	Wiking 630
Melz DLK 23-12—fire fighting ladder / *camion échelle pompiers*	1:90	MP	Wiking 618
VRW—fire engine / *véhicule pompiers*	1:90	MP	Wiking 609
Büssing D 38 (1939)—Berlin double-decker / *bus berlinois à 2 étages*	1:90	MP	Wiking 3730
Mercedes 600, Opel Admiral, BMW 501, Rolls-Royce	1:160	MP	Wiking 9014 set / *ensemble*
Tanker truck / *camion-citerne*	1:160	MP	Wiking 9085
MG TC	1:24	KW	**Wills Finecast (GB)**—
Porsche 911 (1969)	1:43	MW	**X (F)** —also KW, first GT Le Mans '69 / *aussi KW, première GT Le Mans 69*
Porsche 911 (1971)	1:43	MW	X —also KW, first GTS Le Mans '71 / *aussi KW, première GTS Le Mans 71*
Porsche 911 (1972)	1:43	MW	X —also KW, European Championship, Fitzpatrick / *aussi KW, Champ. Europe, Fitzpatrick*
Porsche 911 (1972)	1:43	MW	X —also KW, Le Mans '72 / *aussi KW, Le Mans 72*
Maserati 151	1:43	KW	X —Cunningham team Le Mans '62 / *écurie Cunningham Le Mans 62*
Cadillac (1950)—coupé	1:43	KW	X —'78 model reissue, road version or Cunningham Le Mans '50 / *réédition modèle 78, version routière ou Cunningham Le Mans 50*
Ferrari 512 BB "European University"	1:43	KW	X —Le Mans '81 / *Le Mans 81*
Peugeot 203—coupé	1:43	KR	**XVM (F)** —based on convertible issued in '81 / *sur base cabriolet paru en 81*
Lancia Beta Montecarlo Turbo (1980)	1:43	MM	**Yaxon (I)** 0804 red / *rouge*
Lancia Beta Montecarlo Turbo (1980)	1:43	MM	Yaxon 0805 blue / *bleue*
Ferrari BB "Pozzi-ISO" (1980)—Le Mans	1:43	MM	Yaxon 0806
Ferrari BB "Pozzi-Jolly Club" (1980)	1:43	MM	Yaxon 0807 white / *blanche*
* Honda CBX—road racing type / *compétiton route*	1:8		**Yodel (J)** BK 1004-2800
* Vespa P200E	1:24		Yodel CB 1001-300
* Honda TACT	1:24		Yodel —
* Yamaha Beluga 80 E	1:24		Yodel —
* Suzuki Gemma CS 50 GD	1:24		Yodel —
Nissan Fairlady 280 Z—T-bar roof / *toit T-bar*	1:40	MM	**Yonezawa (J)** G-3—Diapet
Toyota Soarer 2800 GT	1:40	MM	Yonezawa G-1—Diapet
Nissan Leopard 280 X	1:40	MM	Yonezawa G-2—Diapet
Toyota Hilux 4×4—truck / *fourgonnette*	1:40	MM	Yonezawa T-3—Diapet
Isuzu—tanker lorry / *camion-citerne*	1:55	MM	Yonezawa T-12—Diapet
Isuzu—ladder fire engine / *grande échelle pompiers*	1:55	MM	Yonezawa T-20—Diapet
Isuzu—auto carrier semi-trailer / *semi-remorque transport d'autos*	1:55	MM	Yonezawa T-21—Diapet, with 4 cars / *avec 4 autos*
Isuzu—mail van / *fourgon postal*	1:55	MM	Yonezawa T-17—Diapet, decal "Japanese Post" / *décalque «Japanese Post»*
Mitsubishi—power crane / *grue automotrice*	1:60	MM	Yonezawa K-39—Diapet
Nissan Cherry Vanette—mini van / *mini fourgon*	1:35	MM	Yonezawa T-4—Diapet, around 1:40 / *1:40 environ*
Toyota Hi-Ace—camping car / *camper*	1:35	MM	Yonezawa T-6—Diapet
Hitachi Oil Pressure—shovel / *chargeur sur pneus*	1:60	MM	Yonezawa K-56—Diapet
Isuzu—refuse truck / *benne à ordures*	1:55	MM	Yonezawa T-9—Diapet
Japanese Type 74 AC armoured car / *voiture blindée*	1:75	MM	Yonezawa M-3—Diapet, new military M series / *nouvelle série militaire M*
Army Jeep / *jeep armée japonaise*	1:75	MM	Yonezawa M-4—Diapet, with 105 mm field gun / *avec canon 105 mm*
*Honda Tact	1:14	MM	Yonezawa A-2—Diapet, new "Autoby" series A / *nouvelle série «Autoby» A*
"Turbo Series"—gift set / *boîte-cadeau*	1:40	MM	Yonezawa S-6—Diapet, with / *avec* Toyota Soarer Turbo, Nissan Leopard Turbo, Mitsubishi Galant A Turbo, Nissan Bluebird Turbo
Isuzu—crane truck / *camion-grue*	1:55	MM	Yonezawa K-52—Diapet
Isuzu Piazza	1:40	MM	Yonezawa G-4—Diapet
Toyota Celica XX 2800 GT	1:40	MM	Yonezawa G-5—Diapet
Nissan Skyline HT 2000 GT Turbo	1:40	MM	Yonezawa G-6—Diapet
Mitsubishi Mirage Turbo	1:25	MM	Yonezawa G-11—Diapet
Mitsubishi Cordia Turbo	1:28	MM	Yonezawa G-12—Diapet
Military truck 73 type / *camion militaire type 73*	1:75	MM	Yonezawa M-6—Diapet
Neoplan double decker bus / *bus à impériale*	1:60	MM	Yonezawa B-41—Diapet
Toyota Crown—airport taxi / *taxi aéroport*	1:40	MM	Yonezawa P-1—Diapet
Komatsu dump truck HD 1200-M / *dumper*	1:50	MM	Yonezawa T-5—Diapet
Nissan Cherry Vanette / *fourgonette*	1:35	MM	Yonezawa T-8—Diapet
Hitachi oil pressure shovel / *pelleteuse hydraulique*	1:50	MM	Yonezawa K-56—Diapet
*Kawasaki Z 1300	1:23	MM	Yonezawa A-1—Diapet
*Honda Stream Scooter	1:15	MM	Yonezawa A-3—Diapet
Raba 6×4 Artic.—truck with container / *camion avec container*	1:86	MP	unknown **(H)** / *fabricant inconnu*
AMO-F-15 (1928)—truck / *camion*	1:25	KP	unknown **(SU)** / *fabricant inconnu*

MUSEUM MODELS

The Fiat Centro Storico Collection

For the model car enthusiast, the most interesting exhibit in Fiat's 'Centro Storico' is a boat; a reproduction of the *Italterra*, one of the prefabricated Liberty Ships which did so much to supply Britain during the war and which was later fitted with an A 686 Diesel engine, developing 3600 hp, in the course of its transformation into a car carrier in Fiat's own shipyard. In this form it was used to export Fiats to the U.S.
The hull of the model is cut away to show the holds packed with miniature cars — 134 Mercury models, some of the Fiat 1100 (No.13), and some of the Fiat 600 Multipla (No.19), produced round about 1961 and now impossible to find. A real cargo of treasure! There is even a choice of colours and types. In fact Mercury produced the 1100 in at least four versions, differing in their treatment of the grille and rear lights.
The Liberty Ship is only the first item to be encountered on a visit to this most exciting museum from a modeller's point of view. The Centro Storico owns more than 300 reproductions of cars, tractors, construction machinery, busses, trains, aircraft, boats, submarines, postal coaches, marine engines, tanks, and amphibious vehicles. All the models recall the history and development of Fiat, and are shown in display cases which occupy the ground and first floors of the main hall.

A 20-year-old story

The Fiat museum was created in 1961 thanks to the involvement and passion of its founder and Director, Augusto Costantino, who has succeeded in the difficult task of arranging the relics of an enterprise which has, in the course of a 72-year existence, passed through two world wars, the second of which destroyed a large part of its installations. In addition, its leaders have at times been guilty of grave neglect of the company's historical material. For example, it was not until 1961 that a specimen of each Fiat model produced was set aside for safe-keeping — nobody had thought of doing that before. And that's not all; Senator Giovanni Agnelli, the company's third president (from 1920 to 1946) had all the Fiat racing cars destroyed when the company retired from active competition in order to concentrate on mass production in 1927.
Fortunately, the technical and commercial records were by undamaged the war and it is therefore possible to study the sales registers in the museum's vast library for every Fiat model — the very first one records Signor Giovanni Battista Ceirano of Turin as the buyer of the first 3.5 hp car with the chassis number 101. Ceirano was the firm's representative for the Turin region and paid 4000 lire, in two installments, for the first chassis. Even today, sales records are kept for posterity

but for 20 or so years they have been produced by computer rather than by pen and ink as the first one was.

The library gathers together all the technical documents (plans, descriptions, and operating manuals) concerning Fiat production; instruction books and workshop manuals, catalogues and all forms of promotional literature. More than 200 albums hold nearly 100 000 photographs. Documents concerning the purchase of land and property give some impression of the way the enterprise has grown through the years to its present size. Technical drawings alone account for half a million documents; from them it is possible to reconstruct a part for any Fiat product.

Closer to art than technology are the posters, advertisements, and catalogues which have been produced for new models. Some of these items deserve to be in a gallery, if only because of the signatures they bear: Pietro Annigoni, Giorgio di Chirico, Mario Sironi, Felice Casorati.

The library of automobile history contains more than 10 000 publications, some dating from the beginning of the century. They form a vital source of reference for research into the evolution of the automobile, aircraft, and engineering in general.

An historical centre, not a museum

The library forms the very heart of the Centro Storico. But why is this terminology used rather than the traditional 'Museum' title? First, there was no desire to duplicate the activity of the Biscaretti di Ruffia National Motor Museum, which is also in Turin, not far from the Fiat undertaking. Secondly, the aim was to create something dynamic — a living symbol of the continuing strength and vitality of the Fiat name. In fact, the history of an industrial complex such as Fiat is a history of Italy and Europe, fed and embellished by political and social change, fashion, style, taste, and technological evolution.

It was for this reason that the decision was taken to base the collection on a few full-size exhibits, all fully restored and in perfect working order, and numerous scale models and documents. At the same time the building which was to hold the collection, itself of historical interest, was to be preserved in its original form.

Via Chiabrera 20, the Centro Storico's home, was built in 1907 to the designs of the engineer Premoli and originally housed the vehicle finishing department. It was the first extension to the original buildings in the Corso Dante, to the right of the Premoli building. The company's sales offices were opposite what is now the entrance to the Centro Storico, in an 18th century-style building. The clients (of whom there were few in those days) were welcomed in the little palace with all due ceremony and then conducted across the road to take delivery of their new vehicle. Later on the Liberty-styled building of the via Chiabrera was also to house the racing department and to number among its visitors such names as Felice Nazzaro, Vincenzo Lancia, Louis Wagner, and Alessandro Cagno.

After the First War the finishing department was transferred, due to lack of space, to the Lingotto works, where it occupied a five-storey building with a test track on the roof. Via Chiabrera became the spare parts department.

In time, as the growth of Fiat continued, the spares department also outgrew the via Chiabrera premises and the building was used as a gymnastic training centre by Fiat's athletic club.

After the athletes moved out, the great main hall became a depository for unused articles until, at the end of the fifties, the move towards renovation began. A covered space was needed to store the vehicles destined for the new Automobile Museum which was to be completed in 1960. Fiat put the via Chiabrera premises at the disposal of the organisers and it was this turn of events which sowed the idea of a collection of Fiat's museumpieces and documents. The Centro Storico was inaugurated in 1961 and Augusto Costantino, whose brain-child it was, became its first director.

Scale models — a studied choice

Apart from the difficulty of collecting the documents scattered throughout the thousands of offices and factories in the Fiat Group in Turin, the rest of Italy, and the rest of the world, the collection's organisers were faced with the difficulty of deciding on a selection of items to be put on show. Practically, it was impossible to find and show the thousands of different models and types produced by Fiat — even if the choice was limited to automobiles and land-based vehicles.

Thanks to dedicated research work, about 30 vehicles were gathered, each an important landmark in the development not only of Fiat, but also of the automobile industry. There was no desire to collect long lines of cars because this would have reduced the attraction of the museum and limited the possibility of seeing the cars properly. The decision was therefore taken to display the majority of the vehicles in the form of scale models. These exhibits, when not on display elsewhere, are shown on a rota basis in the exhibition hall.

The display gives a representative view of Fiat's history, with the showcases presenting a broad view of the company's evolution in model form. The ground floor, given over to land transport, holds 14 cases; six for cars, one for trains (in addition to a number which shelter one single extra-large model), two for trams and buses, two for motor coaches, one for military vehicles, and two for tractors and construction machinery. On the first floor are to be found the boats, submarines, and aircraft, all to a scale of 1:10 and therefore in many cases too large to be contained in a closed showcase.

The choice of models, which was greater than for any other museum or collection in the world, was not easy and had to be based on cultural considerations similar to those which faced the medieval patrons of the arts who had to decide which of their achievements should be depicted by their artists and craftsmen.

Naturally, to be of value as a true historic document, a scale model should be as accurate as possible in order to provide a proper reference for historians, engineers, and model-makers. It will, in some cases — as in the case of the racing cars which no longer exist — be the only such reference.

All the models in the Fiat centre have that value, belonging not only to the history of the automobile, but also to the history of the model-makers art.

Unified style and scale

In order to give a better impression of the physical aspect of the original, the models are all of a larger scale than that to which we are accustomed. The only examples of the classic 1:43 scale are the Mercury models already mentioned as the cargo of the *Italterra*. A single 1:15 scale model of the famous Mephistopheles is not part of the official collection, but lives in the office of Augusto Costantino.

The scale chosen for the cars is 1:5, and this scale is maintained throughout the collection of 60 models. The smallest, such as the 126 and 'Topolino' measure around 60 cm (23.6 ins) in length, and the biggest, like the 2800 C in its saloon and colonial versions are over a metre (39.3 ins) long. Busses, coaches, and military vehicles are to a scale of 1:10, and the trains are to a scale of 1:15 — but even at this scale they are still of impressive proportions. These are the largest pieces in the collection, so large that they need special display cases. This is true of the 'Pendolino', the Italian State Railways' ultra-modern tilting electric train, a model measuring over two metres. Aircraft are modelled in 1:10 scale, and tractors and construction machines are 1:15.

It would be wrong to assume that the Centro Storico's models were the work of the famous 'master-modellers'. Michele

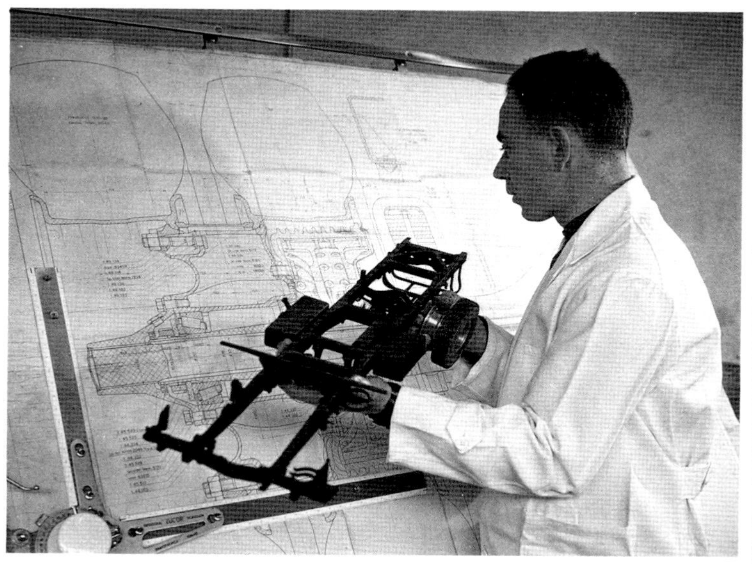

Checking a chassis frame against the original drawings. The model, like all those in the museum, is built in metal to 1:5 scale. Right: Assembly of a Fiat 1300/1500. The doors open to reveal an interior trimmed with the same materials as the real car.

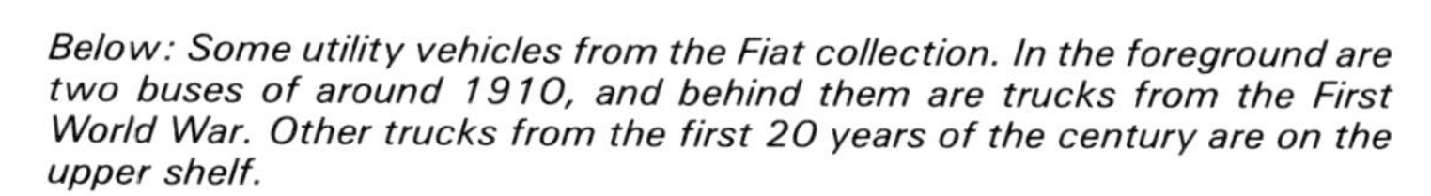

Below: Some utility vehicles from the Fiat collection. In the foreground are two buses of around 1910, and behind them are trucks from the First World War. Other trucks from the first 20 years of the century are on the upper shelf.

The precision of a watchmaker is required to create the detail in the models. On the left is the famous Fiat F-2 which won the French Grand Prix in 1907, built in 1:5 scale by Bruno Reggiani. This is the car which Pocher modelled in their first 1:8 scale kit. In the background are many of the other racing cars of the Centro Storico.
The models of the 804 and 805 built by Bruno Reggiani are the only three-dimensional representations of these cars in existence. The original cars, built in 1922 and 1923, were destroyed in 1927 on the orders of Giovanni Agnelli, president of Fiat at the time.

The 24 hp racer of 1902 was driven by Vincente Lancia and Felice Nazzaro and served as a test bed for the larger-engined cars which followed it. Like the original, the model has wooden wheels.

Conti, Carlo Brianza, or Gerald Wingrove are not represented. Only Manuel Olive-Sans has left his mark with a reproduction of the 508 CS Balilla Coppa d'Oro Spider. This model was made in 1970, and Augusto Costantino still remembers the problems he had in persuading the great Spanish modeller to work on a model of such a size (62 cm/24.4 ins long). "Generally, modellers like Conti or Olive-Sans are not equipped to work on a large scale," says Costantino, "and they are not keen to put a thousand hours' work into one model."
A thousand hours equals three months of uninterrupted work on a basis of 11 hours a day, but the real reason is more likely to be the fear of the dilution of the 'artistic feeling', the creativity, in the face of working in such dimensions. The problem does not lie in the tools and techniques, as the modellers who have worked for Fiat have shown. They are names which are unknown even to the innermost circles of modelling enthusiasts but who have nevertheless undertaken to compete with the 'masters'. Let us take a look at them.

Bruno Reggiani — continuity

Fifty-nine-year-old, Turin-born Bruno Reggiani started professional model-making in 1950 as a builder of architectural models. He started to work with the Centro Storico right at the beginning, in 1961, and has built most of the models on show. He is responsible for all the aircraft, the post-war motor-coaches, and some military vehicles; he has also built a number of cars to a scale of 1:15.
He worked alone, in the workshop behind his model-shop in one of the popular quarters of Turin. Nowadays, his main work for the Centro Storico at an end, he gives his time to the modelling of nuclear installations or test equipment, still for the Fiat Holdings group. He has an annual contract with the Centro Storico for the cleaning and maintenance of the models on show. Obviously, the models are too delicate to be dusted and cleaned by any old cleaning lady. It needs the practised hand of an expert who understands their construction.
The models are in constant need of maintenance. They are sent for display at shows, exhibitions and Fiat premises all over the world, and it is inevitable that they will suffer some damage during transport. In addition, there are always paint scratches, flat tyres, or loose springs. In such cases, Reggiani makes good the damage immediately, and is responsible for the fact that all the models in the centre are in perfect condition.
Bruno Reggiani has built reproductions solely for Fiat, and has devoted between 800 and 1000 hours to each one. The result is that for the past decade or so, he has gone completely without leisure time. The majority of the models are of sheet brass, one millimetre thick, formed on a wooden former, brazed, filled, and then painted. The chassis and suspension are also brass, giving a model which is strong but heavy (up to about 20 kilos — 44 lbs). Fiat specifically asked for the models to be made in metal, so that they would be long-lasting, but the request has put some limitation on the builders from a modelling point of view. Tyres, for instance, cannot be made from real rubber because of its tendency to flatten under weight and to perish under the heat of the lighting. The first models to be made did in fact have real rubber tyres, and it is one of Reggiani's jobs to remove them when they lose their appearance and replace them with new ones from turned Plexiglass which is harder and more durable.
According to Reggiani, weight does not necessarily mean strength; even a heavy model can show fragility if it is removed from its showcase too often. It was this fact that enabled Reggiani to persuade the centre to accept two models — the 127 saloon and 1500 Spider — in Plexiglass, which is both lighter and stronger. The models were constructed using a wooden former, as for brass, over which thin sheets of heated Plexiglass, some three or four millimetres thick, were laid. The resulting parts were then glued together, filled, polished, and painted in the normal manner. Standard Fiat paint is used, with three or four coats polished and smoothed by hand.
Reggiani was responsible for eight of the 10 competition cars, the models of which serve as the only three-dimensional reference following the destruction of the originals. For example, Tarquinio Provini worked from Reggiani's model when producing the current 1:12 scale Protar kit of the 1927 type 806, Fiat's last racing car before their retirement from the sport.
"There is no need," Reggiani says, "for a massive toolkit. I work with a small set of modeller's implements, a small fret-saw, some files, and all the other little instruments that a modeller needs. As for the 'masters' and their predeliction for smaller scales, I don't think it is a question of equipment or tools. Maybe it's because when you work in 1:10 or 1:15 there are fewer details to reproduce. They come up against fewer snags, work more quickly, and can turn out more models for their numerous clients."

Sergio Abrami — enthusiast

"You might say I was weaned on petrol, because I loved cars right from the beginning." That's how 65-year-old Sergio Abrami, Trieste-born and the builder of 16 of the Centro Storico's models, introduced himself. Tractors and construction machinery are his speciality, and he has a special regard for them. From the modeller's point of view, they are particularly challenging because of the amount of mechanical detail which is exposed. Abrami takes up the challenge enthusiastically, and his bulldozers are marvels of realism and detailling.
In 1981 he delivered a 1:15 scale reproduction of the FL 20 bulldozer which, apart from the lack of an engine, was completely operational and had no fewer than 1382 parts in the tracks alone.
Abrami also works in brass shaped over a wooden former. Because of the number and variety of the parts in the models he makes, he often has to use the services of specialists in turning and milling. This means that he needs up to seven months to finish a model and the cost is high — for the FL 20, he spent more than 600 pounds on sub-contracted work and parts.
Abrami used to work for the savings bank in Trieste, and in the 10 years since his retirement, modelling has become his life. He works solely for Fiat, an association which began in 1962. That year he had exhibited a 1:15 scale model of a Lamborghini tractor at a model engineering show and the work was so good (the model is now in the Milan Museum of Science and Technology) that afterwards he received a letter from Fiat enclosing plans of the FL 4 tractor and a request to model it for the Centro Storico.
This was the start if a collaboration that still continues, and which is not only limited to tractors; Abrami made the 1:10 model of a modern Turin bus and two cars, the 1100 Coloniale and the X 1/9, delivered in 1980 and 1975 respectively.
The decision to build the X 1/9 was a capricious one; Abrami had already made some car models, 1:15 scale Benzes and Renaults from the turn of the century, which he had given as presents to friends and relations to mark special occasions such as marriages, but he was not really enthusiastic about them because the bodywork covered the mechanical details which he loved.
He liked the looks of the X 1/9 as soon as he saw it however, and decided he would like to model it in brass and other metals just for the fun of it. Having taken the decision, he suggested to the Centro Storico that they might like to take the model if it turned out right. Needless to say it did and now forms part of the collection.
The Fiat 1100 Coloniale is also of brass construction. This car, with its square lines and large areas of glass, needed extra work to fill and polish the metal perfectly.

The obvious choice for the first model of the Centro Storico: the first Fiat, the 3.5 hp of 1899. Original drawings like this were all the modellers had to work from for many of the models in the collection. Fortunately, however, for those involved in the 3.5 hp scale version, three cars out of the 20 or so made are still in existence (one is at the Museo dell'Automobile, one at the Ford Museum, and one in the Centro Storico itself).

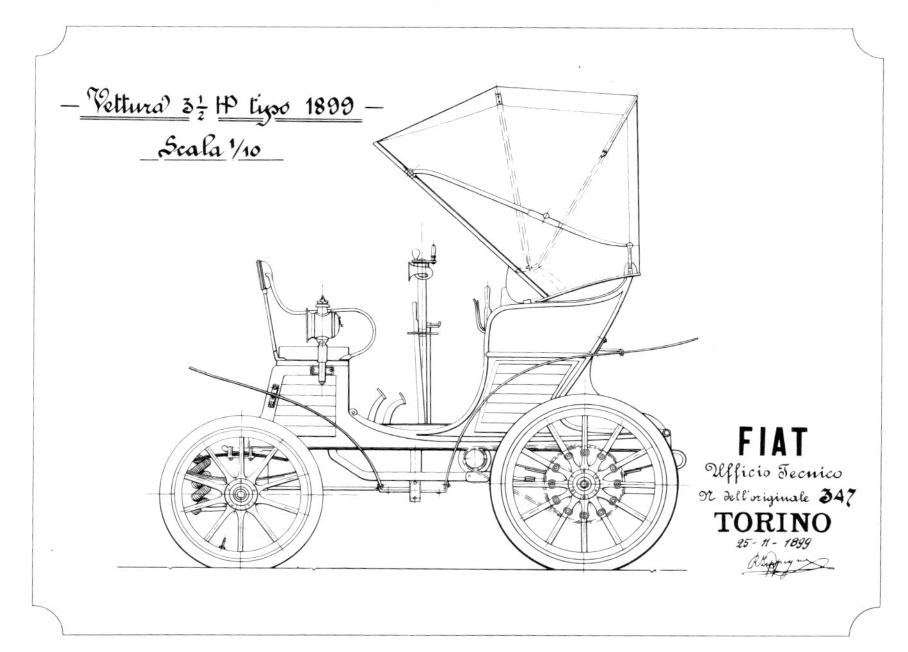

In view of their size, the tyres and wheels also caused Abrami to call upon the help of considerate friends who owned 'professional' lathes. He himself has only hand tools and a small Unomat lathe — "Which I never stop recommending to other modellers," he says with conviction. "I'm a perfectionist," he told me, "and I find pleasure and satisfaction in working in large scale because it gives scope for adding all the details. I feel it is my duty to reproduce all the parts and finicky detail even if they are invisible in the finished model. By the same token, I make no differentiation between the 1:5 scale models and the smaller ones — in my tractors, there are parts so tiny that you can only see them with a magnifiying glass."

Piero Ferré — the professional

In 1976, with the experience and knowledge of 40 years in the business of model-making, Piero Ferré took over control of the small firm which had been started by his father, Mario. Today he no longer works for the Centro Storico, but carries out commissions for other members of the Fiat group, notably Aeritalia, for whom he builds series of 1:100 scale aircraft in silver plate.

Between 1961 and 1966 the Ferré firm built, in its premises at Cinisello, near Milan, models of Fiat cars produced between 1955 (the introduction of the 600) and 1959 (the big 1800/2300 models). The construction material was brass, silver-soldered in the case of the heavier parts such as suspensions and axles, and with tin-soldered bodywork. As with all the Centro Storico models, the doors can be opened to display the interior detail, and realism is followed to such an extent that the same materials as in the full-size car are used wherever possible. Seats are in Vinyl, cloth or leather in the original colours and patterns, even though it was difficult to find hides tanned in the old method for some of the older vehicles.

The house of Ferré has made car models only for Fiat — not by choice, but because no other manufacturer has approached them with a similar commission. All the models are unique apart from the Type Zero, of which three were made. One is in the Turin Automobile Museum, one is in a private collection in Paris, and the third holds pride of place in the Centro Storico's first showcase.

Mario Ferré makes use of professional machine tools, but he is the only one of the centre's suppliers who has a professional rather than an artisanal organisation. In spite of this, it still needed almost 1500 hours work to complete the reproduction of the 1800.

Morselli and Acerbi — the past

The Morselli workshop in Alpignano, a small village on the outskirts of Turin, has the honour of being the birthplace of the first model in the Centro Storico collection. In 1962, the firm supplied the reproduction of the 1899 3.5 hp car, Fiat's first car and the first in its historical collection. At the time Morselli charged the sum of 500 000 lire for the model and the 800 hours of work which it involved. The sum gives some indication of the depreciation of the Italian currency in 20 years; at a conservative estimate, no Italian craftsman of today works for less than 12 to 15 000 lire an hour, and the cost of a model has risen to something in the region of 10 or 12 million lire.

The Morselli establishment also built busses, coaches, two racers (the 1902 24 hp and the 130 hp F2 of 1907), and the first of the tractors, before giving way to Abrami and others when the small company closed as a result of the death of its founder.

Another supplier in the past was the A.P.M. (Allestimenti Plastici e Modelli — Plastic and Model Constructions) company of Aosta headed by Enrico Acerbi, who died prematurely in 1971. Acerbi was a member of the exhibitions department of the Cogne Company, one of Italy's largest steelmakers. Modelling was his hobby, and he made some architectural models for the 'Italia 61' exhibition, held in Turin in 1961 to celebrate the centenary of Italian unity. This brought him to the notice of Fiat, for whom he was to work full-time for around 10 years.

Models of boats and aircraft destined for other parts of the organisation were made of moulded, resin-impregnated, glass wool with the windows formed of plexiglass, but the models for the Centro Storico had to be made in metal, and soldered brass was used in the traditional manner. However, Acerbi did not want to give up his fibreglass techniques completely, and therefore combined the two methods of construction. Structural elements such as the chassis, suspension, and load-bearing structures were made in brass, and the bodywork was made of Polyester reinforced with glass fibre.

The centre's collection holds six models by Enrico Acerbi; the Type 306 bus and the 682 type 2 motor coach in 1:10 scale, and four cars in 1:5 scale. The art of Acerbi and the use of Fibreglass enabled the centre to enlarge its collection with models ranging from the 8 hp car of 1901, through the 508 Ballila saloon and the 13 A to the wooden-sided Giardiniera of 1950.

The models of today

With the build-up of the collection now completed and the models on display, what remains to be done? The question is answered in the basic objectives of the Centro Storico, which is meant to be alive and constantly renewing itself. There is

In 1924, the English driver E.A.D. Eldridge drove this 21.7-litre monster called 'Mephistopheles' to a new world land speed record of 145.96 mph on a public road near Arpajon in France. Sergio Reggiani's model is on show beside the actual car.

In 1914, the 557/14B became the first Fiat racer to be produced with what was considered a normal sized engine — a 4.5-litre, four-cylinder unit producing 135 bhp. The version modelled for the Centro Storico is the short-tailed car which raced in the Targa Florio that year.

The first car produced by Fiat, the 3-1/2 hp of 1899, was also the first model to be made for the collection. Built by a now-defunct small firm from near Turin, Morselli and company, in 1961, it cost 500,000 lire at the time. Today's price would be 20 times that figure.

Below: The smallest model in the collection is of the 1936 500 Topolino which heralded the era of popular cars in Italy.

Bottom: The full sized wheel in the background gives scale to this model of the Fiat Zero of 1912-15.

The 508 Balilla Sport is the only example in the Fiat collection of the work of Spanish master modeller Manuel Olive-Sans.

A photograph from the sixties shows the then new 2300 saloon with a selection of models — 1:5 scale and photographic — of the same era. The girl model admires a 2300 coupé, and among the historic replicas is the museum's first model, the 1899 3-1/2 hp, in the centre. This picture gives a good idea of the impressive size of the 1:5 scale models.

no danger of stagnation in the model collection, for the Fiat company will continue to build new cars, trains, aircraft, and other vehicles — for example, the Panda, modelled by Bruno Reggiani in 1980, is already on display.

It is true that the collection will no longer grow at the speed it did in the sixties, and for some time now, only Reggiani has been building car models. He is almost solely responsible for the 24 models of cars from 1953 to 1980, although some others were built by Ferré, Abrami, and Acerbi.

One element will always be maintained — the rigorous unity of style which presides over the collection. It is a style which comes from the skill and taste of Augusto Costantino who alone has decided which cars should be modelled and in which colours they should be finished. His choice has been made principally on aesthetic grounds, with a view to the future and to the generations who will follow, who will be able to get an impression of the style of the epoch by looking at the models he has chosen. The shapes and colours speak in a simple, universal language and those who are persuaded by them to pursue the subject further will be able to consult the library, where they will find all the hidden technical details which the models cannot show.

The unity of style is also a factor of models in general when they are seen as works of art and not merely miniature representations of reality. It is only necessary to look at the rare examples from the past which have escaped the destruction of the war. There is hardly any difference between one of today's models and its predecessor by 60 years. The model of the Type 3000 tank of 1921, modelled that same year, is perfection now that it has been restored by Reggiani, who himself admits that he was able to learn something from those distant craftsman who built it with such art using the facilities of the factory where the actual tank was built.

This is the true value of a model collection. The graphic arts are influenced by different schools which overlap and change so much in the course of the years that they become unrecognisable; cinema and the theatre are the products of their period; a few months after publication, most books have nothing to teach us. The model by contrast, a result of craftsmanship and technology, like an automobile, always speaks the same language — today and forever.

The early days of Plastic Kits

Plastic kits appeared in America and Europe almost simultaneously at the beginning of the 1950s. Some of the early producers are still very much in business today, but to many of those launching out into the then new and unpredictable field, fortune was less than kind. The collector's shelf is where you'll find their models now, not at your local store. For some this article will be a recollection, for others a discovery, of all those firms that played a part in making the hobby what it is today.

The American Pioneers

Even before kits there were model car builders, but the cars had to be completely built from scratch. When wooden kits first came out after World War II a lot more people turned to the hobby, but the kits still required a skill beyond many people — bodies were just wood blocks, fenders were often cardboard that had to be cut and shaped, and only if you were lucky did you get premolded plastic trim parts. So the advent of the plastic kit in the early 1950s opened the model car field to the USA like no other single factor. All the purchaser had to do was to assemble parts already in the right shape — not that this took no skill at all, but it was a whole lot easier than shaping and finishing raw wood to look like a metal vehicle. The model car hobby had been revolutionized.

Most researchers now agree that the trend in plastic kits was started in 1951 or 1952 with Revell's release of the Highway Pioneers, with molds produced by a firm called Gowland & Gowland. In 1:32 (half as large as the 1950s wooden kits), the Highway Pioneer models were on the crude side by the standards of today, though perhaps not for the time. For the most part, the wheels and tires were one piece, trim parts could be of dubious scale, and only a few models (the hot rods, for example) had engines. Then there was the trouble of having to heat the axle ends to form a hub — and finding a suitable bonding agent for the acetate plastic. To make a really permanent bond with this material, the kit builder had to face the hazards of acetone, seeing 5 Minute Epoxy and the "Super" glues were years in the future. In 1954, though, Revell switched over to styrene plastic, modified some parts for added realism and put each kit into its own styled box. The era of the plastic kit as we know it today was beginning.

As important as the Highway Pioneers are to the model car hobby, their value on the collector's market is not in proportion to their age. The models proved to be very popular in their time and were even reissued in 1960 (in still another style box) for a few more years sales. Many of even the earliest kits can still be purchased for 5 dollars or less in unbuilt form, though there are notable exceptions, such as the Duesenberg, Cord and Bentley.

With the immedite popularity of plastic kits, Revell was not alone in the field for long. One of the first to follow was Hudson Miniatures, producers of some of the first post-war balsa antique car kits. Their Old Timers had been the kits that started many people building model cars, and when they produced the Lil' Old Timers in plastic, 1:32 scale, they made use of Revell's experience and produced a better, more detailed kit. Four models were produced in the first series of 1954, and one of a projected second series. The five known tools — the 1911 Maxwell, 1914 Oldsmobile Curved Dash, 1914 Regal Coupe, 1913 Mercer Raceabout and 1912 Packard Landaulet — were later sold to Revell, who shipped them to England where the kits were released under the Revell logo. They were never released in the USA, unfortunately.

Many of the early 50s pioneers are now long gone and mostly forgotten. Ideal Toys branched out into kits with some rather crude models in several scales. Champion produced a series of 1:32 sports cars in 1953 (later released by Aurora). In 1954 Kaysun (under the name Keepsake Models) released two excellent 1:24 antique cars, a 1902 Rambler Runabout and 1909 Hubmobile — but only the two. Detailing on them is so good they could be released today and not be out of place; they were available from Hawk Models into the late 60s. Premier was another with 1:24 models in 1954, though quality was not the best. In the balsa-kit making business since 1946, Monogram's first plastic kit, a Midget Racer, came out in 1954 in acetate plastic. Monogram is hardly long gone or forgotten, thankfully.

AMT, starting in 1948 as a metal toy firm (hence the name Aluminum Metal Toys) was using acetate plastic by 1949 (styrene wasn't available then) and soon expanded into the promotionals business. Then in 1955 they teamed with Revell to produce the first of the annual car kits, important not only for their immense success, but because they were among the first to contain plated parts. In 1:32, styrene, detailing was truly excellent, the only concession to the times being multi-piece bodies. The kits even contained detailed engines; that was really something for 1955.

The same year, Monogram moved to plated parts as well for their 1:18 Cadillac DeVilles, but the plastic was still acetate which tended to warp badly on these larger scale models.

Revel expanded into what has become America's most popular scale, 1:25, in 1957 with three kits that are now some of the most sought after collectors' items around — built or still boxed. These were a 1957 Cadillace Eldorado (detailing not all it could have been, proportion off a bit and no engine), the Pontiac Club de Mer prototype (perfect except no engine) and a 1957 Ford wagon (just perfect). Despite the multi-piece bodies, these kits were popular releases and justify their showpiece position in today's collections.

American kit history marks 1958 in red letters. This was the year when AMT

Four of the five kits from Hudson Miniatures, one of the first US manufacturers in the field. Construction was easy and detail a bit better than Revell's earlier Highway Pioneers.

This 1914 Stutz Bearcat in 1:32 was sold, like the other early Revell Highway Pioneers, in three different style boxes all told. From the top: the original 1952 release, the 1954 individually boxed version, and the 1960 final reissue.

started producing their own model car kits, no longer in connection with Revell, and began a 20 year tradition. AMT's 1958 kits, considered annual models (models of the current Detroit iron), contained a one-piece styrene molded body, and though not the first to use this idea, AMT were the ones to do it best. The kits were also the first of AMT's 3 in 1 series, which meant the kits could be built showroom stock, custom or racing.

These first AMT kits were still quite unlike the kits being produced today. The chassis was one piece (detail molded in) and there were no engines (some annuals received them in 1960, but it was 1966 before this was standard). Detailing was good for the time, but there were only the minimum number of parts needed to build the model. Custom parts usually consisted of lowering blocks for the chassis, fender skirts, mirrors, spotlights, fins and louvers. Four small flame decals were provided, and the instructions did state: "For additional Chrome or Accessory sets, send 25 cents plus postage to AMT Corporation..." but what these accessories consisted of I don't know — I never found anyone who sent for one. For the racing version, only extra decals were provided to build a NASCAR type; roll bars were included in the 1959 kits.

The 1958 annuals are now very difficult to come by, which is strange, seeing they were still in the line alongside the 1959 ones, much longer than subsequent annual kit production. AMT stopped annual production after the 1977 line, 20 years of the most prized kits in collecting.

Following AMT's great success, Jo-Han, a firm with many interests and a manufacturer of top-quality promotional model cars since 1955, moved into kit retailing in 1959. Like AMT's annuals, Jo-Han's kits were really just the already existing promotionals molded in styrene with a few extra custom parts and decals thrown in the box. For the time, that was all that was needed.

Meanwhile AMT were busy preparing new 1959 annuals and, another big advance, the first model in the Trophy series, a 1932 Ford Model B Roadster. This was a truly exciting time for the hobby as included in the 1.49 dollar package were all the parts needed to build the stock roadster, various types of hot rods, or a dragster; this was considered a 3 in 1 kit, just like the annuals. The Trophy series was in 1:25 with one-piece bodies as well, making two more good reasons for success. History has proved the scale choice was right, and there was no tricky body assembly, making the kit more accessible to the beginner. In addition, the release of the 1932 Ford let all the companies know there was a market for non-contemporary vehicles, and the 1959 hot rod goodies, optional Chrysler Hemi engine and drag parts kept the model state-of-the-art for those who preferred it that way. Needless to add, the 1959 kit and a Sports Roadster version released in 1961 are every collector's dream.

AMT's Trophy series thrived in the 60s and was joined by many similar kits from most of the manufacturers. It is interesting to note Jo-Han never got into the hot rod craze but went directly into classic car kits in the early 60s. Monogram wasn't sleeping either and in the late 50s and early 60s released many exciting plastic kits of hot rods, stock and custom models as well as classics. The model car hobby as we know it today grew its real roots in the 60s, but only because of the pioneering efforts of the companies of the early 50s.

The hobby had seen some changes since those first Highway Pioneers. Although right from the start Revell had been using color plastic to avoid the need for painting, serious modelers weren't going to do without it; and when the plastic changed to styrene to make bonding easier and safer, only enamel paints could be used (acetate would take almost anything). The natural consequence was that companies started to produce their own paints, though modelers had to wait until the end of the 50s before Pactra brought out their spray colors. By this time a lot of kits — AMT's annuals, for example — were molded in white to make painting easier.

By the late 50s kits came with clear parts

Pyro, Strombecker, Les Teuf-Teuf, Europe Model, Merit, Aurora, Record, Les Vieux Tacots, Airfix... so many names that the only 30-year history of plastic kits has seen fall by the wayside. Only Revell, who started it all, and Airfix (at least in name) are still with us.

The Pontiac Club de Mer — GM's 1956 dream car — the 1957 Ford Country Squire station wagon and the 1957 Cadillac Eldorado Brougham: three Revell kits that are now much sought after and sparked off, in 1957, the lasting US prediliction for 1:25 scale.

AMT's Trophy series started the 60s with a vengeance. The 3 in 1 formula meant that modelers could take their choice from three versions of the kit: showroom stock, custom or hot rod. This Ford Tudor sedan went on sale in 1961.

as part of the increasing realism and detail the companies (and modelers) were aiming for, and rubber or vinyl tires would be in the kit box more and more often (though Revell, for one, used plastic right through this period). This was the era when American model contests could still be won by a well built kit out of the box — things like brass frames, working independent suspension, opening everything and super-detailing didn't take over until the mid 60s.

Though not one of the true pioneer companies, no brief history could be complete without mention of MPC (Model Products Corporation). MPC was started by veterans of the model car industry and in 1964 when they released their first car kit (a 1964 Corvette coupe), their ideas were quite advanced. MPC's added realism was quickly duplicated by all the model car companies to take kit building to a standard little removed from that of today.

Europe: The Lost Causes

In Europe, the scene is very different from that in the United States. When a manufacturer puts a new model on the market, it will hope to continue selling that same model for some four or five years at the least, in order to cover the capital costs of production. Other influences are smaller markets, the competitive atmosphere which keeps prices down, and the high capital costs of a wide product range — at least in the more popular fields of aircraft and marine models.

Apart from one or two big firms which have built up an international reputation, like Airfix and Heller, Europe is the continent of lost causes. Who amongst today's younger generation of modellers would recognize the names of Scamold, Kleeware, Aviomodelli or Record? All of these produced kits before 1965, simple productions compared with those which we have become used to today, but now they are all collectors pieces — particularly if they are in their original boxes and not built up. What a strange world we collectors live in!

The first name that must be mentioned in the realm of kits is that of Scamold. Although the kits were in metal rather than plastic, Scamold deserves to be in this history because it was the first company to build what we now call a kit. Based originally at the Brooklands track, Scamold produced models of cars which had become famous through their performances at the cradle of British motor racing, such as a 1934 Maserati, a 1938 Alta four-cylinder, a 1931 Bugatti Type 51 and an E-type ERA of 1934. Scamold sold their models in built-up and kit form, and re-started their operations after the end of the war, but a combination of poor

The original Highway Pioneers series included 30 models in all up to 1956. Note, among the 1954-1955 boxes here, the Ferrari 212 Barchetta — a model you won't find in any manufacturer's current catalog, more's the pity.

Four kits from short-lived US manufacturers: Kaysun's very well detailed Keepsake Miniatures 1902 Rambler in 1:24; two HO models, one of them the Buick Le Sabre, from Ideal's Precision Miniature (not a very apt description) series; an 1877 Shelden in 1:24 from Mod-Ac (actually more wood than plastic); and the 1935 Gilmore Indy winner Special in 1:30 from Best (later released by Aurora).

Monogram released some excellent non-stock Fords in 1959 and 1960 — especially the 1932 Sports Coupe. The Dragster, although well reproduced and then state-of-the-art, looks strange by today's standards.

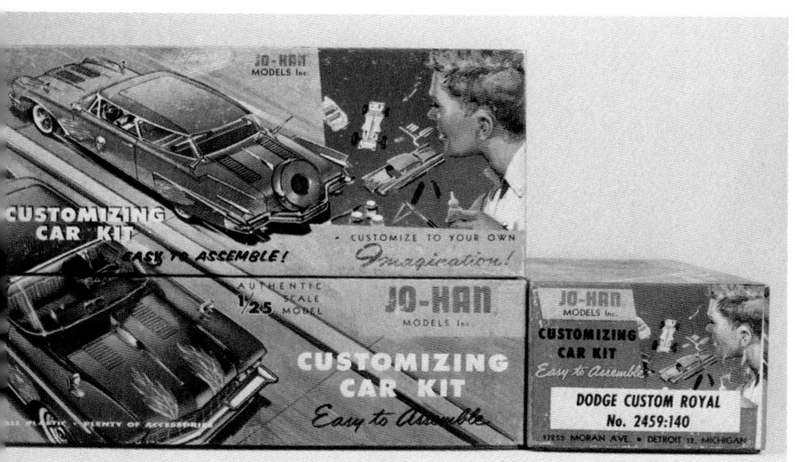

1959 saw the first contemporary car kit to come from Jo-Han, a Dodge Custom Royal, much along the lines of the AMT annual kits of the year before. The box art was rather striking, particularly when viewed from this angle.

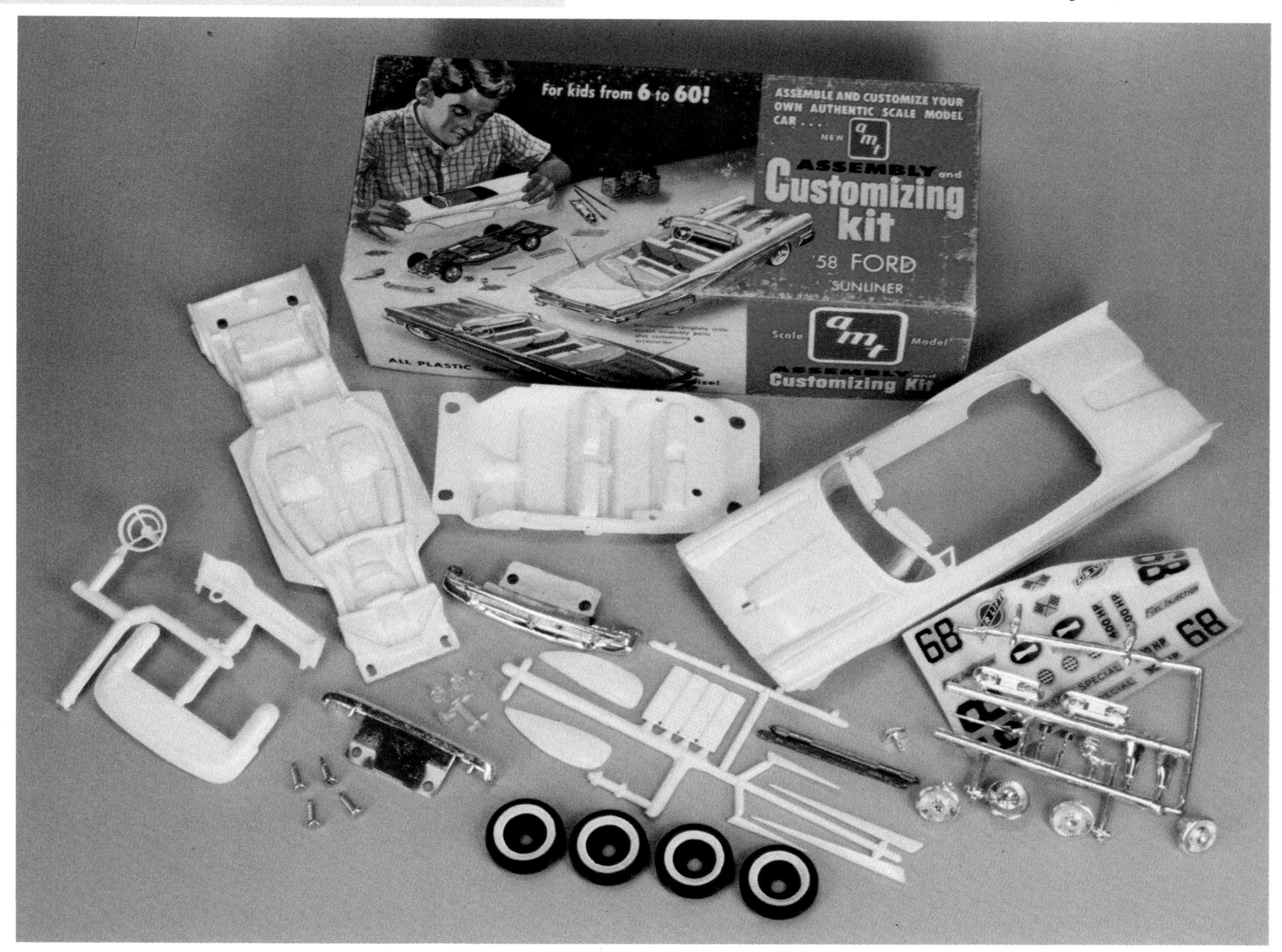

"For kids aged 6 to 60!" said AMT on its 1958 box tops. The kids in question would find inside just an unbuilt styrene promotional model, a few extra custom parts, such as fins and louvers, and decals — flames and racing numbers.

Stutz Bearcat (1914), Aurora Old Timers 1960, 1:16.

Mercedes-Benz 300 SL (1956), Aurora 1961, 1:32.

Citroën Trèfle (1922), Vieux Tacots 1965, 1:32.

Auburn Speedster (1935), Pyro 1960, 1:23.

Ferrari 275 P (1964), Monogram 1965, 1:24.

The 1:30 Indy racers originally released by Best were later reissued by Aurora. This Fuel Injection Special, a 1953 Indy entrant, came out in 1960. With some careful painting these kits, even if a bit dated today, can still look good.

distribution and production techniques (which made building the models a major operation) led to their closure in 1951.
Another early British manufacturer was SMEC (Scale Model Equipment Company) which produced a series of racing cars combining metal and plastic components with a wooden body. The range was attractive, containing 1:32 models of the 1939 GP Mercedes, 1933 3.3-litre Bugatti, 1935 1.5-litre Alta, Alfa Romeo 159, Maserati A6 CGS 2-litre, and Jaguar XK 120, but the difficulties of carving and finishing wooden bodies, combined with poor distribution, saw the death of the marque after only two years.
The plastic kits story really started when a man named Nicholas Koves became involved with the growth of the Glaser (Revell) empire in the United States. Koves had started out in the mattress business before the second world war. During the war he had turned to the manufacture of small plastic items such as cigarette lighter casings and combs. Such was the success of this aspect of the business that he invested in further moulding equipment to increase his output. With the end of the war demand dropped off and Koves began to look around for alternative uses for his machinery. A visit to the US brought him into contact with the early productions of such names as Revell and Hudson, and he realised that here was an outlet for his surplus capacity. He set about the task of converting as soon as he got back to Britain and laid the foundations of the Airfix brand in 1952.
Koves followed almost the same path as Glaser, starting with a range of old timers in 1:32. The first releases, in 1956, were a 1911 Rolls Royce 40/50 Landau and a 1904 Darracq Tonneau. They were followed in 1957 by a 1930 4.5-litre Le Mans Bentley, a 1910 Ford T, a 1905 Rolls Royce Double Phaeton and a 1907 Lanchester Landaulet. Koves was keen to cover a wide range of models and soon there were aircraft, tanks, military vehicles and modern cars. All the kits were simple to assemble and were moulded in a single colour, which allowed prices to be kept very low. These were advantages which other contemporary kit manufacturers sadly lacked, and their professional deficiencies kept many of them hovering on the brink of failure.
An example was Kleeware, a British company which issued, in 1956, a series of kits in which each box contained two models. The idea was a good one but the scale chosen, 1:80, did nothing to make them attractive. The kits were not a success, and neither were the 1:25 models that followed them, despite the fact that the range was an attractive one, comprising such classics as the 1955 Rolls Royce, a 1956 Pegaso Coupé, the 1956 Jaguar XK 120, the 1955 Ferrari Roadster and a 1956 Mercedes 300 SL. The most important of the early British manufacturers was J & L Randall, the makers of the Merit kits. Merit is a name which is well known to collectors because of its range of competition cars, which comprised the Aston Martin DB3S, Connaught Syracuse GP car, Cooper 500 Mk IX, 1956 Grand Prix Ferrari, Le Mans Jagur D-Type, Lotus 11, 1956 GP Maserati, 1955 GP Mercedes, 1956 GP Vanwall, 1956 GP BRM, 1952 Maserati 4 CLT San Remo Grand Prix winner, 1950 GP Simca Gordini, 1950 GP Alfa Romeo Alfetta and 1949 Talbot-Lago GP car. All were definitive classic racing cars, and the kits, which were introduced in 1956, were simple to build. The body was made up of a top, a bottom, and a nose-section, while the other major parts were a seat, fascia panel, steering wheel, axles, wheels and exhausts. Small components such as the windscreen, rear-view mirrors, filler caps and hub nuts completed the kit's contents, together with decals which included representations of spokes which were applied to clear plastic discs to simulate wire wheels where necessary.
Two of the kits, the Talbot-Lago and the Alfetta, were "super kits" with bonnets that were removable to display engine and radiator detail.
Merit also produced old car kits in 1:32; a 1912 Packard, a 1904 Oldsmobile, a 1903 Cadillac, a 1910 Ford T and a 1911 Rolls Royce. It is interesting that both Strombecker and Autolite produced competition car ranges identical to that of Merit, while the French Sitap company produced the Aston Martin, Maserati, Gordini, Cooper, Lotus and Ferrari-Lancia under licence bearing the Sitaplex brand name.
Staying in France, Precisia was an early kit manufacturer, launching 1:32 versions of the Cugnot Fardier of 1796 and the 1899 Gobron Brillé in 1959. The range, which was accompanied by detailed plans and assembly instructions, was marketed under the name of *Les Teuf Teuf*, a French equivalent of the British soubriquet "old crocks". A type 35 B Bugatti was added to the range in 1960 together with an 1898 Peugeot coupé. Despite the high quality of its moulding and the inclusion of a number of parts moulded in black, Precisia has since disappeared.
Similar models were popular; *Les Vieux Tacots*, another "old crocks" style name, introduced a 1904 Darracq in 1957 and followed it two years later with a 1908 Peugeot BB Torpedo, a 1900 De Dion Vis-à-vis and a 1907 Renault limousine. The range grew to such an extent that by the end of the sixties it contained 19 models in 1:32, 1:25 and 1:16. However, its range could not save it from disappearance. It must be pointed out that the plans and instructions were not of a very high standard, although the plastic was of good quality.
Another French company which disappeared in the sixties was Record, which introduced a couple of Renaults, a Dauphine and a Floride, in 1961. Even the inclusion of chromed parts could not save the Paris-based firm from extinction. Europe Model Kit was another attempt which came to nothing, despite the fact that the range included such interesting items as an 1891 Panhard (1964), an 1895 Panhard Coupé (1965), and a Panhard Tonneau of 1905 (1965). They were all in 1:32 and moulded in a single colour. In spite of excellent instructions, the company was yet another Parisian model producer which did not see the decade out.

The first AMT Trophy series kit, the 1932 Ford Roadster, came out in 1959 and was followed a year later by a 1932 Ford V8 Coupe. The first kit was reissued in 1961, but with an operational rumble seat — collectors take note!

The first two Panhards, the 1891 original and the 1895 coupe, were both released by Europe Models in 1:32, in 1964 and 1965, respectively.

Vintage cars, contemporary cars, competition cars (like this Porsche Carrera 6)... The Airfix 1:32 selection was wide and the kits were cheap and excellently made. The good old days?

Record produced only two kits, one of them this 1960 Renault Floride in 1:25, released in 1961. Another French maker, Les Vieux Tacots, was more prolific but didn't last much longer; the 1910 Berliet Coupe de Ville is from 1966.

In Italy it was the Cremona firm of Aviomodelli which started things, in 1963. The models were in 1:30 and represented such interesting vehicles as the 1901 Fiat 12 hp, the 1899 Fiat Vis-à-vis, a 1921 Lancia Lambda and the 1912 Fiat Zero. An innovation at this stage was rubber tyres, but this was not sufficient to keep Aviomodelli from sinking like so many others.

Another company which appeared in 1964, this time in Britain, was Auto Kits, which still exists today under the name it later adopted, Wills Finecast. Although the material was not plastic but metal, the scale was in the realms of the plastic manufacturers at 1:24. The range, which continues to grow slowly, was based on safe subjects such as single-seaters and classic sports cars. The company has never courted the mass market and continues to live on by sales to modellers with specific tastes.

It was not until 1967 that the other giant, Heller, produced its first car and entered the international field. The company's first production was a Renault 16, which was followed by a series which many enthusiasts consider a classic, comprising a Brabham Formula 3, Gordini 500 R8, Ford Mk II, Lotus 49, Brabham F1, McLaren F1, Ferrari P4, Porsche 907, Matra P650, Ferrari 512S, Alpine A 210 Le Mans and a Matra F2. All the models were of exceptional quality, with detailed engines and chassis.

Looking back over the list of models produced by the companies which failed, one is saddened at their demise because it is obvious that they were the work of people who wanted to offer the modeller a selection of subjects which were indicative of highlights in the history of the automobile. Unfortunately, this is not always the case today.

SQUADRA CORSE Ferrari
Modelli:
LE MANS
NÜRBURGRING
SEBRING
SILVERSTONE
MONZA
con ruote e motore di ricambio
DUNLOP
CEAT
14
21
MERCURY

NÜRBURGRING
SILVERSTONE
LE MANS
MONZA
SEBRING
SERIE REGALO
SQUADRA CORSE Ferrari
MERCURY

Gift Sets

The classic collection of miniature cars can cover an infinite range of subjects, a fact which gives the hobby much of its charm, but let me open this article with my own definitions of "classic" and "miniature", to lay the ground rules, as it were.

For the European, such a collection mainly concerns 1:43 die-cast models. There are a number of other scales, but it can be said that 1:43 is the most common (even if it is not always followed very precisely even by the most prestigious manufacturers) with occasional forays into smaller scales down to 1:75.

The British coined a phrase which has gone round the world to describe the ultimate in condition for a model: "mint and boxed", and it is generally accepted that a model with these qualities is worth appreciably more than one in new condition but without a box, or an old, chipped model still in its original box. The description is, of course, only applicable to those models which were originally supplied in a box!

Today it is common to meet collectors who only look for mint, boxed models, but in searching only for perfection, are they not likely to achieve a form of overkill? By collecting only perfect specimens, are they not in danger of nurturing misgivings in the hearts of their fellow collectors? The doubts which can grow after being shown the collection of a more fastidious enthusiast can make your own seem so inadequate. The wisest course is to know your limits and to start as you mean to go on, watching over the quality of the pieces you collect. This is why you should try to find the box; it not only protects the model, it also represents a real piece of history in itself. Keeping a box is to preserve a small piece of time, for often the illustration is an evocative reminder of an era.

However, my purpose here is not to make a plea for the indiscriminate collection of all boxes, but to discuss a specialized aspect of model collecting, that of the group of models assembled together — the gift set.

All the classic names have produced their own gift sets; Tootsietoys, Dinky Toys in both France and Great Britain, Mercury, Tekno, Spot-on, Matchbox, Solido, Manoil, Hubley, Minic, Corgi Toys, Märklin... each has been a regular or occasional producer of such collections.

Gift sets were usually offered to catch the present-buying public at holiday time — most often at Christmas. With their rich decoration, the boxes are evocative of the joy which surrounds such festive occasions. They were often attractive in themselves and enabled the child to extend the limits of his play by providing a selection of models collected around a theme, such as racing, touring, construction equipment or military vehicles. The gift set made it possible to create a game around a theme right away, particularly since the box would often contain accessories such as buildings to cut out, road signs, straw bales, barriers and other components which would add a touch of realism to the nursery carpet or the dining-room table.

There were many such sets, but they never achieved outstanding sales success, no doubt because of their high prices. Now, however, they are actively sought by collectors who want a little more on their shelves than a simple accumulation of individual models.

Gift sets complete a collection and bring to it a history of not only the manufacturer, but even, to some extent, the world. Two examples to support this argument: Just before the outbreak of World War II, Dinky Toys re-issued two of its gift sets — of aircraft and military vehicles — with camouflage colour schemes replacing the bright colours in which they had originally been produced, a reflection of the atmosphere of the

◁ *The numerous collectors of Ferrari models will appreciate this rare Mercury gift set. Introduced in 1966, it contained four versions of the 'Spider', a 250 LM, and spare wheels and engines. (van den Abeele collection)*

The British Budgie Toys range, much less well known than Corgi and Dinky Toys, produced a number of sets at the beginning of the sixties which are now collectors pieces. The cars were in 1:43 and the commercial vehicles approximately 1:76. (Balieu collection)

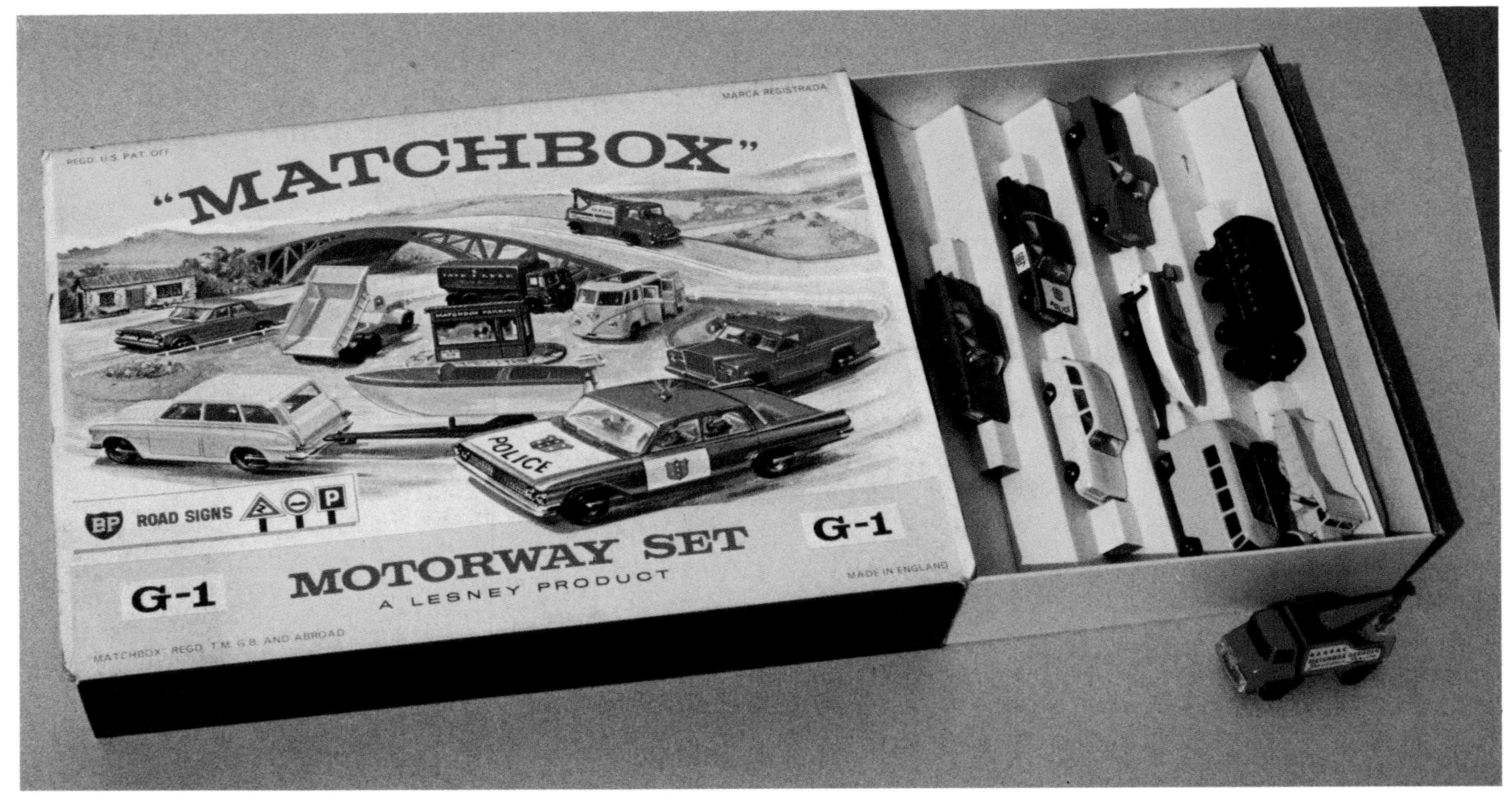

This Matchbox G1 collection dates from 1964. It takes the form of a giant cardboard matchbox decorated with artwork from the packaging produced by the company between 1953 and 1968. It contains nine models, a folding cut-out motorway with road signs to cut out and glue, and a wallet with motorway driving hints for father. It should be remembered that at this time Britain had only just moved into the age of the motorway, and everything connected with high-speed roads was exciting and saleable. (Roulet collection)

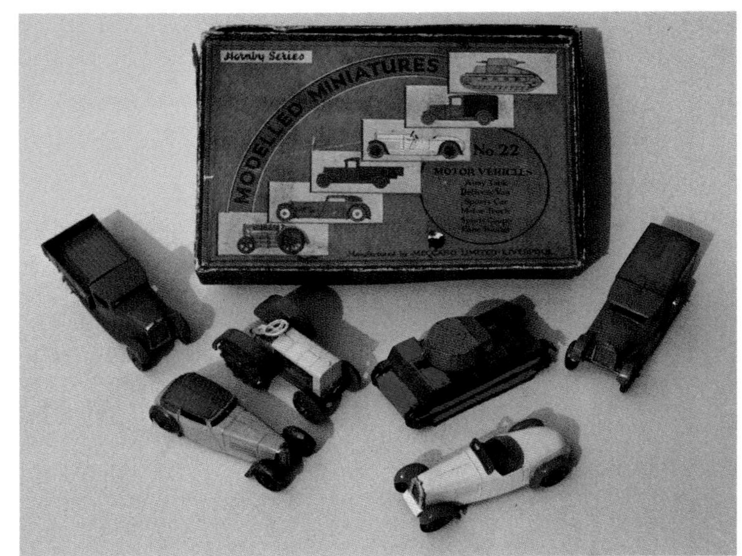

Produced at the end of 1933 or the beginning of 1934, even before the name Dinky Toys had been born, this gift box contained the first six Binns Road productions, forerunners of the many that were to follow. The roadster, coupé, truck, van (built on the same chassis as the truck), Fordson-inspired farm tractor and Vickers-like tank were numbered 22A,B,C,D,E and F, respectively. They were packaged in a simple cardboard box similar to the boxes which carried the models, six at a time, to retailers. (Roulet collection)

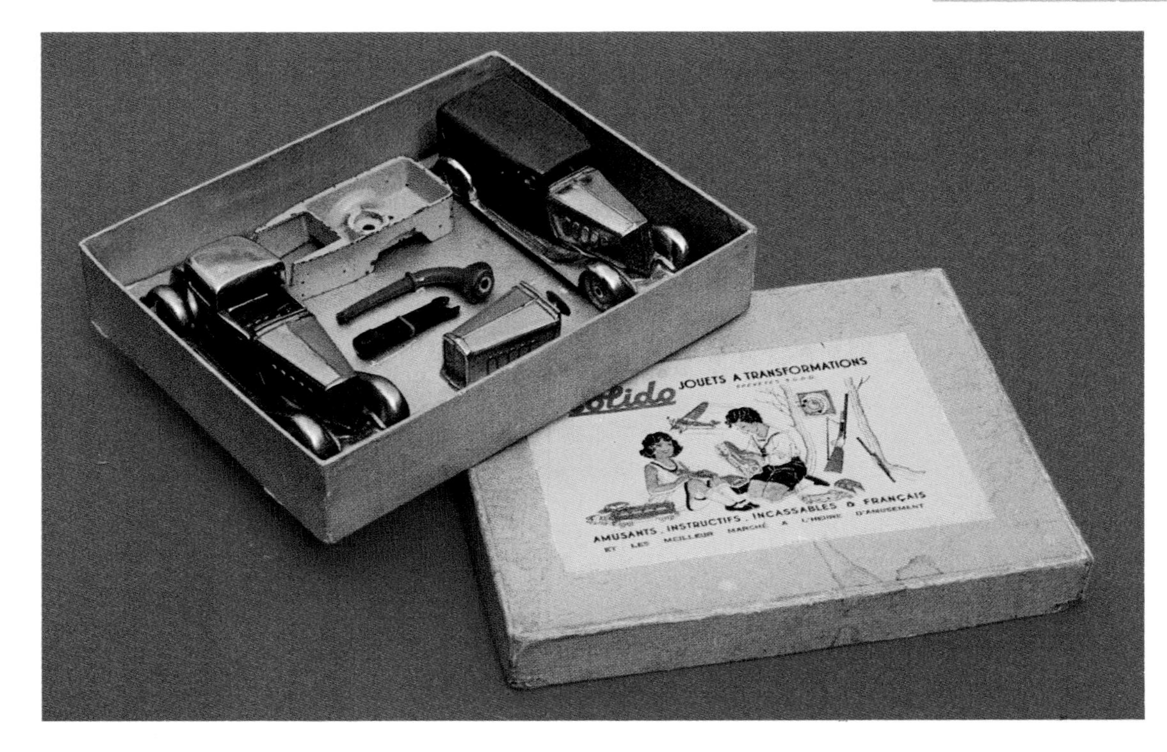

Dating from the same period — 1934 — this Solido Junior 100 set was called the 'Boîte à Transformation (conversion set) A' and sold for 42 francs. The money purchased two complete vehicles, a coupé with the streamlined type 2 chassis and type 2 bonnet (hood), and a delivery van on the type 2 chassis with type 2 bonnet. The spares comprised a breakdown truck body, a crane for this body, and a type 1 bonnet. A spanner, a packet of screws, and an instruction sheet completed the set. (Roulet collection)

times. At the other end of the scale, Tootsietoy's packaging for its gift sets of the thirties was indicative of the brightness of that era in the United States: Tootsietoy Playtime Toys boxes carried a picture of a little boy and girl approaching a doorway marked "Entrance to Playtime". Around them were drawings of popular nursery characters such as Humpty Dumpty, Little Red Riding-hood, Simple Simon and Mother Goose. Each box is a faithful evocation of the times in which it was produced.

It has to be said that sometimes the box tops flattered to deceive, promising joys which the contents were not able to deliver. This was a characteristic of the lesser marques, however, the quality manufacturers providing both packaging and content to a high standard. When commenting on the quality of the packaging, it must be remembered that good boxes meant good sales. The talent expended on the box art and packaging created a demand which was reflected in sales figures. From our point of view, it also ensured that the gift set would be worth collecting.

I should point out that in speaking of boxed sets, I am not referring to the construction kits sold by Märklin, Meccano, Citroën and Dux, among others, nor to plastic kits, which are a study on their own. However, that does not mean that a gift set cannot be construction-based, as evidenced by Corgi's Commer milk-float and Tootsietoy's Build-A-Car sets.

Boxed gift sets are rarer than boxed individual models for obvious reasons: the child would open the box, the models would be dispersed, and the box thrown out with the rest of the Christmas packaging. In addition, not so many were made. On the other hand, gift boxes provided better protection to their contents and it is likely that any that are found in good condition will contain models in perfect shape. The fact that sales were lower may add to the rarity of gift sets, but conversely it also means that there is a good chance that the assiduous collector can find unsold stocks in mint condition.

Human nature being what it is, there is every chance that the blister packs of the last fifteen years or so will find themselves in demand by the next generation of collectors. It is simply a question of childhood memories. The children of the sixties and seventies will surely become collectors and seek to re-live the good times of their childhood with the models they played with then. Not for them the dusty old cardboard boxes of the thirties, forties and fifties! On this subject, it is interesting to note that the tradition has been carried on by the Japanese manufacturers, who could give lessons in faithfulness to more than one of the established European manufacturers. They are joined by the Italian firms of Brumm and Polistil, who have made some tentative moves in this direction, and two British manufacturers, Matchbox and Corgi, who have had gift sets as a permanent feature of their catalogues.

Box-tops adorned with childish scribbles bear evidence to the hands through which many gift sets have passed before reaching the collector's shelf. This is Dinky's No. 4 set, produced between 1953 and 1958 and containing the Alfa Romeo, Cooper Bristol, Ferrari, HWM and Maserati racing cars. (van den Abeele collection)

The Tekno company produced only a few sets at the beginning of its life, under its original Danish ownership. This one, a precursor of the detailed metal kits of today, was in the catalogue under the reference number 799. A larger set (No. 800) contained two trucks, two chassis and seven different types of trailer. (van den Abeele collection)

Cataloguing the complete list of gift sets is a chancy business, but there are a number of them, listed below, which have come to be considered classics, and usually, not surprisingly, contain classic models. Cars, veteran and vintage vehicles, trucks, car transporters and their loads, racing cars, breakdown and rescue sets, agricultural and military collections — not to mention here all the motorcycles, boats and aircraft — all have provided a subject for the countless gift sets produced over the last half century.

In the list which follows, set titles/descriptions have been left in their language of origin to aid identification by the collector.

Collectors have tended to ignore the gift sets produced by Dinky Toys during the sixties, but they often contain rare models. This Goodwood Racing Set comprised an MGB, Porsche 356 Coupé, Austin Healey Sprite and E-type Jaguar and was produced between 1963 and 1965. (van den Abeele collection)

CLASSIC GIFT-SETS

DINKY TOYS (GB)

N°22 Motor Vehicles (Hornby Series), 1933-35
Army Tank, Delivery Van, Sports Car, Motor Truck, Sports Coupe, Farm Tractor.

N°23 Racing Cars, 1936-41
Auto Union, Mercedes-Benz, Speed of the Wind.

N°24 Motor Cars, 1934-40
Models of Series 24, with Ambulance.

N°25 Commercial Motor Vehicles (1), 1934-37
N°25 - a, b, c, d, e, f.

N°25 Commercial Motor Vehicles (2), 1937-41
N°25 - b, d, e, f, g, h.

N°30 Motor Vehicles (1), 1935-37
Models of Series 30, with Ambulance 30f.

N°30 Motor Vehicles (2), 1937-41
idem, but with Caravan 30g

N°33 Mechanical Horse and Five Assorted Trailers, 1935-37

N°33 Mechanical Horse and Four Assorted Trailers, 1937-40
The Box Van was sold separately.

N°36 Motor Cars, 1937-41
Series 36 with drivers, passengers and footman.

N°39 Saloon Cars, 1939-41
Series 39.

N°156 Mechanised Army Set, 1939-41

N°151 Royal Tank Corps Medium Tank Set, 1937-41

N°152 Royal Tank Corps Light Tank Set, 1937-41

N°249 Racing Cars (1), 1953-58
Alfa Romeo, Cooper Bristol, H.W.M., Ferrari, Maserati.

N°249 World Famous Racing Cars (2), 1962-63
Talbot-Lago, Maserati, Ferrari, Alfa Romeo, Vanwall, Cooper Bristol.

N°201 Racing Car Set, 1965-68
Cooper, Lotus, Ferrari, B.R.M. (n°240-241-242-243).

N°149 Sports Cars Gift Set, 1957-59
N°107, 108, 109, 110, 111.

N°121 Goodwood Racing Gift Set, 1963-65
MGB (113), Porsche 356A Coupé (182), Austin Healey Sprite (112), Jaguar E (120).

N°122 Touring Gift Set, 1963-64
Caravan (188), Rambler Station Wagon (193), Jaguar 3.4 l. (195), RAC Motor Cycle Patrol (270), Atlas Kenabrake (295), Healey Sports Boat on trailer (796).

N°123 Mayfair Gift Set, 1963-64
Jaguar Mk 10 (142), Rolls-Royce Silver Wraith (150), Mercedes 220 SE (186), Bentley Type S (194), Rolls-Royce Phantom V (198), Austin Countryman (199).

N°990 Car Transporter and Four Cars Gift Set, 1956-58
Pullmore (982), Hillman Minx (154), Rover 75 (156), Austin Somerset (161), Ford Zephyr (162).

N°957 Fire Service Set, 1959-64
Fire Service Chief's car (257), Fire Engine with Extending Ladder (955), Turntable Fire Escape (956).

N°298 Emergency Services Set, 1963-64
USA Police Car (258), Airport Fire Tender (276), Criterion Ambulances (263 and 277).

N°299 Post Office Services Gift Set, 1958-58
Royal Mail Van (268), Telephone Van (261), Telephone Box (750).

N°697 25-Pounder Field Gun Set
N°686, 687, 688.

N°698 Tank Transporter with Tank
N°660, 651.

N°699 Military Vehicles, 1955-58
N°621, 641, 674, 676.

DINKY TOYS (F)

N°24/1 Coffret en carton jaune, 1935
Yellow box: the six Series 24 models, type I.

N°24/2 Coffret voitures de tourisme, violet avec illustration, 1936-37
Violet, illustrated box: Six Series 24 models, type I or II.

N°24/3 idem, 1938-39
Six Series 24 models, type III.

N°24/4 Coffret de six voitures assorties, en carton bleu, 1940-48
Blue box: Series 24 types III and IV, with metal wheels.

N°24/1956 Coffret cadeau tourisme, type boîte Supertoys, 1956-56
Peugeot 203 saloon (24R), Citroën 2CV (24T), Simca Aronde Elysée (24V), Studebacker Commander 109 Coupé (24Y), Simca Versailles (24Z).

N°24/1957 Coffret cadeau tourisme, type boîte Supertoys, 1957-57
Chrysler New Yorker (24A), Peugeot 403 (24B), Renault Dauphine (24E), Studebacker Commander 109 Coupé (24Y), Simca Versailles (24Z).

Models of Yesteryear and Matchbox: two magic names. To think that only twenty years ago, the shops were full of gift sets like this one, the G-6 gift set, which made its first appearance in 1963. It was the third collection of Models of Yesteryear and contained the Mercer Raceabout (Y7), Bugatti 35 (Y6), Bentley 4.5-litre Le Mans car (Y5), Spyker (Y16) and Rolls Royce Silver Ghost (Y15). (Balieu collection)

A different Matchbox set entirely, but the same G-6 number; Lesney certainly didn't help the collector when they classified their sets! This one was issued in 1964 and contained eight commercial vehicles; a Euclid dumper, refuse truck, a tipper with snow-plough attached, Foden concrete-mixer, Foden tipper, Faun crane truck, a Drott excavator and a TV rental company service van. (Balieu collection)

Two famous Dinky Toy sets, the 22, produced between 1933 and 1935, and the 30 (1935-37), which now only make rare — and expensive — appearances on the market. The 30 set contained six models from the 30 range, including the 30F ambulance in its original form and the 30G caravan in its second version, produced between 1937 and 1941. How many sets like this lie undiscovered in attics? (Basecq collection)

The set which Tootsietoy introduced in 1940 under reference number 5150 was an assortment of ten cars from the 230 series. The Graham alone has become a widely sought collectors piece, so one can imagine the pride of those who have managed to assemble this complete set. (Basecq collection)

The 1933 Tootsietoy catalogue described this set as: "Ten Tootsietoys, all different — colorful — packed the perfection way. A big set of outstanding toys to complete the ever-growing 'Tootsietoy Playtime Toys'." Ever since the introduction of the Number 10 set, in around 1925, gift sets had been an important part of the Tootsietoy range. (Basecq collection)

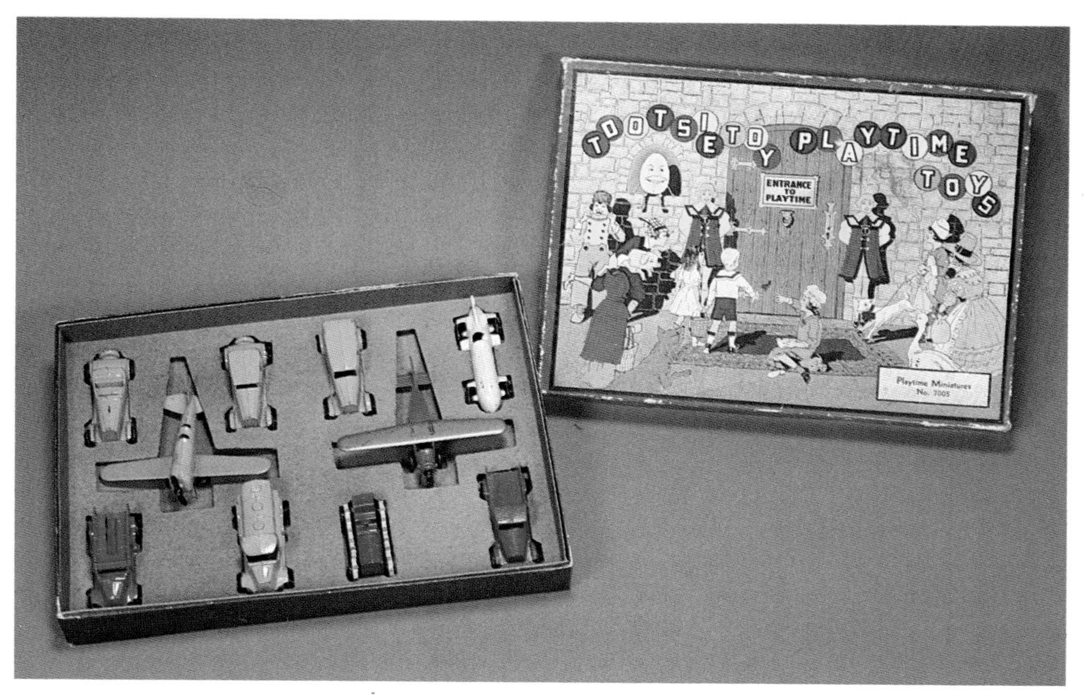

Gift sets often included games, and this Tootsietoy Speedway, produced in 1932, is one of the nicest. In the game, eight different-coloured versions of Malcolm Campbell's Bluebird race round a cardboard track. (Basecq collection)

The GS/24 set from Corgi Toys was produced between 1963 and 1968. It provides the perfect example of a multiplicity of models stemming from the same base being sold in a number of versions as part of the company's normal range. Two Commer chassis were provided, and could be fitted with any of four bodies (a milk float, a pickup, an ambulance or a closed van) to give a total of eight permutations. (Basecq collection)

N°24/1958 Coffret cadeau tourisme, boîte rouge, jaune, verte, noire, 1958-59
Multicoloured box: Peugeot 403 (24B), Citroën DS 19 (24C), Plymouth Belvédère Coupé (24D), Renault Dauphine (24E), Simca Versailles (24Z), later replaced with Citroën DS 19 (24CP) with plastic windows.

503/1 Coffret cadeau tourisme, 1963-64
Peugeot 403 (521), Citroën DS 19 (522), Renault Floride Coupé (543), Simca Aronde (544), De Soto Diplomat (545).

1460 Coffret cadeau tourisme, 1968
Citroën DS 19 Police (501/2), Simca 1500 Break (507), Opel Admiral (513), Alfa Romeo Guilia 1600 Ti.

MATCHBOX (GB)

Gift Set n°1 Commercial Vehicles, 1963
London Bus (5), Sugar Container Truck (10), Land Rover (12), Wreck Truck (13), Ambulance (14), Milk Delivery Truck (21), Long Distance Removal Truck (46), Mobile Refreshment Bar (74).

Gift Set n°2 Car Transporter, 1963
VW Sedan (25), Ford Prefect (30), Ford Fairlane Station Wagon (31), Pontiac Convertible (39), Sports Boat on Trailer (48), Jaguar 3.8 Sedan (65) and Car Transporter (A-2).

Gift Set n°3 Farm and Agricultural, 1963
Caterpillar Bulldozer (K3), Fordson Tractor and Farm Trailer (K11), Combine Harvester (M5), Articulated Cattle Truck (M7).

Gift Set n°4 GP Racepack, 1963
Wreck Truck (13), Ambulance (14), Aston Martin Racing Car (19), Jaguar Racing Car (41), Lyons Maid Ice Cream Mobile Shop (47), Maserati Racing Car (52), E Type Jaguar (32), Ferrari Racing Car (73), B.P. Autotanker (M1), Roadway (R-4).

Gift Set n°5 Military Vehicles, 1963
Saracen Troop Carrier (54), Military Scout Car (61), Military Ambulance (63), 6-wheel Military Crane Truck (64), Saladin Armoured Car (62), Military Radio Truck (68), 10-wheel Transporter with Centurion Tank (M3).

Gift Set n°6 Veteran Cars, 1963
1929 4.5 l. Bentley (Y5), 1923 type 35 Bugatti (Y6), 1913 Mercer Raceabout Sports Car (Y7), 1907 Rolls-Royce Silver Ghost (Y15), 1904 Spyker Veteran Automobile (Y16).

Gift Set n°7 Models of Yesteryear, 1963
1907 London "E" Class Tramcar (Y3), 1905 Shand-Mason Horse-Drawn Fire Engine (Y4), 1912 Packard Landaulet (Y11), 1899 London Horse-Bus (Y12), 1862 "General" Locomotive (Y13).

Gift Set n°8 Civil Engineering, 1963
8-wheel Tipper Truck (K1), Muir-Hill Dumper (K2), Caterpillar Bulldozer (K3), Foden Tipper Truck (K5), Allis-Chalmers Earth Scraper (K6).

Gift Set n°9 Major Pack Set, 1963
Box Truck (M2), Excavator (M4), 18-wheel Tractor and Transporter (M6).

Gift Set n°10 Garage Gift Set, 1963
Dodge Wreck Truck B.P. (13), B.P. Tanker (25), Ford Fairlane Station Wagon (31), Garage Pump and Forecourt (A1), B.P. Service Station (MG1).

In 1964, box presentation was changed and the contents altered, in some cases considerably.

Gift Set n°1 Motorway Set, 1964
10-wheel Quarry Truck (6), Sugar Container Truck (10), Wreck Truck (13), Ford Zephyr (33), Volkswagen Camping Car (34), Vauxhall Victor Estate Car (38), Sports Boat and Trailer (48), Police Car (55), Jeep pick-up Truck (71), Roadway (R-1) and BP Road Signs.

Gift Set n°2 Transporter Set, 1964
Mark Ten Jaguar (28), E Type Jaguar (32), Rolls-Royce (44), Mercedes-Benz 220 S (53), Car Transporter (M-8).

Gift Set n°5 Military Vehicles, 1964
Land Rover (12), Military Personnel Carrier (49), Saracen Troop Carrier (54), Military Scout Car (61), 6-wheel Military Crane Truck (64), Saladin Armoured Car (67), 10-wheel Transporter with Centurion Tank (M-3).

Gift Set n°6 Commercial Truck Set, 1964
10-wheel Quarry Truck (6), Refuse Truck (15), "Mountaineer" Dump Truck with snowplough (16), 8-wheel Tipper (17), Ready-Mix Cement Truck (26), 6-wheel Crane Truck (30), Draft Excavator (58), T.V. Van (62).

Gift Set n°7 Veteran and Vintage Set, 1964
1911 Renault 2-seater (Y2), 1929 4.5 l. Bentley (Y5), 1928 Mercedes-Benz 36/220 (Y10), 1907 Rolls-Royce Silver Ghost (Y15), 1904 Spyker Veteran Automobile (Y16).

Gift Set n°8 Construction Set, 1964
8-wheel Tipper Truck (K1), Curtiss-Wright Rear Dumper (K7), Aveling-Barford Tractor Shovel (K10), Ready-Mix Cement Truck (K13), Jumbo Crane (K14).

Gift Set n°9 Service Station Set, 1964
B.P. Service Station (MG-1), Wreck Truck (13), Ford Zephyr (33), Jeep Pickup Truck (71), Accessory Pack (A-1).

Gift Set n°10 Fire Station Set, 1964
Fire Station (MF-1), Ambulance (14), Fire Chief Car (59), and two Fire Trucks (9).

In 1965, sets n°3-5 were no longer listed. 1966 saw new presentation in blister packaging.

Gift Set n°1 Service Station Set, 1966
M6-1, 13, 31, 64, A-1.

Gift Set n°2 Car Transporter Set, 1966
M-8, 22, 28, 36, 75.

Gift Set n°3 Vacation Set, 1966
12, 23, 27, 42, 45, 48, 56, 68.

Gift Set n°4 Race Track Set, 1966
13, 19 (green), 19 (orange), 29, 41 (white), 41 (yellow), 52 (blue), 52 (red), 54 M-6, Roadway MR-4.

Gift Set n°5 Fire Station Set, 1966
MF-1, 29, 54, 59.

Gift Set n°6 Commercial Truck Set, 1966
16, 17, 25, 26, 30, 69, 70, 71.

Gift Set n°7 Yesteryear Set, 1966
Y1, Y3, Y11, Y14.

Gift Set n°8 King Size Set
K1, K11, K12, K15.

Matchbox changed the boxes almost every year. It should also be noted that model numbers change as new models replace the old but re-use the old numbers.

TOOTSIETOY (USA)

N°10 Auto and Garage Set, ca 1925
4 cars (Sedan, Truck, Roadster, Touring Car) and a folding cardboard garage.

N°170 Interchangeable Truck Set, 1925
One Mack (1921 Mack AC) chassis and three different bodies.

N°5081 Speedway Set, 1932
8 models of Malcom Campbell's Bluebird-1, each in a different colour. 1st type, metal wheels. Cardboard race track.

N°5310 Tootsietoy Trucks Set, 1933
8 different models: Mack Stake Trailer Truck (801), Mack Oil Trailer Truck (802), Mack Van Trailer (803), Mack Coal Truck (804), Graham Wrecker (806), Delivery Cycle (802), Graham Dairy Van (808), Mack Milk Trailer Truck (192).

N°05350 Taxicab Set, 1933
4 Graham Sedan four wheel models (two yellow, two orange) and a wrecker.

N°05300 Motor Set, 1933
10 Graham models: one six-wheel, two five-wheel Coupes, one six-wheel Sedan, two five-wheel Sedans, a five-wheel Roadster, a six-wheel Roadster, a six-wheel Town Car and a Wrecker.

N°05300 Motor Set, 1935
The Roadster or the Town Car was replaced by the Commercial Tyre Van (orange body, brown chassis).

N°05360 Build-A-Car Set, 1933
Five Graham chassis with wide axle channels, five bodies, enough wheels and half-axles to equip five cars. Two sedans, two coupes and a roadster or, in 1938, the Van body.

N° 5210 Truck Set, 1936-38
Torpedo Pickup (1019), Wrecker (1027), two large tank trucks; 1940 pickup truck and station wagon, a large hook and ladder truck, two small trucks and the Waco Navy Bomber.

N°199 Playtime Set, ca 1940
230 series Sedan, Coupe, Roadster and Tanker and an army plane.

N°650 Army Set, 1940
Armoured Car, Supply Truck, cannon, Waco Navy Bomber, nine soldiers.

N°5000 Motor Set, 1940
Two army planes, two Electras, The Big Bluebird, a Ford Wrecker, fourteen 230 series (3 Coupés, 2 Roadsters, 2 Station Wagons, and one of each of the others).

N°5050 Playtime Toy Set, 1940
Seven 230 series (cars and trucks), a Ford Wrecker, army plane and Electra.

N°5100 Playtime Set, 1940
Whole Torpedo series, big ladder and horse truck, Waco Navy Bomber and Mainliner.

N°5150 Motor Set, 1940
Ten models; all the 230 Series: Sedan (230), Coupe (231), Touring Car (232), Roadster (233), Box Truck (234), Oil Truck (235), Hook and Ladder Truck (236), Insurance Patrol (237), Horse Car (238) and Station Wagon (239).

N°750 Jumbo Set, 1941
Torpedo Roadster (1016), Torpedo Coupe (1017), Torpedo Sedan (1018), Torpedo Trans-America Bus (1026 or 1045).

N°5220 Army Set, 1941
Tank, Armoured Car, two Mack Army Trucks, Graham Army Ambulance, Supply Truck, two cannons, two army planes, two miniature bombers and the Waco Bomber.

CORGI TOYS (GB)

Gift Set 1, 1957-62
Car Transporter (1101) with a full load of four cars. British cars till 1959, then American cars and assorted cars in 1962, its last year.

Gift Set 2, 1958-63
Land Rover and Pony Trailer.

Gift Set 3, 1958-63
RAF Land Rover with Thunderbird guided missile on towing trolley.

Gift Set 4, 1958-63
RAF Land Rover, Bloodhound missile, platform and trolley.

Gift Set 5, 1958
Racing cars: Vanwall, B.R.M., Lotus XI.

Gift Set 6, 1959
Bloodhound missile, platform, RAF Land Rover, Thunderbird guided missile, Decca radar scanner, Decca Airfield Radar Truck, Standard Vanguard RAF Car.

Gift Set 7, 1959-63
Farm Tractor and Trailer.

Corgi's "Silverstone Racing Layout", produced between 1961 and 1966, was an unusual gift set which combined cars, figures, plastic construction kits for buildings, and a section of the Silverstone circuit — the Woodcote corner — reproduced here on flexible plastic sheet. It was at the same time complete and yet incomplete, for the actual track was not included. This is another set which leaves collectors with the dilemma of whether they should build the kits or leave them in their original boxes. (van den Abeele collection)

A classic box, filled with classic models. Between 1957 and 1959 — how long ago that seems now! — Dinky Toys offered this line-up of an MG TF, Austin Healey 100, Sunbeam Alpine, Aston Martin DB3S and Triumph TR2 as Gift Set No. 149; a ready-made grid for playroom sports car races. (van den Abeele collection)

Sometimes Dinky Toys produced gift sets complete with illustrated backgrounds; examples of this idea were the petrol pump set and the AA and RAC patrol sets. Another was the Post Office collection, only produced in 1958, which brought together a Royal Mail van, a Post Office Telephones van and a telephone box with figures of a postman and a telephone engineer. (van den Abeele collection)

Tootsietoy was the first company to realize the potential of the car transporter as the basis for a gift set, a trend which many have since followed. (Basecq collection)

A Belgian-made Durseau military band marches through the contents of a Corgi Toy gift set on sale from 1958 to 1963. This kind of set, with many moving parts on the models — here an RAF Land Rover, a Bloodhound missile, its launching platform, and transporter — was particularly popular. (van den Abeele collection)

Matchbox has been a fruitful source of gift sets. This is the G5 set, dating from 1964, and comprises a collection of military vehicles. The parade consists of a Land Rover, a troop transporter, a Saracen armoured personnel carrier, a scout car, a Saladin armoured car, a recovery vehicle, and a tank transporter carrying an impressive Centurion tank. (Balieu collection)

All the pre-war Dinky Toys military vehicle gift sets were constructed along the same lines: a cardboard box with a fold-down front which revealed an interior printed with a countryside scene printed in green. The models were mounted on a baseboard suitably punched to locate them. The box top carried details of the contents and information on the real vehicles on which the models were based. This is set No. 151, described as the 'Royal Tank Corps Medium Tank Set', produced in 1938 and including a Vickers Mk II tank (151A), a Morris covered truck (151B), a mobile kitchen (151C), and a water carrier (152D). (Roulet collection)

Gift Set 8, 1959-62
Massey-Fergusson 65 Farm Tractor, Tipping Farm Trailor and Massey-Fergusson 700 Combine Harvester.

Gift Set 9, 1959-62
Corporal Missile Ramp, Erector and 6×6 Army Truck.

Gift Set 10 ————

Gift Set 11, 1960-64
ERF Dropside Truck and Platform Trailer with loads of bricks, planks and sacks.

Gift Set 12, 1960-65
First Chipperfield Set: Circus Crane Truck and Cage Trailer.

Gift Set 13 ————

Gift Set 14, 1961-65
Jeep FC-150 with overhead service tower, lamp post and workman.

Gift Set 15, 1961-66
Silverstone Racing layout with various components including Vanwall, Lotus XI, B.R.M., Thunderbird Convertible, Mercedes 300 SL Coupe, Aston Martin DB4, Land Rover Breakdown, the three Silverstone buildings, telephone box etc.
Later (after 1963) the Lotus XI was replaced by the Formula One Ferrari.

Gift Set 16, 1961-66
Ecurie Ecosse Transporter with Vanwall, Lotus XI and BRM.

Gift Set 17, 1963-67
Land Rover, Trailer and Formula One Ferrari.

Gift Set 18, 1961-63
Fordson Tractor and Plough.

Gift Set 19, 1962-69
Second Chipperfield Set: Circus Land Rover (a special version not issued separately), with Flat Trailer carrying the Elephant Cage.

Gift Set 20, 1961-63
Golden Guinea Set with Gold-plated Bentley (224), Corvair (223) and Ford Consul (234).

Gift Set 21, 1963-66
ERF Milk Truck and Trailer with Milk Churns.

Gift Set 22, 1963-66
Farm Set with Tipping Farm Trailer, M-F Tractor with Fork, Fordson Tractor, Four Furrow Plough, Combine Harvester, Skip with Milk Churns.

Gift Set 23, 1963-66
Third Chipperfield Set: Flat Trailer, Land Rover Pickup, Bantam Karrier Booking Office (later replaced by Giraffe Transporter), Elephant Cage, Circus Crane Truck, two Circus Cage Wagons.

Gift Set 24, 1963-68
Commer Construction Set: two 15 cwt chassis-cab units and four rear bodies; milk truck, pickup, van and bus.

Gift Set 25, 1963-66
Shell Gas Station, with five cars, three garages and accessories. Also made as a B.P. Gas Station.

Gift Set 28, 1963-66
Bedford Car Transporter, Chevrolet Impala, Mercedes 220 SE Coupe, Fiat 2100, Ford Consul.

Gift Set 38, 1965-67
Monte Carlo Rally Set with 1965 Mini-Cooper, Rover 2000, and Citroën, all three in Monte Carlo Rally trim.

SPOT ON (GB)

PS 4 "Sports Car Set"
MGA, Jaguar XKSS, Triumph TR3, Austin Healey.

PS 5
Meadows Frisky Sport, BMW Isetta, Goggomobile Super.

PS 6 "Miniature Set"
Fiat 500, Goggomobile Super, Austin Seven, NSU Prinz.

PS 7 "Rally Set"
E-type Jaguar, Daimler SP250 Dart, Sunbeam Alpine Convertible, Renault Floride Convertible, Austin Seven, Ford Anglia Saloon.

PS 8 "Shell Pump Set"
RAC Land Rover, Volvo 122S, Ford Anglia Saloon, Rover 3000, Sunbeam Alpine Convertible.

PS 9 "Public Service Set"
Wadham Ambulance, Jaguar Police Car, United Dairies Milk Float, NSU Prinz, RAC Land Rover, Routemaster Bus.

PS 10 "High Street Set"
Rover 3 l, Vauxhall Cresta, Renault Floride Convertible, Daimler SP 250 Dart, Routemaster Bus, United Dairies Milk Float, Fiat 500, Austin Seven, Artic. Bedford 10-ton tanker, Morris 1100.

PS 14 "Presentation Set"
Car, Dinghy and Trailer Set, Austin A40, Mulliner Coach, Sunbeam Alpine Hardtop, Rover 3 l, United Dairies Milk Float.

Gift Set 702
Zephyr Six, Morris 1100 and Canoe, Austin 1800, Dinghy and Trailer.

"Tommy Spot Series"
— all with different folding cardboard pieces (houses, buildings, garages) and figures.

801 "Home"
Hillman Minx, Ford Zephyr Six.

802 "Cops'n Robber"
Jaguar S, BBC 2 Car, robber, policeman.

803 "Services"
Austin 1800, Austin Healey Sprite, garage attendant, mechanic.

804 "Sailing"
Vauxhall Cresta and Dinghy.

805 "Fire"
Land Rover and Trailer, two firemen.

806 "Royal Journey"
Royal Rolls-Royce with H.M. The Queen, The Duke of Edinburgh, driver, footman and six Horse Guards.

807 "Pit Stop"
Mercedes 230 SL, Jaguar S, two drivers.

808 "Motorway Rescue"
Crash Service Land Rover, A.A. Minivan, A.A. man, mechanic.

MÄRKLIN (D)

5521 RG/4, 1936-37
Mercedes racing car (5521/1), Auto Union (5521/2), Auto Union (5521/12), Alfa Romeo (5521/14) and a driver.

5521 LG/4, 1936-37
Touring car (5521/3), Cabriolet (5521/4), Limousine (5521/7) and Truck (5521/19).

5521 G/6, 1936-37
Mercedes racing car (5521/1), Auto Union (5521/2), Touring car (5521/3), Cabriolet (5521/4), Limousine (5521/7), Mercedes racing car (5521/11)..

5521 S/2, 1936-37
Aerodynamic car (5521/6), Mercedes racing car (5521/11), Auto Union (5521/12), Alfa Romeo (5521/14), Bluebird (5521/18) and Truck (5521/19).

MERCURY (I)

N°51 Scatola 8 Pezzi, 1947
Construction kit to build models n°7 (Caravan), 20 (Limousine), 21 (Spider), 22 (Tipper truck), 23 (Crane truck) and 24 (Tanker).

N°45 Scatola 6 Microauto assortiti, 1951?
Limousine (41/a), "Farina" spider (41/b), Lancia Aprilia (41/c), Maserati F1 (42/a), Auto Union (42/b), Mercedes F1 (42/c).

N°46 Scatola 10 Microauto assortiti, 1951?
Limousine (41/a), "Farina" spider (41/b), Lancia Aprilia (41/c), American-type saloon (41/d), Maserati F1 (42/a), Auto Union (42/b), Mercedes F1 (42/c), Tipper truck (43/a) and Tanker (43/b).

N°137A, 1950
Spring-loaded catapault, two special racing cars (Auto Union and Mercedes) and finish signs with metal bases.

N°84 Scatola Scuderia Ferrari, 1966
5 Ferraris (4 Spiders, one 250 LM) with spare wheels and engines.

N°85 Scatola Serie Fiat 850, 1966
Fiat saloon, spider and coupé.

N°82, 1966
Fiat 682 transporter with trailer, with moving parts.

N°83, 1966
Fiat 682 transporter with four cars, moving parts.

N°95, 1966
Fiat 682 transporter, with moving parts.

MEBETOYS (I)

Rallye, 1969
Porsche 912 (A-33), Opel Kadett (A-34), Mini Cooper (A-31) and Lancia Fulvia (A-32).

Prototipi, 1969
Chaparral 2D (A-23), Ford Mk II (A-24), Porsche Carrera 10 (A-25) and Ferrari P4 (A-27).

REVIVAL'S AUTO UNION 16-CYLINDER

After the Alfa Romeo P3 and the Mercedes Benz W 154, the latest product to come from the Casadio brothers is the 16-cylinder Auto Union of 1936-7. The Bologna company was rescued in 1981 by Stefano Serattini and Sandro Bergami, and the kits are now sold under the name "Revival". Like its predecessors, the new kit is to a scale of 1:20.

It was at the end of 1933 when the first news broke of a revolutionary new Grand Prix car from Auto Union, with its engine rear-mounted ahead of the rear axle, all-round independent suspension, a fuel tank mounted between the driver and the engine and a very forward position for the driver. It has to be remembered that this was 1933, not 1983, to prove that there is nothing new in Formula 1! This marvel, which was eventually to be produced in three versions, was powered by a superb engine with 16 cylinders in a 45°V formation. There were two valves per cylinder, operated by a single overhead camshaft mounted in the centre of the V. It operated the exhaust valves by means of pushrods and rockers, but the inlet valves were operated directly. Three different engines were used between 1934 and 1937; the first developed 296 hp from 4360cc, the second extracted 340 hp from 4290cc, and the final type C, which is the one which concerns us, developed 520 hp from 6 litres. Another variation was the R, used in the 1938 record car. Developing 545 hp it had a capacity of 6330cc. Between 1934 and 1937 the three types (A, B and C) took part in 83 races and hill-climbs, gaining 42 victories, notably in the hands of such great drivers as Hans Stuck, Achille Varzi and Bernd Rosemeyer. The C type, the last of the 16 cylinder models before they were replaced by the 12 cylinder D and E types, raced in 1936 and 1937. It took part in 34 races and won half of them. Revival modelled the only remaining example of the car, now in the German Automobile Museum.

Out with your files!

It must be said from the outset that if file work does not appeal to you, this is not the kit for you — particularly in view of the relatively high price. On the other hand, if you enjoy working with metal, fashioning it and finishing it, you will have many hours of satisfaction which will add immeasurably to your model making knowledge.

The Revival kit contains 264 pieces, mainly in metal. Presentation of the kit is good, but moulding quality of both the plastic and metal parts is not above criticism. For this reason, the Auto Union is not a model for the beginner, and the modeller will need a fairly extensive tool kit, particularly a wide selection of fine files of varying shapes and a set of watchmaker's screwdrivers.

The building instructions are satisfactory, but only just, and modelling experience will be helpful. Photographs and drawings of the real car, such as those in these pages, will be more than useful.

Two general points should be made before discussing building the model, because they are applicable throughout the building process. First, it is vital to clean up and check-fit every part, and second, it is indispensable to clean out the holes which are to receive screws. A simple screw in and out will do — gently, because the screws are easy to break. Another general tip is that the movable parts should be given a drop of oil, particularly in the suspension assemblies. Finally, do not forget to equip yourself with epoxy or cyanoacrylate adhesives to join the metal parts.

Assembly

Diagram 1 When joining the left and right sides of the engine block and gearbox, file down the mounting spigot for the water pump pulley so that the two halves fit correctly. Take care not to remove so much material that the spigot is weakened. The casting of the exhaust manifold is not quite perfect, and it will be necessary to separate the pipes with a fine-bladed saw. The small chrome "organ pipes" of the exhaust will need work too; filed at an angle at the bottom to get the right inclination backwards, they will also need to be filed at the top to give the correct angle. The final touch is to take a little material out of their centres to reduce the thickness of the pipe and then paint the interior of the pipe in dark matt grey. (Well adjusted engines do not leave black deposits!) The vertically mounted supercharger is very well reproduced, comprising no less than 26 pieces. The air filter supplied with the kit was not really satisfactory and it was replaced by a mesh held in place with a piece fabricated from white metal of a suitable guage.

Diagram 2 The front chassis cross-member is mounted too far back; it should be on the level of the footboard, not between the seat and the fuel tank. This is not a big fault, but it does spoil the accuracy of the model. When mounting the front axle, which will need a fair amount of filing, take care to clean out the holes for the fixing screws in the chassis and to make the necessary adjustments to the lower parts which receive the suspension springs. Construction of the pedal assembly will show that the bell-crank levers of the brake and clutch pedals are much too long. In fact, that of the brake pedal should not be there, for the pedal operates directly on the master cylinder — a part which is missing from the model.

Assembly of the suspension is complicated and demands great care. The two front suspension arms should not be filed at the point where they join the brake drum except in cases of absolute necessity because if the small ball-joints are made too small they will create a degree of play

An Auto Union team workshop as it might have looked in 1937. In the background is the bodywork for the land speed record car — 6.3 l., 545 hp, one and a quarter tons — in which Rosemeyer averaged 406.3 km/h (252.5 mph) after two runs on the Frankfurt-Darmstadt autobahn on 25 October 1937. The model is still in its out-of-the-box state here, the over-heavy paint job masking a lot of the details. The body of the GP racer has been reworked as described in the main text. Tools and figures in 1:20 come from a Tamiya kit; the trestles were made in balsa.
A lot of work went into the model's engine, especially on the air intake and exhausts. Here Revival supplied only bits of chrome tube which had to be bored out to thin them down and then have the ends filed at an angle so that they would slope backwards.
The two filler caps were filed and turned on a lathe, and the rivets, which had got rubbed away with the paint, were replaced with watchmaker's screws. The two metal windscreen supports were scratchbuilt; the perforations were simulated with matt black paint.

in the system that will make it impossible to keep the front wheels parallel to each other. The transverse bars of the rear suspension should be thinned down and the spring cages cleaned up in order that the suspension can operate freely. This is quite a delicate operation.

Assembly of the steering poses some problems, principally because the worm of the steering gear is mounted off centre on the steering column. The degree of eccentricity is so large that the steering wheel cannot be turned when the steering box is assembled. The only remedy is to clean up the worm gear, but it is likely that this will introduce an unacceptable degree of play at the steering wheel. It is a shame that this has spoiled the manufacturer's efforts to create a steering mechanism that would work.

Diagram 3 The instructions Revival give for fixing the fuel tank mean that it cannot be painted before being fixed in the chassis, and it is therefore difficult to avoid glue marks showing up. It is, however, possible to glue the two halves of the tank together before mounting it in place; sand off the excess glue, paint it, and fix it by simply pushing it into place. The same criticism and subsequent procedure also holds good for the transverse seat supports.

The grille material supplied for the oil and water radiators is too coarse, and is furthermore supplied bent into a plastic bag which makes it difficult to fit. We replaced it with a finer guage of material in brass.

The seat will need to be modified because the backrest is not so rounded as that provided by Revival. Filing it away above the level of the armrests will give it the necessary flatter profile. The covering material was fabric, rather than the leather which Revival have simulated in rubber. In addition, there should be a roll to support the driver's thighs. The seat covering supplied can be utilized to make a cover for the head rest padding.

Diagram 4 The bodywork supplied by Revival can be considerably improved. Although the colour is accurate, the coating of paint is too thick and the moulding quality leaves much to be desired. The real car had a natural aluminium finish which was protected by a coat of clear varnish, so we took the following course. First, the existing paint finish was completely stripped. Then the entire body was filed and rubbed down with fine glasspaper before being polished with a fine metal brush mounted on an electric drill, and finished off with silver polish. The result of these operations is a surface which looks as if it has been chromed. It is an attractive effect, but it is not realistic. Realism is achieved by spraying a couple of coats of matt transparent lacquer (we use Humbrol No. 49) and after these have dried the result is perfect. In the course of polishing the body, the screws which fix the various panels were rubbed away. They were replaced by drilling fine holes with a 0.5 mm drill and opening up the holes to accept watchmaker's screws with a diameter of 0.75 mm. These have heads 1.2 mm in diameter and filled the bill admirably. We also fabricated the fixing points for the front panel with the aid of small rubber rings.

Diagram 5 The dashboard comprises a rev counter and four dials. These were not mounted in circular housings as suggested by Revival, and it will be necessary to remove the four circles moulded in the plastic, together with the rectangle below the two left-hand dials. The pipes for cooling water and oil have to be formed from a brass rod which is folded in three to make it fit in the box — the result is a patience-testing bending job. The fixing rings need not be painted; they were black in the full-size car.

Diagram 6 Once again, the builder will arrive at the final stage marvelling at the quality of the Casadio wire wheels, which are nothing short of perfection. Still, negative comments must be made about the four parts which fix the windscreen in place, and which are nothing like the real thing. We made up two supports from fine metal channels and painted side supports onto a replacement windscreen that we had made up from plastic sheet. Again, watchmaker's screws were used for fixing.

The well detailed tyres will need sanding down to get rid of the whiskers left after moulding. The caps for the various radiators and tanks will also need work to give an appearance of reality — they are, in fact, only roughly finished as supplied. The radiator grille, in plastic, is unfortunately too thick and is too low in comparison to the real thing. It needs to be 25% higher, and correcting this fault means making a new grille.

Having finished the model, we found that we had made a profit of one part which we could not identify on the plan. It was a small handle which didn't seem to fit anywhere. It was regarded as a small dividend for the hundred or so hours of work we had spent on the model!

Building a Revival model is no piece of cake, and it must be reiterated that it is a job for an experienced modeller, otherwise there is a danger of grave disappointment after a great deal of work. For those who have the confidence and the skills to carry out the job, however, there is great satisfaction to be had in a task which is at times nearer to watchmaking or working with jewellery than to merely building a model car.

A valuable photograph for the kit builder; the picture shows that the upper rear part of the engine has been skimped on the Revival Auto Union, that the pipe carrying the cooling liquid is of slightly conical shape, and that the tube carrying the ignition cables is absent from the model, as are the bars which support the radiator. By following the photograph, a number of points can be improved.

NITTO'S HONDA CB 750 F TURBO

Nitto's 1:8 Honda CB 750 F Turbo is made up of over 250 pieces, moulded in glossy black, black, red, aluminium, chrome, clear, clear red and clear orange. The kit is based on the 750 F which appeared last year, and the mouldings are so little changed that there are some twenty or so pieces not used at all in the construction of this model. The kit is well presented, in a box bearing a fine illustration of the bike, which is very helpful when building and painting the model. Our review kit came direct from the manufacturer in Japan, so the instructions were in Japanese, which made the task of building a little more difficult, particularly because they were not as clear as they might be. Versions of the kit exported to Europe and the United States have their instructions in English. A useful section of the leaflet was the page that illustrated every part with its description and reference number.

Satisfactory construction of this kit requires a detailed study of the plans beforehand and a great deal of care during the building procedure. The plans do not indicate those areas of the parts to which cement must be applied, but careful study and a degree of pre-assembly will overcome this and with care a fine result can be achieved, although the finished model is not without its imperfections. One of the problems which arises is because the way in which the parts have been laid out on their stalks has not been sufficiently well thought out, particularly so far as the chrome pieces — which are all on a base of black plastic — are concerned. Two particular examples are the handlebars and the exhaust pipe, on which it is impossible to disguise the ugly black marks left when the parts are removed from their stalk. The only recourse is to Bare-Metal or silver paint, and neither of these remedies is completely effective. Even the "Turbo" decal applied to the exhaust is insufficient to cover the marks. While on the subject of decals, it must be said that those supplied are of high quality, but that the supporting film is a little too matt and shows up on the gloss-finished parts.

Moulding quality is good, but the join between the two halves of the mould is too apparent in many places, requiring extensive trimming work on those parts where it is possible. On some, it is not, particularly the plated ones, and they have to be assembled in a less than perfect state. Painting the model therefore needs a great deal of attention, and it was found that an experienced modeller needed some 30 hours work to achieve a satisfactory result.

Assembly of the engine poses no problems, even if the two elements of the left rear locating stud are some 2 mm out of register. It is a fault which has no influence on the look of the finished model. The aluminium plating was of uneven quality, particularly on the engine, and seemed to have taken much better on the parts formed from black plastic than those in white. The lower engine casing colour is excellent, much better than that of the engine block itself.

There are two ways of approaching construction of the frame: either it can be carefully trimmed and assembled, and then painted red, or it can be left unpainted and assembled with the greatest possible care, avoiding marks from excess glue. In any case, it should be finished off with a coat of Humbrol Fuel Proofer, a clear lacquer which gives the completed assembly an excellent finish. Parts A4 and A5, the mounting brackets for the stand, must be positioned very accurately and we found that the best procedure was to mount the footrest brackets H15 and H16 without cement, then to mount A4 and A5, applying cement only to the central hole which fits over the transversal support of the frame. When the cement is dry, remove H15 and H16 and apply cement to the forward part of A4 and A5 where they form the mounting point for the footrest brackets.

The kit offers the option between battery-operated illuminating head and tail lamps and a more detailed representation of the real machine's battery and fuse gear. We chose the latter and found that the results were particularly good, especially after the detail on the fuse box had been painted in with a very fine brush.

The wheel rims are magnificently reproduced, their colour finish being very good, and the same is true of the tyres. The only painting necessary on the wheel assemblies is to give the centres of the discs a coat of red. Special mention should also be made of the rear suspension units, which are beautifully made and operate perfectly. Nitto have proved with this model that it is perfectly feasible to reproduce a full-size suspension system on a 1:8 model. The springs, which are metal, should be painted red, and give the model real style. The fixing marks for both parts of the shock absorbers cannot be eradicated, but if they are mounted with the marks towards the front they will hardly be noticed.

Mention should also be made of the use of metal for the axles and in the steering, which ensures easy operation. The front suspension is equally easy to build so that it operates satisfactorily, but some care should be taken during assembly that the chromed tubes, E11, are not touched with bare hands; Nitto's chrome is tough, but it does tend to mark easily with fingerprints. The fork casings are of the

But you can't really ride it: this is the model. Nitto's Honda is excellent, though it doesn't have the perfection of a Tamiya (nor, of course, the same scale; Tamiya's big kits are in 1:6). The decal supporting film is a little too matt — most noticeable on the exhaust — but for other things, such as the working suspension and the well detailed engine, all praise is due. The chrome guard on the exhaust was covered with Bare-Metal. Don't forget to paint the fuse box if you want to take advantage of the removable side panels when exhibiting your model.

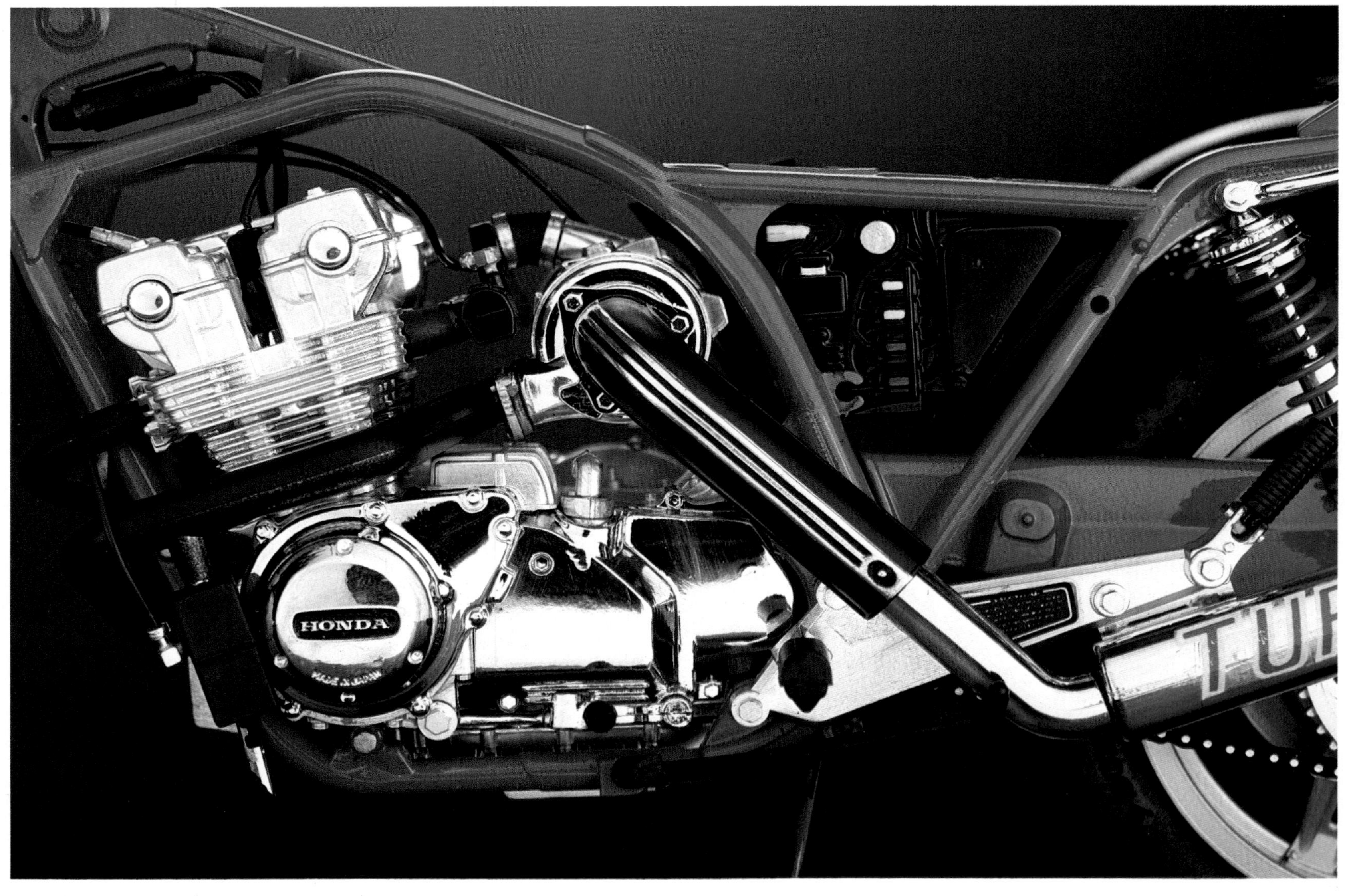

HONDA
TURBO
TURBO
HONDA

correct colour, and will not need painting if the two halves are assembled and cemented carefully.

In the course of building the fork head, it will be noticed that the hole in H6 which receives the left-hand headlamp support, J45, is a little too deep. This was handled by fixing the two supports, J44 and J45, in H6 provisionally, glueing the headlamp and then the upper points of J44 and J45 into the fork triple clamp, I13. Be careful when placing the front wheel that you do not forget H8, the speedometer drive, or you will have to disassemble everything to mount it later. The front mudguard, moulded in glossy black, will have to be painted red for authenticity. H10 and H11, the front indicator mountings, will need some work with a round file to make sure that they fit properly into the lower triple clamp, H16.

The upper part of the exhaust pipe (G14) must be carefully scraped at the point where it is cemented to its support (G23) if a satisfactory fit is to be obtained. This solidity is important when it comes to fixing the "Turbo" decal on the pipe. The two halves of the pipe are an imperfect match, and the appearance of the finished component will be improved by an application of Bare-Metal or aluminium foil. At this stage of assembly it must be noted that the chain guard should also be painted red.

Thus we arrive at the assembly of the pipework for the turbo. Supplied in chrome, it is shown in matt black on the box top, a colour which looks better and gives a better overall look to the model. Watch out when mounting the waste-gate assembly made up of parts I4, I15, H12 and G26. Pipe G26 should be mounted towards the inside, as shown in drawing 14, not facing forwards, as in drawing 19. It is no use looking at the box top for guidance; this assembly is not there.

Although the instructions say that the handlebar controls should be painted matt black, we feel that the natural colour is perfectly suitable, and so long as care is taken in the glueing process, no paint is needed.

Painting the Honda name stamped in the crankcases is an easy matter, requiring only that the rectangle containing the name be painted in black. When the paint begins to dry, take a soft, lint-free cloth dipped in thinners and carefully wipe it across the surface so that it removes the paint from the raised areas only. Take care not to press too hard, or paint will be removed from too much of the area. A final light polish from the same cloth will restore the shine to the plastic and leave the Honda name picked out in chrome against a black background.

The body parts (the two halves of the tank, two side panels, and the saddle tail fairing) are supplied with a glossy black paint finish which had traces of dust in it in the sample we received. Since the tank would show an obvious join with assembled, it was decided to re-paint these components to give an improved finish. The original paint was removed using 1200 wet and dry paper and water, and a fresh coat of glossy black was applied after the two halves had been cemented. The decals were then applied and the whole given a coat of fuel proofer to give a superb finish.

The cables supplied by Nitto are perfectly to scale, a rare find in motorcycle kits, and something which is to be applauded. The final touches are to paint the saddle in satin white, with the fixing points for the lifting strap in chrome, and the result is a fine-looking model. Two small points remain to be noted: parts E2 (the drive-sprocket cover) and J33 (the guide-ring for the speedo drive mounted on the front mudguard) are not marked on the two diagrams in which they appear (16 and 11 respectively). Perhaps this sounds pedantic but it is indicative of the shortcoming of this Nitto kit — the general conception is excellent, but it is let down by faults in small details.

Nitto included this photo (in colour) with the kit. A helpful move, but a photo of the real bike Nitto modelled would have been better. In an exhaustive search of the American and German press — the bike once appeared at the Cologne show — we found not one picture of it. Sad to say, Nitto could supply nothing and, to burn the last bridge, American Turbo Pak, who built the turbo, have now closed down and destroyed all their records, including photographic.

MONOGRAM'S KENWORTH W-900 VIT CONVENTIONAL

King of the Road is the prestigious title awarded by America's truckers to the rugged Kenworth trucks. It's a title justifiably earned by the Kenworth Motor Truck Company with the dependable trucks it has produced since 1923.

Kenworth's roots go back to the Gerliner Manufacturing Company that was established in Portland, Oregon, in 1915. Two years later the company changed its name to Gersix, and the location was changed from Portland to Seattle, Washington. Then in 1923 the two principle stockholders of Gersix, H.W. Kent and W.K. Worthington, combined their last names and formed Kenworth Motors Truck Corporation.

In 1944 Kenworth became a wholly owned subsidiary of the Pacific Car and Foundry Company (PACCAR). Peterbilt is also a subsidiary of PACCAR, but fierce competition remains between these two fine truck manufacturers. Though they both have the same parent company, they are operated as separate businesses with each striving to produce the best quality truck available through engineering, testing, and listening to the requests of modern day truckers.

Ease of maintenance, ruggedness and the ability to get the job done are not the only considerations in updating and adding new features to the Kenworths. Driver comfort, appearance and lightweight construction are also important factors.

This is especially true of rigs designed for independent truckers, and Kenworths certainly fall into this category. Although some large fleets use Kenworths, most are purchased by small fleets and owner/operators. Kenworth, bearing this in mind, has been innovative in making available many options designed to appeal to this segment of the buying public. One option is what Kenworth calls VIT — Very Important Truck. This includes a walk-in double sleeper, deluxe interior with high-back air-ride seats and of course a wide variety of exterior paint schemes, colors and interior color combinations. The VIT package is available on both the W-900 highway conventional and the K 100 cabover. It was introduced in 1974 and has been one of the most popular options ever since.

The producers of *Moving On*, a popular American TV series that followed the travels of a trucker, chose the Kenworth W-900 Conventional VIT as the star of its series. AMT released a model of the *Moving On* Kenworth in 1:25 scale a few years back, but it lacked the double sleeper and thus wasn't authentic.

In August 1981 Monogram released the second in its series of 1:16 scale trucks, a Kenworth W-900 Conventional with the VIT package included. This followed a Peterbilt 359 Conventional, which was released in 1980, and will be joined by a Kenworth W-900 Aerodyne Conventional in September 1982. Monogram probably chose the Peterbilt and the Kenworths as its first issues in 1:16 scale because they have turned out to be the best sellers among the many brand names released in both 1:25 and 1:32 scale. This, too, indicates the popularity of the Kenworth.

Monogram's Kenworth is a large kit, 20 inches (50 cm) long, whereas a Conventional in 1:25 scale would be only from 10 to 12 inches (25 to 30 cm) in length depending on the wheelbase. This larger size naturally lends itself to details, first in what the manufacturers can include in the moldings and second in what the modeler can add.

The kit is entirely plastic and does not include metal parts among the total of 272 parts plus decals and instructions to be found in the box. It is molded in two colors. The chassis and engine is black and the hood/cab/sleeper parts are red.

Plated parts are of two varieties; the traditional bright chrome pieces and the rest in a dull finish which gives the appearance of polished aluminum. The plated parts are well done and the molding on all parts is crisp and virtually free of flash. There are some clear plastic parts too, of course. The tires are vinyl one-piece Michelin radials and have an authentic appearance. The decals included are in four colors, orange, brown, butterscotch and black, as pictured on the kit's box art.

The kit features a 450-horsepower Caterpillar 3408 Diesel with a displacement of 1099 cubic inches (18 litres). The truck rides on Kenworth's Airglide 100 suspension which provides a comfortable ride on eight air bags.

By following the instructions included and taking one's time, a realistic model will result, but with additional effort an even better replica can be built. Since a Kenworth can be ordered with a wide variety of optional components and can even be ordered with a customer-designed paint scheme in a limitless choice of colors, it is correct to build or paint your model in a variety of ways. In other words, you can build and paint your truck to your specifications just as you can order it the way you want Kenworth to create it for you. Naturally, this must be done within the realm of the available options keeping in mind you want the finished model to look like a genuine big rig you might see on the road.

Although most of the instruction sheet sequences and painting tips are correct, a few improvements can be made. For example, in step 30 the instructions indicate orange should be painted as the background color of the numbers on the emblems that are molded on the heads. The correct color for this is yellow.

Kenworth paints all its engines white. A Detroit, Cummins or Caterpiller Diesel cannot be distinguished by its color in a Kenworth. After examining a number of real trucks, it was discovered that the transmission may be painted either white, to match the engine, or following the basic body color.

As indicated in step 37, the radiator should be painted aluminum. However, part 99, the radiator shield, should be painted white.

As mentioned earlier, Monogram has added the feature of polished-aluminum-like plated parts. The fuel tanks are one of the major components utilizing this feature. Since either polished aluminum or chrome tanks can be ordered for the Kenworths, this is a correct option. However, when a brushed aluminum tank is used, it is usually mounted with chrome mounting straps, and a layer of rubber is placed between these chrome straps and the tank. To obtain this look, the straps which are molded on the tanks should first be painted black. Next, chrome tape should be placed on top of the painted black surface, allowing the edges to show.

Chrome tape should also be used on the air filters for their mounting straps.

The quarter fenders on most of Ken-

The interior trim on the W-900 cab — viewed here from the walk-in sleeper box — makes it look more like a deluxe limousine than a utility truck. Monogram molded the dash in some detail, but it takes a few hours of careful painting to reproduce the wood panels, chrome instrument trim and numerous control switches. Right: Detail of the mirrors, air filters and exhaust stacks — all of them giant size — that surround the cab. Below: the biggest turbocharged Diesel found on American trucks, the CAT 3408. Monogram's reproduction of it lacks many details and it would surely have been easy enough in 1:16 scale to include the various cables and lines.

The King of the Road — the W-900 Conventional VIT, every independent trucker's dream and Kenworth's pride and joy — a minimum of 75,000 dollars worth of Big Rig. The one here (top) has a roof spoiler and shows the correct proportions for the radio's antennas — we substituted piano wire for Monogram's oversize plastic parts on our model. Above: The kit before the antennas were replaced and the spoiler added. The pogo stick — a device designed to support the air and electric lines to the trailer, as shown at left — should be added at the rear of the cab and surely should have been included in Monogram's kit.

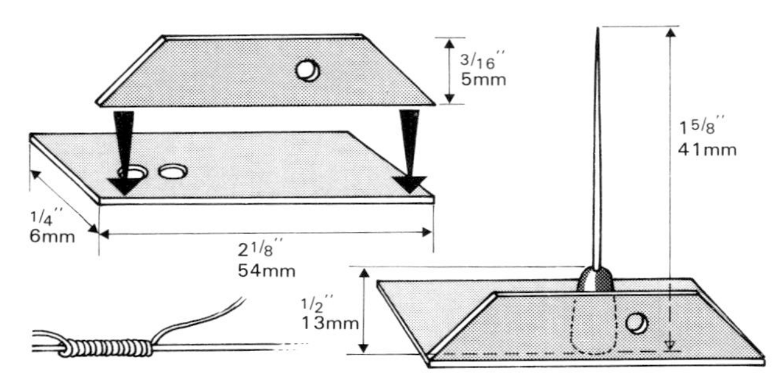

To model the pogo stick, cut out two sheets of polystyrene to the size indicated on the diagram, punch three holes for the cables and glue the pieces edge to edge at right angles to each other. Then cut out a 1/2 inch piece from a plastic kit runner and round off the top where a 1/8 inch diameter aluminum rod will be glued on. The cables, here fine electric wires, should be wound tightly around a toothpick to give them the proper shape before mounting.

worth's luxury trucks are chrome and not the body color as indicated in steps 49 and 50 of the instructions. On most of the new Kenworths, the top portion is now white instead of black, with the Kenworth name in red lettering. Commercially available red transfer lettering can be used to accomplish this task.
The clear lenses included in the kit that are used on the marker lamps, tail lamps and turn signals should be painted the proper colors. Marker lamps and front of turn signals should be amber. The tail lamps and rear of turn signals should be red. A suitable medium to accomplish this is the glass stain marketed by a number of manufacturers including Pactra. It should be available in a well stocked craft shop.
One mistake in numbering was discovered in step 70. Parts 257 and 46, the support braces for the mirrors, should be switched. Part 46 should be used on the drivers side mirror and part 270 should be used on the curbside mirror.
Semi-gloss black paint is an important part in detail-painting the Kenworth W-900. Areas that should be painted black include the windshield rubber molding, the background of the Kenworth emblems located on the sides of the hood and sleeper, the end of the exhaust stacks, the rubber stripping on top of the cowl on which the hood rests and, using a thinned wash, the grill.
As indicated earlier, multicolor custom-designed paint schemes are familiar sights on the Kenworth VITs. These can be accomplished by masking the designs of your choice and using the colors you prefer. It is recommended that a fine-width tape of complementary color be used between the various colors painted on your miniature rig. This accomplishes two things; first, it covers the area between the colors where a bit of seepage may have occurred under the tape used for masking and second, by using the right choice of colors, it adds to the color scheme.
Our truck was painted using cans of spray paints. Two coats of light grey auto primer were applied to all the non-plated parts. Duplicolor auto touch-up paints were used to apply the color scheme and design we chose for our truck. The chassis was given three coats of T90 universal black metallic. The hood/cab/sleeper parts of the truck were first painted with three coats of DS-TO 50 medium metallic green. The truck was then masked with Scotch magic tape in three steps with DS-FM 190 deep, almost black, green, DS-TO 53 lime green and DS-GM 243 gold lime green being added in that order.
Green, orange and light blue matt crepe tape manufactured by Chartpak was then applied to complete the color scheme.
If you want to add a personal touch to your truck by naming it after yourself or giving it a ficticious company name, or to copy the lettering of a real truck, you should use transfer lettering or decals.
Additional details such as pogo stick, air and electric line, roof mounted air deflector, hood mounted bug deflector, engine plumbing and brake lines are missing from the kit but can be added fairly easily to this large scale model. Schedules being what they are, not all of these could be included in the model pictured here.
A bug deflector was cemented to the hood of our model. It was cut out of a sheet of green transparent acetate originally designed to be used as a color sheet for an overhead projector. Chrome tape was applied to the bottom edge of the deflector and it was cemented to the hood using a cyanoacrylate adhesive. The deflector is an optional item that many truckers add to their rigs.
The pogo stick was constructed from sheet plastic, aluminum tubing and insulated small gauge stranded wire. The deck plate was moved back so it was against the fifth wheel plate and the pogo stick cemented in place in front of the deck plate.
In comparison to the other truck models that are available today, Monogram's Kenworth Conventional is an excellent kit. The parts fit together well without requiring excessive work and time. However, there are still a few areas we would like to see improved in this kit in particular and in many truck kits in general. For example, some of the transparent plastic parts should be molded in amber and red instead of clear plastic, and the fuel tanks should be molded differently — preferably as a complete unit minus one end. This would require only one end to be cemented in place and would eliminate the distracting parting lines so clearly seen as a verticle line on the ends of the tanks. It would also be desirable to have the various pipes (particularly the exhaust and air breather) molded as a solid piece, if possible, thus eliminating the parting lines which result when cementing the halves together. An additional feature we'd like to see added to the kit would be two lengths of fine piano wire in scale for the CB antenna. The plastic pieces included are too thick, and were replaced with suitable piano wire on our model.
Since Monogram released this fine model, Kenworth has updated its W-900 Conventional truck, adding many engineering improvements and giving it some changes in appearance. Not content to rest on its many past achievements, Kenworth continues to be a leader in the trucking industry worthy of that proud King of the Road title.

The W-900 VIT's sleeper box is covered throughout in imitation leather. Access to the cab is through the curtains (on the left), past the generous storage space; the door here is to the outside. All this plush upholstery is not just for show, mind — it also helps keep out the noise of things like the compressor on a reefer trailer.

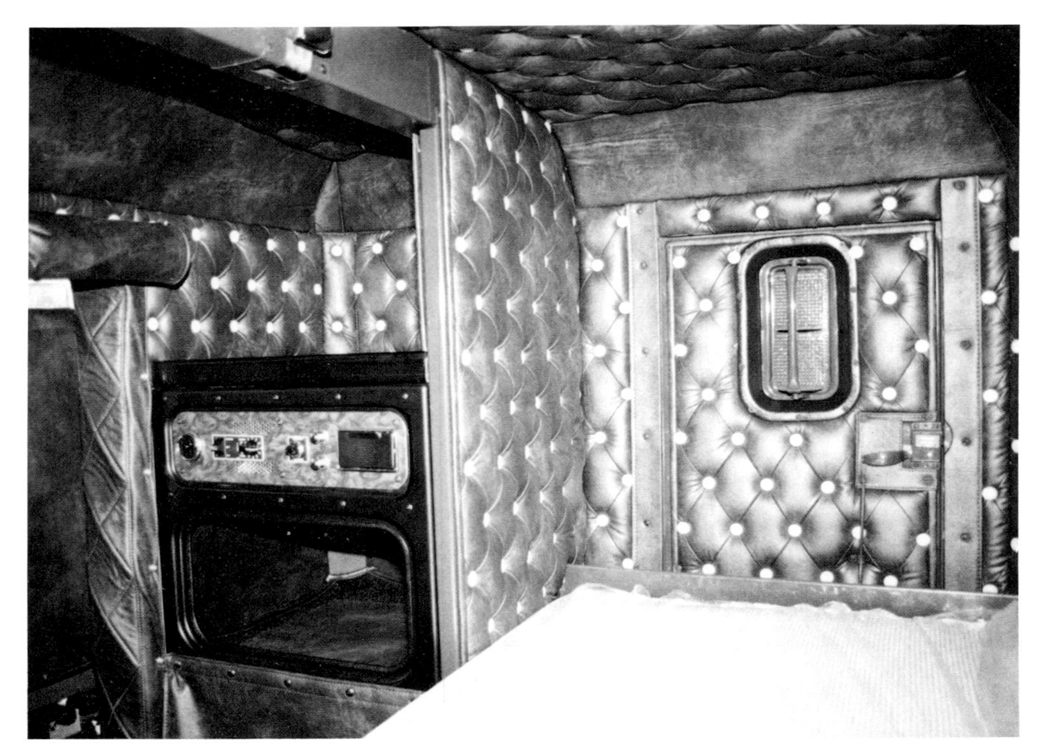

ESCI'S MERCEDES-BENZ 450 SLC BANDAMA

In 1977 Mercedes-Benz entered four 280 E saloons in the London-Sydney rally, quite an event because it had been over two decades since the German manufacturer had been active in automobile competition. The results were sufficiently good for Mercedes to decide to enter the world championship, with their 450 SLC, specially prepared to take the beating of international rallying. In 1979 a 450 crewed by Mikkola and Hertz was entered for the Safari Rally in Kenya. They finished in an encouraging second place behind Mehta's Datsun. After a short pause to correct transmission problems revealed in the Safari, four 450s were entered in the Bandama Rally, to be driven by Mikkola, Waldegaard, Preston and Cowan. The cars performed unbelievably well, finishing in the first four places, with second places in New Zealand and Argentina's Codassur Rally coming later. Then came a decision which surprised everyone: Mercedes decided to withdraw from the rally scene completely at the end of 1980.

The Bandama Rally in Ivory Coast is among the toughest in the world. Like the London-Sydney, Safari and Paris-Dakar it is a pure rally, which means the highest possible speed in bad country, with navigation not as important as in such events as the Monte Carlo Rally. In these rough-country rallies the cars take terrible punishment and need comprehensive modifications as far as components such as suspension and transmission are concerned. The engine and transmission are well protected from the underside and the gearboxes are beefed-up considerably. Often, sufficient engine cooling is a problem because of the heat, and extra air filters are needed to deal with the ever present dust. The passenger compartment is made safer with a roll cage which also stiffens the body, thus improving the endurance. Rallies like this eat tyres, so it's obvious that running such cars can cost a small fortune, and they are not something for private people. Rally cars that stand a chance of winning cost four to five times their catalogue price, plus the cost of the service teams, spare parts, gas and so on. In fact, the only way most people can get their hands on one is by building a plastic kit — so let's try!

The Esci 1/24 scale kit of the Bandama 450 is quite simple and with a little attention can be made into a fine looking model. The Cartograph decals provided are as usual of excellent quality and encourage the builder to do his best. Here's how I made my Rally Mercedes.

I started by cleaning up the body. Moulding seams were carefully scraped off with a sharp knife, sanded with fine emery paper and finally polished with fine steel wool. Next I applied the decals according to the instructions and set the coachwork aside for the decals to dry for 24 hours. Meanwhile I assembled the engine and other small parts. When the decals were dry I washed off all the excess glue. After this the body was given a coat of matt varnish (any type will do, diluted with 50 percent thinner). This coat serves to protect the plastic when weathering, because thinner eats plastic. The varnish should be allowed to dry for about three days. Meanwhile, the bonnet (hood) was spray painted matt black and the decals applied.

When the varnish was dry the body was given a wash with thinned Raw Umber oil paint. This was allowed to dry for a few minutes and then neatly wiped off with a rag damped with a little turpentine until only a little paint remained in the grooves and a light film covered the rest, giving the impression of dirt and producing in the model an effect of depth. When the oil paint was completely dry the details could be painted. Afterwards a coat of semi-gloss varnish was applied to seal everything off and the whole was set aside to dry.

After assembly of the engine it was spray painted with a mixture of 60 percent silver and 40 percent black, as were the wheel rims. This coat was sealed with matt varnish and set aside to dry for a couple of days. These parts were also given a wash with Raw Umber, wiped off when still wet, and when dry they were drybrushed with silver paint.

To drybrush — the word means exactly what it indicates — take a wide, flat brush, dip it in thick unstirred paint taken from the bottom of the paint jar, wipe the brush on a dust-free rag until it leaves no more streaks and then gently float it over the parts to be treated. This technique is excellent for bringing out detail, because the paint only adheres to raised parts. You should therefore always drybrush with a lighter shade than the base colour of the parts.

The engine was finished by painting the detail. For the exhaust manifold I used Humbrol Brown Matt 29.

Next the interior and chassis were assembled, keeping the rollbar, seats and dashboard apart. These were spray painted matt black and, when dry, gently polished to obtain a semi-gloss sheen. Dashboard details were painted before

Even though a picture can speak a thousand words, and in this case show with what artistry François Verlinden transformed the Esci kit into a miniature version of the real car, only his text can reveal the craftsman's secrets. Note especially the tiny traces of rust on the bonnet, the stains on the windscreen and the impeccable weathering on the bodywork. The same care went into the interior with its safety belts and maps, the engine in all its perfection, and the diorama base with its rocks and mud. Just for the record, two errors in Esci's decals; Suède instead of Sweden and Thorszelius misspelt without the S.

The real car or the model? Only one detail betrays the 1:24 kit: a slight moulding fault on the wing mirror. But can't you just feel the wind drying that bush, don't you get some of the dust of Africa's wide-open spaces in your eyes?

This photo of the Mikkola/Hertz car — one of the four Mercedes 450 SLCs in the Bandma Rally 1979 — shows a couple of details Esci didn't include; protective metal spats in front, mud flaps on front and back wheels, and radio antenna. Still, there's nothing to stop you making your own from a sheet of polystyrene and a hair from a nylon brush.

assembling the whole. Leather parts like the steering wheel and gear-lever cover were lightly drybrushed with Burnt Sienna oil paint. The safety belts were cut from paper tape, painted, decals applied and fixed to the rollbar and seats. A couple of road maps cut from a pocket diary added realism, as did the chipped paint effect on the engine hood and other areas. (To achieve this chipped effect, a dark metal colour, a mixture of black and silver, is applied with a fine pointed brush. It's also a good way to make scratches.)
The engine was now mounted together with the exhaust pipes. The latter were painted with Humbrol Matt 29 and drybrushed with Humbrol Rust Matt 62. The transparent parts were fitted to the body, but not before I had cut a template to match the areas covered by the wipers and sprayed the windshield very lightly with Humbrol Matt 29.
Now the body could be fixed to the chassis. The tyres were made matt with steel wool, mounted on the rims and fixed to the chassis. The tail lights were painted red from the inside and, with the mirrors, wipers and door handles, fixed in place; the headlight reflectors were painted silver and the transparencies glued in. I made headlight guards from fine wire mesh and glued them to the tubular frame. I also applied the chipped paint effect to this frame and the engine-transmission guard. Some rust stains (unthinned Burnt Sienna) on the underside gave the final touch.
To simulate the coat of red-brown Bandama dust I sprayed a very light coat of Humbrol Matt 62 Rust on the front and flanks of the car. Such a job should be done very carefully because a heavy coat would spoil all the previous detailing and weathering.
You can make a diorama baseplate out of any simple piece of hardboard, plywood or its equivalent cut to the appropriate size. A 1 cm wide edge is taped off, and rough terrain is made with plaster or modelling clay of some kind applied with a knife or slice. Here, some pebbles and large pieces of gravel were pressed in this paste to simulate rocks. Then some sand and fine gravel were sprinkled on and the whole was wetted with a mixture of white glue, water and red-brown waterbase paint, thus fixing all the ground material. The tyre tracks were made with a tyre from the spares box. Finally, the model was pressed into the prepared base, the tape on the edges carefully removed and the whole assembly set aside to dry.
The Esci model — a definitive reproduction of what is, being the last of the competition Mercedes, a historic car — provides an ideal opportunity for using the weathering techniques so dear to specialist and military modellers. Easy to build, as finely moulded as we have come to expect from this Italian firm and, with top-quality decals, this kit will take a proud place in any modern car collection and perhaps turn a few more modelling hearts towards rally cars.

Conscientious modellers with a bent for superdetail have plenty to go on here. The Mercedes team photo of the interior of the 450 SLC rally car shows clearly the non-series steering wheel — three spokes instead of four — the speed pilot, trip master, radio and microphone, and roof-mounted map-reading light.

★★ TAMIYA

past, present and future

Mr Yoshio Tamiya — known throughout the company and the plastic model business as Y — is the man who created Tamiya at a time in his life when most other men would have been contemplating retirement.

Since the appearance of its first Formula 1 model, the R273 Honda, in the mid sixties, Tamiya has steadily established itself as the company by which other model-car makers are judged. With a range which has now grown to cover a wide variety of racing and road vehicles, Tamiya is perhaps best known for its 1:12 Formula 1 cars. Each new addition to the range is eagerly awaited by enthusiastic modellers because of the unique blend of accuracy, high quality materials, realism, and sheer building pleasure it will provide. On the two-wheel side, Tamiya's 1:6 motorcycle kits are similarly well regarded, while recent years have seen the company's range of radio control models bringing a new standard of realism to radio control car racing.

The man who brought all this about, Yoshio Tamiya, was born on 15 May 1905 in Shizuoka City, the town where he has spent all his life and which is still the headquarters of the company which bears his name. His father was an enterprising businessman whose main interests lay in the production of Japanese tea. The tea business left two lifelong interests with the young Yoshio Tamiya — from the machinery used to process the tea came a fascination with all forms of mechanisms, and from the end product itself came a love of the tea ceremony, that unique custom which embodies so much of the Japanese philosophy in its combination of tranquility, contemplation, and the appreciation of beauty. To its devotees, each element of the tea ceremony combines to create the perfection of the whole — the comparison with a superb kit is obvious, and perhaps gives an insight into the Tamiya philosophy.

When Yoshio was twenty, his father gave him 2000 yen, which he spent on the purchase of a Ford Model T truck. At this time rickshaws and horse-drawn vehicles were the main means of transport in Shizuoka, and the would-be transport operator found strong resistance from the more traditional enterprises — no doubt as much influenced by his youth as by his use of new-fangled methods. Young Yoshio had inherited his father's business skills however, and by 1930 he had a thriving business. Like the rest of the world, Japan was hit by an economic depression in 1932 and 1933, but careful management saw the business, by now one of the biggest in the area, safely through it. In 1939, the effects of the war between China and Japan were beginning to be felt, and a government decree was issued which called for small transport companies to join together to form larger groups. In line with instructions, the Tamiya enterprise was linked with those of two of his friends, but a later decree required that these newly-created units should come together once more to form even bigger groupings. In the Shizuoka area, fourteen companies were forced into a single entity.

Shunsaku Tamiya, son of Y. Tamiya, is president of the Tamiya Plastic Model Company and the man in charge of its day-to-day running. A graduate in criminal law, he joined the company in 1958. By combining modern business methods with an enthusiasm for models and model-making he has helped the company to keep in touch with public taste.

Yoshio Tamiya was appointed a director of the new company, but after a year he resigned in a disagreement over policy. The same year he saw his bus services taken over by a combination of government policy and enforced take-over. In a few short months everything he had worked for since he was twenty had disappeared.

By now Japan was involved in the Second World War and Tamiya set up a factory to produce sub-assemblies for fighter aircraft. On 19 June 1945 Shizuoka City was the target of a raid by U.S. Air Force B-29s, and the factory was completely destroyed. The end of the war came soon after, and with it the insurance which had been taken out against war risks became just so much useless paper. With debts amounting to 60,000 yen, Yoshio Tamiya was presented with the task of starting his business life all over again.

Following the advice of friends, the field which Tamiya took to in an effort to rebuild his business was that of timber. He set up a sawmill, and then had to buy an area of forest in order to provide his mill with raw material. For three years he

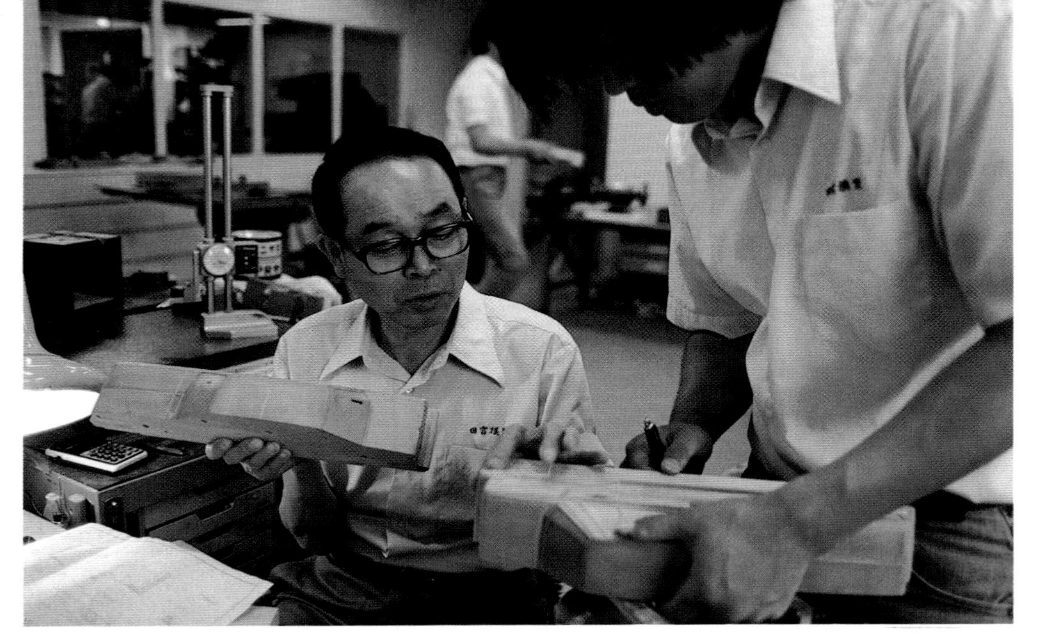

Midway between the designer's board and the finished mould. This is where the drawings are translated into three dimensions for the first time and the designer can get a better idea of how the finished model will look. One designer is responsible for each model right the way through, from the first pencil strokes on a blank paper to the final successful test shots from the injection moulding machine. Personal pride that his model is just right ensures that each designer upholds Tamiya's high quality standards.

This NASCAR Dodge was Tamiya's first tentative step in modelling competition cars. The overall shape is evidence of the fact that the modellers were already doing a good job, but when you compare the decals with those on such modern Tamiya kits as the Porsche 935, the progress made is obvious.

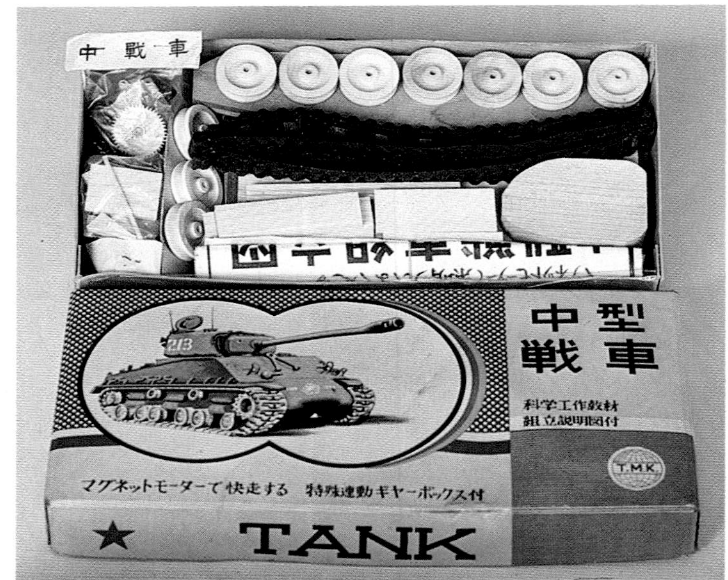

This tank kit marked Tamiya's transition from a timber company to a model-making company. With its wooden body and rubber tracks it sold in sufficient numbers to show that a market for scale models existed. Military models still form the backbone of the Tamiya range and are the company's most consistent sellers.

The high quality of Tamiya's box art is well known. The paintings are prepared at the Shizuoka headquarters by company employees, and this policy of self-sufficiency also covers such fields as photography and catalogue production, all of which is done in house.

The lower floors of Tamiya's giant administration and technical centre house a series of injection-moulding machines which are used for the test shots of new models. Once new moulds have been passed for production here they go on to the production department or to one of the many independent moulders who work on the job of turning out components for the company.

These are the first modellers to get their hands on every new Tamiya kit. Their full-time job is to build models for test and display purposes, and their skill is so developed that they are able to build even the most complex models in a fraction of the time the average amateur would need. Despite the fact that they spend all their working hours making models, they — like everyone else at the company headquarters — are enthusiastic modellers in their own time.

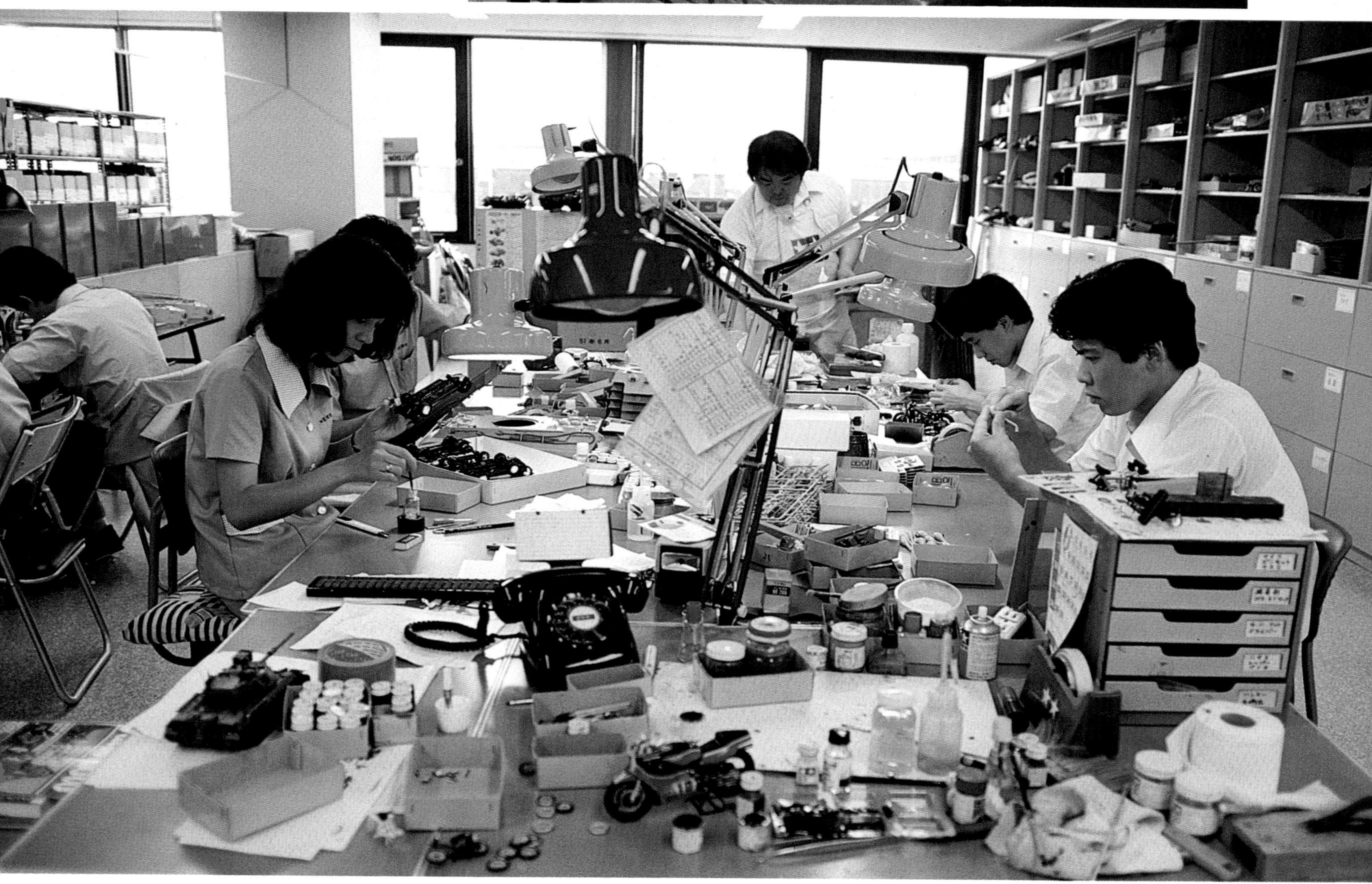

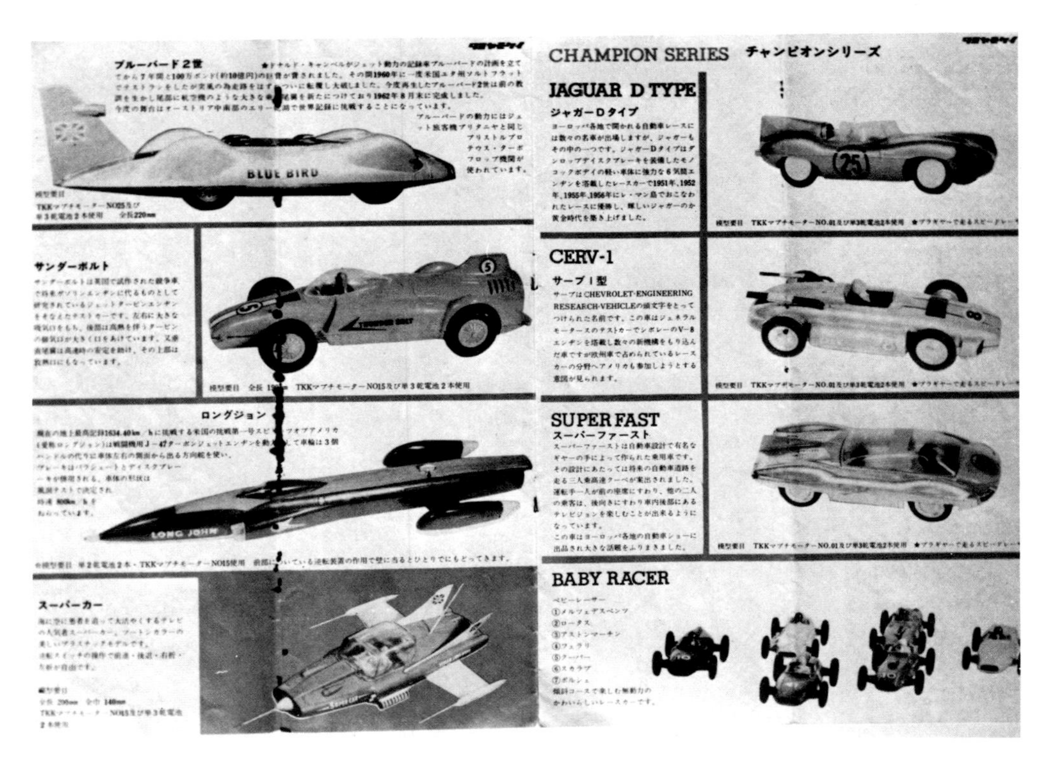

A Tamiya sales leaflet of the early sixties combines reality and fantasy with models like the Bluebird record car, Chevrolet CERV 1 dream car, Jaguar D-type, and the Supercar featured in a contemporary British children's TV series.

hardly saw his desk, joining his casual labourers as they cut and trimmed the timber. In 1948 Mr Tamiya's elder sister's son, Fumiwaka Tamiya, came home from a concentration camp in Siberia and set up a new department for the manufacture of wooden models. It might not have been appreciated as such at the time, but it was a historic step.

There was another major setback ahead however, for in October of 1951 the factory and a large stock of timber was destroyed in a fire. It was a disconsolate Yoshio Tamiya who sat down with local bank chairman Kitaro Otano at his home soon after the fire. Talking more as a friend than as a banker, Mr Otano counselled Mr Tamiya against taking a loan. "Sell for cash, buy on credit, and build up the confidence of your customers," was the message he gave, and it was a message which Mr Tamiya still lives by.

Within two months, the sawmill was operating again, and as time went by the model department became more and more successful. It was so successful, in fact, that when raw material became scarce in 1953, it was decided to close down the sawmill and concentrate on models. In 1958, soon after Yoshio Tamiya's son Shunsaku joined the company in charge of the Planning Department, they produced their first plastic model kits. A new era had begun.

In the years that followed Shunsaku Tamiya began to take a more important part in the company's development, and his father made a number of visits to the USA and Europe in order to study the market and local products — at that time acknowledged as the best in the world. The firm was making good progress in the Japanese domestic market, and in 1966 it took on the task of expanding its exports sales and duly appointed a number of distributors. Many of those distributors still handle Tamiya products and have grown with the company.

In 1967, Tamiya made its first official appearance at the Nuremberg Toy Fair. Although its main line of products was — and remains — the 1:35 Military Miniature series of tanks and military vehicles, the company was becoming well known for its Formula 1 cars. Starting with the Honda, and followed by the Matra MS 11 and 1968 Ferrari, the name of Tamiya was becoming synonymous with complexity and accuracy (although there was a rare lapse of accuracy as far as the Matra was concerned — Jackie Stewart never drove the Matra-engined MS 11 in a race, as one might infer from the box art and decals).

Since then the company has gone from strength to strength with a range to meet all tastes. Yoshio Tamiya, now 77 years old, is still Chairman of the board, but day-to-day control of the company lies with Shunsaku Tamiya, President of the Tamiya Plastic Model Company since Fumiwaka Tamiya's death in 1977. Two more of Yoshio Tamiya's sons are also involved in the company's operations, sharing their father's interest in models and model-making as a hobby and a business. A symbol of the stature of the Tamiya company today, only 24 years after its first tentative steps in the field of plastic kits, is the impressive new building which houses the Engineering Division. The massive entrance hall contains some of the full-size vehicles which served as references for the Tamiya designers who were turning them into plastic kits. On the top floor, safe from prying eyes, there is a test track laid out for prototype radio controlled models. In between lie the many departments which go to make up the totally self-contained unit which produces every Tamiya kit. Here are the designers, the mould-makers, all the researchers, the artists who produce the box art, the men who write and photograph the instruction books, and the many others who also have a part to play.

In typical Japanese fashion, the president's desk is just like any other in the large open-plan office, and so are those of the other senior executives in the same area. It is easy to see that this is a team operation, and any of the designers can put forward their ideas for future models. Since someone has to take the responsibility, the final decision as to which projects shall be followed through is taken by the president, and he has a track record which shows an incredible understanding of what the market will want.

Once the decision has been taken, the project is handed to the design team. If possible, an example of the original is procured and stripped down to its component parts. This is a simple matter when the vehicle concerned is a new car from a Japanese factory, or a racing motorcycle from Yamaha in Iwata, just down the road, but it is not so easy when it is something like the Renault Formula 1 car. Renault was not prepared to provide drawings of the car, so Tamiya had to work from photographs taken at race tracks. The most difficult job the designers have ever had was a Russian tank which had to be reproduced with only five photographs as reference!

Once the designer has completed the mould drawings, he rolls them up and takes them downstairs with him to the next floor, where all the moulds are produced. He will set up his drawings on a board in the mould-making shop and will stay there until the moulds have been completed and final approval has been given the test shots produced from them. In this way the designer has a personal involvement in every model for which he is responsible, an involvement which carries right through to the finished product. It is

Experience has shown that the simplest way to prepare a new kit is to strip down the full-size vehicle and prepare drawings from the components. Once this job has been completed, the vehicles make interesting conversation pieces for company headquarters, like this P 34 Tyrrell, Porsche 911 and Ford Mutt which grace Tamiya's entrance hall, together with body panels from Tyrrell, Wolf and Lotus Formula 1 cars.

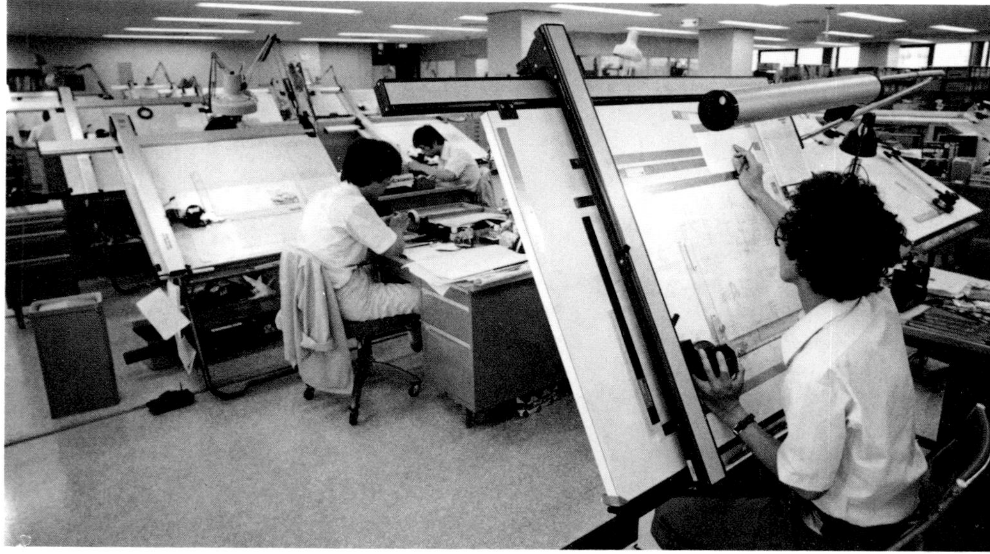

The design department at Tamiya covers one complete floor of the engineering building. Members of the design staff are allotted projects which they see through from the initial measurements of the prototype to the successful moulding of the first sets of parts.

typical of the high standards of Tamiya moulding that no flash is accepted, even on the stalks which support the parts. Modellers whose memories go back even only a few years will appreciate the savings in time — and accuracy — which this exactitude means; gone are the days when instruction sheets read "Remove the part from the stalk and carefully remove all flash." Thanks to companies like Tamiya, with their increasingly higher standards, today's modellers know no such jobs.

An important aspect of the design process is the way in which the parts are laid out on the stalk, and this is an area which receives a great deal of attention. The layout of the parts is not only decided in view of the relative size of the parts and the space available for them; the way in which the molten plastic will flow during the moulding process must also be considered, as must the way in which the various clusters of parts will fit together when they are put into the box, avoiding the danger of contact damage during shipment. Another important aspect given that plastic is petroleum based is that waste should be cut to the minimum, thus reducing unnecessary cost. The general hard work put into detailing by the designer and mould-maker is obvious to the modeller, but their extra attention tends to go unnoticed.

There are over 20 designers at Tamiya, all capable of working on any kind of model. Sometimes a designer will specialize in one field of modelling because of his personal enthusiasm for a particular type of vehicle, but in the main, versatility is the keyword.

Like many Japanese businesses, Tamiya operates with a relatively small work force and relies on a large number of subcontractors who supply it with components. There are some 600 or so small injection-moulders in the Shizuoka area who supply the company with parts. The majority of them are former Tamiya employees who have been set up in business by the company's policy of offering senior employees the opportunity to start on their own with Tamiya equipment that has been replaced by more modern plant before the end of its useful life. In addition to these local suppliers, Tamiya also draws on some 2000 other companies around the country.

Tamiya's product quality is not achieved by secret production processes or space-age technology, but by pure and simple high standards. Certainly these standards require that the company is equipped with the most up-to-date equipment, but it is the thinking and conviction behind the use of that equipment, rather than the equipment itself, which achieves the required quality. There is an unspoken philosophy which says that if the results will not be perfect, then Tamiya will not undertake the job.

Tamiya's commitment to quality has brought its own reward, and the company currently sells some 35,000 kits per day in Japan and 65 other countries. It comes as a shock to a westerner, used to seeing Tamiya kits in every model shop and regarding the company as one of the biggest sellers, to find that only 30 percent of production is exported, and the Japanese market is by far the most important in terms of quantity and profit. Exports are growing slowly, however, and the company's executives are well aware of the possibilities such trade could hold for Tamiya. There is a continuing dialogue with the distributors in other countries, and Tamiya personnel make a number of trips abroad each year in order to keep in touch with what is happening. There is evidence that the market is an expanding one as more people realize the pleasure to be derived from building a realistic model.

Tamiya's policy is to stick with the realistic end of the market. TV tie-ins are not part of its marketing philosophy, and the firm prefers to turn out kits which will

Overleaf: Photographed in the factory's own studio, the full range of classic Tamiya 1:12 models. They are arranged chronologically, starting in the top left-hand corner with John Surtees' F1 Honda of 1967 and providing a review of motor sport over nearly fifteen years. After the Honda, the other models are: Lotus 49, Porsche 908, Lotus 49B, Matra MS 11, Lola T70, Ferrari 312B, Datsun 240 Z, Tyrrell-Ford 003, Datsun 240Z.G., J.P.S. Lotus 72D, Texaco Marlboro McLaren M23, Yardley McLaren M23, Martini Brabham BT-44B, Ferrari 312T, Porsche 934 Turbo RSR, Tyrrell Project 34, Lotus J.P.S. MkIII, Martini Porsche 935 Turbo, Wolf WR-1, Ferrari 312T4, and the Renault RE20. ▷

HONDA
SURTEES
GRAHAM HILL
TEAM LOTUS
TAKI RACING TEAM
JAPAN
NISSAN MOTOR
elf
Shell
YARDLEY
YARDLEY McLAREN
MARTINI
brabham
GOODYEAR
HEUER
Agip
MARTINI PORSCHE
MARTINI RACING
DUNLOP
Walter Wolf Racing
Castrol

10
LOTUS FORD
5
MATRA F1
John Player Special
TEXACO-Marlboro
TEXACO
5
Marlboro
GOOD YEAR
8
Jägermeister
MAX MORITZ
24
elf
3
Valvoline
5
MICHELIN
RENAULT elf
11
Agip
16
RENAULT

have a long life. The Military Miniatures series is a prime example of this thinking, with a wide range of realistic models to a common scale. The appeal is directed at the dedicated modeller, and sales are regular and long-term rather than spectacular and short. The same policy shapes the company's thinking on its Formula 1 range, with each car staying in the range for a long time.

A common question asked by committed European and American modellers is why Tamiya have no Grand Prix cars from the past in their range — it would seem that in terms of a vehicle which could have a long production run, unaffected by the vagaries of fashion, a Maserati 250F or an E.R.A. would be ideal. The answer to this one lies in the 70 percent of Tamiya sales made in Japan. The Japanese market is largely unaware of historic racing cars, but is very aware of what is happening in Formula 1 today. A vast range of well-produced racing magazines whet the appetites of Japanese modellers for such kits as the Ferrari 312T4 and Renault RE20. Tamiya would be foolish not to cater to this already existing desire, and one can only hope that as exports to the west become more important the company will think more about historic cars.

It is an interesting reflection on the way in which the market is influenced to hear that in the past couple of years the demand for Formula 1 cars has dropped significantly, no doubt as a reflection of the public's disgust at all the political wrangling which has overshadowed the racing. The new trend, reflecting public interest in the real thing, is towards 1:12 motorcycles, both road and racing, and 1:24 passenger cars. In response to this shift of opinion, Tamiya will only be issuing one F1 car per year, in 1:12 *or* 1:20, and will be stepping up its production of motorcycles and saloon cars.

Handiwork is the secret of successful mould making, and skilled craftsmen will spend hours polishing the mould surfaces with a number of tools and products depending on the degree of detail and the job in hand. This picture shows work proceding on the preparation of the mould for the 1:12 Yamaha YZR 500 Grand Prix motorcycle (note the drive chain and sprockets at the bottom left hand corner of the picture).

Everywhere you look in the Tamiya design centre there are models in assembled or half-assembled form. This department is not only responsible for designing the models, but also for producing the instruction leaflets that accompany the kits and explain the intricacies of construction in words and pictures.

What can the modeller expect in future kits — how can one improve on what many feel to be perfection? It would seem that the first changes will come from developments in electronics. Light-emitting diodes (LEDs) are now small enough to provide scale-size light sources for models, and we should soon see accessory kits which will give operating lights and turn signals for cars and realistic flashes for the gun-barrels of tanks.

The trend towards complexity seen in Tamiya's F1 cars and 1:6 motorcycles is likely to continue. Not only have younger modellers become more skilled, and thus able to cope with the detail; the work involved in such kits and the sense of achievement in their completion have taken them out of the world of "toys" and widened their appeal to adults. The average age of Tamiya's customers used to range from 10 to 16 — it now runs from 10 to 25.

Although the actual building is the biggest part of the attraction of a model once it has been bought, the purchase decision is still most influenced by the appeal of what is portrayed, so we can expect models to continue to be made of interesting vehicles rather than purely for the modelling challenge they present. However, the main improvement will still come from the same source from which most improvements flow — experience and improving technology.

This then is the past, present, and future of Tamiya. It is a company where everyone, from the founder and president down, is an enthusiast. Everybody at the Shizuoka factory makes models for their own amusement and satisfaction, and this involvement in the hobby shows in the attitude of the personnel and the kits they produce. Their enthusiasm breeds perfection and brings in profits — surely an ideal situation in the hobby industry. The Tamiya family's business sense is tempered by a love of the product and, in the time since they produced their first plastic kit in 1958, respect for the modellers of the world who have shared in their success.

In a way, they are victims of that success, for every modeller has a pet prototype which he would like to see produced as a kit to Tamiya standards, and Tamiya executives must harden themselves to a never-ending succession of pleas of "Why don't you make..." every time they meet an enthusiast. My request? Well, Mr Tamiya, if we can't have a Maserati 250F, how about a model of that Model T truck that started it all back in 1925?

THE PROFESSIONAL MODELLER

An interview with J.-P. Magnette

Belgium can pride itself on always having been in the forefront of motor vehicle production and assembly, and even though it no longer has domestic manufacturers of the quality of Minerva and FN, it still houses highly efficient assembly plants for many of the major manufacturers.
Following on that tradition is a small assembly plant which has been established since 1977 some 30 kilometers (18 miles) to the east of Brussels. However, this is not the usual type of building one would expect to find in an industrial estate, but an assembly plant to 1:43 scale, split between a student's bedroom and the back of a garage.
The site is an attractive white house in the countryside of Brabant, a green and pleasant region which reminds many people of the English county of Sussex. Among the trees and bushes of the peaceful garden I made the acquaintance of Jean-Paul Magnette, a man of unusual talent and skill. Twenty-five years old, black hair, spectacles with narrow metal frames, a lop-sided smile, and a white apron on which the enthusiast can make out spots of colour like Ferrari red and Bugatti blue. This is the man who files, polishes, glues, assembles, modifies, paints and decorates a range of model cars — of which 90 percent, in the best Belgian tradition, are exported.
In the bedroom, shelves hold a batch of Porsche 935 "Moby Dick" racers which await packing. On the corner of the table a dozen Alfa Romeo 33s shiver in their nakedness, awaiting the red coats they will receive in the spray booth. The bookshelves hold serried ranks of books and magazines which contain all the vital reference material. All over the place are paintbrushes, files, tweezers, tubes and pots of paint, and crowded like flowers in old cream and yoghurt pots are bunches of colourful decals. It was in this setting, with a glass of traditional Belgian beer, that I sat down to interview this one-man production line.
Jean-Paul Magnette described how he started in what is now his business. "I started off like any other boy, with an interest in model cars — Dinky Toys in particular — and when I grew older I started to build plastic kits. I was very attracted towards models that were more realistic than the ordinary toy cars I played with. After ruining quite a few kits, I finally began to achieve satisfactory results and my friends began to comment on the quality of my work. Encouraged by their praise, I took some of my models to the owner of a model shop in Brussels and he was sufficiently impressed to buy some from me and exhibit them in the shop, where they drew the attention of his customers. That's when I began to see that there was a demand for my work.
At the time, I was still a student of law and I saw modelling purely and simply as a hobby, but the demand for models became more pressing and my studies less and less interesting until the point in 1977 when I had to take a decision about my future. I set myself up on my own and began to work. My hobby had become my business."
With that background information about the man and how he started established, I took a draught of my beer, switched on my tape recorder, and settled down to interview Jean-Paul in earnest. The transcription of our conversation says it all.

AYBM: Do you consider that there is sufficient demand that one can look upon model-making as a profession?

JPM: Yes; it's all because of the problem of time. Collectors just can't keep up with current production and they start to come up against the well known problem of cupboards full of unmade kits. What is supposed to be a pastime becomes a chore. That's what gave me my start, because collectors were very happy to find someone who would build their kits for them. Obviously there are any number of small builders who will do that, but they only work in an irregular fashion. I'm available practically 24 hours a day, and I do nothing else. In the beginning, I was building small quantities — two of this, three of that — but I soon saw that it wasn't profitable to rely solely on the market I could find in Brussels. Even the whole of Belgium wasn't really enough, and I began to realize that I had to start working on a bigger scale. Then by chance I met a dealer from Paris who was interested in a nice 1:12 kit of the Alex-

A very specialized workshop built into a garage: the professional home of Jean-Paul Magnette. At the back, the painting booth (originally a car-garage shot-blasting cabin) and compressor; on the right, the bench where the kits are put together; on the left, the paint store.

ander Calder BMW M1 made in Japan by Otaki. He asked me to work for him and it was through him that I met André-Marie Ruf and began to build his models in quantity.

AYBM: A hot question, this one — what do you think is the future for kits?

JPM: Personally, I think that there are enormous possibilities. People are thinking more before they buy and they are no longer buying any old thing, so there is a selection process in operation. There is also a great improvement in the quality of kits — just look at one of the early John Day productions alongside one of today's kits. There is great competition between manufacturers, so they have to improve quality to keep up. New manufacturers start up and old ones close down. The biggest problem comes from production techniques, moulding in particular. Most firms produce in small, irregular, quantities but, among others, Western Models and AMR are real professionals with a regular clientèle for their models. Certainly the current economic crisis will have repercussions on the business and will cause a slowing-down in demand, especially from the younger modellers, because it is difficult for a 15- or 16-year-old to pay 1000 Belgian francs (20 dollars) for a kit, and unfortunately there are many toy firms whose products were the mainstay of a beginner's collection in the old days that have just ceased to exist. Perhaps I'm being over-optimistic, but I believe the kit has a healthy future.

AYBM: You say that most manufacturers produce in small, irregular quantities, and yet what do we see in the shop windows? Always the same Ferraris and Porsche 935s!

JPM: Yes, that's a good example; there are far too many doubles. What is needed is a certain amount of co-operation between the manufacturers. It is possible, because some of them already do it. On the other hand, others set out to produce the same models as their competitors just as soon as they learn what their rivals plan to introduce, in the hope that they can make it faster and better than the other company. The result for the collector is uncertainty and discouragement, because he does not know which model to choose and he cannot afford to buy them all. This profusion of doubles puts the collector off to the point where he becomes interested in larger scale plastic kits, where there isn't the same confusion, or turns to the more serious mass production manufacturers.

AYBM: In this battle between plastic kits and metal kits, which side are you on?

JPM: I receive hardly any orders for plastic kits to be built up apart from a few display models for shops. I know that there is a certain reticence on the part of collectors so far as plastic kits are concerned because there is a general impression that plastic will not last, but I wonder what will become of some white metal kits after a few years — I think there might be some unpleasant surprises in store. On the other hand, it must be said that plastic — and resin in particular — enables much finer detail to be reproduced than in metal and that it is easier to assemble, with much less preparation necessary. Resin is more fragile, but I think that technical progress will make it more solid.

AYBM: What scale do you work in?

JPM: Only in 1:43, because I am a specialist in building models to this scale. All my tools are chosen because of their suitability for work on models of this size, and this enables me to achieve a degree of automation. At first, I built a lot of Tamiya 1:12 kits, and I learnt the business through them. At the moment, there is such a glut of 1:43 models that there is a move towards scales like 1:24, which enable a builder to create real masterpieces, like the Western Models Maserati 250F. The detail is reproduced more effectively and they don't take up too much space on the shelf. They have a spectacular side that you can never achieve in 1:43.

AYBM: Because of the nature of your work, I suppose that you must have to be a colour specialist?

JPM: Colour is a very special topic. It's a long time since I stopped working with small pots of paint like the ones which you see in model shops, except for finishing small parts. Now I have a professional-quality spray booth with a compressor and a spray gun. I do a great deal of research into different paint products in order to find those that are best suited to work on models, and it's not easy. The method I use at present is to give a model three coats, one of primer

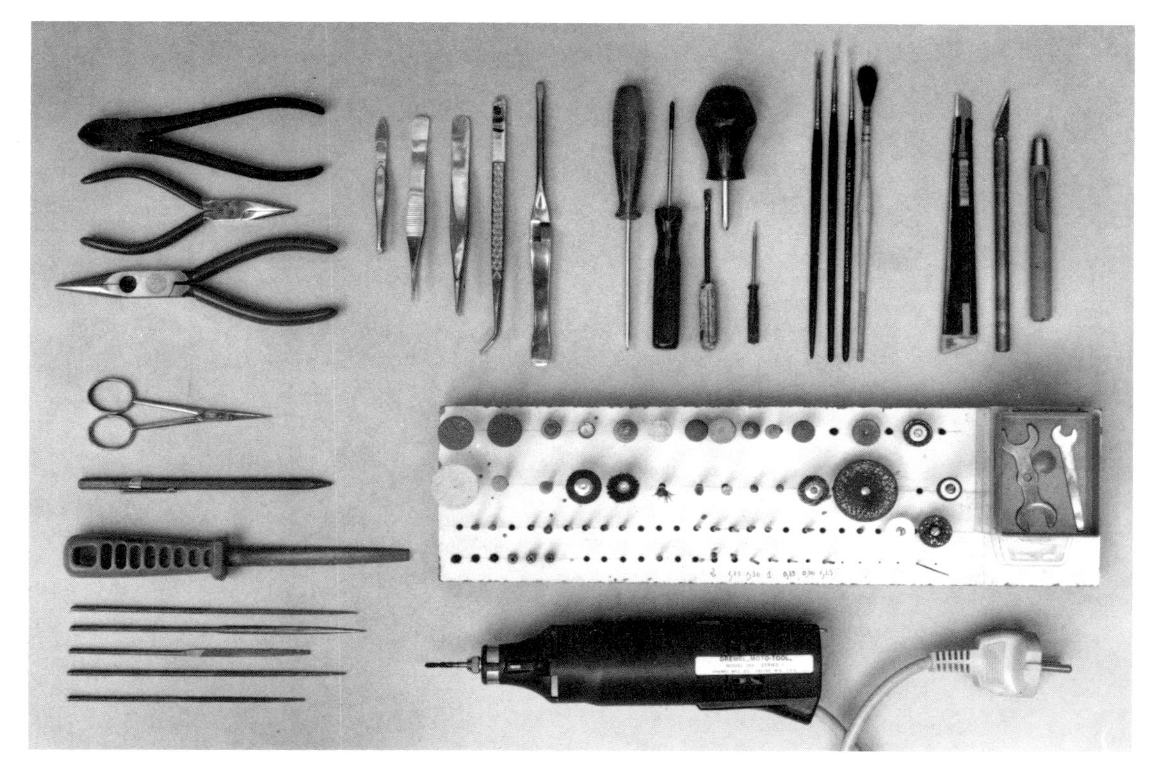

The professional modeller's basic tool kit. "It's not always possible to find exactly what's needed. The tools that are generally available are not always solid and reliable." Still, according to Magnette, the Dremel drill is well adapted to modellers' needs.

For aesthetic reasons, Magnette wasn't wearing his protective mask for this photo. The spray booth is, of course, "fitted with an extractor fan, which is absolutely necessary, not only for reasons of hygiene, but also to extract the overspray and any dust that might be floating about."

Some American firms produce a complete range of professional-quality equipment: booths, extractor fans, compressors and spray guns. This small Paasche booth, No BBF-2' (24 × 18 × 18 ins), is ideal for modellers. It is not exported.

The amateur kit-builder's nightmare... and Jean-Paul Magnette's bread and butter. He builds models in series of up to two or three hundred.

and two of top colour. For the primer I use a cellulose paint which has good sticking power, covers well, and dries quickly. For the finishing coats, I use a synthetic enamel which gives a glossy finish but which dries more slowly. Synthetic enamel is better than acrylic finishes because they don't have such a good finish or high gloss. Acrylic needs to be finished off with polish, and that's not always possible on small surfaces.

So far as colour is concerned, that's enough to make you tear your hair out. To do it right, you have to see the real car. Photographs, even in colour, can't be trusted. You have to make the colours a little lighter, because the small surface of a model has a tendency to make the colour look darker. For instance, Alfa Romeo red is almost bordeau when you put it on a 1:43 model. Fortunately, in most cases I can get hold of the manufacturer's colour specification, and from that I can find the shade that is exactly right for the model and which will give the impression of the colour of the real car. I'm not colour-blind, but I do find it difficult to get blues and greens just right.

AYBM: Do you use brushes, aerosols, or spray-guns?

JPM: Like all modellers, I started out with brushes, and the results were disastrous. It's a technique that is very difficult to master, and you really have to have the knack to get a good result. The problems of brush painting are many: spots, runs, dust... You have to use the paint very thin, but that makes the dust more obvious. If you use the paint thick, it takes longer to dry and you run the danger of having dust settle on the model during the drying process. And you have to use a new brush every time! In short, brush painting is very difficult, and I would advise people to use an airbrush or aerosols, which I use for detail work and for painting a number of small pieces when I need them in quantity.

I don't think it is possible to get a professional finish with brushes. The biggest problem is that of dust specks. If you are going to avoid them, you have to thoroughly clean the model. First, take off all the dust with a very clean soft brush. Then degrease all the surfaces with acetone or white spirit and a perfectly clean cloth. If you want to give a model a real show-room finish you can give it a coat of clear lacquer after you have put the decals on, but I don't do it often because I fel that it makes the model too show-room and it doesn't look realistic, especially on competition cars. After you have painted a car, you should always put it in a box pierced with holes to keep it out of the dust but still able to dry.

AYBM: You have progressed from brushes to a spray-gun. What does your professional equipment consist of?

JPM: My painting equipment is a very important part of my business. I had to make a considerable investment in order to achieve satisfactory results. After a number of false starts, my equipment is now based on an Italian Dari compressor of 8 kg pressure. This model has the advantage of variable pressure and is capable of continuous work. It has a large capacity, but it will operate on a very fine spray for the small areas it has to cover. The compressor is a 1 hp unit and it has a 10 kg reserve of air; it's a machine that is perfectly suited to series work and I can do two or three hundred models at a time quite easily, without having to worry about the pressure or the output. As for my spray booth, it is actually a small shot-blasting cabin similar to those that you find in garages. It has a volume of about one cubic meter, which makes it big enough for even large-scale models. Of course, it is fitted with an extractor fan, which is absolutely necessary, not only for reasons of hygiene, as is the mask I wear for painting, but also to extract the overspray and any dust that might be floating about.

AYBM: What about your spray guns?

JPM: I use the same kind of spray gun that body repairers use for retouching. There are different types of gun, depending on the bore of the nozzle which actually sprays the paint. For finishing off details or touching-up, I use a fine spray. For small production runs, I use a medium gun, but for runs of more than 10 models I will use a bigger gun. The main thing to bear in mind is not to skimp on the quality of your equipment.

AYBM: You say don't cut down on quality, but that naturally means expense. How much did your equipment cost?

JPM: The booth cost me 40,000 Belgian francs (800 dollars) with the extractor hood, a compressor will cost around 15,000 francs (300 dollars), and the spray gun will cost between 5000 and 6000 francs (100-200 dollars) for a good one. One thing I have to point out is that it is very difficult to find one source from which you can buy all your painting equipment, including the booth, extractor, compressor and gun. I had to shop around to find all the various elements which were best suited to my needs. I know there are specialists like the Paasche company in the USA who can provide a complete range, but you have to go there and order the stuff yourself because nobody imports it into Europe.

AYBM: From a practical point of view, how do you go about painting a series of models?

JPM: Apart from the chassis, which I paint in batches because they do not need so much care in finishing, I paint bodies one by one. The main thing is to have the coats of paint as thin as possible, because that's the only way you can avoid spots and runs.

AYBM: Are there any hints which you can give to the ordinary modeller who does not have your specialized equipment?

JPM: The success of a model doesn't just depend on the finishing coat. I cannot stress too much the importance of preparing the model for painting. This is a process where patience should always be the rule. Perfect trimming and rubbing-down and an absolutely clean surface are vital for success. The priming coat will show up any surface defects, which can be put right at this stage. I find that Duplicolor matt grey aerosol primer is very good for this job. The working temperature is also important. You will get a better gloss finish if the model is heated during the drying process, for instance by putting it under an electric lamp. Whatever you do, you should not really try to paint at temperatures below 20°C (68°F).

AYBM: Do plastic kits call for a different technique?

JPM: Painting models in polystyrene plastic calls for much more care. I would advise modellers to experiment on a piece of scrap stalk in order to find out how the plastic reacts to the primer, which should be applied in very thin coats to allow it to dry quickly. If you put on a coat that is too thick you run the risk of melting the plastic. Duplicolor primer is OK, but you must be careful how you use it. Humbrol varnish is very good for top coats.

Resin models, on the other hand, present fewer problems and can be handled in the same way as white metal. The one thing to remember is that you must never use paint-stripper if you make a mistake. If you have to take paint off, use a cloth dipped in acetone and rubbed quickly over the surface to be cleaned. If you want a metallic finish, use an aerosol from a car accessory shop and give it a final coat of clear varnish to bring up the shine and give the finish depth.

AYBM: Have you any experience of restoring old models?

JPM: My speciality is building kits, and I don't have too much experience of restoring old models, but I have done a few. The technique is the same as that I use for kits. The first thing to do is to strip the model down entirely and to strip off all the old paint with paint-stripper. I find that Duplicolor stripper works well on oven-fired finishes such as those found on most of the commercially produced zamac models. The paint that has been loosened by the stripper must be cleaned off in a bath of cold water with a small wire brush. It is best to wear gloves when you are doing this, because the stripper can damage your skin.

As we talked, we had moved into the garden, where photographer Eric de Ville was taking shots of Jean-Paul's model of the 1951 Le Mans Cadillac Sedan. Flat on his stomach among the daffodils, he was searching for the ideal angle to show the car against a realistic background. "Never mind floodlights," he muttered, "natural light is the only way." But in Belgium, natural light is not always as bright or as plentiful as it might be, and before long we were in the middle of a typical spring shower. "You know," said Jean-Paul, "our climate often gives me problems with drying paint. Even in the workshop, sometimes the humidity interferes with the drying process of certain paints. I often have to put them in the oven — and with a resin model, that needs a great deal of care!"

Back indoors, I continued my interview by asking Jean-Paul "Apart from painting equipment, which seems to be no problem, do you meet difficulties in finding the other tools necessary for your work?

JPM: In fact, it is fairly difficult, because it's not always possible to find exactly what's needed. The tools that are generally available are not always solid and reliable. Tools for the mass production of models as a specialized trade don't exist, and professional tools cannot be adapted.

I'm thinking of drills, knives, and sanders; there is a small drill made by Dremel on the market which is designed for use by modellers, and I use one for certain jobs, but for others I use a Black & Decker professional model which gives better performance when I have to drill or polish 300 models at a time.

I spend a lot of time either looking for suitable tools or trying to make my own. However, I must not be too defeatist, because progress is being made in this area. For instance, look at the softening agents for decals from America that are so useful when applying the necessarily numerous decals to competition cars. Most amateur modellers will find that the tools currently available to them are satisfactory, but in my case, I have to have access to a tool kit that will enable me to work on large numbers of models at one time. Because of this, I study everything that could help me achieve standardization or even automation.

AYBM: Such automation must enable you to save time. What is the average time

Sam and Miles Collier drove Cadillac Sedan No. 3 to 10th position in the 1950 Le Mans 24-hour race. This 1:43 version is an AMR creation assembled by Magnette.

Variations on a theme: the Solido-based Alfa Romeo 33. The recent disappearance of some of the industrial makers will cut the number of transkits available, and professionals such as Magnette will rely more and more on the semi-industrial and specialist craftsmen.

it takes you to complete a model — and what are your records?

JPM: When I am producing models in bulk, three or four hundred at a time, it needs two or three hours per model from the time I take the parts out of the box to the time I put the completed model back in. As for records, the quickest model to assemble is the AMR Ferrari GTO and the longest is the Ferrari BB 512 from the same company, which contains no less than 97 parts. But it is not always the most detailed models that take the longest time to build. You can spend much longer on some of the less sophisticated kits whose moulding quality is not so high.

AYBM: How could the kit manufacturers make your job easier?

JPM: There has been real progress lately, particularly where small accessories are concerned. For instance, headlamps moulded in a single resin block. Previously, you had to cut the headlamp shape out of thin Plexiglass and try to stick it on as best you could. Photo-etched parts have improved the finish of models considerably by making them more realistic and thus more attractive. At the same time, they make them easier to build. Today every kit manufacturer is trying to turn out more precise and more detailed models. The Porsche Targa from MRF is a good example of this trend — the details are very well reproduced and the number of parts is not excessive. The rear-view mirrors are moulded in one piece with the bodywork, the chassis moulding also includes the front seats and the rear luggage area. This shows that it is possible to make very detailed models without complicating the building process with lots of small parts that have to be fixed. This is the way the manfacturers should be going, I think.

AYBM: Would you be prepared to share all the experience you have accumulated during your career?

JPM: I've already thought about that. Certainly I am ready to accept any form of co-operation. One could perhaps open a school of model-making — why not? The problem is to know how many people would be interested, to find premises, and to work out some kind of curriculum. Anyway, it's an idea to keep in mind.

AYBM: How do you foresee the future of the profession in the current economic situation?

JPM: Not being a kit manufacturer myself, I am completely dependent on the production of the specialists, and I think that they will have no trouble in expanding their production, because the demand is still there in spite of the crisis. Technically, I am equipped to produce a larger output, but unfortunately the manufacturers always stick to the same types of models. It's the problem of the Porsches and Ferraris we spoke of earlier. When he makes models like that, a manufacturer knows he can sell them, so there is a temptation not to make anything else. On the other hand, there are modellers like André-Marie Ruf who only make models which please them, without thinking whether they are going to sell fifty or three thousand. Such as they are, the quality manufacturers will continue to thrive, but there has been a cleaning-up process in the profession, and that will continue. Looking to other countries, I see markets like France and Italy that show a great deal of life, and promise to continue in this manner.

AYBM: Does your profession provide you with a livelihood? What would you do if kits or specialized models disappeared from the market?

JPM: At the moment, let's say that I'm making enough to live an independent life. I am even preparing to move into a new workshop. If specialist models disappeared from the market there would always be something else to do. Models are not limited to 1:43 scale automobiles; there are aircraft, ships... who knows, I could always become a journalist!

AYBM: One final indiscreet question: do you have a hobby outside of model cars?

JPM: Music and the cinema. I listen to an enormous amount of music as I work, and I suit it to the work in hand: lively music for mass production, when I need to get a move on, and something calmer when I'm working on a job that needs patience and attention to detail.

Not even a 1981 German Championship race would have featured as many "Moby Dick" Porsche 935s on the grid as this... one of the many series of AMR models Magnette has assembled, painted and decorated for French craftsman André-Marie Ruf.

World list of model cars

"A complete revision — a total re-make with additions, improvements, and refinements..." That's what we said a year ago in the introduction to our lists of models. We also said the job would not be a simple one — how right we were!
We had hoped to offer collectors new lists of model cars to complete the work started by Jacques Greilsamer and Bertrand Azeme in their *World Catalogue of Model Cars*, lists classified by alphabetical order and chronology. The idea was simple but the method was less than trouble-free; instead of simplifying matters, we made them more confusing...
Justifiably, our critics were scathing, and the only right thing to do is to start all over again from zero.
The new lists are still worldwide in their coverage, as complete as we can make them, and alphabetically arranged under makers' names. Our new policy is to cover one letter per year, starting — naturally enough — with A. In this way we shall have covered the complete alphabet in a mere 26 years, thus ensuring at least one regular feature throughout the first quarter-century of the life of the *Automobile Year Book of Models*.
The new policy will completely replace the system used last year, and we ask our readers to regard last year as a false start so far as our catalogue section is concerned. The new scheme, allied to the annual lists of new models which are an integral part of our annual, will enable enthusiasts to keep their records up to date and thus have an inventory of current and past productions. We crave your indulgence for last year, and hope that our new-style catalogue section will be of sufficient interest and use to make up for a past mistake.

Countries where models are produced are abbreviated as follows:

AUS	Australia
B	Belgium
BR	Brazil
CDN	Canada
CH	Switzerland
CS	Czechoslovakia
D	German Federal Republic
DDR	German Democratic Republic
DK	Denmark
E	Spain
F	France
GB	Great Britain
GR	Greece
H	Hungary
HK	Hong Kong
I	Italy
IL	Israel
IND	India
J	Japan
NL	Netherlands
P	Portugal
PL	Poland
S	Sweden
SF	Finland
SU	USSR
USA	United States
YU	Yugoslavia

Référence du fabricant / *Manufacturer's Reference*	Désignation / *Designation*	Type	*Type*	Date de la voiture / *Date of car*	Date du modèle / *Date of model*	Echelle / *Scale*

ABC (CARLO BRIANZA) — I

Matière / *Material:* Résine / *Resin*

1	Fiat	Prototype à turbine	*Prototype with turbine*	1954	1974	1/43
2a	Alfa Romeo	2300 cc, 8 C «Mille Miglia»	*2300 cc, 8 C "Mille Miglia"*	1932	1975	1/43
2b	Alfa Romeo	2300 cc, 8 C civile	*2300 cc, 8 C road car*	1932	1975	1/43
3	Lancia	Augusta	*Augusta*	1934	1975	1/43
4	Alfa Romeo	512/12 cyl. GP expérimentale	*512/12 cyl. GP prototype*	1940	1975	1/43
5	Mercedes	Type SSK «Papler»	*Type SSK "Papler"*	1929	1976	1/43
6	Volkswagen	«Kübelwagen» (grise ou sable)	*"Kübelwagen" (grey or sand)*	1938	1974	1/43
7	Alfa Romeo	P3, carénée, 1re circuit Avus, Guy Moll	*P3, streamlined, 1st Avus circuit, Guy Moll*	1934	1978	1/43
8	Fiat	«806» Grand Prix	*"806" Grand Prix*	1927	1977	1/43
9	Buick	Type «Bug», Indianapolis	*"Bug" type, Indianapolis*	1920	1979	1/43
10	Alfa Romeo	Type «coloniale»	*"Coloniale" type*	1938	1981	1/43
11a	Alfa Romeo	33 TT 12 «Willy Kauhsen Racing Team», Champ. du monde, courte, Dijon	*33 TT 12 "Willy Kauhsen Racing Team", World Champion, short tail, Dijon*	1975	1975	1/43
11b	Alfa Romeo	33 TT 12 «WKRT», Champ. du monde, longue, Monza	*33 TT 12, "WKRT", World Champion, long tail, Monza*	1975	1975	1/43
12	Tecno	PA/123 «Martini», F1	*PA/123 "Martini", F1*	1973	1976	1/43
13	Ferrari	340, Mexico, Carrera Pan. Am..	*340 Mexico, Carrera Pan. Am.*	1952	1977	1/43
14	Alfa Romeo	GTZ 2	*GTZ 2*	1965	1978	1/43
15	Alfa Romeo	1750 cc, gazogène «Mille Miglia»	*1750 cc, gas, "Mille Miglia".*	1933	1978	1/43
16	Alfa Romeo	1750 cc, gazogène, civile	*1750 cc, gas, road car*	1933	1979	1/43
17	Ferrari	250 GT «SWB»	*250 GT "SWB"*	1960	1981	1/43

Notes:

7	Alfa Romeo	2300 cc, 8C, Pescara	*2300 cc, 8C, Pescara.*	?	?	1/43
9b	OM	Type 665, berline	665 type, saloon	1924	?	1/43
10	Lancia	3 RO, modèle 102, Autocarro	*3 RO, model 102, Autocarro.*	1938	?	1/43

Modèles à monter / *Kits*

K1	Ferrari	312 T2, F1, prototype	*312 T2, F1, prototype*	1975	1976	1/43

Série spéciale (100 exemplaires numérotés) / *Special series (100 numbered models of each)*

100/1	Brabham	BT 46, F1 «Martini», prototype présentation presse, août 1977	*BT 46, F1 "Martini", prototype press presentation, August 1977*	1977	1978	1/43
100/2	Alfa Romeo	«Disco volante» coupé	*"Disco volante" coupé*	1952	1978	1/43

ABINGDON CLASSICS — GB

Matière / *Material:* *White metal*

Première série: Voitures de sport et berlines / *Series 1: Standard sports and saloons.*

1	MG	TC, Midget, ouverte	*TC, Midget, open*	1946	—	1/43
2	MG	TC, Midget, ouverte	*TC, Midget, open*	1949	—	1/43
3	MG	TC, Midget, avec capote.	*TC, Midget, with hood*	1946	—	1/43
4	MG	TC, Midget, avec capote.	*TC, Midget, with hood*	1949	—	1/43
5	MG	TD, Midget, ouverte, roues pleines	*TD, Midget, open, disc wheels*	1953	—	1/43
6	MG	TD, Midget, avec capote, roues pleines	*TD, Midget, with hood, disc wheels.*	1953	—	1/43
7	MG	TD, Midget, ouverte, roues à rayons	*TD, Midget, open, wire wheels*	1953	—	1/43
8	MG	TD, Midget, avec capote, roues à rayons	*TD, Midget, with hood, wire wheels.*	1953	—	1/43
9	MG	A Twin Cam, ouverte, roues à papillon	*A, Twin Cam, open, centre lock disc wheels*	1958	—	1/43
10	MG	A Twin Cam, avec capote, roues à papillon	*A, Twin Cam, with hood, centre lock disc wheels*	1958	—	1/43
11	MG	A Twin Cam, avec hardtop, roues à papillon	*A, Twin Cam, with hardtop, centre lock disc wheels*	1958	—	1/43

□ = fabricant de maquettes à construire

□ = *manufacturer of model kits*

Référence du fabricant *Manufacturer's Reference*	Désignation *Designation*	Type	*Type*	Date de la voiture *Date of car*	Date du modèle *Date of model*	Echelle *Scale*
12	MG	A Twin Cam, ouverte, roues à papillon	*A, Twin Cam, open, centre lock disc wheels*	1960	—	1/43
13	MG	A Twin Cam, avec capote, roues à papillon	*A, Twin Cam, with hood, centre lock disc wheels*	1960	—	1/43
14	MG	A Twin Cam, avec hardtop, roues à papillon	*A, Twin Cam, with hardtop, centre lock disc wheels*	1960	—	1/43
15	MG	A, 1500, ouverte, roues à rayons	*A, 1500, open, wire wheels*	1956	—	1/43
16	MG	A, 1500, avec capote, roues à rayons	*A, 1500, with hood, wire wheels*	1956	—	1/43
17	MG	A, 1500, avec hardtop, roues à rayons	*A, 1500, with hardtop, wire wheels*	1956	—	1/43
18	MG	A, 1500, ouverte, roues pleines	*A, 1500, open, disc wheels*	1956	—	1/43
19	MG	A, 1500, avec capote, roues pleines	*A, 1500, with hood, disc wheels*	1956	—	1/43
20	MG	A, 1500, avec hardtop, roues pleines	*A, 1500, with hardtop, disc wheels*	1956	—	1/43
21	MG	A, 1600 Mk1, ouverte, roues à rayons	*A, 1600 Mk1, open, wire wheels*	1960	—	1/43
22	MG	A, 1600 Mk1, avec capote, roues à rayons	*A, 1600 Mk1, with hood, wire wheels*	1960	—	1/43
23	MG	A, 1600 Mk1, avec hardtop, roues à rayons	*A, 1600 Mk1, with hardtop, wire wheels*	1960	—	1/43
24	MG	A, 1600 Mk1, ouverte, roues pleines	*A, 1600 Mk1, open, disc wheels*	1960	—	1/43
25	MG	A, 1600 Mk1, avec capote, roues pleines	*A, 1600 Mk1, with hood, disc wheels*	1960	—	1/43
26	MG	A, 1600 Mk1, avec hardtop, roues pleines	*A, 1600 Mk1, with hardtop, disc wheels*	1960	—	1/43
27	MG	A, 1600 Mk2, ouverte, roues à rayons	*A, 1600 Mk2, open, wire wheels*	1962	—	1/43
28	MG	A, 1600 Mk2, avec capote, roues à rayons	*A, 1600 Mk2, with hood, wire wheels*	1962	—	1/43
29	MG	A, 1600 Mk2, avec hardtop, roues à rayons	*A, 1600 Mk2, with hardtop, wire wheels*	1962	—	1/43
30	MG	A, 1600 Mk2, ouverte, roues pleines	*A, 1600 Mk2, open, disc wheels*	1962	—	1/43
31	MG	A, 1600 Mk2, avec capote, roues pleines	*A, 1600 Mk2, with hood, disc wheels*	1962	—	1/43
32	MG	A, 1600 Mk2, avec hardtop, roues pleines	*A, 1600 Mk2, with hardtop, disc wheels*	1962	—	1/43
33	MG	A, 1600 Mk2 de luxe, ouverte, roues à papillon	*A, 1600 Mk2, de luxe, open, center lock, disc wheels*	1962	—	1/43
34	MG	A, 1600 Mk2 de luxe, avec capote, roues à papillon	*A, 1600 Mk2, de luxe, with hood, center lock, disc wheels*	1962	—	
35	MG	A, 1600 Mk2 de luxe, avec hardtop, roues à papillon	*A, 1600 Mk2, de luxe, with hardtop, centre lock, disc wheels*	1962	—	1/43
36	MG	PA, 4 pl. sport, ouverte	*PA, 4-seater sports, open*	1934	—	1/43
37	MG	PA, 4 pl. sport, avec capote	*PA, 4-seater sports, with hood.*	1934	—	1/43
38	MG	PB, 4 pl. sport, ouverte	*PB, 4-seater sports, open*	1936	—	1/43
39	MG	PB, 4 pl. sport, avec capote	*PB, 4-seater sports, with hood.*	1936	—	1/43
40	MG	PA, 2 pl. sport, ouverte	*PA, 2-seater sports, open*	1934	—	1/43
41	MG	PA, 2 pl. sport, avec capote	*PA, 2-seater sports, with hood.*	1934	—	1/43
42	MG	PB, 2 pl. sport, ouverte	*PB, 2-seater sports, open*	1936	—	1/43
43	MG	PB, 2 pl. sport, avec capote	*PB, 2-seater sports, with hood.*	1936	—	1/43

Deuxième série: Voitures de courses / *Series two: Racing cars.*

Référence du fabricant	Désignation	Type	*Type*	Date de la voiture	Date du modèle	Echelle
1	MG	TC Midget de course	*TC Midget racer*	1948	—	1/43
2	MG	R Midget	*R type Midget*	1935	—	1/43
3	MG	Ex 182 «A» Le Mans, nº 41 Lockett/Miles	*Ex 182 "A" Le Mans, No. 41 Lockett/Miles*	1955	—	1/43
4	MG	Ex 182 «A» Le Mans, nº 42 Jacobs/Flynn	*Ex 182 "A" Le Mans, No. 42 Jacobs/Flynn*	1955	—	1/43
5	MG	Ex 182 «A» Le Mans, nº 64 Lund/Waeffler	*Ex 182 "A" Le Mans, No. 64 Lund/Waeffler*	1955	—	1/43
6	MG	Ex 181 «Goutte d'eau» de record, S. Moss	*Ex 181 "Teardrop", record car, S. Moss*	1957	—	1/43
7	MG	Ex 181 «Goutte d'eau» de record, P. Hill	*Ex 181 "Teardrop", record car, P. Hill*	1959	—	1/43

Référence du fabricant / *Manufacturer's Reference*	Désignation / *Designation*	Type	*Type*	Date de la voiture / *Date of car*	Date du modèle / *Date of model*	Echelle / *Scale*

Troisième série: Exemplaires numérotés de 1 à 800 avec courte histoire de la voiture / *Series three: Limited edition of 800 each model, short history of car included.*

1	MG	PA «Airline»	*PA "Airline"*	1935	—	1/43
2	MG	PB «Airline»	*PB "Airline"*	1936	—	1/43

Quatrième série: Promotionnels / *Series four: Promotionals.*

1	MG	Châssis type M, «High Speed Service Van»	*M type chassis, "High Speed Service Van"*	1930	—	1/43
2	MG	Châssis type M, «Abingdon Classics»	*M type chassis, "Abingdon Classics"*	1930	—	1/43
3	MG	Châssis type M, «MGCC Golden Jubilee»	*M type chassis, "MGCC Golden Jubilee"*	1930	—	1/43
4	MG	Châssis type M, «25e anniversaire MG club hollandais»	*M type chassis, "Dutch MG Car Club 25th anniversary*	1930	—	1/43

ABM — I

Matière / *Material:* Résine / *Resin*

1	Tyrell	F1 «P 34», GP Suède	*F1 "P 34", Swedish GP*	1976	1977	1/43
2	Tyrell	F1 «P 34», GP Argentine «FNCB»	*F1 "P 34", Argentine GP "FNCB"*	1977	1977	1/43
3	Tyrell	F1 «P 34», GP Espagne «FNCB»	*F1 "P 34", Spanish GP "FNCB"*	1977	1977	1/43
4	Tyrell	F1 «007», GP Italie «Gulf-Rondini», A. Pesenti Rossi	*F1 "007", Italian GP "Gulf-Rondini", A. Pesenti Rossi*	1976	1977	1/43
5	Tyrell	F1 «P 34», GP Autriche «FNCB», radiateurs frontaux	*F1 "P 34", Austrian GP "FNCB", front radiators*	1977	1977	1/43
6	Tyrell	F1 «006/2» «Elf»	*F1 "006/2" "Elf"*	1973	1977	1/43
7	Tyrell	F1 «007» «Elf»	*F1 "007" "Elf"*	1974	1977	1/43
8	Tyrell	F1 «007/2» «Elf»	*F1 "007/2" "Elf"*	1975	1977	1/43
9	Tyrell	F1 «007», GP Afrique du Sud «Lexington», Ian Sheckter	*F1 "007", South African GP "Lexington", Ian Sheckter*	1975	1977	1/43
10	Tyrell	F1 «007/2», GP Allemagne «Gulf-Rondini», A. Pesenti Rossi	*F1 "007/2", German GP "Gulf-Rondini", A. Pesenti Rossi*	1976	1977	1/43
11	Tyrell	F1 «P 34», présentation à la presse	*F1 "P 34", press presentation*	1975	1977	1/43
12	March	F1 «2.4.0», 6 roues	*F1 "2.4.0.", six wheels*	1977	1977	1/43
13	March	F1 «771», Merzario	*F1 "771", Merzario*	1977	1977	1/43
14	Tyrell	F1 «008», présentation à la presse	*F1 "008", press presentation*	1977	1977	1/43
—	Brabham	Alfa Romeo, 1re GP Suède, «aspirateurs», N. Lauda	*Alfa Romeo, 1st, Swedish GP "Fan Car", N. Lauda*	1978	1978	1/43

ACE ☐ GB

Matière / *Material:* *White metal*

1	MG	B roadster MKS 1/2	*B roadster MKS 1/2*	1962/69	1980	1/43
2	MG	B roadster MK 2.	*B roadster MK 2.*	1969/72	1980	1/43
3	MG	B roadster MK 3.	*B roadster MK 3.*	1971/74	1980	1/43
4	MG	B roadster MK 4 AB	*B roadster MK 4 AB*	1974	1980	1/43
5	MG	C MK	*C MK*	1967	1980	1/43
6	MG	A 1500	*A 1500*	1958	1980	1/43
7	MG	Ex 135 «Humbug» de record	*Ex 135 "Humbug", record car*	—	1980	1/43

ACE ☐ USA

Matière / *Material:* Bois / *Wood*

1R	«Pickup»	Roadster	*Roadster*	—	—	—
2R	Jalopy	Roadster	*Roadster*	—	—	—
3R	Ford	Modèle T Hotrod	*Model T Hotrod*	—	—	—
4R	Racer	Voiture course piste cendrée.	*Dirt track.*	—	—	—
5R	Racer	Midget	*Midget*	—	—	—
6R	Racer	Midget	*Midget*	—	—	—

Référence du fabricant / *Manufacturer's Reference*	Désignation / *Designation*	Type	*Type*	Date de la voiture / *Date of car*	Date du modèle / *Date of model*	Echelle / *Scale*
7R	Jeep	Jeepster décapotable	*Jeepster convertible*	1948	1948	1/24
8R	MG	TD	*TD*	—	—	—
10R	Racer	Midget de luxe	*Deluxe Midget*	—	—	—
15R	Ford	Sportsman décapotable	*Sportsman convertible*	1946	1946	1/24
20R	Hot Rod	Roadster	*Roadster*	—	—	—
25R	Jaguar	XK (probablement 120)	*XK (probably 120)*	—	—	—
30R	Chevrolet	Corvette	*Corvette*	1953-54	—	1/24
49R	Ford	Club coupé	*Club coupé*	1949	—	—
146		Roadster	*Roadster*	—	—	—
242	Jeep	Armée américaine	*US army*	—	—	—
246	Jeep	Version civile	*Civilian*	—	—	—

ADAM'S □ USA

Matière / *Material:* Polystyrène / *Polystyrene*

Référence du fabricant / *Manufacturer's Reference*	Désignation / *Designation*	Type	*Type*	Date de la voiture / *Date of car*	Date du modèle / *Date of model*	Echelle / *Scale*
K-150	Honest John	Fusée	*Rocket missile*	1956	1957	1/50
K-151	M-40	Canon de 155 mm	*155 mm gun*	1944	1957	1/50
K-152		Plate-forme pour obusier de 105 mm	*105 mm howitzer gun emplacement*	1943	1957	1/50
K-153	T-131	Canon atomique de 280 mm	*280 mm atomic cannon*	1955	1957	1/50
K-154	Hawk	Batterie de fusées	*Missile battery*	1956	1958	1/50
K-156	M-1	Canon antiaérien de 120 mm	*120 mm anti-aircraft gun*	1945	1958	1/50
K-157		Véhicule de débarquement LVT US	*US Marine Corps LVT*	1943	1958	1/50
K-159	Hawk	Transport de fusée	*Missile carrier*	1956	1958	1/50

ADVENT □ USA

Matière / *Material:* Plastique / *Plastic*

Les maquettes Advent ont été produites à partir de moules Revell et furent vendues à un prix réduit. Un grand nombre d'entre elles étaient dépourvues de pièces chromées.
Advent kits were produced from Revell tools and sold for a budget price. Many of these did not contain plated parts.

Référence du fabricant / *Manufacturer's Reference*	Désignation / *Designation*	Type	*Type*	Date de la voiture / *Date of car*	Date du modèle / *Date of model*	Echelle / *Scale*
2701	Chevrolet	Vega «Snake Funny Car»	*Vega "Snake Funny Car"*	—	1979	1/32
2702	Dragster	«Mongoose» dragster	*"Mongoose" rail dragster*	—	1979	1/32
2703	Chevrolet	Vega «Jungle Jim» fantaisie.	*Vega "Jungle Jim" funny car*	—	1979	1/32
2704	Dragster	«Jade Grenade» dragster	*"Jade Grenade" rail dragster*	—	1979	1/32
3001	Triumph	TR4	*TR4*	1961	1979	1/32
3002	Austin Healey	3000	*3000*	1962	1979	1/32
3003	MG			1963	1979	1/32
3004	Sunbeam	Alpine	*Alpine*	1963	1979	1/32
3101	Datsun	240-Z	*240-Z*	1971	1979	1/25
3102	Jaguar	XK-E décapotable	*XK-E convertible*	1961	1979	1/25
3103	Porsche	911	*911*	—	1979	1/25
3104	Chevrolet	Corvette (en fait un modèle 1959)	*Corvette (really a 1959)*	1960	1979	1/25
3111	Ford	Ranchero (carrosserie spéciale)	*Ranchero (custom)*	1957	1979	1/25
3112	Ford	Skyliner hardtop décapotable	*Skyliner hardtop convertible.*	1959	1979	1/25
3113	Chevrolet	Camaro «Killer Camaro» fantaisie	*Camaro "Killer Camaro" funny car.*	1971	1979	1/25
3114	Ford	Mustang «Boss Mustang» fantaisie	*Mustang "Boss Mustang" funny car.*	—	1979	1/25
3115	Ford	Thames camionnette «Jungle Fever» dragster	*Thames panel truck "Jungle Fever" dragster*	1951	1979	1/25
3116	Ford	Anglia «Hot Blooded» dragster	*Anglia "Hot Blooded" gas coupe dragster*	1951	1979	1/25
3121	Ford	T sedan hotrod	*T sedan street rod*	1926	1979	1/25
3122	Ford	T phaeton hotrod	*T phaeton street rod*	1927	1979	1/25
3123	Ford	A camionnette hotrod	*A panel delivery street rod*	1931	1979	1/25
3124	Ford	A pickup hotrod	*A pickup street rod*	1929	1979	1/25
3131		«Double Trouble» (anciennement «Mysterion»)	*"Double Trouble" (former "Mysterion")*	—	1979	1/25
3132		«Yellow Fever» (anciennement «Outlaw»)	*"Yellow Fever" (former "Outlaw")*	—	1979	1/25
3133	Ford	T «The Rodfather» (anciennement Tweedie Pie»)	*T "The Rodfather" (former "Tweedie Pie")*	—	1979	1/25

Référence du fabricant / *Manufacturer's Reference*	Désignation / *Designation*	Type	*Type*	Date de la voiture / *Date of car*	Date du modèle / *Date of model*	Echelle / *Scale*
3134		«Medicine Man» fourgonnette de livraison	*"Medicine Man" cab delivery*	—	1979	1/25
3141	Porsche	914	*914*	—	1979	1/25
3142	Volkswagen	Véhicule course Baja	*"Baja Bug" racer*	—	1979	1/25
3143	Datsun	510 «BRE/Datsun» (Pete Brock)	*510 "BRE/Datsun" (Pete Brock)*	—	1979	1/25
3144	Volkswagen	Fourgonnette (carrosserie spéciale)	*Van (custom microbus)*	1964	1979	1/25

AGM — GB

Matière / *Material:* Résine / *Resin*

Référence	Désignation	Type	*Type*	Date voiture	Date modèle	Echelle
1	De Soto	Suburban Sedan	*Suburban Sedan*	1948	1976	1/43
2	Bristol	450 Le Mans, carénée, 1954	*450 Le Mans, 1954*	1954	1976	1/43
3	De Soto	Suburban Sedan, taxi de New York	*Suburban Sedan, New York taxi*	1948	1977	1/43

AIRFIX □ GB

Matière / *Material:* Plastique / *Plastic*

Série 1 / *Series 1:* Voitures anciennes / *Veteran cars*

Référence	Désignation	Type	*Type*	Date voiture	Date modèle	Echelle
74-01440-7	Ford	T Runabout	*T Runabout*	1910	1957	1/32
71-01441-0	Rolls-Royce	Landau 40/50 CV	*Landau 40/50 HP*	1911	1956	1/32
72-01442-3	Bentley	4,5 l compresseur Le Mans	*4.5 l. supercharged Le Mans*	1930	1957	1/32
75-01445	Rolls-Royce	Double phaéton	*Double phaeton*	1905	1957	1/32
76-01446	Lanchester	Landaulet	*Landaulet*	1907	1957	1/32
77-01447	Morris	Cowley «Bullnose»	*Cowley "Bullnose"*	1923	1959	1/32
78-01448-1	Mercedes	Roadster	*Roadster*	1904	1962	1/32
79-01449-4	De Dietrich	Paris-Vienne	*Paris-Vienna*	1902	1966	1/32
60-01450-4	Ford	T	*T*	1912	1966	1/32

Série 1 / *Series 1:* Voitures modernes / *Modern cars*

Référence	Désignation	Type	*Type*	Date voiture	Date modèle	Echelle
M1C	Sunbeam	Rapier	*Rapier*	1960	1961	1/32
M2C	Austin Healey	Sprite Mk 1	*Sprite Mk 1*	1958	1961	1/32
M3C	Renault	Dauphine	*Dauphine*	1958	1962	1/32
M4C-01404-1	Morris	Mini Minor	*Mini Minor*	1962	1962	1/32
M5C-01405-4	Jaguar	Type E, hardtop	*E-type, hardtop*	1961	1963	1/32
M6C-01406-7	Volkswagen	1200 berline	*1200 saloon*	1957	1964	1/32
M7C-01407-0	MG	1100	*1100*	1962	1965	1/32
M8C-01408-3	Ford	Cortina Lotus	*Cortina Lotus*	1964	1965	1/32
M9C	Bond	Bug 700 E	*Bug 700 E*	—	—	1/32

Série 2 / *Series 2:* Voitures historiques / *Historical motor vehicles*

Référence	Désignation	Type	*Type*	Date voiture	Date modèle	Echelle
02441-3	Alfa Romeo	8 cyl. 2300	*2300 cc 8-cyl.*	1931	—	1/32
02442-6	De Dietrich	Paris-Vienne	*Paris-Vienna*	1902	—	1/32
02443-9	Ford	Runabout modèle T	*Model T Runabout*	1912	—	1/32
02444-2	Rolls-Royce	Landau	*Landau*	1911	—	1/32
02445-5	Darracq	Tonneau	*Tonneau*	1905	—	1/32
02446-8	Bentley	4,5 l compresseur	*4.5 l. supercharged*	1930	—	1/32
02447-1	Rolls-Royce	Double phaéton	*Double phaeton*	1905	—	1/32
02448-4	Lanchester	Landaulet	*Landaulet*	1907	—	1/32
02450-7	Morris	Cowley	*Cowley*	1926	—	1/32

Série 2 / *Series 2:* Voitures modernes / *Modern cars*

Référence	Désignation	Type	*Type*	Date voiture	Date modèle	Echelle
M 201 C	Ford	Zodiac Mk III	*Zodiac Mk III*	1962	1963	1/32
M 202 C	Triumph	TR 4 A.	*TR 4 A.*	1965	1966	1/32
M 203 C	MG	B	*B*	1965	1966	1/32
M 204 C	Triumph	Herald	*Herald*	1965	1967	1/32
M 205 C-02405-7	Ferrari	250 LM	*250 LM*	1965	1965	1/32
M 207 C-02407-6	Porsche	Carrera 6	*Carrera 6*	—	—	1/32
M 208 C-02408-6	Mercedes-Benz	280 SL	*280 SL*	—	—	1/32

Référence du fabricant *Manufacturer's Reference*	Désignation *Designation*	Type	*Type*	Date de la voiture *Date of car*	Date du modèle *Date of model*	Echelle *Scale*
02409-9	Ford	3 l, Alan Mann	*3 l. Alan Mann's.*	—	—	1/32
02410-9	Ford	Escort	*Escort*	—	—	1/32
02411-2	Porsche	917	*917*	—	—	1/32
02412-5	Bugle	Buggy de plage	*Beach buggy*	—	—	1/32
02413-8	Bond	Bug 700 E	*Bug 700 E*	—	—	1/32
02414-1	Morris	Mini Minor	*Mini Minor*	—	—	1/32
02415-4	Jaguar	Type E	*E-type*	—	—	1/32
02418-3	Ford	Cortina Lotus	*Cortina Lotus*	—	—	1/32
Série 3 / *Series 3:* Voitures modernes / *Modern cars*						
M 301 C-03401-8	Jaguar	420	*420*	—	—	1/32
M 302 C	Vauxhall	Victor Estate	*Victor Estate*	—	—	1/32
03403-4	Ford	Capri	*Capri*	—	—	1/32
03404-7	Austin	Maxi	*Maxi*	—	—	1/32
03405	Morris	Marina TC	*Marina TC*	—	—	1/32
03406-3	Maserati	Indy	*Indy*	—	—	1/32
03410-2	Aston Martin	DB 6	*DB 6*	—	—	1/32
03411-5	Mercedes-Benz	280 SL	*280 SL*	—	—	1/32
03412-8	Porsche	Carrera 6	*Carrera 6*	—	—	1/32
Série 3 / *Series 3:* Voitures historiques / *Historical model cars*						
03441-6	Vauxhall	Prince Henry	*Prince Henry*	1911	—	1/32
03442-9	Bugatti	Type 35 B	*35 B type*	—	—	1/32
03443-2	MG	Magnette K 3	*Magnette K 3*	1932	—	1/32
Série 4 / *Series 4:* Voitures fantaisie / *Customized cars*						
04401-1	Kansas Cruiser	—	—	—	—	1/24
04402-4	Night Prowler	—	—	—	—	1/24
04403-7	Krackle Kat	—	—	—	—	1/24
04404-0	Rebel Rouser	—	—	—	—	1/24
Série 5 / *Series 5:* Voitures historiques / *Veteran auto series*						
572	Dennis	Voiture de pompiers	*Fire engine*	1914	1962	1/32
573	AEC	Autobus londonien, classe B ou transport de troupes militaires	*Type B bus "Old Bill Bus" (military version)*	1910-14	1965	1/32
Série 6 / *Series 6:* Véhicules à moteur / *Motor vehicles*						
06442-8	Dennis	Voiture de pompiers	*Fire engine*	1914	1962	1/32
06443-1	AEC	Autobus londonien, classe B	*London type B bus*	1910	1962	1/32
Série 6 / *Series 6:* Voitures de rallye / *Rally cars*						
06405-9	Lancia	Stratos «Alitalia»	*Stratos "Alitalia"*	—	—	1/24
06406-2	Triumph	TR 7 «British Leyland»	*TR 7 "British Leyland"*	—	—	1/24
06407-5	Ferrari	365 Boxer NART	*365 Boxer NART*	—	—	1/24
06408-8	Porsche	934/5 «Vaillant-Kremer»	*934/5 "Vaillant-Kremer"*	—	—	1/24
06413-0	Maserati	Bora	*Bora*	—	—	1/24
06414-3	Mazda	RX-7	*RX-7*	—	—	1/24
06415-6	Porsche	935 «Moby Dick» écurie Martini	*935 "Moby Dick" Martini team*	—	—	1/24
06424-0	Renault	Alpine A 110 (snap'n glue kit)	*Alpine A 110 (snap'n glue kit)*	—	—	1/24
06425-3	Maserati	Boomerang	*Boomerang*	—	—	1/24
06426-6	BMW	3,5 CSL	*3.5 CSL*	—	—	1/24
06427-9	De Tomaso	Pantera	*Pantera*	—	—	1/24
Série 6 / *Series 6:* Classiques américaines / *American car classics*						
06404-6	Stutz	Bearcat 6,5 l	*6.5 l. Bearcat*	—	—	1/25

Référence du fabricant / *Manufacturer's Reference*	Désignation / *Designation*	Type	*Type*	Date de la voiture / *Date of car*	Date du modèle / *Date of model*	Echelle / *Scale*
Série 7 / *Series 7:* Voitures de rallye / *Rally cars*						
07401-0	Maserati	Merak	*Merak*	—	—	1/24
07402-3	Lotus	Elite	*Elite*	—	—	1/24
07404-9	BMW	M1 Procar H. Stuck	*M1 Procar H. Stuck*	—	—	1/24
07406-5	Datsun	280 ZX	*280 ZX*	—	—	1/24
Série 7 / *Series 7:* «Echelle de l'élite» / *"Scale Elite"*						
721	Chevrolet	Corvette Stingray	*Corvette Stingray*	—	—	1/24
722	Ford	«Woodie»	*"Woodie"*	1929	—	1/24
732	Toyota	«James Bond»	*"James Bond"*	—	—	1/24
Série 8 / *Series 8:* «Echelle de l'élite» / *"Scale Elite"*						
821	Lincoln	«Gangbuster»	*"Gangbuster"*	1929	—	1/24
823	Aston Martin	DB 5 «James Bond»	*DB 5 "James Bond"*	—	—	1/24
826	Dodge	Charger	*Charger*	1967	—	1/24
827	Pontiac	GTO	*GTO*	1967	—	1/24
828	Ford	Mustang Fastback	*Mustang Fastback*	1967	—	1/24
829	Ford	«J» prototype carr. transparente	*"J" prototype transparent body*	1967	—	1/24
830	Chevrolet	Mako Shark Mk IV	*Mako Shark Mk IV*	—	—	1/24
831	Monkeemobile	—	—	—	—	1/24
Série 8 / *Series 8:* Classiques américaines / *American car classics*						
08440-8	Chrysler	Imperial Custom Eight	*Imperial Custom Eight*	1932	—	1/25
08441-1	Lincoln	Roadster	*Roadster*	1927	—	1/25
Série 16 / *Series 16:* Voitures au 1/16 / *1:16 scale cars*						
16402-7	Lamborghini	Countach	*Countach*	1971	—	1/16
Série 16 / *Series 16:* Camions au 1/32 / *1:32 scale trucks*						
16401-4	Ford	C 900, écurie Ferrari	*C 900, Ferrari racing team*	—	—	1/32
16401-8	Ford	C 800, écurie Porsche	*C 800, Porsche racing team*	—	—	1/32
Série 20 / *Series 20:* «Echelle des connaisseurs» / *Connoisseurs 1:12 scale*						
09398-1 20440-8	Bentley	4,5 l compresseur Le Mans	*4.5 l. supercharged Le Mans*	1930	—	1/12
Série motos / *Motorcycles series*						
02481	Ariel	Arrow	*Arrow*	—	—	1/16
02480	Honda	CB 450	*CB 450*	—	—	1/16
03480	BSA	C 15	*C 15*	—	—	1/16
04480	BMW	R 69	*R 69*	—	—	1/16
11480	Honda	CB 750	*CB 750*	—	—	1/8
09480	Suzuki	TM 400 J Cyclone	*TM 400 J Cyclone*	—	—	1/8
11481	Honda	750 course	*750 road racer*	—	—	1/8
20480	Norton	750 Commando	*750 Commando*	—	—	1/8
20481	BMW	R 75/5	*R 75/5*	—	—	1/8
20482	Norton	750 Commando SS	*750 Commando SS*	—	—	1/8
20483	BMW	R 60/5 police	*R 60/5 police*	—	—	1/8

ALT BERLIN □ E

Matière / *Material:* Plastique / *Plastic*

Référence du fabricant / *Manufacturer's Reference*	Désignation / *Designation*	Type	*Type*	Date de la voiture / *Date of car*	Date du modèle / *Date of model*	Echelle / *Scale*
111001	Fiat	Autobus	*Bus*	1925	—	1/87
111002	Berliner	Taxi «Orix»	*"Orix" Taxi*	1907	—	1/87
111003	Le Zèbre			1907	—	1/87

Référence du fabricant / *Manufacturer's Reference*	Désignation / *Designation*	Type	*Type*	Date de la voiture / *Date of car*	Date du modèle / *Date of model*	Echelle / *Scale*
111004	Ford	Type «T»	*"T" type*	1916	—	1/87
111005	Opel	Laubfrosch/Citroën 5 CV	*Laubfrosch/Citroën 5 CV*	1923	—	1/87
111006	Rolls-Royce	Phantom 1	*Phantom 1*	1925	—	1/87
111007	Hispano-Suiza			1907	—	1/87
111008	Studebacker	Big Six	*Big Six*	1916	—	1/87
111009	Fiat	Balilla	*Balilla*	1934	—	1/87
111010	Citroën	11 BL, Légère	*11 BL, Legere*	1936	—	1/87
111011	Bugatti	Type 57 Stelvio	*"57", Stelvio type*	1937	—	1/87
111012	Lancia	Aprilia	*Aprilia*	1938	—	1/87

AMERICANA MINIATURES □ GB

Matière / *Material:* *White metal*

1	Dodge	Décapotable, «14 D»	*Convertible, "14 D"*	1940	1975	1/43
2	Kaiser	Darin sport	*Darin 2 seater sports*	1956	1975	1/43
3	Cord	Beverly sedan	*Beverly sedan*	1937	1975	1/43
4a	Chevrolet	Corvette	*Corvette*	1956/57	1975	1/43
4b	Chevrolet	Corvette (remoulée)	*Corvette (re-molded)*	1956/57	1981	1/43
5	La Salle	Sedan	*Sedan*	1940	1975	1/43
6	Studebacker	Avanti	*Avanti saloon*	—	1976	1/43
7	Plymouth	Coupé	*Coupé*	1931	1976	1/43
8	Cord	L 29 roadster	*L 29 roadster*	1929	1976	1/43
9	Kurtis	500 sport	*500 sports*	1954	1978	1/43
10	Austin-Nash	Metropolitan	*Metropolitan*	1954/61	1980	1/43
11	Muntz	Jet roadster	*Jet roadster*	1954	1980	1/43
12	Studebacker	Starlight coupé	*Starlight coupé*	1950	1980	1/43
13	Chevrolet	Styleline sedan	*Styleline sedan*	1950	1980	1/43

AMR (André-Marie Ruf) — F

Matière / *Material:* *White metal*

1	Porsche	Carrera turbo Le Mans	*Carrera turbo Le Mans*	1974	1975	1/43
2	Jaguar	XJ 12, limousine	*XJ 12, saloon*	1975	1976	1/43
3	Ferrari	Berlinetta Boxer	*Berlinetta Boxer*	1974	1976	1/43
4	Porsche	917 «Cochon rose», Le Mans (pour Grelley)	*917 "Pink Pig" Le Mans (for Grelley)*	1971	1976	1/43
5	Chevrolet	Corvette Greenwood «Big 1», Le Mans	*Corvette Greenwood "Big 1" Le Mans*	1976	1978	1/43
6	Ferrari	250 GTO Tour de France	*250 GTO Tour de France*	1964	1981	1/43

AMR-X □ F

Matière / *Material:* *White metal*

1	BMW	2002 Schnitzer, groupe II	*2002 Schnitzer, Gr. 2*	1974	—	1/43
2a	Alpine	1800, Tour de Corse (Larrousse)	*1800 cc, Tour de Corse (Larrousse)*	1974	—	1/43
2b	Alpine	1800, Tour de Corse (Nicolas)	*1800 cc, Tour de Corse (Nicolas)*	1975	—	1/43
3	Ferrari	BB NART, Sebring	*BB NART, Sebring*	1975	—	1/43
4	Chevrolet	Corvette Greenwood «Spirit of 76», Atlanta	*Corvette Greenwood "Spirit of 76", Atlanta race*	1976	—	1/43
5	Porsche	Turbo 2,2 l «00», Danny Ongais, Daytona	*Turbo 2,2 l "00" Danny Ongais, Daytona*	1977	—	1/43
6	Ferrari	BB NART, Le Mans	*BB NART, Le Mans*	1977	—	1/43
7a	Porsche	934 «TAG», Daytona	*934 "TAG", Daytona*	1976	—	1/43
7b	Porsche	934 IMSA «Brumos», Daytona	*934 IMSA "Brumos", Daytona*	1977	—	1/43
8	Porsche	Turbo, Watkins Glen	*Turbo, Watkins Glen*	1974	—	1/43
9	Chevrolet	Corvette «Mancuso», Watkins Glen	*Corvette "Mancuso", Watkins Glen*	1977	—	1/43
10	Porsche	935 «Moby Dick», Le Mans	*935 "Moby Dick", Le Mans*	1978	—	1/43
11	Ferrari	512 BB, Luigi Chinetti, Le Mans	*512 BB, Luigi Chinetti, Le Mans*	1978	—	1/43
12	Alpine	A 210 Le Mans, 1re Indice	*A 210 Le Mans, 1st Index*	1965	—	1/43
13	Chevrolet	Corvette Greenwood «Lifesaver», Le Mans	*Corvette Greenwood "Lifesaver", Le Mans*	1976	—	1/43
14	Chevrolet	Corvette Heinz «Confédérée», Daytona	*Corvette Heinz "Rebel Flag", Daytona*	1972	—	1/43

Référence du fabricant *Manufacturer's Reference*	Désignation *Designation*	Type	*Type*	Date de la voiture *Date of car*	Date du modèle *Date of model*	Echelle *Scale*
15	Chevrolet	Corvette Greenwood «First National City Bank», Le Mans	*Corvette Greenwood "First National City Bank", Le Mans*	1974	—	1/43
16	Chevrolet	Monza IMSA Cord, Daytona	*Monza IMSA Cord, Daytona*	1978	—	1/43
17	Chevrolet	Monza IMSA Al Holbert	*Monza IMSA Al Holbert*	1978	—	1/43
18	Chevrolet	Monza «Budweiser», Watkins Glen.	*Monza "Budweiser", Watkins Glen.*	1978	—	1/43
19	Ferrari	512 BB NART, Daytona	*512 BB NART, Daytona*	1979	—	1/43
20	Ferrari	512 BB NART, Le Mans	*512 BB NART, Le Mans*	1979	—	1/43
21	Rondeau	Cosworth 3 l «ITT-Oceanic», Le Mans	*Cosworth 3 l "ITT-Oceanic", Le Mans*	1979	—	1/43
22	Rondeau	Cosworth 3 l «Merlin Plage», Le Mans	*Cosworth 3 l "Merlin Plage", Le Mans*	1979	—	1/43
23	Rondeau	Cosworth 3 l «VSD», Le Mans.	*Cosworth 3 l "VSD", Le Mans.*	1979	—	1/43
24	WM	Prototype, Le Mans	*Prototype, Le Mans*	1979	—	1/43
25	BMW	3.20 «Rodenstock» Winkelhock, gr. 5.	*3.20 "Rodenstock" Winkelhock, Gr. 5*	1979	—	1/43
26	Alpine	A.210 Le Mans	*A.210 Le Mans*	1968/69	—	1/43
27	Rondeau	Cosworth 3 l «ITT-Le Point», 1er Le Mans	*Cosworth 3 l "ITT-Le Point", 1st Le Mans*	1980	1980	1/43
28	Rondeau	Cosworth 3 l «Belga», 3e Le Mans (Gyl).	*Cosworth 3 l "Belga", 3rd Le Mans (Gyl).*	1980	1980	1/43
29	Chevrolet	Corvette, D. Rowe, Daytona.	*Corvette, D. Rowe, Daytona.*	1980	1980	1/43
30	Lotus	Europe gr. 5 «Minolta», Ertl	*Europa Gr. 5 "Minolta", Ertl.*	1979	1980	1/43
31	Ferrari	512 BB, «Bellancauto», Le Mans	*512 BB, "Bellancauto", Le Mans*	1980	1980	1/43
32	Porsche	911 S, civile	*911 S, road car*	—	1980	1/43
33	Lancia	Beta, Tour d'Italie «Alitalia»	*Beta, Tour d'Italie "Alitalia"*	1979	1980	1/43
34	Lancia	Beta, Tour d'Italie Röhrl/ Villeneuve	*Beta, Tour d'Italie Röhrl/ Villeneuve*	1979	1980	1/43
35	Renault	R 5 turbo gr. 4, Tour de France	*R 5 turbo Gr. 4, Tour de France*	1980	1981	1/43
36	Porsche	911 S «Brumos», 1re Sebring	*911 S "Brumos", 1st Sebring*	1972	1981	1/43
37	Porsche	911 S Le Mans	*911 S Le Mans*	1972	1981	1/43
38	Porsche	911 S «SEB», Monte Carlo	*911 S "SEB", Monte Carlo*	1972	1981	1/43
39	Porsche	911 S Kremer, Le Mans.	*911 S Kremer, Le Mans.*	1971	1981	1/43
40	Renault	R 5 turbo gr. 4, 1re Monte Carlo	*R 5 turbo, Gr. 4, 1st Monte Carlo*	1981	1981	1/43
41	Peugeot	202, civile	*202, road car, saloon.*	—	1981	1/43
42	Maserati	Tipo 151 Le Mans	*Tipo 151 Le Mans.*	1962	1981	1/43
43	Porsche	911, 1re GT, Le Mans	*911, 1st GT, Le Mans*	1969	1981	1/43
44	Porsche	911, 1re GTS, Le Mans	*911, 1st GTS, Le Mans.*	1971	1981	1/43
45	Porsche	911, Kremer no 25, Le Mans.	*911, Kremer No. 25, Le Mans*	1972	1981	1/43
46	Porsche	911 S, Kremer no 80, Le Mans.	*911 S, Kremer No. 80, Le Mans*	1972	1981	1/43
47a	Ferrari	512 BB «European University», Le Mans	*512 BB "European University", Le Mans*	1981	1981	1/43
47b	Cadillac	Le Mans, Cunningham	*Le Mans, Cunningham*	1950	1981	1/43
48	Porsche	935 «Moby Dick», Joest Racing	*935 "Moby Dick", Joest Racing*	1981	1981	1/43

AMR-X-F1 □ F

Matière / *Material:* *White metal*

Référence du fabricant *Manufacturer's Reference*	Désignation *Designation*	Type	*Type*	Date de la voiture *Date of car*	Date du modèle *Date of model*	Echelle *Scale*
XF.1-1	Ferrari	F1 «312 T5»	*F1 "312 T5"*	1980	1980	1/43
XF.1-2	Arrows	F1 «A 3», «Warsteiner».	*F1 "A 3", "Warsteiner".*	1980.	.1980	1/43
XF.1-3	Fittipaldi	F1 «F 8», «Skoll»	*F1 "F 8", "Skoll"*	1980	1980	1/43

AMR-X-NOSTALGIA □ F

Matière / *Material:* *White metal*

Référence du fabricant *Manufacturer's Reference*	Désignation *Designation*	Type	*Type*	Date de la voiture *Date of car*	Date du modèle *Date of model*	Echelle *Scale*
01	Ferrari	250 GTO, conduite à gauche, version Silverstone, Tour de France, 12 h. Sebring et Le Mans	*250 GTO, left-hand drive (Silverstone, Tour de France, Sebring 12 hours and Le Mans versions).*	1962	1980	1/43
02	Ferrari	250 GTO, conduite à droite	*250 GTO, right-hand drive*	1962	1980	1/43
03	Ferrari	250 GT «SWB», civile	*250 GT "SWB", road car*	1961	1980	1/43
04	Ferrari	250 GT «SWB», conduite à droite Tour de France	*250 GT "SWB", right-hand drive Tour de France*	1961-62	1980	1/43
05	Ferrari	250 GT «SWB», conduite à droite TT (Moss), Le Mans (Moss-Hill)	*250 GT "SWB", right-hand drive TT (Moss), Le Mans (Moss-Hill).*	1961	1980	1/43

Référence du fabricant *Manufacturer's Reference*	Désignation *Designation*	Type	*Type*	Date de la voiture *Date of car*	Date du modèle *Date of model*	Echelle *Scale*
06	Ferrari	250 GT «SWB», conduite à gauche nº19-20, Le Mans . .	*250 GT "SWB", left-hand drive No. 19-20, Le Mans . . . . .*	1961	1980	1/43
07	Ferrari	250 GT «SWB», conduite à gauche nº 14-16, Le Mans, nº 6 TT (Parkes).	*250 GT "SWB", left-hand drive No. 14-16, Le Mans, No. 6 TT (Parkes) . . . .*	1961	1980	1/43
08a	Ferrari	250 GTO, conduite à gauche, Laguna Seca	*250 GTO, left-hand drive, Laguna Seca . . . .*	1963	1980	1/43
08b	Ferrari	250 GTO, conduite à gauche, Targa Florio	*250 GTO, left-hand drive, Targa Florio . . . .*	1962	1980	1/43

AMR-X-TENARIV □ F

Matière / *Material:* *White metal*

Référence du fabricant	Désignation	Type	*Type*	Date de la voiture	Date du modèle	Echelle
1a	Renault	F2 «Elf», Championne Europe, Jabouille.	*F2 "Elf", European Championship, Jabouille . . .*	1976	1977	1/43
1b	Renault	F2 «Elf», Michel Leclère	*F2 "Elf", Michel Leclère version*	1976	1977	1/43
2a	Martini	F2 «MK 19», René Arnoux . . .	*F2 "MK 19", René Arnoux's car*	1976	1977	1/43
2b	Martini	F2 «MK 19», Patrick Tambay . .	*F2 "MK 19", Patrick Tambay's car . . . .*	1976	1977	1/43
3a	March	F2 «762», «Jägermeister». . . .	*F2 "762", "Jägermeister". . . .*	1976	1977	1/43
3b	March	F2 «762», «Caixa».	*F2 "762", "Caixa". . . . . . .*	1976	1977	1/43
3c	March	F2 «762», «Scaini»	*F2 "762", "Scaini" . . . . . .*	1976	1977	1/43
4a	Chevron	F2 «B 35», «Gitanes», Laffite . .	*F2 "B 35", "Gitanes", Laffite . .*	1976	1977	1/43
4b	Chevron	F2 «B 35», «Alpquell», Binder . .	*F2 "B 35", "Alpquell", Binder . .*	1976	1977	1/43
5	Renault	F1 «RSO1», GP Zandvoort . . .	*F1 "RSO1", Zandvoort GP . . .*	1977	1978	1/43
6	ATS	F1 «PC 4», Jean-Pierre Jarrier . .	*F1 "PC 4", Jean-Pierre Jarrier's car . . . .*	1977	1978	1/43
7	Shadow	Cosworth F1 «DN 8», 1re GP Autriche, Alan Jones.	*Cosworth F1 "DN 8", 1st Austrian GP, Alan Jones . . .*	1977	1978	1/43
8	Hesketh	Cosworth F1 «308 E», «Penthouse» Rupert Keegan .	*Cosworth F1, "308 E", "Penthouse" Rupert Keegan .*	1977	1978	1/43
9a	Martini	F2 «MK 22», Arnoux ou Pironi .	*F2 "MK 22", Arnoux or Pironi . .*	1977	1978	1/43
9b	Martini	F2 «MK 22», Martini Team Everest.	*F2 "MK 22", Martini Team Everest. . . . .*	1977	1978	1/43
10a	Kauhsen	F2 «Renault», Klaus Ludwig. . .	*F2 "Renault", Klaus Ludwig. . .*	1977	1978	1/43
10b	Kauhsen	F2 «Toshiba», Michel Leclère . .	*F2 "Toshiba", Michel Leclère . .*	1977	1978	1/43
11a	Chevron	F2 «B 40», «ICI», Patrick Tambay	*F2 "B 40", "ICI", Patrick Tambay*	1977	1978	1/43
11b	Chevron	F2 «B 40», «Stebel», Ricardo Patrese	*F2 "B 40", "Stebel", Ricardo Patrese . . . .*	1977	1978	1/43
11c	Chevron	F2 «B 40», «Opert», Jacques Laffite	*F2 "B 40", "Opert", Jacques Laffite . . . .*	1977	1978	1/43
12a	March	F2 «772», «Sarca», Pessenti-Rossi	*F2 "772", "Sarca", Pessenti-Rossi . . . .*	1977	1978	1/43
12b	March	F2 «772», «Le Marquis», Colombo.	*F2 "772", "Le Marquis", Colombo. . . . .*	1977	1978	1/43
13	Williams	F1 «FW 06», Alan Jones	*F1 "FW 06", Alan Jones . . . .*	1978	1979	1/43
14	Brabham	Alfa Romeo F1 «BT 46», Lauda	*Alfa Romeo F1 "BT 46", Lauda*	1978	1979	1/43
15	Surtees	F1 «TS 20», «Beta» ou «Durex»	*F1 "TS 20", "Beta" or "Durex" .*	1978	1978	1/43
16	Ligier	Matra F1 «JS 7», 1re GP Suède, Jacques Laffite	*Matra F1 "JS 7", 1st Swedish GP, Jacques Laffite . . . . .*	1977	1978	1/43
17	Lotus	F1 «79», 1re GP Hollande, Mario Andretti	*F1 "79", 1st Dutch GP, Mario Andretti . . . .*	1978	1979	1/43
18	Ligier	F1 «JS 11», 1re GP Brésil ou Argentine	*F1 "JS 11", 1st Brasilian or Argentine GP . . . .*	1979	1979	1/43
19	Tyrrell	F1 «009»	*F1 "009" . . . .*	1979	1979	1/43
20	Brabham	Alfa Romeo «BT 48», F1	*Alfa Romeo F1 "BT 48" . . . .*	1979	1979	1/43
21	McLaren	F1 «M 28», J. Watson	*F1 "M 28", J. Watson . . . . .*	1979	1979	1/43
22	Renault	F1 «RS 11/12», 1re GP France, Jean-Pierre Jabouille	*F2 "RS 11/12", 1st French GP, Jean-Pierre Jabouille . . . .*	1979	1979	1/43
23	Williams	F1 «FW 07», GP Monaco, Alan Jones	*F1 "FW 07", Monaco GP, Alan Jones . . . .*	1979	1979	1/43
24	Arrows	F1 «A 2», «Warsteiner».	*F1 "A 2", "Warsteiner". . . . .*	1979	1980	1/43
25	Ensign	F1 «MN 179», Gaillard-Surer . .	*F1 "MN 179", Gaillard-Surer . .*	1979	1980	1/43
26	Williams	F1 «FW 07 B», 1re GP Angleterre Clay Regazzoni	*F1 "FW 07 B", 1st British GP Clay Regazzoni . . . . . .*	1980	1980	1/43
27	Ligier	F1 «JS 11/15», GP Argentine . .	*F1 "JS 11/15", Argentine GP . .*	1980	1980	1/43

Référence du fabricant / *Manufacturer's Reference*	Désignation / *Designation*	Type	*Type*	Date de la voiture / *Date of car*	Date du modèle / *Date of model*	Echelle / *Scale*

AMR-VOITURE □ F

Matière / *Material:* *White metal*

1	Ligier	Maserati «JS 2», Le Mans	*Maserati "JS 2", Le Mans*	1974	1978	1/43
2	Ligier	Maserati Tour de France	*Maserati, Tour de France*	1974	1978	1/43
3	Ligier	Maserati «Gitanes», Le Mans	*Maserati "Gitanes", Le Mans*	1975	1978	1/43

AMT □ USA

Matière / *Material:* Plastique / *Plastic*

AMT utilisait du Tenite — un acétate — pour tous ses modèles à volant jusqu'en 1961. Du polystyrène fut utilisé pour toutes les maquettes plastiques des modèles annuels dès 1958. Le terme «télécommande» indique qu'il s'agit d'un modèle à pile télécommandé; ces modèles étaient les mêmes que ceux à volant.
AMT used Tenite plastic — an acetate — on all their flywheel models to 1961. Styrene plastic was used on all the annual kits, the models that started in 1958. Remote is used to indicate a battery operated remote controlled model car. These are the same as the flywheel models with the exception of the motivation power.

A remonter/ *Keywind*

	Ford	Custom cond. int. 4 portes	*4 doors custom sedan*	1949	1949	1/25
	Plymouth	Conduite intérieure 4 portes	*4 doors sedan*	1949	1949	1/25
	Ford	Custom conduite intérieure 4 portes (télécommande)	*4 doors custom sedan (remote)*	1949	1949	1/25
	Plymouth	Conduite intérieure 4 portes (télécommande)	*4 door sedan (remote)*	1949	1949	1/25
	Ford	Custom cond. int. 4 portes	*4 doors custom sedan*	1950	1950	1/25
	Plymouth	Conduite intérieure	*Sedan*	1950	1950	1/25
	Studebaker	Conduite intérieure	*Sedan*	1950	1950	1/25
	Ford	Custom conduite intérieure 4 portes (télécommande)	*4 doors custom sedan (remote)*	1951	1951	1/25
	Studebaker	Conduite intérieure	*Sedan*	1951	1951	1/25
	Pontiac	Conduite intérieure	*Sedan*	1951	1951	1/2?

Les modèles de Pontiac 1951/1952 sont à une échelle inférieure au 1/25.
AMT's Pontiac models for 1951/1952 are smaller than 1/25 scale.

	Ford	Custom conduite intérieure 4 portes (télécommande)	*4 doors custom sedan (remote)*	1951	1951	1/25
	Ford	Conduite intérieure 4 portes	*4 doors sedan*	1952	1952	1/25
	Studebaker			1952	1952	1/25
	Pontiac			1952	1952	1/2?

Modèles à volant/ *Flywheels*

	Ford	Conduite intérieure 4 portes	*4 doors sedan*	1953	1953	1/25
	Ford	Décapotable	*Convertible*	1953	1953	1/25
	Ford	Décapotable (Indy Pace Car)	*Convertible (Indy Pace Car)*	1953	1953	1/25
	Studebaker	Coupé Starliner	*Starliner coupé*	1953	1953	1/25
	Pontiac	2 portes hardtop	*2 doors hardtop*	1953	1953	1/25
	Buick			—	—	—

Maquettes à construire/ *Kits*

	Ford	Décapotable (Indy Pace Car)	*Convertible (Indy Pace Car)*	1953	1953	1/25
		Boîte de trois kits contenant Ford décapotable, Pontiac et Studebaker	*Three car kit (Two-Tine kit) with Ford convertible/Pontiac and Studebaker*	1953	1953	1/25

Modèles à volant/ *Flywheels*

129	Buick	Roadmaster conduite intérieure	*Roadmaster sedan*	1954	1954	1/25
130	Ford	Custom conduite intérieure	*Custom sedan*	1954	1954	1/25
131	Studebaker	Starliner	*Starliner*	1954	1954	1/25
132	Pontiac	Catalina hardtop	*Catalina hardtop*	1954	1954	1/25
133	Ford	Custom conduite intérieure (peinture deux tons)	*Custom sedan (two-tone paint)*	1954	1954	1/25
134	Studebaker	Starliner (peinture deux tons)	*Starliner (two-tone paint)*	1954	1954	1/25

Référence du fabricant *Manufacturer's Reference*	Désignation *Designation*	Type	*Type*	Date de la voiture *Date of car*	Date du modèle *Date of model*	Echelle *Scale*
135	Pontiac	Catalina hardtop (peinture deux tons)	*Catalina hardtop (two-tone paint)*	1954	1954	1/25
136	Buick	Roadmaster conduite intérieure (peinture deux tons)	*Roadmaster sedan (two-tone paint)*	1954	1954	1/25
222	Ford	Thunderbird décapotable	*Thunderbird convertible*	1955	1954	1/25
333	Ford	Sunliner décapotable	*Sunliner convertible*	1954	1954	1/25
444	Buick	Skylark décapotable	*Skylark convertible*	1954	1954	1/25
700	Ford	Custom conduite intérieure (télécommande)	*Custom sedan (remote)*	1954	1954	1/25
701	Studebaker	Starliner (télécommande)	*Starliner (remote)*	1954	1954	1/25
702	Pontiac	Catalina hardtop (télécommande)	*Catalina hardtop (remote)*	1954	1954	1/25
703	Buick	Roadmaster conduite intérieure (télécommande)	*Roadmaster sedan (remote)*	1954	1954	1/25

Maquettes à construire (boîte de trois)/*Kits (three car sets)*

Référence du fabricant *Manufacturer's Reference*	Désignation *Designation*	Type	*Type*	Date de la voiture *Date of car*	Date du modèle *Date of model*	Echelle *Scale*
500	Ford décapotable/Pontiac/Studebaker		*Ford convertible/Pontiac/ Studebaker*	1954	1954	1/25
501	Buick Roadmaster/Ford décapotable/Pontiac		*Buick Roadmaster/Ford convertible/Pontiac*	1954	1954	1/25
502	Ford conduite intérieure/Buick décapotable/Pontiac		*Ford sedan/Buick convertible/ Pontiac*	1954	1954	1/25

Modèles à volant/*Flywheels*

Cette année-là, AMT livre ses modèles avec des intérieurs, même lorsqu'il s'agit de conduites intérieures. Quelques modèles étaient disponibles avec ou sans intérieur. Seuls les Nos 133, 134, 136, 137, 600, 601 en étaient dépourvus.
This year, AMT put interiors in cars other than convertibles. Some models were both ways. Only 133, 134, 136, 137, 600 and 601 came without interiors.

Référence du fabricant *Manufacturer's Reference*	Désignation *Designation*	Type	*Type*	Date de la voiture *Date of car*	Date du modèle *Date of model*	Echelle *Scale*
55F	Ford	Victoria conduite intérieure	*Victoria sedan.*	1955	1955	1/25
66D	Dodge	Royal Lancer conduite intérieure	*Royal Lancer sedan*	1955	1955	1/25
77C	Cadillac	Coupé de ville hardtop	*Coupé de ville hardtop*	1955	1955	1/25
133	Ford	Victoria conduite intérieure	*Victoria sedan.*	1955	1955	1/25
134	Studebaker	Starliner conduite intérieure	*Starliner sedan*	1955	1955	1/25
136	Buick	Roadmaster conduite intérieure	*Roadmaster sedan*	1955	1955	1/25
137	Dodge	Royal Lancer conduite intérieure	*Royal Lancer sedan*	1955	1955	1/25
138	Cadillac	Coupé de ville	*Coupé de ville*	1955	1955	1/25
222	Ford	Thunderbird décapotable	*Thunderbird convertible*	1955	1955	1/25
333	Ford	Sunliner décapotable	*Sunliner convertible*	1955	1955	1/25
444	Buick	Century décapotable	*Century convertible*	1955	1955	1/25
600	Ford	Victoria conduite intérieure (télécommande)	*Victoria sedan (remote)*	1955	1955	1/25
601	Studebaker	Starliner conduite intérieure (télécommande)	*Starliner sedan (remote)*	1955	1955	1/25
700	Ford	Victoria conduite intérieure (télécommande)	*Victoria sedan (remote)*	1955	1955	1/25
704	Ford	Sunliner décapotable (télécommande)	*Sunliner convertible (remote)*	1955	1955	1/25
705	Buick	Century décapotable (télécommande)	*Century convertible (remote)*	1955	1955	1/25
706	Dodge	Royal Lancer conduite intérieure (télécommande)	*Royal Lancer sedan (remote)*	1955	1955	1/25
707	Cadillac	Coupé de ville (télécommande)	*Coupé de ville (remote)*	1955	1955	1/25
708	Ford	Thunderbird décapotable (télécommande)	*Thunderbird convertible (remote)*	1955	1955	1/25

Maquettes à construire/*Kits*

Référence du fabricant *Manufacturer's Reference*	Désignation *Designation*	Type	*Type*	Date de la voiture *Date of car*	Date du modèle *Date of model*	Echelle *Scale*
300	Ford	Thunderbird décapotable (maquette de styling)	*Thunderbird convertible (styling kit)*	1955	1955	1/25
500	Dodge/Ford Thunderbird/Buick Roadmaster			1955	1955	1/25
501	Cadillac/Buick décapotable — *convertible* — Ford Victoria			1955	1955	1/25

Référence du fabricant / *Manufacturer's Reference*	Désignation / *Designation*	Type	*Type*	Date de la voiture / *Date of car*	Date du modèle / *Date of model*	Echelle / *Scale*

Modèles à volant/*Flywheels*

Les modèles suivants étaient livrés sans intérieur: 133, 134, 136, 138, 139, 600 et 601.
The following models came with no interior: 133, 134, 136, 138, 139, 600 and 601.

Référence du fabricant	Désignation	Type	*Type*	Date de la voiture	Date du modèle	Echelle
44B	Buick	Roadmaster hardtop	*Roadmaster hardtop . . . . . .*	1956	1956	1/25
55F	Ford	Victoria conduite intérieure . . .	*Victoria sedan. . . . .*	1956	1956	1/25
66D	Dodge	Royal Lancer hardtop	*Royal Lancer hardtop . . . . .*	1956	1956	1/25
77C	Cadillac	Coupé de ville	*Coupé de ville . . . .*	1956	1956	1/25
88C	Continental	Mark II hardtop	*Mark II hardtop . . . .*	1956	1956	1/25
133	Ford	Victoria conduite intérieure . . .	*Victoria sedan. . . . .*	1956	1956	1/25
134	Studebaker	Golden Hawk conduite intérieure	*Golden Hawk sedan . . . . . .*	1956	1956	1/25
136	Buick	Roadmaster hardtop	*Roadmaster hardtop . . . . . .*	1956	1956	1/25
137	Dodge	Royal Lancer hardtop	*Royal Lancer hardtop . . . . .*	1956	1956	1/25
138	Cadillac	Coupé de ville	*Coupé de ville . . . .*	1956	1956	1/25
139	Continental	Mark II hardtop	*Mark II hardtop . . . .*	1956	1956	1/25
222	Ford	Thunderbird décapotable	*Thunderbird convertible . . . .*	1956	1956	1/25
333	Ford	Sunliner décapotable	*Sunliner convertible . . . . . .*	1956	1956	1/25
444	Buick	Century décapotable	*Century convertible . . . . . .*	1956	1956	1/25
600	Ford	Victoria conduite intérieure (télécommande)	*Victoria sedan (remote) . . . .*	1956	1956	1/25
601	Studebaker	Golden Hawk conduite intérieure (télécommande)	*Golden Hawk sedan (remote) . .*	1956	1956	1/25
700	Ford	Victoria conduite intérieure (télécommande)	*Victoria sedan (remote) . . . .*	1956	1956	1/25
703	Buick	Roadmaster hardtop (télécommande)	*Roadmaster hardtop (remote) . .*	1956	1956	1/25
704	Ford	Sunliner décapotable (télécommande)	*Sunliner convertible (remote) . .*	1956	1956	1/25
705	Buick	Century décapotable (télécommande)	*Century convertible (remote) . .*	1956	1956	1/25
706	Dodge	Royal Lancer hardtop (télécommande)	*Royal Lancer hardtop (remote) .*	1956	1956	1/25
707	Cadillac	Coupé de ville (télécommande)	*Coupé de ville (remote) . . . .*	1956	1956	1/25
708	Ford	Thunderbird décapotable (télécommande)	*Thunderbird convertible (remote)*	1956	1956	1/25
709	Continental	Mark II hardtop (télécommande)	*Mark II hardtop (remote) . . . .*	1956	1956	1/25

Maquettes à construire/*Kits*

Référence du fabricant	Désignation	Date de la voiture	Date du modèle	Echelle
501	Cadillac/Continental/Buick décapotable — *convertible*	1956	1956	1/25

Modèles à volant/*Flywheels*

Première apparition des modèles SMP — Scale Model Products — reproduisant des voitures de la GM. Etant distribués par AMT et catalogués dans les catalogues des dépositaires AMT, nous les répertorions parmi les modèles AMT.
This was the first year for SMP — Scale Model Products — models of GM cars. Because they were marketed by AMT and are listed on AMT's dealer sheets, they are considered along with the AMT models.

Les modèles suivants sont sans intérieur: 133, 136, 139, 140, 141, 142, 600, 609, 610, 611 et 641.
The following models came without interior: 133, 136, 139, 140, 141, 142, 600, 609, 610, 611 and 641.

Référence du fabricant	Désignation	Type	*Type*	Date de la voiture	Date du modèle	Echelle
44B	Buick	Roadmaster hardtop	*Roadmaster hardtop . . . . . .*	1957	1957	1/25
55F	Ford	Fairlane 500 hardtop.	*Fairlane 500 hardtop. . . . . .*	1957	1957	1/25
88C	Continental	Mark II hardtop	*Mark II hardtop . . . .*	1957	1957	1/25
99C	Chevrolet	Bel Air hardtop	*Bel Air hardtop . . . .*	1957	1957	1/25
00P	Pontiac	Star Chief hardtop	*Star Chief hardtop. . . . . . .*	1957	1957	1/25
133	Ford	Fairlane 500 hardtop.	*Fairlane 500 hardtop. . . . . .*	1957	1957	1/25
136	Buick	Roadmaster hardtop	*Roadmaster hardtop . . . . . .*	1957	1957	1/25
139	Continental	Mark II hardtop	*Mark II hardtop . . . .*	1957	1957	1/25
140	Chevrolet	Bel Air hardtop	*Bel Air hardtop . . . .*	1957	1957	1/25
141	Chevrolet	Station-wagon	*Station wagon . . . .*	1957	1957	1/25
142	Pontiac	Star Chief hardtop	*Star Chief hardtop. . . . . . .*	1957	1957	1/25
222	Ford	Thunderbird décapotable	*Thunderbird convertible . . . .*	1957	1957	1/25
333	Ford	Sunliner décapotable	*Sunliner convertible . . . . . .*	1957	1957	1/25
444	Buick	Century décapotable.	*Century convertible . . . . . .*	1957	1957	1/25
666	Pontiac	Star Chief décapotable	*Star Chief convertible . . . . .*	1957	1957	1/25
777	Chevrolet	Bel Air décapotable	*Bel Air convertible. . . . . . .*	1957	1957	1/25

Référence du fabricant / *Manufacturer's Reference*	Désignation / *Designation*	Type	*Type*	Date de la voiture / *Date of car*	Date du modèle / *Date of model*	Echelle / *Scale*
600	Ford	Fairlane 500 hardtop (télécommande)	*Fairlane 500 hardtop (remote)* . .	1957	1957	1/25
609	Continental	Mark II hardtop (télécommande)	*Mark II hardtop (remote)*	1957	1957	1/25
610	Chevrolet	Bel Air hardtop (télécommande)	*Bel Air hardtop (remote)*	1957	1957	1/25
611	Pontiac	Star Chief hardtop (télécommande)	*Star Chief hardtop (remote)*. . .	1957	1957	1/25
641	Chevrolet	Station-wagon (télécommande)	*Station wagon (remote)*	1957	1957	1/25
700	Ford	Fairlane 500 hardtop (télécommande)	*Fairlane 500 hardtop (remote)*. .	1957	1957	1/25
703	Buick	Roadmaster hardtop (télécommande)	*Roadmaster hardtop (remote)* . .	1957	1957	1/25
704	Ford	Sunliner décapotable (télécommande)	*Sunliner convertible (remote)* . .	1957	1957	1/25
705	Buick	Century décapotable (télécommande)	*Century convertible (remote)* . .	1957	1957	1/25
708	Ford	Thunderbird décapotable (télécommande)	*Thunderbird convertible (remote)*	1957	1957	1/25
708	Continental	Mark II hardtop (télécommande)	*Mark II hardtop (remote)*	1957	1957	1/25
710	Chevrolet	Bel Air hardtop (télécommande)	*Bel Air hardtop (remote)*	1957	1957	1/25
711	Pontiac	Star Chief hardtop (télécommande)	*Star Chief hardtop (remote)*. . .	1957	1957	1/25
712	Pontiac	Star Chief décapotable (télécommande)	*Star Chief convertible (remote)* .	1957	1957	1/25
714	Chevrolet	Bel Air décapotable (télécommande)	*Bel Air convertible (remote)*. . .	1957	1957	1/25
Maquettes à construire/*Kits*						
501	Thunderbird/Continental/Buick Century			1957	1957	1/25
	Chevrolet	Bel Air hardtop	*Bel Air hardtop*	1957	1957	1/25
	Pontiac	Star Chief hardtop.	*Star Chief hardtop*.	1957	1957	1/25
	Chevrolet	Bel Air décapotable	*Bel Air convertible*.	1957	1957	1/25
	Pontiac	Star Chief décapotable	*Star Chief convertible*	1957	1957	1/25
Modèles à volant/*Flywheels*						
CT1	Chevrolet	Apache camionnette	*Apache pickup*	1958	1958	1/25
11E	Edsel	Pacer hardtop.	*Pacer hardtop*.	1958	1958	1/25
22M	Imperial	Crown hardtop	*Crown hardtop*	1958	1958	1/25
33S	Chevrolet	Nomad station-wagon	*Nomad station wagon*	1958	1958	1/25
44B	Buick	Roadmaster hardtop	*Roadmaster hardtop*	1958	1958	1/25
55F	Ford	Fairlane hardtop.	*Fairlane hardtop*.	1958	1958	1/25
66T	Ford	Thunderbird hardtop	*Thunderbird hardtop*	1958	1958	1/25
88C	Continental	Mark III hardtop.	*Mark III hardtop*.	1958	1958	1/25
99C	Chevrolet	Impala hardtop	*Impala hardtop*	1958	1958	1/25
00P	Pontiac	Bonneville hardtop	*Bonneville hardtop*	1958	1958	1/25
111	Chevrolet	Corvette décapotable	*Corvette convertible*	1958	1958	1/25
222	Ford	Thunderbird décapotable	*Thunderbird convertible*	1958	1958	1/25
333	Ford	Sunliner décapotable	*Sunliner convertible*	1958	1958	1/25
444	Buick	Roadmaster décapotable	*Roadmaster convertible*	1958	1958	1/25
666	Pontiac	Bonneville décapotable.	*Bonneville convertible*	1958	1958	1/25
777	Chevrolet	Impala décapotable	*Impala convertible*.	1958	1958	1/25
888	Edsel	Pacer décapotable.	*Pacer convertible*	1958	1958	1/25
999	Imperial	Crown décapotable	*Crown convertible*.	1958	1958	1/25
600	Ford	Fairlane hardtop (télécommande/ sans intérieur)	*Fairlane hardtop (remote/no interior)*	1958	1958	1/25
603	Buick	Roadmaster hardtop (télécommande/sans intérieur)	*Roadmaster hardtop (remote/no interior)*	1958	1958	1/25
610	Chevrolet	Impala hardtop (télécommande/ sans intérieur)	*Impala hardtop (remote/no interior)*	1958	1958	1/25
611	Pontiac	Bonneville hardtop (télécommande/sans intérieur)	*Bonneville hardtop (remote/no interior)*	1958	1958	1/25
700	Ford	Fairlane hardtop (télécommande)	*Fairlane hardtop (remote)*. . . .	1958	1958	1/25
703	Buick	Roadmaster hardtop (télécommande)	*Roadmaster hardtop (remote)* . .	1958	1958	1/25
710	Chevrolet	Impala hardtop (télécommande)	*Impala hardtop (remote)*	1958	1958	1/25
711	Pontiac	Bonneville hardtop (télécommande)	*Bonneville hardtop (remote)* . .	1958	1958	1/25

Référence du fabricant / *Manufacturer's Reference*	Désignation / *Designation*	Type	*Type*	Date de la voiture / *Date of car*	Date du modèle / *Date of model*	Echelle / *Scale*
Maquettes à construire/*Kits*						
501	Ford/Pontiac/Continental (sortie non confirmée/*release is questionable*)			1958	1958	1/25
3FK	Ford	Fairlane 500 décapotable	*Fairlane 500 convertible*	1958	1958	1/25
3FKHT	Ford	Fairlane 500 hardtop	*Fairlane 500 hardtop*	1958	1958	1/25
4BK	Buick	Roadmaster décapotable	*Roadmaster convertible*	1958	1958	1/25
4BKHT	Buick	Roadmaster hardtop	*Roadmaster hardtop*	1958	1958	1/25
6PK	Pontiac	Bonneville décapotable	*Bonneville convertible*	1958	1958	1/25
6PKHT	Pontiac	Bonneville hardtop	*Bonneville hardtop*	1958	1958	1/25
7CK	Chevrolet	Impala décapotable	*Impala convertible*	1958	1958	1/25
7CKHT	Chevrolet	Impala hardtop	*Impala hardtop*	1958	1958	1/25
8EK	Edsel	Pacer décapotable	*Pacer convertible*	1958	1958	1/25
8EKHT	Edsel	Pacer hardtop	*Pacer hardtop*	1958	1958	1/25
9MK	Imperial	Crown décapotable	*Crown convertible*	1958	1958	1/25
Modèles à volant/*Flywheels*						
11FO-HT	Ford	Galaxie hardtop	*Galaxie hardtop*	1959	1959	1/25
12FO-THT	Ford	Thunderbird hardtop	*Thunderbird hardtop*	1959	1959	1/25
22ED-HT	Edsel	Corsair hardtop	*Corsair hardtop*	1959	1959	1/25
33ME-HT	Mercury	Park Lane hardtop	*Park Lane hardtop*	1959	1959	1/25
44CO-HT	Continental	Mark IV hardtop	*Mark IV hardtop*	1959	1959	1/25
55BU-HT	Buick	Invicta hardtop	*Invicta hardtop*	1959	1959	1/25
66PO-HT	Pontiac	Bonneville hardtop	*Bonneville hardtop*	1959	1959	1/25
77CH-HT	Chevrolet	Impala hardtop	*Impala hardtop*	1959	1959	1/25
78CH-SW	Chevrolet	Station-wagon	*Station wagon*	1959	1959	1/25
79CH-AT	Chevrolet	Apache camionnette	*Apache pickup*	1959	1959	1/25
88IM-HT	Imperial	Hardtop	*Hardtop*	1959	1959	1/25
111FO-C	Ford	Galaxie Sunliner décapotable	*Galaxie Sunliner convertible*	1959	1959	1/25
112FO-TC	Ford	Thunderbird décapotable	*Thunderbird convertible*	1959	1959	1/25
222ED-C	Edsel	Corsair décapotable	*Corsair convertible*	1959	1959	1/25
333ME-C	Mercury	Park Lane décapotable	*Park Lane convertible*	1959	1959	1/25
444CO-C	Continental	Mark IV décapotable	*Mark IV convertible*	1959	1959	1/25
555BU-C	Buick	Invicta décapotable	*Invicta convertible*	1959	1959	1/25
666PO-C	Pontiac	Bonneville décapotable	*Bonneville convertible*	1959	1959	1/25
777CH-C	Chevrolet	Impala décapotable	*Impala convertible*	1959	1959	1/25
778CH-CV	Chevrolet	Corvette décapotable	*Corvette convertible*	1959	1959	1/25
888IM-C	Imperial	Décapotable	*Convertible*	1959	1959	1/25
Maquettes à construire/*Kits*						
1CK	Ford	Galaxie Sunliner décapotable	*Galaxie Sunliner Convertible*	1959	1959	1/25
1HTK	Ford	Galaxie hardtop	*Galaxie hardtop*	1959	1959	1/25
1TCK	Ford	Thunderbird décapotable	*Thunderbird convertible*	1959	1959	1/25
1THK	Ford	Thunderbird hardtop	*Thunderbird hardtop*	1959	1959	1/25
2CK	Edsel	Corsair décapotable	*Corsair convertible*	1959	1959	1/25
2HTK	Edsel	Corsair hardtop	*Corsair hardtop*	1959	1959	1/25
3CK	Mercury	Park Lane décapotable	*Park Lane convertible*	1959	1959	1/25
3HTK	Mercury	Park Lane hardtop	*Park Lane hardtop*	1959	1959	1/25
4CK	Continental	Mark IV décapotable	*Mark IV convertible*	1959	1959	1/25
4HTK	Continental	Mark IV hardtop	*Mark IV hardtop*	1959	1959	1/25
5CK	Buick	Invicta décapotable	*Invicta convertible*	1959	1959	1/25
5HTK	Buick	Invicta hardtop	*Invicta hardtop*	1959	1959	1/25
6CK	Pontiac	Bonneville décapotable	*Bonneville convertible*	1959	1959	1/25
6HTK	Pontiac	Bonneville hardtop	*Bonneville hardtop*	1959	1959	1/25
7CK	Chevrolet	Impala décapotable	*Impala convertible*	1959	1959	1/25
7HTK	Chevrolet	Impala hardtop	*Impala hardtop*	1959	1959	1/25
7CV	Chevrolet	Corvette décapotable	*Corvette convertible*	1959	1959	1/25
7CHK	Chevrolet	Corvette hardtop	*Corvette hardtop*	1959	1959	1/25
8CK	Imperial	Décapotable	*Convertible*	1959	1959	1/25
8HTK	Imperial	Hardtop	*Hardtop*	1959	1959	1/25
160	Ford	Leva Car Mach I (prototype)	*Leva Car Mach I (prototype)*	1959	1959	1/16
Maquettes série Trophy/*Trophy series kits*						
132	Ford	Modèle B roadster	*Model B roadster*	1932	1959	1/25
159	Speed Boat	Avec remorque	*With trailer*	1959	1959	1/25

Référence du fabricant / *Manufacturer's Reference*	Désignation / *Designation*	Type	*Type*	Date de la voiture / *Date of car*	Date du modèle / *Date of model*	Echelle / *Scale*
Modèles à volant/ *Flywheels*						
10	Ford	Falcon conduite intérieure	*Falcon sedan*	1960	1960	1/25
11	Ford	Special Starliner hardtop	*Special Starliner hardtop*	1960	1960	1/25
12	Ford	Thunderbird hardtop	*Thunderbird hardtop*	1960	1960	1/25
13	Ford	F-100 camionnette	*F-100 pickup*	1960	1960	1/25
22	Edsel	Ranger hardtop	*Ranger hardtop*	1960	1960	1/25
33	Mercury	Park Lane hardtop	*Park Lane hardtop*	1960	1960	1/25
44	Continental	Mark V hardtop	*Mark V hardtop*	1960	1960	1/25
55	Buick	Invicta hardtop	*Invicta hardtop*	1960	1960	1/25
66	Pontiac	Bonneville hardtop	*Bonneville hardtop*	1960	1960	1/25
70	Chevrolet	Corvair conduite intérieure	*Corvair sedan*	1960	1960	1/25
76	Chevrolet	El Camino camionnette	*El Camino pickup*	1960	1960	1/25
77	Chevrolet	Impala hardtop	*Impala hardtop*	1960	1960	1/25
78	Chevrolet	Nomad station-wagon	*Nomad station wagon*	1960	1960	1/25
79	Chevrolet	Apache camionnette	*Apache pickup*	1960	1960	1/25
88	Imperial	Hardtop	*Hardtop*	1960	1960	1/25
90	Chrysler	Valiant conduite intérieure	*Valiant sedan*	1960	1960	1/25
111	Ford	Special Sunliner décapotable	*Special Sunliner convertible*	1960	1960	1/25
112	Ford	Thunderbird décapotable	*Thunderbird convertible*	1960	1960	1/25
222	Edsel	Ranger décapotable	*Ranger convertible*	1960	1960	1/25
333	Mercury	Park Lane décapotable	*Park Lane convertible*	1960	1960	1/25
444	Continental	Mark V décapotable	*Mark V convertible*	1960	1960	1/25
555	Buick	Invicta décapotable	*Invicta convertible*	1960	1960	1/25
666	Pontiac	Bonneville décapotable	*Bonneville convertible*	1960	1960	1/25
777	Chevrolet	Impala décapotable	*Impala convertible*	1960	1960	1/25
888	Imperial	Décapotable	*Convertible*	1960	1960	1/25
Maquettes à construire/ *Kits*						
1060	Ford	Falcon conduite intérieure	*Falcon sedan*	1960	1960	1/25
1160	Ford	Special Starliner hardtop	*Special Starliner hardtop*	1960	1960	1/25
1260	Ford	Thunderbird hardtop	*Thunderbird hardtop*	1960	1960	1/25
1360	Ford	F-100 camionnette	*F-100 pickup*	1960	1960	1/25
2260	Edsel	Ranger hardtop	*Ranger hardtop*	1960	1960	1/25
3060	Mercury	Comet conduite intérieure	*Comet sedan*	1960	1960	1/25
3360	Mercury	Park Lane hardtop	*Park Lane hardtop*	1960	1960	1/25
4460	Continental	Mark V hardtop	*Mark V hardtop*	1960	1960	1/25
5560	Buick	Invicta hardtop	*Invicta hardtop*	1960	1960	1/25
6660	Pontiac	Bonneville hardtop	*Bonneville hardtop*	1960	1960	1/25
7060	Chevrolet	Corvair conduite intérieure	*Corvair sedan*	1960	1960	1/25
7660	Chevrolet	El Camino camionnette	*El Camino pickup*	1960	1960	1/25
7760	Chevrolet	Impala hardtop	*Impala hardtop*	1960	1960	1/25
7860	Chevrolet	Corvette hardtop	*Corvette hardtop*	1960	1960	1/25
7960	Chevrolet	Apache camionnette	*Apache pickup*	1960	1960	1/25
8860	Imperial	Hardtop	*Hardtop*	1960	1960	1/25
9060	Chrysler	Valiant conduite intérieure	*Valiant sedan*	1960	1960	1/25
11160	Ford	Special Sunliner décapotable	*Special Sunliner convertible*	1960	1960	1/25
11260	Ford	Thunderbird décapotable	*Thunderbird convertible*	1960	1960	1/25
22260	Edsel	Ranger décapotable	*Ranger convertible*	1960	1960	1/25
33360	Mercury	Park Lane décapotable	*Park Lane convertible*	1960	1960	1/25
44460	Continental	Mark V décapotable	*Mark V convertible*	1960	1960	1/25
55560	Buick	Invicta décapotable	*Invicta convertible*	1960	1960	1/25
66660	Pontiac	Bonneville décapotable	*Bonneville convertible*	1960	1960	1/25
77760	Chevrolet	Impala décapotable	*Impala convertible*	1960	1960	1/25
77860	Chevrolet	Corvette décapotable	*Corvette convertible*	1960	1960	1/25
88860	Imperial	Décapotable	*Convertible*	1960	1960	1/25
Maquettes série Trophy/ *Trophy series kits*						
125	Ford	Modèle T roadster/coupé abaissé	*Model T roadster/chopped coupé*	1925	1960	1/25
140	Ford	Coupé	*Coupé*	1940	1960	1/25
232	Ford	Coupé 5 glaces (V8)	*5 windows coupé (V8)*	1932	1960	1/25
Modèles à friction / *Frictions*						
F-111	Ford	Galaxie Sunliner décapotable	*Galaxie Sunliner convertible*	1961	1961	1/25

Référence du fabricant / *Manufacturer's Reference*	Désignation / *Designation*	Type	*Type*	Date de la voiture / *Date of car*	Date du modèle / *Date of model*	Echelle / *Scale*
F-121	Ford	Galaxie hardtop	*Galaxie hardtop*	1961	1961	1/25
F-131	Ford	F-100 camionnette	*F-100 pickup*	1961	1961	1/25
F-211	Ford	Thunderbird décapotable	*Thunderbird convertible*	1961	1961	1/25
F-221	Ford	Thunderbird hardtop	*Thunderbird hardtop*	1961	1961	1/25
F-311	Mercury	Monterey décapotable	*Monterey convertible*	1961	1961	1/25
F-321	Mercury	Monterey hardtop	*Monterey hardtop*	1961	1961	1/25
F-411	Lincoln	Continental 4 portes décapotable	*Continental 4 door convertible*	1961	1961	1/25
F-421	Lincoln	Continental 4 portes hardtop	*Continental 4 door hardtop*	1961	1961	1/25
F-511	Buick	Invicta décapotable	*Invicta convertible*	1961	1961	1/25
F-521	Buick	Invicta hardtop	*Invicta hardtop*	1961	1961	1/25
F-611	Pontiac	Bonneville décapotable	*Bonneville convertible*	1961	1961	1/25
F-621	Pontiac	Bonneville hardtop	*Bonneville hardtop*	1961	1961	1/25
F-711	Chevrolet	Impala décapotable	*Impala convertible*	1961	1961	1/25
F-721	Chevrolet	Impala hardtop 4 portes	*Impala hardtop 4 door*	1961	1961	1/25
F-730	Chevrolet	El Camino camionnette	*El Camino pickup*	1960	1961	1/25
F-731	Chevrolet	Apache camionnette	*Apache pickup*	1961	1961	1/25
F-811	Chrysler	Imperial décapotable	*Imperial convertible*	1961	1961	1/25
F-821	Chrysler	Imperial hardtop	*Imperial hardtop*	1961	1961	1/25
F-911	Chevrolet	Corvette décapotable	*Corvette convertible*	1961	1961	1/25
F-1031	Ford	Falcon Ranchero camionnette	*Falcon Ranchero pickup*	1961	1961	1/25
F-1061	Ford	Falcon conduite intérieure	*Falcon sedan*	1961	1961	1/25
F-3061	Mercury	Comet conduite intérieure	*Comet sedan*	1961	1961	1/25
F-5041	Buick	Station-wagon spécial	*Special station wagon*	1961	1961	1/25
F-6061	Pontiac	Tempest conduite intérieure	*Tempest sedan*	1961	1961	1/25
F-7061	Chevrolet	Corvair hardtop	*Corvair hardtop*	1961	1961	1/25
F-8061	Plymouth	Valiant hardtop	*Valiant hardtop*	1961	1961	1/25

Maquettes à construire, modèles de l'année / *Annual kits*

Référence du fabricant / *Manufacturer's Reference*	Désignation / *Designation*	Type	*Type*	Date de la voiture / *Date of car*	Date du modèle / *Date of model*	Echelle / *Scale*
K-111	Ford	Galaxie Sunliner décapotable	*Galaxie Sunliner convertible*	1961	1961	1/25
K-121	Ford	Galaxie Starliner hardtop	*Galaxie Starliner hardtop*	1961	1961	1/25
K-131	Ford	F-100 camionnette	*F-100 pickup*	1961	1961	1/25
K-211	Ford	Thunderbird décapotable	*Thunderbird convertible*	1961	1961	1/25
K-311	Mercury	Monterey décapotable	*Monterey convertible*	1961	1961	1/25
K-321	Mercury	Monterey hardtop	*Monterey hardtop*	1961	1961	1/25
K-411	Lincoln	Continental 4 portes décapotable	*Continental 4 door convertible*	1961	1961	1/25
K-421	Lincoln	Continental 4 portes hardtop	*Continental 4 door hardtop*	1961	1961	1/25
K-511	Buick	Invicta décapotable	*Invicta convertible*	1961	1961	1/25
K-521	Buick	Invicta hardtop	*Invicta hardtop*	1961	1961	1/25
K-611	Pontiac	Bonneville décapotable	*Bonneville convertible*	1961	1961	1/25
K-621	Pontiac	Bonneville hardtop	*Bonneville hardtop*	1961	1961	1/25
K-711	Chevrolet	Impala décapotable	*Impala convertible*	1961	1961	1/25
K-721	Chevrolet	Impala hardtop	*Impala hardtop*	1961	1961	1/25
K-730	Chevrolet	El Camino camionnette	*El Camino pickup*	1960	1961	1/25
K-731	Chevrolet	Apache camionnette	*Apache pickup*	1961	1961	1/25
K-811	Chrysler	Imperial décapotable	*Imperial convertible*	1961	1961	1/25
K-821	Chrysler	Imperial hardtop	*Imperial hardtop*	1961	1961	1/25
K-911	Chevrolet	Corvette décapotable	*Corvette convertible*	1961	1961	1/25
K-921	Chevrolet	Corvette hardtop	*Corvette hardtop*	1961	1961	1/25
K-1031	Ford	Falcon ranchero camionnette	*Falcon Ranchero pickup*	1961	1961	1/25
K-1061	Ford	Falcon conduite intérieure	*Falcon sedan*	1961	1961	1/25
K-3061	Mercury	Comet conduite intérieure	*Comet sedan*	1961	1961	1/25
K-5041	Buick	Station-wagon spécial	*Special station wagon*	1961	1961	1/25
K-6061	Pontiac	Tempest 4 portes conduite intérieure	*Tempest 4 door sedan*	1961	1961	1/25
K-7061	Chevrolet	Corvair Monza hardtop	*Corvair Monza hardtop*	1961	1961	1/25
K-8061	Plymouth	Valiant hardtop	*Valiant hardtop*	1961	1961	1/25

Maquettes série Styline / *Styline Series kits*

Référence du fabricant / *Manufacturer's Reference*	Désignation / *Designation*	Type	*Type*	Date de la voiture / *Date of car*	Date du modèle / *Date of model*	Echelle / *Scale*
S121	Ford	Galaxie (Club Victoria hardtop)	*Galaxie (Club Victoria hardtop)*	1961	1961	1/25
S221	Ford	Thunderbird hardtop	*Thunderbird hardtop*	1961	1961	1/25
S1031	Ford	Falcon ranchero camionnette	*Falcon Ranchero pickup*	1961	1961	1/25

Modèles à friction / *Frictions*

Référence du fabricant / *Manufacturer's Reference*	Désignation / *Designation*	Type	*Type*	Date de la voiture / *Date of car*	Date du modèle / *Date of model*	Echelle / *Scale*
F112	Ford	Galaxie 500 Sunliner décapotable	*Galaxie 500 Sunliner convertible*	1962	1962	1/25

Référence du fabricant / *Manufacturer's Reference*	Désignation / *Designation*	Type	*Type*	Date de la voiture / *Date of car*	Date du modèle / *Date of model*	Echelle / *Scale*
F212	Ford	Thunderbird Sports Roadster décapotable	*Thunderbird Sports Roadster convertible*	1962	1962	1/25
F522	Buick	Elektra 225 hardtop	*Elektra 225 hardtop*	1962	1962	1/25
F622	Pontiac	Bonneville hardtop	*Bonneville hardtop*	1962	1962	1/25
F912	Chevrolet	Corvette décapotable	*Corvette convertible*	1962	1962	1/25
F1062	Ford	Falcon conduite intérieure	*Falcon sedan*	1962	1962	1/25
F3062	Mercury	Comet conduite intérieure	*Comet sedan*	1962	1962	1/25
F5042	Buick	Station-wagon spécial	*Special station wagon*	1962	1962	1/25
F6012	Pontiac	Tempest décapotable	*Tempest convertible*	1962	1962	1/25

Maquettes à construire, modèles de l'année / *Annual kits*

Les numéros de référence précédés de la lettre S indiquent qu'il s'agit de modèles semblables à ceux de la série Styline; les boîtes comportaient plus de pièces hors série et coûtaient plus cher que les kits standard.
Kits numbers preceded with the letter S are considered Styline Series models. These kits had more custom parts and cost more than a regular kit.

Référence du fabricant / *Manufacturer's Reference*	Désignation / *Designation*	Type	*Type*	Date de la voiture / *Date of car*	Date du modèle / *Date of model*	Echelle / *Scale*
K112	Ford	Galaxie 500 décapotable	*Galaxie 500 convertible*	1962	1962	1/25
S121	Ford	Galaxie 500 hardtop	*Galaxie 500 hardtop*	1962	1962	1/25
K132	Ford	F-100 camionnette	*F-100 pickup*	1962	1962	1/25
K162	Ford	Fairlane 500 conduite intérieure	*Fairlane 500 sedan*	1962	1962	1/25
K212	Ford	Thunderbird décapotable	*Thunderbird convertible (sports roadster)*	1962	1962	1/25
S222	Ford	Thunderbird hardtop	*Thunderbird hardtop*	1962	1962	1/25
K312	Mercury	Monterey décapotable	*Monterey convertible*	1962	1962	1/25
K322	Mercury	Monterey hardtop	*Monterey hardtop*	1962	1962	1/25
K362	Mercury	Meteor conduite intérieure	*Meteor sedan*	1962	1962	1/25
K412	Lincoln	Continental 4 portes décapotable	*Continental 4 door convertible*	1962	1962	1/25
K422	Lincoln	Continental 4 portes hardtop	*Continental 4 door hardtop*	1962	1962	1/25
K512	Buick	Elektra 225 décapotable	*Elektra 225 convertible*	1962	1962	1/25
K522	Buick	Elektra 225 hardtop	*Elektra 225 hardtop*	1962	1962	1/25
K612	Pontiac	Bonneville décapotable	*Bonneville convertible*	1962	1962	1/25
S622	Pontiac	Bonneville hardtop	*Bonneville hardtop*	1962	1962	1/25
K712	Chevrolet	Impala décapotable	*Impala convertible*	1962	1962	1/25
S722	Chevrolet	Impala hardtop	*Impala hardtop*	1962	1962	1/25
K732	Chevrolet	Apache camionnette	*Apache pickup*	1962	1962	1/25
K812	Chrysler	Imperial Crown décapotable	*Imperial Crown convertible*	1962	1962	1/25
K822	Chrysler	Imperial Crown hardtop	*Imperial Crown hardtop*	1962	1962	1/25
K912	Chevrolet	Corvette décapotable	*Corvette convertible*	1962	1962	1/25
S922	Chevrolet	Corvette hardtop (pas de hardtop de série dans le kit)	*Corvette hardtop (no stock hardtop in kit)*	1962	1962	1/25
S1062	Ford	Falcon Futura conduite intérieure	*Falcon Futura sedan*	1962	1962	1/25
S3062	Mercury	Comet conduite intérieure	*Comet sedan*	1962	1962	1/25
K5042	Buick	Station-wagon spécial	*Special station wagon*	1962	1962	1/25
K6012	Pontiac	Tempest Le Mans décapotable	*Tempest Le Mans convertible*	1962	1962	1/25
K6022	Pontiac	Tempest Le Mans conduite intérieure	*Tempest Le Mans sedan*	1962	1962	1/25
K7012	Chevrolet	Chevy II Nova décapotable	*Chevy II Nova convertible*	1962	1962	1/25
K7022	Chevrolet	Chevy II Nova décapotable	*Chevy II Nova convertible*	1962	1962	1/25
S7052	Chevrolet	Corvair Monza coupé	*Corvair Monza coupé*	1962	1962	1/25
S8062	Plymouth	Valiant Signet hardtop	*Valiant Signet hardtop*	1962	1962	1/25

Modèles à friction / *Frictions*

La liste de ces modèles 1963 pourrait ne pas être complète, les données d'usine faisant défaut.
The listing of 1963 Frictions may not be complete as no factory literature could be found.

Référence du fabricant / *Manufacturer's Reference*	Désignation / *Designation*	Type	*Type*	Date de la voiture / *Date of car*	Date du modèle / *Date of model*	Echelle / *Scale*
	Ford	Galaxie 500 XL hardtop	*Galaxie 500 XL hardtop*	1963	1963	1/25
	Ford	Thunderbird décapotable	*Thunderbird (sports roadster) convertible*	1963	1963	1/25
	Buick	Elektra décapotable	*Elektra convertible*	1963	1963	1/25
	Pontiac	Bonneville hardtop	*Bonneville hardtop*	1963	1963	1/25
	Plymouth	Valiant Signet hardtop	*Valiant Signet hardtop*	1963	1963	1/25

Maquettes à construire, modèles de l'année / *Annual kits*

Référence du fabricant / *Manufacturer's Reference*	Désignation / *Designation*	Type	*Type*	Date de la voiture / *Date of car*	Date du modèle / *Date of model*	Echelle / *Scale*
05-163	Ford	Fairline 500 hardtop	*Fairline 500 hardtop*	1963	1963	1/25
05-363	Mercury	Meteor hardtop	*Meteor hardtop*	1963	1963	1/25

Référence du fabricant / *Manufacturer's Reference*	Désignation / *Designation*	Type	*Type*	Date de la voiture / *Date of car*	Date du modèle / *Date of model*	Echelle / *Scale*
05-613	Pontiac	Tempest Le Mans décapotable. .	*Tempest Le Mans convertible . .*	1963	1963	1/25
5623	Pontiac	Tempest Le Mans hardtop . . .	*Tempest Le Mans hardtop . . .*	1963	1963	1/25
05-713	Chevrolet	Chevy II Nova décapotable . . .	*Chevy II Nova convertible . . .*	1963	1963	1/25
5723	Chevrolet	Chevy II Nova hardtop	*Chevy II Nova hardtop . . . . .*	1963	1963	1/25
06-113	Ford	Galaxie 500 XL décapotable. . .	*Galaxie 500 XL convertible . . .*	1963	1963	1/25
6123	Ford	Galaxie 500 XL hardtop (pavillon style fastback) . . .	*Galaxie 500 XL hardtop (fastback style roof) . . . . .*	1963	1963	1/25
06-213	Ford	Thunderbird décapotable	*Thunderbird convertible (sports roadster). . . . .*	1963	1963	1/25
6223	Ford	Thunderbird hardtop.	*Thunderbird hardtop. . . . . .*	1963	1963	1/25
06-313	Mercury	Monterey décapotable	*Monterey convertible . . . . .*	1963	1963	1/25
6323	Mercury	Marauder hardtop (pavillon style fastback).	*Marauder hardtop (fastback style roof) . . . .*	1963	1963	1/25
06-413	Lincoln	Continental 4 portes décapotable	*Continental 4 door convertible. .*	1963	1963	1/25
6423	Lincoln	Continental 4 portes conduite intérieure.	*Continental 4 door sedan . . . .*	1963	1963	1/25
06-513	Buick	Elektra décapotable	*Elektra convertible. . . . . . .*	1963	1963	1/25
6523	Buick	Elektra hardtop	*Elektra hardtop . . . .*	1963	1963	1/25
06-553	Buick	Riviera hardtop	*Riviera hardtop . . . .*	1963	1963	1/25
06-613	Pontiac	Bonneville décapotable.	*Bonneville convertible . . . . .*	1963	1963	1/25
6623	Pontiac	Bonneville hardtop	*Bonneville hardtop . . . . . .*	1963	1963	1/25
06-713	Chevrolet	Impala SS décapotable	*Impala SS convertible . . . . .*	1963	1963	1/25
6723	Chevrolet	Impala SS hardtop.	*Impala SS hardtop. . . . . . .*	1963	1963	1/25
06-813	Chrysler	Imperial Crown décapotable. . .	*Imperial Crown convertible . . .*	1963	1963	1/25
6823	Chrysler	Imperial Crown hardtop	*Imperial Crown hardtop . . . .*	1963	1963	1/25
06-913	Chevrolet	Corvette Sting Ray décapotable	*Corvette Sting Ray convertible. .*	1963	1963	1/25
6923	Chevrolet	Corvette Sting Ray coupé. . . .	*Corvette Sting Ray coupé. . . .*	1963	1963	1/25
8133	Ford	F-100 camionnette (avec kart) .	*F-100 pickup (with go-cart) . .*	1963	1963	1/25
08-733	Chevrolet	Fleetside camionnette (avec moto Triumph)	*Fleetside pickup (with Triumph cycle) . . . .*	1963	1963	1/25
08-743	Chevrolet	Chevy II Nova station-wagon . .	*Chevy II Nova station wagon . .*	1963	1963	1/25

Consulter la liste Junior Trophy / Craftsman pour les autres modèles de l'année 1963.
See also Jr. Trophy / Craftsman Series for additional 1963 annual models.

Modèles à friction / *Frictions*

La liste de ces modèles 1964 pourrait ne pas être complète, les données d'usine faisant défaut.
The listing of 1964 Frictions may not be complete as no factory literature could be found.

Référence du fabricant / *Manufacturer's Reference*	Désignation / *Designation*	Type	*Type*	Date de la voiture / *Date of car*	Date du modèle / *Date of model*	Echelle / *Scale*
	Ford	Galaxie 500 XL décapotable. . .	*Galaxie 500 XL convertible . . .*	1964	1964	1/25
	Ford	Thunderbird hardtop.	*Thunderbird hardtop. . . . . .*	1964	1964	1/25
	Ford	Fairlane 500 hardtop.	*Fairlane 500 hardtop. . . . . .*	1964	1964	1/25
	Pontiac	Grand Prix hardtop	*Grand Prix hardtop . . . . . .*	1964	1964	1/25
	Chevrolet	Impala SS décapotable	*Impala SS convertible . . . . .*	1964	1964	1/25
	Chevrolet	Chevelle Malibu SS hardtop. . .	*Chevelle Malibu SS hardtop. . .*	1964	1964	1/25

Maquettes à construire, modèles de l'année / *Annual kits*

Référence du fabricant / *Manufacturer's Reference*	Désignation / *Designation*	Type	*Type*	Date de la voiture / *Date of car*	Date du modèle / *Date of model*	Echelle / *Scale*
5014	Oldsmobile	F-85 Cutlass décapotable. . . .	*F-85 Cutlass convertible . . . .*	1964	1964	1/25
5024	Oldsmobile	F-85 Cutlass hardtop	*F-85 Cutlass hardtop . . . . .*	1964	1964	1/25
5114	Ford	Falcon Sprint décapotable . . .	*Falcon Sprint convertible . . . .*	1964	1964	1/25
5124	Ford	Falcon Sprint hardtop	*Falcon Sprint hardtop . . . . .*	1964	1964	1/25
5164	Ford	Fairlane 500 hardtop.	*Fairlane 500 hardtop. . . . . .*	1964	1964	1/25
5614	Pontiac	Tempest Le Mans décapotable. .	*Tempest Le Mans convertible . .*	1964	1964	1/25
5624	Pontiac	Tempest Le Mans GTO hardtop	*Tempest Le Mans GTO hardtop*	1964	1964	1/25
6114	Ford	Galaxie 500 XL décapotable (avec phares fonctionnant) . .	*Galaxie 500 XL (with working headlights). . . . .*	1964	1964	1/25
6124	Ford	Galaxie 500 XL hardtop (avec phares fonctionnant).	*Galaxie 500 XL hardtop (with working headlights) . . . . .*	1964	1964	1/25
6154	Ford	Mustang hardtop/décapotable. .	*Mustang hardtop/convertible . .*	1964	1964	1/25
6214	Ford	Thunderbird décapotable	*Thunderbird convertible . . . .*	1964	1964	1/25
6224	Ford	Thunderbird hardtop.	*Thunderbird hardtop. . . . . .*	1964	1964	1/25
6314	Mercury	Park Lane décapotable	*Park Lane convertible . . . . .*	1964	1964	1/25
6324	Mercury	Marauder hardtop	*Marauder hardtop . . . .*	1964	1964	1/25
6414	Lincoln	Continental 4 portes décapotable	*Continental 4 door convertible. .*	1964	1964	1/25
6424	Lincoln	Continental 4 portes conduite intérieure.	*Continental 4 door sedan . . . .*	1964	1964	1/25

Référence du fabricant *Manufacturer's Reference*	Désignation *Designation*	Type	*Type*	Date de la voiture *Date of car*	Date du modèle *Date of model*	Echelle *Scale*
6514	Buick	Wildcat décapotable	*Wildcat convertible*	1964	1964	1/25
6524	Buick	Wildcat hardtop	*Wildcat hardtop*	1964	1964	1/25
6554	Buick	Riviera hardtop	*Riviera hardtop*	1964	1964	1/25
6614	Pontiac	Bonneville décapotable	*Bonneville convertible*	1964	1964	1/25
6624	Pontiac	Bonneville hardtop	*Bonneville hardtop*	1964	1964	1/25
6654	Pontiac	Grand Prix hardtop	*Grand Prix hardtop*	1964	1964	1/25
6714	Chevrolet	Impala SS décapotable (avec phares fonctionnant)	*Impala SS convertible (with working headlights)*	1964	1964	1/25
6724	Chevrolet	Impala SS hardtop (avec phares fonctionnant)	*Impala SS hardtop (with working headlights)*	1964	1964	1/25
6814	Chrysler	Imperial décapotable	*Imperial convertible*	1964	1964	1/25
6824	Chrysler	Imperial hardtop	*Imperial hardtop*	1964	1964	1/25
6914	Chevrolet	Corvette Sting Ray décapotable (avec remorque)	*Corvette Sting Ray convertible (with trailer)*	1964	1964	1/25
6924	Chevrolet	Corvette Sting Ray coupé (avec remorque)	*Corvette Sting Ray coupé (with trailer)*	1964	1964	1/25
8734	Chevrolet	Chevelle El Camino camionnette	*Chevelle El Camino pickup*	1964	1964	1/25
8744	Chevrolet	Chevelle Malibu station-wagon	*Chevelle Malibu station wagon*	1964	1964	1/25

Consulter la liste Junior Trophy / Craftsman pour les autres modèles de l'année en 1964.
See also Jr. Trophy / Craftsman Series for additional 1964 annual models.

Modèles à friction / *Frictions*

Référence du fabricant *Manufacturer's Reference*	Désignation *Designation*	Type	*Type*	Date de la voiture *Date of car*	Date du modèle *Date of model*	Echelle *Scale*
	Ford	Galaxie 500 XL décapotable	*Galaxie 500 XL convertible*	1965	1965	1/25
	Ford	Thunderbird décapotable	*Thunderbird convertible*	1965	1965	1/25
	Ford	Mustang hardtop	*Mustang hardtop*	1965	1965	1/25
	Mercury	Marauder hardtop	*Marauder hardtop*	1965	1965	1/25
	Chevrolet	Impala SS hardtop	*Impala SS hardtop*	1965	1965	1/25
	Plymouth	Barracuda fastback	*Barracuda fastback*	1965	1965	1/25

Maquettes à construire, modèles de l'année / *Annual kits*

Référence du fabricant *Manufacturer's Reference*	Désignation *Designation*	Type	*Type*	Date de la voiture *Date of car*	Date du modèle *Date of model*	Echelle *Scale*
5025	Oldsmobile	Dynamic 88 hardtop	*Dynamic 88 hardtop*	1965	1965	1/25
5115	Ford	Falcon Futura Sprint décapotable	*Falcon Futura Sprint convertible*	1965	1965	1/25
5125	Ford	Falcon Futura Sprint hardtop	*Falcon Futura Sprint hardtop*	1965	1965	1/25
5165	Ford	Fairlane 500 hardtop	*Fairlane 500 hardtop*	1965	1965	1/25
5615	Pontiac	GTO Tempest hardtop décapotable	*GTO Tempest hardtop convertible*	1965	1965	1/25
5725	Chevrolet	Corvair Corsa hardtop	*Corvair Corsa hardtop*	1965	1965	1/25
6025	Dodge	Coronet 500 hardtop	*Coronet 500 hardtop*	1965	1965	1/25
6115	Ford	Galaxie 500 XL décapotable	*Galaxie 500 XL convertible*	1965	1965	1/25
6125	Ford	Galaxie 500 XL hardtop	*Galaxie 500 XL hardtop*	1965	1965	1/25
6155	Ford	Mustang 2+2 fastback	*Mustang 2+2 fastback*	1965	1965	1/25
6215	Ford	Thunderbird décapotable	*Thunderbird convertible*	1965	1965	1/25
6225	Ford	Thunderbird hardtop	*Thunderbird hardtop*	1965	1965	1/25
6325	Mercury	Park Lane hardtop	*Park Lane hardtop*	1965	1965	1/25
6415	Lincoln	Continental 4 portes décapotable	*Continental 4 door convertible.*	1965	1965	1/25
6425	Lincoln	Continental 4 portes conduite intérieure	*Continental 4 door sedan*	1965	1965	1/25
6525	Buick	Wildcat hardtop	*Wildcat hardtop*	1965	1965	1/25
6555	Buick	Riviera hardtop	*Rivieral hardtop*	1965	1965	1/25
6625	Pontiac	Bonneville hardtop	*Bonneville hardtop*	1965	1965	1/25
6655	Pontiac	Grand Prix hardtop	*Grand Prix hardtop*	1965	1965	1/25
6715	Chevrolet	Impala SS409 décapotable	*Impala SS409 convertible.*	1965	1965	1/25
6725	Chevrolet	Impala SS409 hardtop	*Impala SS409 hardtop*	1965	1965	1/25
6815	Chrysler	Imperial décapotable	*Imperial convertible*	1965	1965	1/25
6825	Chrysler	Imperial hardtop	*Imperial hardtop*	1965	1965	1/25
6855	Chrysler	Barracuda fastback	*Barracuda fastback*	1965	1965	1/25
6915	Chevrolet	Corvette Sting Ray décapotable	*Corvette Sting Ray convertible.*	1965	1965	1/25
6925	Chevrolet	Corvette Sting Ray coupé	*Corvette Sting Ray coupé*	1965	1965	1/25
8735	Chevrolet	Chevelle El Camino camionnette	*Chevelle El Camino pickup*	1965	1965	1/25
8745	Chevrolet	Chevelle Malibu station-wagon	*Chevelle Malibu station wagon*	1965	1965	1/25

Consulter la liste Junior Trophy / Craftsman pour les autres modèles de l'année en 1965.
See also Jr. Trophy / Craftsman Series for additional 1965 annual models.

Référence du fabricant / *Manufacturer's Reference*	Désignation / *Designation*	Type	*Type*	Date de la voiture / *Date of car*	Date du modèle / *Date of model*	Echelle / *Scale*
Modèles à friction / *Frictions*						
	Ford	Galaxie 500 XL hardtop	*Galaxie 500 XL hardtop*	1966	1966	1/25
	Ford	Thunderbird hardtop	*Thunderbird hardtop*	1966	1966	1/25
	Ford	Mustang hardtop	*Mustang hardtop*	1966	1966	1/25
	Mercury	Marauder hardtop	*Marauder hardtop*	1966	1966	1/25
	Chevrolet	Impala SS396 hardtop	*Impala SS396 hardtop*	1966	1966	1/25
	Plymouth	Barracuda fastback	*Barracuda fastback*	1966	1966	1/25
Maquettes à construire, modèles de l'année / *Annual kits*						
5126	Ford	Falcon Futura conduite intérieure	*Falcon Futura sedan*	1966	1966	1/25
5166	Ford	Fairlane 500 hardtop	*Fairlane 500 hardtop*	1966	1966	1/25
5726	Chevrolet	Corvair Corsa hardtop	*Corvair Corsa hardtop*	1966	1966	1/25
6116	Ford	Galaxie 500 XL décapotable	*Galaxie 500 XL convertible*	1966	1966	1/25
6126	Ford	Galaxie 500 XL hardtop	*Galaxie 500 XL hardtop*	1966	1966	1/25
6156	Ford	Mustang hardtop/décapotable	*Mustang hardtop/convertible*	1966	1966	1/25
6166	Ford	Mustang 2+2 fastback	*Mustang 2+2 fastback*	1966	1966	1/25
6216	Ford	Thunderbird décapotable	*Thunderbird convertible*	1966	1966	1/25
6226	Ford	Thunderbird hardtop (et décapotable)	*Thunderbird hardtop (and convertible)*	1966	1966	1/25
6326	Mercury	Park Lane hardtop	*Park Lane hardtop*	1966	1966	1/25
6356	Mercury	Comet Cyclone GT hardtop	*Comet Cyclone GT hardtop*	1966	1966	1/25
6426	Lincoln	Continental 4 portes conduite intérieure	*Continental 4 door sedan*	1966	1966	1/25
6526	Buick	Wildcat hardtop	*Wildcat hardtop*	1966	1966	1/25
6556	Buick	Riviera hardtop	*Riviera hardtop*	1966	1966	1/25
6566	Buick	Skylark GS hardtop	*Skylark GS hardtop*	1966	1966	1/25
6716	Chevrolet	Impala SS396 décapotable	*Impala SS396 convertible*	1966	1966	1/25
6726	Chevrolet	Impala SS396 hardtop	*Impala SS396 hardtop*	1966	1966	1/25
6816	Chrysler	Imperial décapotable	*Imperial convertible*	1966	1966	1/25
6856	Plymouth	Barracuda fastback	*Barracuda fastback*	1966	1966	1/25
6916	Chevrolet	Corvette Sting Ray décapotable	*Corvette Sting Ray convertible*	1966	1966	1/25
6926	Chevrolet	Corvette Sting Ray coupé	*Corvette Sting Ray coupé*	1966	1966	1/25
Modèles à friction / *Frictions*						
9127	Ford	Galaxie 500 XL hardtop	*Galaxie 500 XL hardtop*	1967	1967	1/25
9227	Ford	Thunderbird hardtop	*Thunderbird hardtop*	1967	1967	1/25
9287	Ford	Mustang fastback	*Mustang fasback*	1967	1967	1/25
9447	Buick	Riviera hardtop	*Riviera hardtop*	1967	1967	1/25
9667	Oldsmobile	Toronado hardtop	*Toronado hardtop*	1967	1967	1/25
9727	Chevrolet	Impala hardtop	*Impala hardtop*	1967	1967	1/25
Maquettes à construire, modèles de l'année / *Annual kits*						
5127	Ford	Falcon Sports Coupé SP	*Falcon Sports Coupé SP*	1967	1967	1/25
5167	Ford	Fairlane GT hardtop	*Fairlane GT hardtop*	1967	1967	1/25
5327	Mercury	Cougar GT hardtop	*Cougar GT hardtop*	1967	1967	1/25
5727	Chevrolet	Corvair Monza hardtop	*Corvair Monza hardtop*	1967	1967	1/25
6117	Ford	Galaxie 500 XL décapotable	*Galaxie 500 XL convertible*	1967	1967	1/25
6127	Ford	Galaxie 500 XL hardtop	*Galaxie 500 XL hardtop*	1967	1967	1/25
6167	Ford	Mustang GT fastback	*Mustang GT fastback*	1967	1967	1/25
6227	Ford	Thunderbird hardtop	*Thunderbird hardtop*	1967	1967	1/25
6367	Mercury	Comet Cyclone GT hardtop	*Comet Cyclone GT hardtop*	1967	1967	1/25
6427	Lincoln	Continental 4 portes conduite intérieure	*Continental 4 door sedan*	1967	1967	1/25
6557	Buick	Riviera hardtop	*Riviera hardtop*	1967	1967	1/25
6627	Chevrolet	Camaro SS350 Rally Sport hardtop	*Camaro SS350 Rally Sport hardtop*	1967	1967	1/25
6717	Chevrolet	Impala SS427 décapotable	*Impala SS427 convertible*	1967	1967	1/25
6727	Chevrolet	Impala SS427 hardtop	*Impala SS427 hardtop*	1967	1967	1/25
6857	Plymouth	Barracuda Formula S fastback	*Barracuda Formula S fastback*	1967	1967	1/25
6917	Chevrolet	Corvette Sting Ray décapotable	*Corvette Sting Ray convertible*	1967	1967	1/25
6927	Chevrolet	Corvette Sting Ray coupé	*Corvette Sting Ray coupé*	1967	1967	1/25
6937	Oldsmobile	Toronado hardtop	*Toronado hardtop*	1967	1967	1/25
8747	Chevrolet	Fleetside camionnette	*Fleetside pickup*	1967	1967	1/25

Référence du fabricant *Manufacturer's Reference*	Désignation *Designation*	Type	*Type*	Date de la voiture *Date of car*	Date du modèle *Date of model*	Echelle *Scale*
Modèles à friction / *Frictions*						
9128	Ford	Galaxie 500 XL hardtop	*Galaxie 500 XL hardtop*	1968	1968	1/25
9228	Ford	Thunderbird hardtop	*Thunderbird hardtop*	1968	1968	1/25
9428	Lincoln	Continental conduite intérieure	*Continental sedan*	1968	1968	1/25
9668	Oldsmobile	Toronado hardtop	*Toronado hardtop*	1968	1968	1/25
Maquettes à construire, modèles de l'année / *Annual kits*						
2568	AMC	AMX coupé (n'a peut-être pas été commercialisé sous cette référence)	*AMX coupé (may not have been released under this number)*	1968	1968	1/25
5128	Ford	Falcon coupé sport	*Falcon sports coupé*	1968	1968	1/25
5168	Ford	Fairlane Torino fastback	*Fairlane Torino fastback*	1968	1968	1/25
5328	Mercury	Cougar GT XR-7 hardtop	*Cougar GT XR-7 hardtop*	1968	1968	1/25
5628	Chevrolet	Chevelle SS396 hardtop	*Chevelle SS396 hardtop*	1968	1968	1/25
5728	Chevrolet	Corvair Monza hardtop	*Corvair Monza hardtop*	1968	1968	1/25
5768	Pontiac	Firebird 400 hardtop/décapotable	*Firebird 400 hardtop/convertible*	1968	1968	1/25
6128	Ford	Galaxie 500XL hardtop	*Galaxie 500XL hardtop*	1968	1968	1/25
6228	Ford	Thunderbird hardtop	*Thunderbird hardtop*	1968	1968	1/25
6428	Lincoln	Continental conduite intérieure	*Continental sedan*	1968	1968	1/25
6558	Buick	Riviera hardtop	*Riviera hardtop*	1968	1968	1/25
6618	Chevrolet	Camaro hardtop/décapotable	*Camaro hardtop/convertible.*	1968	1968	1/25
6728	Chevrolet	SS427 hardtop (pas de série)	*SS427 hardtop (non stock)*	1968	1968	1/25
6928	Chevrolet	Corvette coupé/décapotable	*Corvette coupé/convertible*	1968	1968	1/25
6938	Oldsmobile	Toronado hardtop	*Toronado hardtop*	1968	1968	1/25
Y901	Ford	Thunderbird hardtop	*Thunderbird hardtop*	1969	1969	1/25
Y902	Ford	XL hardtop	*XL hardtop*	1969	1969	1/25
Y903	Ford	Falcon Futura coupé	*Falcon Futura coupé*	1969	1969	1/25
Y904	Ford	Torino fastback	*Torino fastback*	1969	1969	1/25
Y905	Ford	Mustang Mach I fastback	*Mustang Mach I fastback*	1969	1969	1/25
Y907	Lincoln	Continental conduite intérieure	*Continental sedan*	1969	1969	1/25
Y908	Mercury	Cougar XR-7 hardtop	*Cougar XR-7 hardtop*	1969	1969	1/25
Y909	Chevrolet	Impala SS hardtop	*Impala SS hardtop*	1969	1969	1/25
Y910	Chevrolet	Chevelle SS396 hardtop	*Chevelle SS396 hardtop*	1969	1969	1/25
Y911	Chevrolet	Corvair Monza hardtop	*Corvair Monza hardtop*	1969	1969	1/25
Y912	Chevrolet	Corvette coupé	*Corvette coupé*	1969	1969	1/25
Y913	Chevrolet	Camaro SS396 hardtop.	*Camaro SS396 hardtop.*	1969	1969	1/25
Y914	Chevrolet	Chevelle El Camino camionnette	*Chevelle El Camino pickup*	1969	1969	1/25
Y915	Buick	Riviera hardtop	*Riviera hardtop*	1969	1969	1/25
Y916	Buick	Wildcat hardtop	*Wildcat hardtop*	1969	1969	1/25
Y917	Buick	Opel GT coupé	*Opel GT coupé*	1969	1969	1/25
Y922	AMC	AMX 390 coupé.	*AMX 390 coupé.*	1969	1969	1/25
Y925	Chevrolet	Fleetside CST/10 camionnette	*Fleetside CST/10 pickup*	1969	1969	1/25
Y718	Chevrolet	Corvette décapotable	*Corvette convertible*	1970	1970	1/25
Y720	Chevrolet	Camaro SS396 hardtop.	*Camaro SS396 hardtop.*	1970	1970	1/25
Y722	AMC	AMX coupé	*AMX coupé*	1970	1970	1/25
Y723	Oldsmobile	Toronado hardtop	*Toronado hardtop*	1970	1970	1/25
Y729	Ford	Mustang Mach I fastback	*Mustang Mach I fastback*	1970	1970	1/25
Y732	Chevrolet	Corvette coupé	*Corvette coupé*	1970	1970	1/25
Y733	Chevrolet	Fleetside CST/10 camionnette	*Fleetside CST/10 pickup*	1970	1970	1/25
Y735	Buick	Opel GT coupé	*Opel GT coupé*	1970	1970	1/25
Y736	Oldsmobile	442 hardtop	*442 hardtop*	1970	1970	1/25
Y739	Chevrolet	Impala SS454 hardtop	*Impala SS454 hardtop*	1970	1970	1/25
Série Motor City Stocker / *Motor City Stocker Series*						
X851	Ford	LTD hardtop	*LTD hardtop*	1970	1970	1/25
X852	Chevrolet	Chevelle hardtop	*Chevelle hardtop*	1970	1970	1/25
X853	Buick	Wildcat hardtop	*Wildcat hardtop*	1970	1970	1/25
X854	Ford	Cobra hardtop	*Cobra hardtop*	1970	1970	1/25
X855	Ford	Thunderbird hardtop	*Thunderbird hardtop*	1970	1970	1/25
X856	Chevrolet	Monte Carlo hardtop	*Monte Carlo hardtop*	1970	1970	1/25
Maquettes à construire, modèles de l'année / *Annual kits*						
T112	Chevrolet	Vega station-wagon (voiture fantaisie Vagabond)	*Vega station wagon (Vagabond funny car)*	1971	1971	1/25

Référence du fabricant *Manufacturer's Reference*	Désignation *Designation*	Type	*Type*	Date de la voiture *Date of car*	Date du modèle *Date of model*	Echelle *Scale*
T114	Ford	Mustang Mach I fastback	*Mustang Mach I fastback . . . .*	1971	1971	1/25
T115	Ford	Pinto station-wagon	*Pinto station wagon . . . . . .*	1971	1971	1/25
T116	Ford	Torino Cobra hardtop	*Torino Cobra hardtop . . . . .*	1971	1971	1/25
T117	Chevrolet	Chevelle SS454 hardtop	*Chevelle SS454 hardtop . . . .*	1971	1971	1/25
T118	Ford	Thunderbird hardtop	*Thunderbird hardtop . . . . . .*	1971	1971	1/25
T119	Chevrolet	Monte Carlo hardtop	*Monte Carlo hardtop . . . . . .*	1971	1971	1/25
T120	GMC	Sierra Grande camionnette . . .	*Sierra Grande pickup . . . . . .*	1971	1971	1/25
T121	Buick	Opel GT coupé	*Opel GT coupé . . . .*	1971	1971	1/25
T347	AMC	Gremlin conduite intérieure fantaisie	*Gremlin sedan funny car . . . .*	1970	1971	1/25
T179	Dodge	Charger «Nitro Charger» fantaisie	*Charger "Nitro Charger" funny car . . . .*	1972	1972	1/25
T335	Ford	Mustang Mach I fastback	*Mustang Mach I fastback . . . .*	1972	1972	1/25
T337	Ford	Pinto conduite intérieure	*Pinto sedan . . . .*	1972	1972	1/25
T343	Buick	Opel GT coupé	*Opel GT coupé . . . .*	1972	1972	1/25
T355	Chevrolet	Chevelle SS454 hardtop	*Chevelle SS454 hardtop . . . .*	1972	1972	1/25
T356	Chevrolet	Monte Carlo hardtop	*Monte Carlo hardtop . . . . . .*	1972	1972	1/25
T359	Chevrolet	Camaro SS hardtop	*Camaro SS hardtop . . . . . .*	1972	1972	1/25
T361	Chevrolet	Corvette coupé	*Corvette coupé . . . .*	1972	1972	1/25
T364	GMC	Sierra Grande camionnette . . .	*Sierra Grande pickup . . . . . .*	1972	1972	1/25
T365	Chevrolet	Nova SS conduite intérieure . . .	*Nova SS sedan . . . .*	1972	1972	1/25
T366	Chevrolet	Corvette décapotable	*Corvette convertible . . . . . .*	1972	1972	1/25
T372	AMC	Javelin/AMX (compétition Trans Am)	*Javelin/AMX (Trans Am racer) .*	1972	1972	1/25
T381	Chevrolet	Vega station-wagon (fantaisie) fourgonnette en option	*Vega station wagon (funny car) van options . . . .*	1972	1972	1/25
T518	Chevrolet	Fourgonnette Chevrolet 30 . . .	*Chevy van 30 . . . .*	1972	1972	1/25
T416	Chevrolet	Camaro SS 350 hardtop	*Camaro SS 350 hardtop . . . .*	1973	1973	1/25
T420	Chevrolet	Corvette Sting Ray coupé	*Corvette Sting Ray coupé . . . .*	1973	1973	1/25
T422	Ford	Pinto coupé	*Pinto coupé . . . .*	1973	1973	1/25
T423	Buick	Opel GT coupé	*Opel GT coupé . . . .*	1973	1973	1/25
T424	Chevrolet	Vega station-wagon «Kammback» fantaisie	*Vega station wagon "Kammback Funny Car" . . . .*	1973	1973	1/25
T425	Ford	Mustang Mach I fastback	*Mustang Mach I fastback . . . .*	1973	1973	1/25
T426	Chevrolet	Corvette Sting Ray décapotable	*Corvette Sting Ray convertible . .*	1973	1973	1/25
T427	AMC	Gremlin conduite intérieure «Lou Azar» fantaisie	*Gremlin sedan "Lou Azar Funny Car" . . . .*	1973	1973	1/25
T547	Chevrolet	Chevyvan 30 «Drag Van»	*Chevyvan 30 "Drag Van" . . . .*	1973	1973	1/25
T345	AMC	Javelin AMX hardtop	*Javelin AMX hardtop . . . . .*	1974	1974	1/25
T346	Ford	Mustang II fastback	*Mustang II fastback . . . . . .*	1974	1974	1/25
T354	Chevrolet	Corvette Sting Ray décapotable	*Corvette Sting Ray convertible . .*	1974	1974	1/25
T367	Chevrolet	Corvette Sting Ray coupé	*Corvette Sting Ray coupé . . . .*	1974	1974	1/25
T368	AMC	Gremlin X fantaisie	*Gremlin X funny car . . . . . .*	1974	1974	1/25
T370	Ford	Pinto Runabout conduite intérieure	*Pinto Runabout sedan . . . . .*	1974	1974	1/25
T371	Chevrolet	Vega station-wagon fantaisie . .	*Vega station wagon funny car . .*	1974	1974	1/25
T388	Chevrolet	Camaro 350 hardtop	*Camaro 350 hardtop . . . . . .*	1974	1974	1/25
T387	Ford	F-350 Super camionnette	*F-350 Super pickup . . . . . .*	1975	1975	1/25
T451	AMC	Gremlin X conduite intérieure . .	*Gremlin X sedan . . . .*	1975	1975	1/25
T452	AMC	Matador X conduite intérieure . .	*Matador X sedan . . . .*	1975	1975	1/25
T454	Ford	Pinto Runabout conduite intérieure	*Pinto Runabout sedan . . . . .*	1975	1975	1/25
T455	Ford	Mustang II fastback	*Mustang II fastback . . . . . .*	1975	1975	1/25
T456	Chevrolet	Corvette Sting Ray coupé	*Corvette Sting Ray coupé . . . .*	1975	1975	1/25
T457	Chevrolet	Vega station-wagon fantaisie . .	*Vega station wagon funny car . .*	1975	1975	1/25
T458	Chevrolet	Camaro hardtop	*Camaro hardtop . . . .*	1975	1975	1/25
T460	Chevrolet	Corvette Sting Ray décapotable	*Corvette Sting Ray convertible . .*	1975	1975	1/25
T465	Ford	Pinto Runabout conduite intérieure	*Pinto Runabout sedan . . . . .*	1976	1976	1/25
T466	AMC	Gremlin X conduite intérieure . .	*Gremlin X sedan . . . .*	1976	1976	1/25
T467	AMC	Matador X conduite intérieure . .	*Matador X sedan . . . .*	1976	1976	1/25
T468	Chevrolet	Corvette coupé	*Corvette coupé . . . .*	1976	1976	1/25
T469	Chevrolet	Monza 2+2 fastback	*Monza 2+2 fastback . . . . . .*	1976	1976	1/25
T470	Ford	Mustang II Mach I fastback . . .	*Mustang II Mach I fastback . . .*	1976	1976	1/25
T471	Chevrolet	Vega station-wagon fantaisie . .	*Vega station wagon funny car . .*	1976	1976	1/25
T472	Chevrolet	Nova hatchback	*Nova hatchback . . . .*	1976	1976	1/25
T473	Chevrolet	Camaro Rally Sport hardtop . . .	*Camaro Rally Sport hardtop . . .*	1976	1976	1/25
T474	Mercury	Capri II Ghia 2.8 coupé	*Capri II Ghia 2.8 coupé . . . . .*	1976	1976	1/25

Référence du fabricant *Manufacturer's Reference*	Désignation *Designation*	Type	*Type*	Date de la voiture *Date of car*	Date du modèle *Date of model*	Echelle *Scale*
T475	Chevrolet	Corvette décapotable (la production des Corvettes décapotables prit fin en 1975)	*Corvette convertible (real Corvette convertible production stopped in 1975)*	1976	1976	1/25
T476	Ford	F-350 Super camionnette	*F-350 Super pickup*	1976	1976	1/25
T480	AMC	Matador conduite intérieure	*Matador sedan*	1977	1977	1/25
T481	Ford	Econoline 150 fourgon	*Econoline 150 van*	1977	1977	1/25
T482	Ford	F-350 Ranger XLT camionnette	*F-350 Ranger XLT pickup*	1977	1977	1/25
T483	Chevrolet	Corvette coupé	*Corvette coupé*	1977	1977	1/25
T484	AMC	Pacer station-wagon	*Pacer station wagon*	1977	1977	1/25
T485	Ford	Pinto Runabout conduite intérieure	*Pinto Runabout sedan*	1977	1977	1/25
T486	Mercury	Capri II «S» 2.8 coupé (version Midnight)	*Capri II "S" 2.8 coupé (Midnight version)*	1977	1977	1/25
T487	Ford	Mustang II fastback	*Mustang II fastback*	1977	1977	1/25
T488	Chevrolet	Monza 2+2 fastback	*Monza 2+2 fastback*	1977	1977	1/25
T489	Chevrolet	Nova hatchback	*Nova hatchback*	1977	1977	1/25
T490	Chevrolet	Camaro Rally Sport hardtop	*Camaro Rally Sport hardtop*	1977	1977	1/25
T491	Chevrolet	Vega station-wagon fantaisie	*Vega station wagon funny car*	1977	1977	1/25

Jr. Trophy/Craftsman – modèles de l'année / *Jr. Trophy/Craftsman Series (Annuals)*

Référence du fabricant *Manufacturer's Reference*	Désignation *Designation*	Type	*Type*	Date de la voiture *Date of car*	Date du modèle *Date of model*	Echelle *Scale*
4110	Ford	Falcon Futura décapotable	*Falcon Futura convertible*	1963	1963	1/25
4310	Mercury	Comet S222 décapotable	*Comet S222 convertible*	1963	1963	1/25
4710	Chevrolet	Corvair Monza 900 décapotable	*Corvair Monza 900 convertible*	1963	1963	1/25
4820	Plymouth	Valiant Signet 200 hardtop	*Valiant Signet 200 hardtop*	1963	1963	1/25
4324	Mercury	Comet Caliente hardtop	*Comet Caliente hardtop*	1964	1964	1/25
4724	Chevrolet	Chevelle Malibu SS hardtop	*Chevelle Malibu SS hardtop*	1964	1964	1/25
4754	Chevrolet	Corvair Monza Spyder hardtop	*Corvair Monza Spyder hardtop*	1964	1964	1/25
4824	Plymouth	Valiant Signet 200 hardtop	*Valiant Signet 200 hardtop*	1964	1964	1/25
4001	Plymouth	Valiant Signet hardtop	*Valiant Signet hardtop*	1965	1965	1/25
4002	Chevrolet	Chevelle Malibu hardtop	*Chevelle Malibu hardtop*	1965	1965	1/25
4003	Chevrolet	Chevy II Nova SS hardtop	*Chevy II Nova SS hardtop*	1965	1965	1/25

Jr. Trophy/Craftsman – série standard / *Jr. Trophy/Craftsman Series (Regular Series)*

Référence du fabricant *Manufacturer's Reference*	Désignation *Designation*	Type	*Type*	Date de la voiture *Date of car*	Date du modèle *Date of model*	Echelle *Scale*
J-257	Ford	Thunderbird hardtop/ décapotable	*Thunderbird hardtop/convertible*	1957	1962	1/25
04-029	Edsel	Corsair hardtop	*Corsair hardtop*	1959	1963	1/25
04-129	Ford	Galaxie hardtop	*Galaxie hardtop*	1959	1963	1/25
04-529	Buick	Invicta hardtop	*Invicta hardtop*	1959	1963	1/25
04-740	Chevrolet	Nomad station-wagon	*Nomad station wagon*	1960	1963	1/25
4010	Ford	Starliner hardtop	*Starliner hardtop*	1960	1965	1/25
4011	Pontiac	Bonneville hardtop	*Bonneville hardtop*	1960	1965	1/25
4012	Mercury	Park Lane décapotable	*Park Lane convertible*	1959	1965	1/25
4013	Chevrolet	Impala décapotable	*Impala convertible*	1959	1965	1/25
4031	Buick	Skylark GS hardtop	*Skylark GS hardtop*	1966	1967	1/25
4032	Ford	Thunderbird hardtop	*Thunderbird hardtop*	1966	1967	1/25
4033	Chevrolet	Impala SS hardtop	*Impala SS hardtop*	1963	1967	1/25
4034	Ford	Galaxie 500 XL hardtop	*Galaxie 500 XL hardtop*	1964	1967	1/25
4035	Lincoln	Continental Mark IV hardtop	*Continental Mark IV hardtop*	1959	1967	1/25
4036	Chevrolet	Chevy II Nova 400 station-wagon	*Chevy II Nova 400 station wagon*	1963	1967	1/25
4037	Ford	Thunderbird hardtop/ décapotable	*Thunderbird hardtop/convertible*	1957	1967	1/25
4038	Mercury	Comet Caliente hardtop	*Comet Caliente hardtop*	1964	1967	1/25
C101	Lincoln	Continental Mark IV hardtop	*Continental Mark IV hardtop*	1959	1968	1/25
C102	Chevrolet	Chevy II Nova 400 station-wagon	*Chevy II Nova 400 station wagon*	1963	1968	1/25
C103	Ford	Thunderbird hardtop/ décapotable	*Thunderbird hardtop/convertible*	1957	1968	1/25
C104	Mercury	Comet Caliente hardtop	*Comet Caliente hardtop*	1964	1968	1/25
C105	Pontiac	Bonneville hardtop	*Bonneville hardtop*	1960	1968	1/25

Maquettes à construire, série Trophy / *Trophy kits*

En 1963, de nouveaux numéros de référence à 4 chiffres apparaissent sur les listes de prix AMT pour les maquettes série Trophy. Si les emballages originaux continuent à être utilisés, les nouveaux numéros cependant commencent à figurer sur les boîtes à un certain moment, entre 1963 et

Référence du fabricant *Manufacturer's Reference*	Désignation *Designation*	Type	*Type*	Date de la voiture *Date of car*	Date du modèle *Date of model*	Echelle *Scale*

1965. Puisqu'il s'agit des mêmes maquettes que les kits originaux, nous n'indiquons ici les nouveaux numéros que pour mémoire. Le même phénomène semble s'être produit en 1968 lorsque AMT adopta une numérotation précédée de la lettre T (à ne pas confondre avec les références précédées elles aussi d'un T utilisées pour quelques-uns des premiers kits Trophy). Les kits Trophy de cette époque sont aujourd'hui difficiles à trouver; personne actuellement en place chez AMT ne se souvient exactement sous quelle forme les nouveautés 1968 furent commercialisées. Il semble bien pourtant que seuls les numéros changèrent alors – comme ce fut le cas en 1963 – les emballages restant ceux utilisés auparavant. Les listes de prix d'alors portent les deux numéros de référence – sans doute comme sur les boîtes elles-mêmes –, la référence originale figurant entre parenthèses avant le nouveau chiffre précédé de la lettre T. Les choses se compliquent dès 1971 : AMT attribue à un certain nombre de nouveaux kits des anciens numéros de référence déjà utilisés pour des maquettes sorties en 1968. Un grand nombre de ces premiers numéros avec T ne figurèrent jamais dans la liste des produits pour 1969. Ceux qui y figurèrent furent répertoriés comme ayant été commercialisés en 1968. Les références en T de 1968 absentes de la liste des produits en 1969 figurent sur les listes que nous avons dressées et sont accompagnées du numéro de référence original auquel le lecteur voudra bien se reporter.
In 1963 AMT's price lists started showing new four digit numbers for the Trophy series kits. These kits were retailed in boxes with the same style artwork as before but also had the new number added sometime between 1963 and 1965. As the contents had scarcely been changed, we list these new numbers here purely for reference and direct the reader to the original release. In 1968 AMT changed over to a series of "T" numbers (not to be confused with the earlier T for Trophy). Unfortunately, nobody now with AMT knows what was released in what form in 1968, although it is unlikely that box artwork was changed; because AMT's listings have both numbers, the box may also be presumed to have both, with the original number in parentheses before the new T-number. However, starting in 1971, AMT re-used some of the 1968 T-numbers, many of which in fact never made it to their 1969 Product Directory. In our listings here, a 1968 T-release which AMT still listed as such in 1969 appears simply as a 1968 T-release; 1968 T-allocations out of use by 1969 appear here with a cross-reference to the original release, with a second entry here under the same T-number describing a subsequent release thus labelled.

Référence du fabricant *Manufacturer's Reference*	Désignation *Designation*	Type	*Type*	Date de la voiture *Date of car*	Date du modèle *Date of model*	Echelle *Scale*
36	Ford	Roadster/coupé toit abaissé	*Roadster/chopped top coupé*	1936	1961	1/25
125	Ford	Roadster/coupé toit abaissé	*Roadster/chopped top coupé*	1925	1960	1/25
A125	Ford	Phaéton	*Phaeton*	1932	1973	1/25
T126	Hussein	Can Am voiture de course	*Can Am racer*	1964	1968	1/25
T127	McLaren	Elva Can Am voiture de course	*Elva Can Am racer*	1965	1968	1/25
T128	Chaparral II	Can Am voiture de course	*Can Am racer*	1965	1968	1/25
T128	Ford	Modèle T coupé	*Model T coupé*	1925	1974	1/25
T129	Ford	Roadster/Ala Kart	*Roadster/Ala Kart*	1929	1962	1/25
T129	Lola	70 Can Am voiture de course	*70 Can Am racer*	1964	1968	1/25
A129	Ford	Roadster	*Roadster*	1929	1973	1/25
T131	Ford	Galaxie hardtop	*Galaxie hardtop*	1961	1969	1/25
132	Ford	Modèle B roadster	*Model B roadster*	1932	1959	1/25
T132	Ford	Thunderbird décapotable	*Thunderbird convertible*	1960	1969	1/25
A132	Ford	Roadster	*Roadster*	1932	1973	1/25
T133	Mercury	Park Lane hardtop	*Park Lane hardtop*	1960	1969	1/25
T133	Ford	Tudor conduite intérieure	*Tudor sedan*	1932	1975	1/25
T-134	Ford	Camionnette	*Pickup*	1934	1962	1/25
T134	Ford	Galaxie 500 hardtop	*Galaxie 500 hardtop*	1962	1969	1/25
T134	Ford	Coupé (hotrod)	*Coupé (street rod)*	1934	1976	1/25
T135	Ford	Falcon Ranchero camionnette (en fait un modèle 1961)	*Falcon Ranchero pickup (really a 1961)*	1962	1969	1/25
T136	Buick	Elektra 225 hardtop	*Elektra 225 hardtop*	1962	1969	1/25
A136	Ford	Coupé/roadster	*Coupé/roadster*	1936	1973	1/25
T137	Ford	Mustang hardtop	*Mustang hardtop*	1966	1969	1/25
A137	Chevrolet	Coupé	*Coupé*	1937	1973	1/25
T138	Buick	Skylark GS hardtop	*Skylark GS hardtop*	1966	1969	1/25
T139	Ford	Thunderbird hardtop	*Thunderbird hardtop*	1963	1969	1/25
140	Ford	Coupé	*Coupé*	1940	1960	1/25
T140	Pontiac	Bonneville hardtop	*Bonneville hardtop*	1960	1969	1/25
A140	Ford	Coupé	*Coupé*	1940	1973	1/25
T141	Mercury	Comet Caliente hardtop	*Comet Caliente hardtop*	1964	1969	1/25
T141	Chevrolet	Décapotable	*Convertible*	1937	1975	1/25
T142	Buick	Invicta hardtop	*Invicta hardtop*	1959	1969	1/25
T142	Ford	Modèle T Depot Hack (Woody)	*Model T Depot Hack (Woody)*	1923	1976	1/25
T143	Ford	Modèle T «Hotrod» pompiers	*Model T "Hotrod" fire-truck*	1927	1973	1/25
T144	Ford	Conduite intérieure	*Sedan*	1939-40	1974	1/25
T145	Ford	Camionnette	*Pickup*	1934	1974	1/25
T146	Ford	Falcon coupé fantaisie («Super Bird»)	*Falcon coupé funny car ("Super Bird")*	1969	1969	1/25
T147	Ford	Autolite BF-42 Special (prototype Mach I)	*Autolite BF-42 Special (Mach I prototype)*	—	1969	1/25
T147	Ford	Coupé 5 glaces	*Five window coupé*	1932	1975	1/25

Référence du fabricant *Manufacturer's Reference*	Désignation *Designation*	Type	*Type*	Date de la voiture *Date of car*	Date du modèle *Date of model*	Echelle *Scale*
T148	Chrysler	Western camionnette (Imperial décapotable)	*Western pickup (Imperial convertible)*	1966	1968	1/25
T148	Plymouth	Coupé	*Coupé*	1941	1977	1/25
T-149	Ford	Club coupé	*Club coupé*	1949	1962	1/25
T149	Ford	Commerciale	*Sedan delivery*	1940	1974	1/25
T-150	Ford	Décapotable	*Convertible*	1950	1962	1/25
F150	Chevrolet	Chevelle hardtop fantaisie	*Chevelle hardtop funny car*	1965	1968	1/25
T150	Chevrolet	Chevelle hardtop fantaisie «Time Machine»	*Chevelle hardtop funny car "Time Machine"*	1965	1969	1/25
T150	Ford	Modèle B roadster	*Model B roadster*	1932	1976	1/25
F151	Chevrolet	II Nova hardtop fantaisie	*II Nova hardtop funny car*	1965	1968	1/25
T151	Chevrolet	II Nova fantaisie «Twister»	*II Nova funny car "Twister"*	1965	1969	1/25
F152	Plymouth	Barracuda fastback fantaisie	*Barracuda fastback funny car*	1966	1968	1/25
T152	Plymouth	Barracuda fastback fantaisie «Hemi Hustler»	*Barracuda fastback funny car "Hemi Hustler"*	1966	1969	1/25
F153	Ford	Mustang fastback fantaisie	*Mustang fastback funny car*	1966	1968	1/25
T153	Ford	Mustang fastback fantaisie «Mustang 427»	*Mustang fastback funny car "Mustang 427"*	1966	1969	1/25
T153	Willys	Coupé	*Coupé*	1940	1976	1/25
F154	Ford	Falcon hardtop fantaisie	*Falcon hardtop funny car*	1965	1968	1/25
T154	Lotus-Ford	Dan Gurney Indy 500 voiture de course	*Dan Gurney Indy 500 racer*	1963	1976	1/25
F155	Mercury	Cyclone hardtop fantaisie	*Cyclone hardtop funny car*	1967	1968	1/25
T155	Mercury	Cyclone hardtop fantaisie	*Cyclone hardtop funny car*	1967	1972	1/25
F156	Studebaker	Commander hardtop fantaisie	*Commander hardtop funny car*	1953	1968	1/25
T156	Chevrolet	II Nova (série Street Freak) «Rat Packer»	*II Nova (Street Freak series) "Rat Packer"*	1965	1975	1/25
T-157	Ford	Fairlane 500 hardtop	*Fairlane 500 hardtop*	1957	1963	1/25
F157	Chevrolet	Corvair hardtop fantaisie «Che ZOOOM»	*Corvair hardtop funny car "Che ZOOOM"*	1968	1968	1/25
T157	Ford	Mustang fastback (série Street Freak) «High Roller»	*Mustang fastback (Street Freak series) "High Roller"*	1966	1975	1/25
F158	Edsel	Pacer hardtop fantaisie	*Pacer hardtop funny car*	1958	1968	1/25
T158	Buick	Opel GT coupé	*Opel GT coupé*	1973	1975	1/25
159	—	Bateau à moteur sur remorque	*Speed Boat with trailer*	1959	1959	1/25
T159	Chevrolet	Corvair hardtop	*Corvair hardtop*	1969	1975	1/25
160	Ford	Leva Car Mach I (prototype)	*Leva Car Mach I (prototype)*	1959	1959	1/16
T160	Plymouth	Barracuda fastback (série Street Freak) «Mad Mackarel»	*Barracuda fastback (Street Freak series) "Mad Mackarel"*	1966	1975	1/25
T-161	—	Double dragster (coupé Fiat caréné)	*Double dragster (Fiat coupé streamlined)*	—	1962	1/25
F161	Pontiac	Tempest hardtop fantaisie «Farmer»	*Tempest hardtop funny car "Farmer"*	1963	1968	1/25
T161	Mercury	Comet Cyclone (série Street Freak) «Psyclone»	*Comet Cyclone (Street Freak series) "Psyclone"*	1967	1975	1/25
F162	Oldsmobile	F/85 décapotable «Streaker» fantaisie	*F/85 convertible "Streaker" funny car*	1965	1968	1/25
T162	Agajanian's	Willard Battery Indy car (Parnelli/Jones)	*Willard Battery Indy car (Parnelli/Jones)*	1963	1976	1/25
A163	Chevrolet	Corvette coupé	*Corvette coupé*	1963	1973	1/25
T164	Fiat	Drag coupé «Fiatsco»	*Drag coupé "Fiatsco"*	—	1976	1/25
T165	Plymouth	Modifiée version course	*Early modified racer*	1936	1975	1/25
T166	Chevrolet	Modifiée version course	*Early modified racer*	1937	1975	1/25
T167	Ford	Modifiée version course	*Early modified racer*	1940	1975	1/25
T168	Grant King	Sprint voiture de course	*Sprint racer*	—	1975	1/25
T169	—	Sprint voiture de course «Pole Cat»	*Sprint racer "Pole Cat"*	—	1975	1/25
T170	—	«Drifter» voiture de course	*Super modified "Drifter" racecar*	—	1975	1/25
T171	—	Dragster «Copperhead» à moteur arrière	*"Copperhead" rear engined rail dragster*	—	1972	1/25
T171	—	«Groove Boss» voiture de course	*Super modified "Groove Boss" racecar*	—	1976	1/25
T172	—	Dragster «Turbosonic» à turbine	*"Turbosonic" turbine rail dragster*	—	1972	1/25
T173	—	«Flying Wedge» dragster	*"Flying Wedge" rail dragster*	—	1972	1/25
T174	Tommy Ivo's	Dragster à moteur arrière	*Rear engined rail dragster*	—	1972	1/25
T175	AMC	Gremlin modifiée version course	*Gremlin modified racer*	1976	1976	1/25
T176	Steve Mc Gee's	Dragster à moteur arrière	*Rear engined rail dragster*	—	1974	1/25
T177	Ford	Victoria pompiers	*Victoria "Fire Chief Car"*	1932	1972	1/25
T178	Ford	Modèle T (police)	*Model T touring ("Police Car")*	1927	1972	1/25
T180	Ford	Mustang modifiée version course	*Mustang modified racer*	1965	1976	1/25

Référence du fabricant / *Manufacturer's Reference*	Désignation / *Designation*	Type	*Type*	Date de la voiture / *Date of car*	Date du modèle / *Date of model*	Echelle / *Scale*
T181	Chevrolet	Conduite intérieure modifiée version course	*Sedan modified racer.*	1935	1976	1/25
T182	Volkswagen	Volksvan (caricature)	*Volksvan (caricature)*	—	1971	1/25
T183	—	Roamin' Chariot (caricature)	*Roamin' Chariot (caricature)*	—	1971	1/25
T184	—	Lil' Stogie (caricature)	*Lil' Stogie (caricature)*	—	1971	1/25
T184	Willys	Camionnette	*Pickup.*	1940	1977	1/25
T185	—	Lil' Hot Dogger (caricature)	*Lil' Hot Dogger (caricature)*	—	1971	1/25
T186	Chevrolet	Chevelle (modifiée version course stock-car)	*Chevelle (modified stocker racer)*	1965	1972	1/25
T187	Pontiac	GTO (modifiée version course stock-car)	*GTO (modified stocker racer)*	1965	1971	1/25
T188	Ford	Falcon (modifiée version course stock-car)	*Falcon (modified stocker racer)*	1969	1971	1/25
T189	Buick	Skylark (modifiée version course stock-car)	*Skylark (modified stocker racer)*	1966	1970	1/25
T190	Oldsmobile	Olds 88 (modifiée version course stock-car)	*Olds 88 (modified stocker racer)*	1965	1971	1/25
T191	Ford	Fairlane (modifiée version course stock-car)	*Fairlane (modified stocker racer)*	1965	1970	1/25
T192	Chevrolet	Impala (modifiée version course stock-car)	*Impala (modified stocker racer)*	1966	1971	1/25
T193	Ford	Galaxie (modifiée version course stock-car)	*Galaxie (modified stocker racer)*	1964	1970	1/25
T194	Ford	Torino (modifiée version course stock-car)	*Torino (modified stocker racer)*	1969	1971	1/25
T195	Volkswagen	«Lug Bug» dépanneuse (caricature).	*"Lug Bug" wrecker (caricature)*	—	1971	1/25
T196	—	Lil' Beetle Bus (caricature)	*Lil' Beetle Bus (caricature)*	—	1970	1/25
T197	Volkswagen	«Bugaboo» dragster (carrosserie conduite intérieure)	*"Bugaboo" rail dragster (sedan body)*	—	1971	1/25
T198	Chevrolet	«Stingaree» Corvette dragster	*"Stingaree" Corvette rail dragster*	—	1971	1/25
T199	Ford	«Infini-T» carrosserie T dragster	*"Infini-T" T-bodied rail dragster*	—	1971	1/25
T200	Chevrolet	«Boondocker» Blazer	*"Boondocker" Blazer*	1971	1976	1/25
T201	Chevrolet	«The Candidate» Corvette coupé fantaisie (F201 sur certaines listes de prix)	*"The Candidate" Corvette coupé funny car (Also listed as F201 on some early price lists)*	1967	1968	1/25
T201	Dodge	«Vantasy» fourgon camping (base Deora)	*"Vantasy" custom camper (Deora-based)*	1965	1976	1/25
T202	—	«Sand Kat» (dragster)	*"Sand Kat" (sand dragster)*	—	1968	1/25
T203	—	«Sand Bagger» (dragster)	*"Sand Bagger" (sand dragster)*	—	1968	1/25
T204	Oldsmobile	442 hardtop	*442 hardtop*	1969	1969	1/25
T205	Lotus-Ford	Indy 500 voiture de course (pour l'inauguration du circuit Michigan International Speedway, série limitée)	*Indy 500 racer (for Michigan International Speedway opening, limited release)*	1963	1968	1/25
T205	Volkswagen	«Streetle Beetle» (carrosserie conduite intérieure spéciale)	*"Streetle Beetle" (custom sedan)*	—	1975	1/25
T206	Ford	Mustang «Warren Top Trans Am» voiture de course	*Mustang "Warren Top Trans Am racer"*	1973	1973	1/25
T210	Willys	Fourgon de livraison version hotrod «Lunge Box»	*Panel delivery "Lunge Box" street rod.*	1933	1976	1/25
T212	—	Lil' Cash Box (caricature).	*Lil' Cash Box (caricature).*	1970	1972	1/25
T213	GMC	«Jimmy» station-wagon	*"Jimmy" wagon*	1970	1970	1/25
T214	Tommy Ivo's	Dragster	*Rail dragster*	—	1970	1/25
T215	Ford	Pinto «Mini Musclecar» conduite intérieure.	*Pinto "Mini Musclecar" sedan.*	1974	1974	1/25
T216	AMC	Gremlin «Mini Musclecar» conduite intérieure.	*Gremlin "Mini Musclecar" sedan*	1974	1974	1/25
T218	Ford	Coupé «Flower Power» (Michael J. Pollard)	*Coupé roadster "Flower Power" (Michael J. Pollard)*	1936	1968	1/25
T219	Ford	Roadster «More Bonnie & Clyde».	*Sports roadster "More Bonnie & Clyde".*	1932	1968	1/25
T219	AMC	Pacer station-wagon (carrosserie spéciale)	*Pacer wagon (custom)*	1977	1977	1/25
T220	Ford	Victoria «Bonnie & Clyde»	*Victoria "Bonnie & Clyde"*	1932	1968	1/25
T220	AMC	Matador coupé «AMT-X».	*Matador coupé "AMT-X".*	1977	1977	1/25
T221	Ford	Galaxie 500 XL hardtop «Daytona Sportsman»	*Galaxie 500 XL hardtop "Daytona Sportsman"*	1964	1969	1/25
T221	AMC	Gremlin conduite intérieure «Custom GT».	*Gremlin sedan "Custom GT"*	1976	1977	1/25

Référence du fabricant / *Manufacturer's Reference*	Désignation / *Designation*	Type	*Type*	Date de la voiture / *Date of car*	Date du modèle / *Date of model*	Echelle / *Scale*
T222	Chevrolet	Impala SS hardtop «Street Custom»	*Impala SS hardtop "Street Custom"*	1964	1969	1/25
T223	Chevrolet	Impala hardtop «voiture chef pompiers»	*Impala hardtop "Fire Chief Car"*	1970	1971	1/25
T223	Ford	Mustang II fastback «Python»	*Mustang II fastback "Python"*	1977	1977	1/25
T224	Dune Buggy	Lil' Bo' Weevil	*Lil' Bo' Weevil*	—	1970	1/25
T224	Mercury	Capri II conduite intérieure «Cafe Racer»	*Capri II sedan "Cafe Racer"*	1977	1977	1/25
T225	Pontiac	Bonneville hardtop «Custom Show»	*Bonneville hardtop "Custom Show"*	1965	1969	1/25
T225	Ford	Pinto conduite intérieure «Pintera»	*Pinto sedan "Pintera"*	1976	1976	1/25
T226	Mercury	Park Lane hardtop «Street Custom»	*Park Lane hardtop "Street Custom"*	1966	1969	1/25
T226	Chevrolet	Camaro «Z-76» carrosserie spéciale	*Camaro "Z-76" custom*	1976	1976	1/25
T227	Ford	LTD conduite intérieure (police routière)	*LTD sedan (Interceptor police car)*	1970	1971	1/25
T228	—	Mademoiselle Secret Agent 97 (même version que celle de «Man from UNCLE»)	*Mademoiselle Secret Agent 97 (same as "Man from UNCLE")*	1966	1968	1/25
T229	Dodge	Deora «Alexander's Drag Time»	*Deora "Alexander's Drag Time"*	1967	1968	1/25
T229	Dodge	Dart Sportsman voiture de course (Richard Petty)	*Dart Sportsman racer (Richard Petty)*	—	1976	1/25
T230	Dodge	Deora «Topless Pickup»	*Deora "Topless Pickup"*	1965	1968	1/25
T230	Plymouth	Duster «Kit Car Racer» (Jim Cushman)	*Duster "Kit Car Racer" (Jim Cushman)*	—	1976	1/25
T231	Dodge	Deora «Lil' Covered Wagon»	*Deora "Lil' Covered Wagon"*	1965	1968	1/25
T231	Dodge	Dart Sportsman voiture de course (Warren Stewart)	*Dart Sportsman racer (Warren Stewart)*	—	1977	1/25
232	Ford	Coupé 5 glaces	*Five window coupé*	1932	1960	1/25
T232	Ford	Mark II voiture de course	*Mark II racer*	—	1968	1/25
T232	Thomas Flyer	Vainqueur course New York–Paris	*New York to Paris race winner*	1908	1976	1/25
T233	Ford	Camionnette «Hillbilly Hauler»	*Pickup "Hillbilly Hauler"*	1934	1968	1/25
T233	Plymouth	Valiant «Scamp Kit Car Racer»	*Valiant "Scamp" Kit Car Racer*	—	1977	1/25
T234	George Barris	Surf Rod	*Surf Rod*	—	1968	1/25
T234	Ford	Camionnette pont à pieux	*Stake pickup*	1934	1977	1/25
T235	Ford	Thunderbird «Here Comes the Judge»	*Thunderbird "Here Comes the Judge"*	1957	1968	1/25
T236	Chevrolet	El Camino camionnette de camping	*El Camino camper pickup*	1959	1968	1/25
T237	Ford	Torino décapotable (pace car d'Indianapolis 1968)	*Torino convertible (Indy Pace Car 1968)*	1968	1969	1/25
T238	Chevrolet	Corvette coupé	*Corvette coupé*	1967	1969	1/25
T239		Buggy «T. Vee» (à moteur VW)	*Dune buggy "T. Vee" (VW powered)*	—	1969	1/25
240	Ford	Conduite intérieure	*Sedan*	1939-40	1961	1/25
T240	SSXR	Fireball 500 (voiture film George Barris)	*Fireball 500 (George Barris movie car)*	1966	1968	1/25
T240	Ford	Ranchero (carrosserie spéciale, en fait modèle 1961)	*Ranchero (custom, really a 1961)*	1962	1977	1/25
T241	Ford	«Super Stang» (série Gasser) (ancienne Mach I)	*"Super Stang" (Gasser series) (old Mach I)*	—	1969	1/25
T242	Willys	Coupé (série Gasser)	*Coupé (Gasser series)*	1940	1968	1/25
T243	Ford	Coupé (série Gasser)	*Coupé (Gasser series)*	1936	1968	1/25
T243	Chevrolet	«Monzilla» Monza fantaisie	*"Monzilla" Monza funny car*	1976	1976	1/25
T244	Chevrolet	Coupé (série Gasser)	*Coupé (Gasser series)*	1937	1968	1/25
T244	Pontiac/Chevrolet	Astre/Vega fantaisie	*Astre/Vega funny car*	1976	1976	1/25
T245	Studebaker	Commander hardtop (série Gasser)	*Commander hardtop (Gasser series)*	1953	1968	1/25
T245	Ford/Mercury	Pinto/Bobcat fantaisie	*Pinto/Bobcat funny car*	1976	1977	1/25
T246	Ford	Crown Victoria hardtop (série Gasser)	*Crown Victoria hardtop (Gasser series)*	1956	1968	1/25
T246	Chevrolet	Chevyvan 30 «Candy Van»	*Chevyvan 30 "Candy Van"*	1973	1975	1/25
T247	Chevrolet	Bel Air hardtop (série Gasser)	*Bel Air hardtop (Gasser series)*	1957	1968	1/25
T248	Chevrolet	Corvette «Sock it To Me»	*Corvette "Sock it To Me"*	1962	1968	1/25
T249	Ford	Modèle T touring «Hillbilly Hot Rod»	*Model T touring "Hillbilly Hot Rod"*	1927	1968	1/25
T250	Piranha	Dragster (cf. référence 910)	*Dragster (refer to 910 release)*	—	—	—

Référence du fabricant *Manufacturer's Reference*	Désignation *Designation*	Type	*Type*	Date de la voiture *Date of car*	Date du modèle *Date of model*	Echelle *Scale*
T250	Chevrolet	El Camino camionnette	*El Camino pickup*	1965	1975	1/25
T251	Sunbeam	Get Smart (cf. référence 912)	*Get Smart (refer to 912 release)*	—	—	—
T252	Dodge	Deora (cf. référence 2030)	*Deora (refer to 2030 release)*	—	—	—
T252	Dodge	Deora camionnette (Alexander Bros)	*Deora pickup (Alexander Bros)*	1965	1971	1/25
T253	Mercedes-Benz	300 SL coupé «Autobahn»	*300 SL coupé "Autobahn"*	1954	1968	1/25
T253	Ford	Commerciale	*Sedan delivery*	1940	1976	1/25
T254	Ford	Roadster/Ala Kart «Mod Rod»	*Roadster/Ala Kart "Mod Rod"*	1929	1968	1/25
T255	Ford	Coupé 5 glaces «Snake Eyes» (cf. référence 2132)	*Five window coupé "Snake Eyes" (refer to 2132 release*	—	—	—
T255	Eagle	Gurney/Jorgensen (vainqueur Indianapolis 1975)	*Gurney/Jorgensen (1975 Indy Winner)*	1975	1975	1/25
T256	Ford	Mach I prototype (cf. référence 2148)	*Mach I prototype (refer to 2148 release)*	—	—	—
T256	McLaren	Johnny Rutherford «Gatorade» (deuxième Indianapolis 1975)	*Johnny Rutherford "Gatorade" (1975 2nd place Indy finisher)*	1975	1975	1/25
T257	Don Garlits'	Wynn's Jammer dragster (cf. référence 2167)	*Wynn's Jammer rail dragster (refer to 2167)*	—	—	—
T257	Don Garlits'	Wynn's Jammer dragster	*Wynn's Jammer rail dragster*	1964	1970	1/25
T258	—	«Hippie Hemi» dragster	*"Hippie Hemi" rail dragster*	—	1968	1/25
T259	Chevrolet	Astro I (voiture de rêve Chevrolet)	*Astro I (Chevy prototype show car)*	—	1968	1/25
T260	Ford	Modèle T roadster (cf. référence 2225, sans doute jamais commercialisée)	*Model T roadster (refer to 2225, likely never issued)*	—	—	—
T260	McLaren	Johnny Rutherford vainqueur Indianapolis 1974	*Johnny Rutherford 1974 Indy Winner*	1974	1975	1/25
T261	Ford	Club coupé (cf. référence 2249)	*Club coupé (refer to 2249 release)*	1949	1968	1/25
T261	Ford	Club coupé «Tijuana Taxi»	*Club coupé "Tijuana Taxi"*	1949	1969	1/25
T261	Penske	Gam 2/Norton Spirit voiture course Indianapolis	*Gam 2/Norton Spirit Indy racer*	1976	1976	1/25
T262	Studebaker	Commander hardtop (cf. référence 2253) «Mr. Speed»	*Commander hardtop (refer to 2253) "Mr. Speed"*	1953	—	—
T262	Studebaker	Commander hardtop «Double Whammy»	*Commander hardtop "Double Whammy"*	1953	1971	1/25
T263	Ford/Willys	Conduite intérieure/coupé «Show 'N' Go» (cf. référence 2232)	*Sedan/coupé "Show 'N' Go" (refer to 2232)*	1932	1940	—
T263	Penske Eagle	Peter Revson Sunoco DX voiture course Indianapolis	*Peter Revson Sunoco DX Indy racer*	1974	1974	1/25
T264	Ford	Camionnette (cf. référence 2234)	*Pickup (refer to 2234 release)*	1934	—	—
T264	Penske McLaren	Gary Bettenhausen Sunoco DX voiture course Indianapolis	*Gary Bettenhausen Sunoco DX Indy racer*	1974	1974	1/25
T265	Ford	Coupé/roadster (cf. référence 2336)	*Coupé/roadster (refer to 2336 release)*	1936	—	—
T265	Eagle	Patric Racing Eagle voiture course Indianapolis	*Patric Racing Eagle Indy racer*	1974	1975	1/25
T266	Ford	Coupé (cf. référence 2340)	*Coupé (refer to 2340)*	1940	—	—
T266	Ford	Coupé (série Gasser) (avec disque)	*Coupé (Gasser series) (with record)*	1940	1969	1/25
T267	Ford	Victoria «Lil' Vicky» (cf. référence 2342)	*Victoria "Lil' Vicky" (refer to 2342 release)*	1932	—	—
T267	Ford	«Iron Horse» Mustang (prototype Ford Mach I)	*"Iron Horse" Mustang (Ford Mach I prototype)*	—	1975	1/25
T268	Chevrolet	El Camino camionnette «Drag Camper»	*El Camino pickup "Drag Camper"*	1965	1968	1/25
T269	Ford	Décapotable «Show Boat» (cf. référence 2350)	*Convertible "Show Boat" (refer to 2350 release)*	—	—	—
T269	Ford	Thunderbird hardtop/décapotable	*Thunderbird hardtop/convertible*	1966	1974	1/25
T270	Ford	Camionnette «Wild Cat» (cf. référence 2353)	*Pickup "Wild Cat" (refer to 2353 release)*	1953	—	—
T270	Ford	Camionnette «Baja Patrol»	*Pickup "Baja Patrol"*	1953	1969	1/25
T271	Ford	Crown Victoria hardtop «Haulin Vicky» (cf. référence 2356)	*Crown Victoria hardtop "Haulin Vicky" (refer to 2356 release)*	1956	—	—
T271	Ford	Crown Victoria hardtop	*Crown Victoria hardtop*	1956	1969	1/25
T272	Ford	Thunderbird (cf. référence 2357)	*Thunderbird (refer to 2357 release)*	1957	—	—
T272	Chevrolet	Bel Air décapotable	*Bel Air convertible*	1951	1977	1/25

Référence du fabricant / *Manufacturer's Reference*	Désignation / *Designation*	Type	*Type*	Date de la voiture / *Date of car*	Date du modèle / *Date of model*	Echelle / *Scale*
T273	Chevrolet	Impala hardtop «Ala Impala» (cf. référence 2358)	*Impala hardtop "Ala Impala" (refer to 2358 release)*	1958	—	—
T273	Chevrolet	Impala hardtop	*Impala hardtop*	1958	1969	1/25
T274	Chevrolet	El Camino camionnette «Shaker» (cf. référence 2359)	*El Camino pickup "Shaker" (refer to 2359 release)*	1959	—	—
T275	Fiat/Streamliner	Anciens modèles dragsters doubles	*Old double dragsters*	1961	1968	1/25
T276	Bill Cushenbery	Silhouette	*Silhouette*	1962	1968	1/25
T277	Studebaker	Avanti coupé (cf. référence 2364)	*Avanti coupé (refer to 2364 release)*	1963	—	—
T278	Ford	Conduite intérieure «Joker» (cf. référence 2440)	*Sedan "Joker" (refer to 2440 release)*	1939-40	—	—
T278	Ford	Conduite intérieure (série Gasser)	*Sedan (Gasser series)*	1939-40	1969	1/25
T279	Mercury	Coupé «Merc» (cf référence 2449)	*Coupé "Merc" (refer to 2449 release)*	1949	—	—
T280	Chevrolet	Bel Air hardtop	*Bel Air hardtop*	1957	1968	1/25
T281	Ford	Galaxie Sunliner décapotable	*Galaxie Sunliner convertible.*	1961	1968	1/25
T282	—	«Hull Raiser» bateau de course (cf. référence 2463)	*"Hull Raiser" dragboat (refer to 2463 release)*	—	—	—
T283	Chevrolet	Chevelle station-wagon «Dragon-wagon» (cf. référence 2465)	*Chevelle wagon "Dragon-wagon" (refer to 2465).*	1965	—	—
T283	Chevrolet	Chevelle station-wagon «Surf Wagon»	*Chevelle wagon "Surf Wagon"*	1965	1969	1/25
T284	Ford	Modèle T touring «Touring 'T'» (cf. référence 2527)	*Model T touring "Touring 'T'" (refer to 2527)*	1927	—	—
T284	Chevrolet	Fleetline conduite intérieure	*Fleetline sedan*	1951	1976	1/25
T285	Ford	Fairlane 500 hardtop	*Fairlane 500 hardtop*	1957	1968	1/25
T286	Pontiac	GTO hardtop/décapotable	*GTO hardtop/convertible*	1965	1968	1/25
T287	Ford	Sports roadster (cf. référence 2632)	*Sports roadster (refer to 2632 release)*	1932	—	—
T287	Chevrolet	Corvette décapotable	*Corvette convertible*	1955	1976	1/25
T288	Chevrolet	Coupé «Stovebolt» (cf. référence 2637)	*Coupé "Stovebolt" (refer to 2637 release)*	—	—	—
T288	Chevrolet	Coupé	*Coupé*	1937	1969	1/25
T289	Chevrolet	Nomad station-wagon	*Nomad wagon*	1955	1968	1/25
T290	Chevrolet	Corvette (cf. référence 5662, sans doute jamais commercialisée)	*Corvette (refer to 5662, likely never issued)*	1962	—	—
T290	Ford	Club coupé	*Club coupé*	1949	1975	1/25
T291	—	Man from UNCLE (cf. référence 912)	*Man from UNCLE (refer to 912 release)*	—	—	—

Il est plus que probable que parmi les références T250 à T291 sorties en 1968, les numéros T258, T259, T275, T276, T280, T285, T286, T289 ont reçu un nouvel emballage en 1969.
It is highly likely the following T250/T291 1968 releases received new box art in 1969: T258, T259, T275, T276, T280, T285, T286, T289.

Référence du fabricant / *Manufacturer's Reference*	Désignation / *Designation*	Type	*Type*	Date de la voiture / *Date of car*	Date du modèle / *Date of model*	Echelle / *Scale*
T291	Mercury	Coupé	*Coupé*	1949	1975	1/25
T292	Ford	Commerciale	*Sedan delivery*	1940	1968	1/25
T293	Willys	«Ohio» George Montgomery coupé dragster	*"Ohio" George Montgomery drag coupé*	1933	1968	1/25
T294	AMC	AMC coupé	*AMC coupé*	1968	1968	1/25
T294	AMC	AMX coupé «AMXpress»	*AMX coupé "AMXpress"*	1969	1969	1/25
T294	AMC	AMX coupé «AMX Express»	*AMX coupé "AMX Express"*	1970	1970	1/25
T295	Ford	F-100 camionnette (camping)	*F-100 pickup (with camper cap)*	1963	1968	1/25
T295	Chevrolet	Bel Air hardtop	*Bel Air hardtop*	1951	1976	1/25
T296	Ford	Shelby Mustang GT 500 fastback (avec disque)	*Shelby Mustang GT 500 fastback (with record)*	1968	1968	1/25
T297	Pontiac	Bonneville hardtop «Polyglasser»	*Bonneville hardtop "Polyglasser"*	1962	1969	1/25
T298	Dodge	Deora Cabana camper	*Deora Cabana camper*	1965	1968	1/25
T299	Meyers	Manx Dune Buggy	*Manx Dune Buggy*	—	1968	1/25
T300	Meyers	Tow'd Toadster Dune Buggy	*Tow'd Toadster Dune Buggy*	—	1970	1/25
T301	Buick	Riviera hardtop «Che Riviera»	*Riviera hardtop "Che Riviera"*	1965	1969	1/29
T302	—	Lil' Gasser (caricature)	*Lil' Gasser (caricature)*	—	1970	1/25
T303	Oldsmobile	Dynamic 88 hardtop «Havana Banana»	*Dynamic 88 hardtop "Havana Banana"*	1965	1969	1/25
T304	—	Lil' Mixer (caricature)	*Lil' Mixer (caricature)*	—	1970	1/25
T305	—	Lil' Yeller School Bus (caricature)	*Lil' Yeller School Bus (caricature)*	—	1970	1/25

Référence du fabricant / *Manufacturer's Reference*	Désignation / *Designation*	Type	*Type*	Date de la voiture / *Date of car*	Date du modèle / *Date of model*	Echelle / *Scale*
T306	Willys	Fourgonnette de livraison «Van-Tastic» dragster	*Delivery van "Van-Tastic" dragster*	1933	1969	1/25
T307	Ford	Mustang «Long Nose» fantaisie	*Mustang "Long Nose" funny car*	1963	1971	1/25
T308	Chevrolet	Nova station-wagon «Crew Wagon»	*Nova wagon "Crew Wagon"*	1963	1969	1/25
T308	Chevrolet	Nova station-wagon «Bossa Nova» fantaisie	*Nova wagon "Bossa Nova" funny car.*	1963	1971	1/25
T309	—	Graveyard Ghoul Duo (Munster Coach et Dragula)	*Graveyard Ghoul Duo (Munster Coach and Dragula)*	—	1969	1/25
T310	Ford	Fairlane hardtop.	*Fairlane hardtop.*	1965	1969	1/25
T310	Chevrolet	Corvette décapotable	*Corvette convertible*	1953	1976	1/25
T311	Willys	Camionnette/coupé	*Pickup/coupé.*	1940	1969	1/25
T312	Chevrolet	Chevelle El Camino camionnette (course «caisse à savon»)	*Chevelle El Camino pickup (Soap Box Derby)*	1969	1969	1/25
T313	Ford	Cobra roadster «King Cobra»	*Cobra roadster "King Cobra"*	1964	1969	1/25
T314	Ford	Camionnette/pont à pieux	*Pickup/stake truck.*	1934	1969	1/25
T315	Volkswagen	«Superbug» (série Gasser, carrosserie conduite intérieure spéciale)	*"Superbug" (Gasser series, custom sedan)*	—	1969	1/25
T316	Chevrolet	Décapotable	*Convertible.*	1937	1969	1/25
T317	Chevrolet	Chevelle SS454 hardtop	*Chevelle SS454 hardtop*	1970	1970	1/25
T318	—	«Fire Bug» camion pompiers (ancienne ZZR)	*"Fire Bug" fire truck (old ZZR)*	—	1969	1/25
T319	Ford	Modèle T «Cop Out» fourgon cellulaire	*Model T panel "Cop Out" paddy wagon.*	1925	1969	1/25
T320	Ford	Thunderbird hardtop (voiture fantaisie à moteur Allison)	*Thunderbird hardtop (Allison engined funny car)*	1969	1969	1/25
T321	Ford	Cobra hardtop (base Torino)	*Cobra hardtop (Torino-based).*	1970	1970	1/25
T322	Pontiac	Grand Prix hardtop	*Grand Prix hardtop*	1965	1969	1/25
T322	Ford	F-350 camionnette «Star Truk»	*F-350 super pickup "Star Truk"*	1975	1975	1/25
T323	—	«Surf Van» fourgonnette (commercialisée brièvement comme «Horse Hide Hauler»	*"Surf Van" panel truck (out briefly as "Horse Hide Hauler")*	—	1969	1/25
T324	Ford	Phaéton	*Phaeton*	1932	1969	1/25
T325	Ford	Modèle T «Cinder Bug» camion de pompiers	*Model T "Cinder Bug" fire truck*	1927	1969	1/25
T326	Chevrolet	Monte Carlo hardtop.	*Monte Carlo hardtop.*	1970	1970	1/25
T327	Ford	Pinto conduite intérieure fantaisie «Crazy Horse».	*Pinto sedan funny car "Crazy Horse".*	1971	1971	1/25
T328	Ford	Galaxie 500 XL hardtop «Sweet Bippie»	*Galaxie 500 XL hardtop "Sweet Bippie"*	1966	1969	1/25
T329	Ford	Modèle T «Fruit Wagon» roadster	*Model T "Fruit Wagon" roadster*	1925	1969	1/25
T330	Chevrolet	Camionnette Fleetside avec compartiment camping	*Fleetside pickup with camper*	1969	1969	1/25
T331	Buick	Opel GT coupé	*Opel GT coupé*	1970	1970	1/25
332	Ford	Sports roadster	*Sports roadster*	1932	1961	1/25
T332	Ford	Cobra hardtop/décapotable (base Torino)	*Cobra hardtop/convertible (Torino-based)*	1969	1969	1/25
T333	Chevrolet	Camaro décapotable (pace car Indianapolis 1969)	*Camaro convertible (1969 Indy pace car).*	1969	1969	1/25
T334	Ford	Galaxie 500 XL hardtop «Jolly Green Gasser»	*Galaxie 500 XL hardtop "Jolly Green Gasser"*	1965	1969	1/25
T334	Pontiac	Grand Prix hardtop «Grand Slam»	*Grand Prix hardtop "Grand Slam"*	1965	1975	1/25
T336	Chevrolet	Blazer station-wagon «River Rat».	*Blazer wagon "River Rat".*	1970	1970	1/25
T338	Lincoln	Continental décapotable «Beard of Paradise»	*Continental convertible "Beard of Paradise"*	1965	1969	1/25
T338	Chevrolet	Impala hardtop «Heavy Chevy»	*Impala hardtop "Heavy Chevy"*	1970	1975	1/25
T339	Chevrolet	Corvette hardtop/décapotable «AcCellerator»	*Corvette hardtop/convertible "AcCellerator"*	1968	1969	1/25
T340	Chevrolet	Blazer station-wagon «Crew Chief»	*Blazer wagon "Crew Chief".*	1970	1972	1/25
T341	Ford	Mustang fastback «Mach Won!» fantaisie	*Mustang fastback "Mach Won!" funny car.*	1970	1970	1/25
T342	Mercury	Cougar hardtop «High Country Cougar» fantaisie	*Cougar hardtop "High Country Cougar" funny car.*	1969	1969	1/25
T344	Chevrolet	Camaro hardtop «Funnyhugger» fantaisie	*Camaro hardtop "Funnyhugger" funny car.*	1969	1970	1/25

Référence du fabricant *Manufacturer's Reference*	Désignation *Designation*	Type	*Type*	Date de la voiture *Date of car*	Date du modèle *Date of model*	Echelle *Scale*
T345	Chevrolet	Corvette décapotable	*Corvette convertible*	1969	1969	1/25
T346	Chevrolet	Corvair Monza hardtop	*Corvair Monza hardtop*	1969	1969	1/25
T347	AMC	Gremlin conduite intérieure fantaisie	*Gremlin sedan funny car*	1971	1970	1/25
T348	Ford	Maverick conduite intérieure «Right On» Pro Stock voiture de course	*Maverick sedan "Right On" Pro Stock racer*	1970	1973	1/25
T349	—	«Digger Cuda» dragster (carrosserie sur base Barracuda)	*"Digger Cuda" dragster (Barracuda-based body)*	—	1970	1/25
T350	Piranha	Race Team (cf. référence 916)	*Race Team (refer to 916 release)*	—	—	—
T350	Ford	Mustang II «The Champ» fantaisie	*Mustang II "The Champ" funny car*	1974	1975	1/25
T351	Plymouth	«Mopower» fantaisie	*"Mopower" funny car*	—	1975	1/25
T352	Chevrolet	Corvette «Dragray» fantaisie	*Corvette "Dragray" funny car*	—	1975	1/25
T353	Ford	Cobra camionnette «Cobra Race Team» (cf. référence 2953)	*Cobra pickup "Cobra Race Team" (refer to 2953 release)*	1953/64	—	—
T353	Ford	Décapotable	*Convertible*	1950	1975	1/25
T354	—	Roadster Indianapolis Team Chevelle El Camino/roadster Indianapolis (cf. référence 2965)	*Indy Roadster Team Chevelle El Camino/Indy roadster (refer to 2965 release)*	1965	—	—
T356	Ford	Mustang II «Troja Horse» fantaisie	*Mustang II "Troja Horse" funny car*	—	1976	1/25
T357	—	Drag Combo Chevy II Nova Indianapolis fantaisie + Nova wagon	*Indy Drag Combo Chevy II Nova funny car + Nova wagon*	1963/65	1968	1/25
T357	Dodge	Challenger «Hamtown Hemi» fantaisie	*Challenger "Hamtown Hemi" funny car*	—	1973	1/25
T358	Cal Drag Combo	Ford Galaxie 500 XL hardtop + Falcon fantaisie	Ford Galaxie 500 XL hardtop + Falcon funny car	1964/65	1968	1/25
T358	AMC	Hornet «Draggin' Fly» fantaisie	*Hornet "Draggin' Fly" funny car*	—	1973	1/25
T360	Chevelle Drag Team	Chevy Impala + Chevelle fantaisie	*Chevy Impala + Chevelle funny car*	1963/65	1969	1/25
T362	Indy 500 Combo	Roadster Indianapolis + Lotus/Ford voiture course Indianapolis	*Indy Roadster + Lotus/Ford Indy Racer*	1963	1969	1/25
T363	—	Amtronic (transporteur futuriste)	*Amtronic (futuristic transporter)*	—	1969	1/25
T365	Chevrolet	Nova SS conduite intérieure (suite de série modèle de l'année 1972)	*Nova SS sedan (continuation of 1972 Annual release)*	1972	1972	1/25
T369	Buick	Opel GT coupé «Mini Musclecar»	*Opel GT coupé "Mini Musclecar"*	1973	1973	1/25
T372	AMC	Javelin/AMX Mark Donohue voiture de course	*Javelin/AMX Mark Donohue racer*	1972	1972	1/25
T373	Chevrolet	Malibu «Bobby Allison» voiture de course NASCAR	*Malibu "Bobby Allison" NASCAR racer*	1973	1973	1/25
T374	Chevrolet	Corvair Monza hardtop	*Corvair Monza hardtop*	1969	1972	1/25
T375	Ford	Maverick «Maxi Mav» dragster	*Maverick "Maxi Mav" rail dragster*	—	1972	1/25
T376	—	Koo-Koo-Kar (caricature)	*Koo-Koo-Kar (caricature)*	—	1972	1/25
T377	—	Depth Charger (caricature)	*Depth Charger (caricature)*	—	1972	1/25
T378	—	Flame Out (caricature)	*Flame Out (caricature)*	—	1972	1/25
T379	Pontiac	Ventura II coupé	*Ventura II coupé*	1972	1972	1/25
T380	Pontiac	Firebird hardtop/décapotable + bateau Quartermasters	*Firebird hardtop/convertible + ski drag boat "Quartermasters"*	1968	1968	1/25
T380	Chevrolet	Laguna «Donnie Allison» voiture de course NASCAR	*Laguna "Donnie Allison" NASCAR racer*	—	1974	1/25
T380	Chevrolet	Malibu «Donnie Allison» voiture de course NASCAR	*Malibu "Donnie Allison" NASCAR racer*	—	1976	1/25
T382	Chevrolet	Nova conduite intérieure «Novacaine» fantaisie	*Nova sedan "Novacaine" funny car*	1972	1972	1/25
T383	Ford	Torino hardtop «El Toro» fantaisie	*Torino hardtop "El Toro" funny car*	1971	1972	1/25
T384	Chevrolet	Camaro hardtop «Funnyhugger II» fantaisie	*Camaro hardtop "Funnyhugger II" funny car*	1969	1972	1/25
T385	Ford	Mustang II GT fastback	*Mustang II GT fastback*	1974	1974	1/25
T386	Chevrolet	Chevelle El Camino camionnette «Gear Hustler»	*Chevelle El Camino pickup "Gear Hustler"*	1965	1972	1/25

Référence du fabricant *Manufacturer's Reference*	Désignation *Designation*	Type	*Type*	Date de la voiture *Date of car*	Date du modèle *Date of model*	Echelle *Scale*
T389	Chevrolet	Corvette «John Greenwood» GT voiture de course	*Corvette "John Greenwood" GT racer*	1968	1973	1/25
T390	Ford	Camionnette (modifiée Stocker Hauler)	*Pickup (modified Stocker Hauler)*	1953	1971	1/25
T391	Ford	Torino hardtop voiture de course NASCAR	*Torino hardtop NASCAR racer.*	1972	1973	1/25
T392	Ford	Thunderbird (série Modern Classics)	*Thunderbird (Modern Classics series)*	1957	1974	1/25
T393	Chevrolet	Corvette (en fait un modèle 1960) décapotable	*Corvette (really a 1960) convertible*	1959	1974	1/25
T394	Chevrolet	Fourgon Chevrolet 30 «Nirvana»	*Chevyvan 30 "Nirvana"*	1973	1975	1/25
T395	Chevrolet	Chevelle «Gordon Johncock» voiture de course NASCAR	*Chevelle "Gordon Johncock" NASCAR racer*	—	1974	1/25
T396	Studebaker	Commander hardtop (série Modern Classics)	*Commander hardtop (Modern Classics series)*	1953	1975	1/25
T397	Ford	Shelby Cobra GT 500 Mustang (série Modern Classics)	*Shelby Cobra GT 500 Mustang (Modern Classics series)*	1968	1974	1/25
T398	Chevrolet	El Camino camionnette	*El Camino pickup*	1959	1974	1/25
T399	Tommy Ivo's	Streamliner dragster	*Streamliner rail dragster*	—	1973	1/25
T400	—	«Two Much» (dragster)	*"Two Much" (rail dragster)*	—	1973	1/25
T400	Ford	Modèle T fourgonnette de livraison	*Model T delivery van.*	1923	1977	1/25
T401	—	Lil' Gypsy Wagon (caricature)	*Lil' Gypsy Wagon (caricature)*	—	1972	1/25
T401	Chevrolet	Fourgon Chevrolet 30 «Xtasy»	*Chevyvan 30 "Xtasy"*	1973	1977	1/25
T402	—	Royal Rail (caricature)	*Royal Rail (caricature)*	—	1972	1/25
T402	Chevrolet	Fourgon Chevrolet 30 «Sun Chaser»	*Chevyvan 30 "Sun Chaser"*	1973	1977	1/25
T403	—	Hemi Howler (caricature)	*Hemi Howler (caricature)*	—	1972	1/25
T403	Chevrolet	Fourgon Chevrolet 30 «Foxy Box»	*Chevyvan 30 "Foxy Box"*	1973	1977	1/25
T404	Buick	Riviera hardtop «Low Rider»	*Riviera hardtop "Low Rider"*	1965	1973	1/25
T405	Ford	Pinto conduite intérieure «Crazy Horse II» fantaisie	*Pinto sedan "Crazy Horse II" funny car.*	1973	1973	1/25
T406	Willys	Fourgonnette dragster	*Panel truck dragster*	1933	1974	1/25
T407	Ford	Galaxie 500 XL hardtop	*Galaxie 500 XL hardtop*	1965	1974	1/25
T408	Chevrolet	Impala SS hardtop «Street Shaker»	*Impala SS hardtop "Street Shaker"*	1964	1973	1/25
T409	GMC	Camionnette	*Stepside pickup*	1972	1976	1/25
T410	Ford	Camionnette	*Pickup.*	1953	1973	1/25
T411	Chevrolet	Chevelle Malibu wagon «Superwagon»	*Chevelle Malibu wagon "Superwagon"*	1965	1973	1/25
T412	Mercedes-Benz	300 SL coupé (série Modern Classics)	*300 SL coupé (Modern Classics series)*	1954	1974	1/25
T412	Ford	F-350 Ranger camionnette «Boonie Boss»	*F-350 Ranger pickup "Boonie Boss"*	1977	1977	1/25
T413	Studebaker	Avanti coupé (série Modern Classics)	*Avanti coupé (Modern Classics series)*	1963	1974	1/25
T413	Ford	F-350 Ranger camionnette «Tuff Truk»	*F-350 Ranger pickup "Tuff Truk"*	1977	1977	1/25
T414	Ford	Cobra roadster (série Modern Classics)	*Cobra roadster (Modern Classics series)*	1964	1974	1/25
T415	Chevrolet	Chevelle SS 454 hardtop «Red Alert»	*Chevelle SS 454 hardtop "Red Alert"*	1972	1972	1/25
T417	Matra/Brabham	II (moules Heller)	*II (tooling from Heller)*	—	1969	1/24
T418	Gordini/Alpine	R8/A210 (moules Heller)	*R8/A210 (tooling from Heller)*	—	1970	1/24
T418	Ford	Econoline 150 fourgonnette «Vantom»	*Econoline 150 van "Vantom"*	1976	1976	1/25
T419	Ferrari/Porsche	330/P4/907	*330/P4/907*	—	1970	1/24
T419	—	«Skorpion» dragster style GT	*"Skorpion" GT styled rail dragster*	—	1972	1/25
T419	Ford	Econoline 150 fourgonnette «Hyper Hut» carrosserie spéciale	*Econoline 150 van "Hyper Hut" custom*	1977	1977	1/25
T420	Ford	Econoline 150 fourgonnette «Cockoo Nest» carrosserie spéciale	*Econoline 150 van "Cockoo Nest" custom*	1977	1977	1/25
T421	Chevrolet	Monte Carlo «Bobby Allison» voiture de course NASCAR	*Monte Carlo "Bobby Allison" NASCAR racer*	1972	1972	1/25

Référence du fabricant / *Manufacturer's Reference*	Désignation / *Designation*	Type	*Type*	Date de la voiture / *Date of car*	Date du modèle / *Date of model*	Echelle / *Scale*
T421	Ford	Econoline 150 fourgonnette «Disco Van» carrosserie spéciale	*Econoline 150 van "Disco Van" custom*	1977	1977	1/25
T428	GMC	«Jimmy» station-wagon «Bushwacker» (avec moto trail)	*"Jimmy" wagon "Bushwacker" (with trail bike)*	1970	1973	1/25
T429	Chevrolet	Laguna «Benny Parson» voiture de course NASCAR	*Laguna "Benny Parson" NASCAR racer*	—	1974	1/25
T430	AMC	Matador «Penske» voiture de course NASCAR	*Matador "Penske" NASCAR racer*	1974	1974	1/25
T434	Chevrolet	Monza 2+2 fastback «Double Deuce»	*Monza 2+2 fastback "Double Deuce"*	1975	1975	1/25
T435	Mercury	Capri II coupé	*Capri II coupé*	1975	1975	1/25
T437	AMC	Matador conduite intérieure «Mighty Mat»	*Matador sedan "Mighty Mat"*	1975	1975	1/25
T438	Chevrolet	Nova Pro Stock voiture de course	*Nova Pro Stock racer.*	1975	1975	1/25
T439	Chevrolet	10 (fourgon de police)	*Chevyvan 10 (Police van)*	1973	1973	1/25
T440	Ford	Mustang II fastback «Hell Drivers»	*Mustang II fastback "Hell Drivers"*	1974	1974	1/25
T441	Chevrolet	Camaro hardtop «Joie Chitwood» Cascadeurs	*Camaro hardtop "Joie Chitwood" Thrill Show*	1974	1974	1/25
T442	Willys	Coupé/camionnette «Mean Machine»	*Coupé/pickup "Mean Machine"*	1940	1973	1/25
T443	Chevrolet	Malibu «Lennie Pond» voiture de course NASCAR	*Malibu "Lennie Pond" NASCAR racer*		1975	1/25
T444	Ford	Club coupé Cascadeurs	*Club coupé "Thrill Show"*	1950	1973	1/25
T445	Ford	Décapotable Cascadeurs	*Convertible "Thrill Show"*	1950	1973	1/25
T446	Mercury	Coupé Cascadeurs	*Coupé "Thrill Show".*	1949	1973	1/25
T447	Ford	C-900 tracteur avec remorque Haulaway «Thrill Show»	*C-900 tractor Haulaway trailer "Thrill Show" transporter*	—	1973	1/25
T448	Ford	Camion transporteur + T 405 Pinto fantaisie	*Transporter truck + T 405 Pinto funny car.*	1973	1973	1/25
T461	Ford	Modèle T touring «Laurel & Hardy»	*Model T "Laurel & Hardy"*	1927	1976	1/25
T462	Ford	Modèle T roadster «Laurel & Hardy»	*Model T roadster "Laurel & Hardy"*	1925	1976	1/25
T501	Shelby Drag Team	Ford XL + Shelby GT 500 Mustang	*Ford XL + Shelby GT 500 Mustang*	1968/69	1969	1/25
T506	Chevrolet	Fourgon premiers secours Chevrolet 30	*Rescue van (Chevyvan 30)*	1970	1971	1/25
T517	Chevrolet	Fourgon camping Chevrolet 30 «Open Road Camper»	*Chevyvan 30 "Open Road Camper"*	1970	1971	1/25
T550	Chevrolet	«Red Alert Racing Team» fourgon Chevrolet 30 + T 415 Chevelle	*"Red Alert Racing Team" Chevyvan 30 + T 415 Chevelle*	1972/73	1973	1/25
T561	Chevrolet	«Aquarod Race Team» fourgon Chevrolet 30 + bateau de course	*"Aquarod Race Team" Chevyvan 30 + drag boat*	1973	1975	1/25
T565	AMC/Chevrolet	«Penske Race Team» Matador voiture de course NASCAR + fourgon Chevrolet 30/remorque	*"Penske Race Team" Matador NASCAR racer + Chevyvan 30/trailer*	1973	1974	1/25
T566	Ford	«Mod Ford Racing Team» Ford F-350 Ranger camionnette + vieille Ford modifiée	*"Mod Ford Racing Team" Ford F-350 Ranger pickup + early Ford modified*	1940/75	1975	1/25
T567	Ford	«Grant King Race Team» Ford camionnette + Grant King Sprint voiture de course	*"Grant King Race Team" Ford pickup + Grant King Sprint racer*	1953	1976	1/25
T569	Ford/Dodge	«Richard Petty Race Team» LN-8000 transporteur + Dart voiture de course Petty	*"Richard Petty Race Team" LN-8000 transporter + Petty Dart racer*	—	1977	1/25
T-757	Chevrolet	Bel Air hardtop	*Bel Air hardtop*	1957	1963	1/25
901	—	Munster Koach (série TV)	*Munster Koach (TV car)*	—	1965	1/25
902	—	Wackie Woodie (Krazy Kustom)	*Wackie Woodie (Krazy Kustom)*	—	1965	—
903	—	Va-Va Vette (Krazy Kustom)	*Va-Va Vette (Krazy Kustom).*	—	1965	—
904	Porter	My Mother The Car (show car feuilleton TV)	*My Mother The Car (TV show car)*	—	1966	1/25
905	—	Drag-U-La (show car feuilleton TV)	*Drag-U-La (TV show car)*	—	1966	1/25

Référence du fabricant / *Manufacturer's Reference*	Désignation / *Designation*	Type	*Type*	Date de la voiture / *Date of car*	Date du modèle / *Date of model*	Echelle / *Scale*
906	—	ZZR Roadster (voiture vedette film)	*ZZR Roadster (movie car)*	—	1967	1/25
907	Ford	Mustang décapotable «Sony & Cher»	*Mustang convertible "Sony & Cher"*	1966	1967	1/25
910	Piranha	Dragster	*Dragster*	—	1967	1/25
911	Plymouth	Barracuda «Fireball 500» (voiture vedette film)	*Barracuda "Fireball 500" (movie car)*	—	1967	1/25
912	—	Man From UNCLE (show car feuilleton TV)	*Man From UNCLE (TV show car)*	1966	1967	1/25
913	—	Girl From UNCLE (show car feuilleton TV)	*Girl From UNCLE (TV show car)*	1966	1967	1/25
914	Chrysler	Imperial «The Hero» (show car feuilleton TV)	*Imperial "The Hero" (TV show car)*	1966	1967	1/25
915	Chevrolet	Corvette «THE Cat» décapotable	*Corvette "THE Cat" convertible*	1967	1967	1/25
916	Piranha	Equipe de dragster (Piranha dragster + Man From UNCLE car)	*Drag Team set (Piranha dragster + Man From UNCLE car)*	1966	1967	1/25
925	Sunbeam	Get Smart (show car feuilleton TV)	*Get Smart (TV show car)*	1966	1967	1/25
2001	Volkswagen	Golf	*Rabbit sedan*	1978	1978	1/25
2002	Volkswagen	Scirocco conduite intérieure	*Scirocco sedan*	1978	1979	1/25
2003	Sunbeam	Tiger	*Tiger*	1966	1979	1/25
2004	Mazda	RX-7 (snap kit)	*RX-7 (snap kit)*	1980	1980	1/25
2015	—	Emballage de Noël comprenant 2167 + 2180 + 2190 et 6 pots de peinture	*Christmas Set (included 2167 + 2180 + 2190 + 6 cans of paint)*	—	1967	1/25
2020	Aston Martin	Ulster (moules Matchbox)	*Ulster (Matchbox tool)*	1934	1979	1/32
2021	Bugatti	Type 59 (moules Matchbox)	*Type 59 (Matchbox tool)*	—	1979	1/32
2022	Porsche	917-10 (moules Matchbox)	*917-10 (Matchbox tool)*	1973	1979	1/32
2023	Jaguar	SS100 (moules Matchbox)	*SS100 (Matchbox tool)*	1935	1979	1/32
2024	Surtees	T516/03 voiture de course (moules Matchbox)	*T516/03 racer (Matchbox tool)*	—	1979	1/32
2025	MG	TC roadster (moules Matchbox)	*TC roadster (Matchbox tool)*	1948	1979	1/32
2030	Dodge	Deora carrosserie spéciale camionnette (Alexander Bros.)	*Deora custom pickup (Alexander Bros.)*	1966	1967	1/25
2032	Dodge	Deora «Alexanders Drag Time»	*Deora "Alexanders Drag Time"*	1966	1967	1/25
2033	Dodge	Deora «Topless Pickup»	*Deora "Topless Pickup"*	1966	1967	1/25
2034	Dodge	Deora «Lil' Covered Wagon»	*Deora "Lil' Covered Wagon"*	1966	1967	1/25
2050	Porsche	917-10 «Penske Can Am racer» (moules Matchbox)	*917-10 "Penske Can Am racer" (Matchbox tool)*	1973	1979	1/32
2053	Studebaker	Commander hardtop	*Commander hardtop*	1953	1965	1/25
2064	Studebaker	Avanti coupé	*Avanti coupé*	1963	1965	1/25
2065	Mercedes-Benz	300 SL coupé	*300 SL coupé*	1954	1965	1/25
2125	Ford	Modèle T roadster/coupé abaissé (cf. référence 125)	*Model T roadster/chopped coupé (refer to 125 release)*	1925	—	—
2127	Ford	T touring XR-6 roadster	*T touring XR-6 roadster*	1927	1964	1/25
2128	Ford	Modèle A Tudor conduite intérieure	*Model A Tudor sedan*	1928	1964	1/25
2129	Ford	Modèle A roadster/AlaKart (cf. référence T-129)	*Model A roadster/AlaKart (refer to T-129 release)*	1929	—	—
2132	Ford	Coupé 5 glaces	*Five window coupé*	1932	1967	1/25
2134	Ford	Camionnette (cf. référence T-134)	*Pickup (refer to T-134 release)*	1934	—	—
2136	Ford	Roadster/coupé abaissé (cf. référence 36)	*Roadster/chopped coupé (refer to 36 release)*	1936	—	—
2140	Ford	Coupé (cf. référence 140)	*Coupé (refer to 140 release).*	1940	—	—
2148	Ford	Mach I (show car prototype Mustang)	*Mach I (Mustang prototype show car)*	—	1967	1/25
2149	Ford	Club coupé (cf. référence T-149)	*Club coupé (refer to T-149 release)*	1949	—	—
2150	Ford	Décapotable (cf. référence T-150)	*Convertible (refer to T-150 release)*	1950	—	—
2153	Ford	Camionnette	*Pickup*	1953	1964	1/25
2156	Ford	Crown Victoria hardtop	*Crown Victoria hardtop*	1956	1965	1/25
2157	Ford	Fairlane 500 hardtop (cf. référence T-157)	*Fairlane 500 hardtop (refer to T-157 release)*	1957	—	—
2161	—	Double dragster (cf. référence T-161)	*Double dragster (refer to T-161)*	—	—	—
2162	Bill Cushenbery	Silhouette (& remorque)	*Silhouette (& trailer)*	—	1964	1/25
2163	—	Bateau de course avec remorque	*Dragboat with trailer*	—	1964	1/25

Référence du fabricant / *Manufacturer's Reference*	Désignation / *Designation*	Type	*Type*	Date de la voiture / *Date of car*	Date du modèle / *Date of model*	Echelle / *Scale*
2164	—	Wild Dream/King T carrosserie spéciale	*Wild Dream/King T custom*	—	1965	1/25
2165	Car Craft	Dream Rod	*Dream Rod*	—	1965	1/25
2166	George Barris	Surf Woody	*Surf Woody*	—	1965	1/25
2167	Don Garlits'	Wynn's Jammer dragster (série Checkered Flag)	*Wynn's Jammer rail dragster (Checkered Flag series)*	—	1965	1/25
2168	—	Hippie Hemi dragster	*Hippie Hemi rail dragster*	—	1967	1/25
2170	Ford	Cobra roadster	*Cobra roadster*	1964	1965	1/25
2178	Chevrolet	Astro I (show car prototype Chevrolet	*Astro I (Chevy prototype show car)*	—	1967	1/25
2180	Lotus-Ford	Voiture de course Indianapolis (série Checkered Flag)	*Indy racer (Checkered Flag series)*	1963	1965	1/25
2190	Agajanian's	Willard Battery Special (voiture de course Indianapolis) (série Checkered Flag)	*Willard Battery Special (Indy racer) (Checkered Flag series)*	1963	1965	1/25
2201	Buick	Riviera hardtop	*Riviera hardtop*	1969	1977	1/25
2202	Mercury	Cougar XR-7 hardtop	*Cougar XR-7 hardtop*	1969	1977	1/25
2203	Chevrolet	Impala SS hardtop	*Impala SS hardtop*	1964	1977	1/25
2204	Ford	Galaxie 500 XL hardtop	*Galaxie 500 XL hardtop*	1966	1977	1/25
2205	Chevrolet	Corvette décapotable	*Corvette convertible*	1962	1977	1/25
2206	Mercury	Park Lane hardtop	*Park Lane hardtop*	1966	1977	1/25
2207	Ford	Mustang hardtop	*Mustang hardtop*	1966	1977	1/25
2208	Ford	Thunderbird hardtop/ décapotable	*Thunderbird hardtop/convertible*	1966	1977	1/25
2209	Pontiac	Bonneville hardtop	*Bonneville hardtop*	1965	1977	1/25
2210	Ford	XL hardtop	*XL hardtop*	1969	1977	1/25
2211	Chevrolet	Chevelle SS 396 décapotable	*Chevelle SS 396 convertible*	1969	1977	1/25
2212	Chevrolet	Chevelle SS 396 hardtop	*Chevelle SS 396 hardtop*	1969	1969	1/25
2213	Chevrolet	T-Top Camaro hardtop	*T-Top Camaro hardtop*	1977	1977	1/25
2214	Chevrolet	Monza SS (version routière carrosserie style IMSA)	*Monza SS (IMSA style) street custom*	1977	1978	1/25
2215	Ford	Shelby GT 500 Mustang «Snakebite»	*Shelby GT 500 Mustang "Snakebite"*	1968	1979	1/25
2217	Mikado	RX-7 (carrosserie spéciale Mazda RX-7) (snap kit)	*RX-7 (custom Mazda RX-7) (snap kit)*	1980	1980	1/25
2218	Plymouth	Horizon TC 3 conduite intérieure	*Horizon TC 3 sedan*	1980	1980	1/25
2225	Ford	Modèle T roadster/coupé	*Model T roadster/coupé*	1925	1965	1/25
2232	Ford	Coupé 5 glaces (cf. référence 232)	*Five window coupé (refer to 232 release)*	1932	—	—
2240	Ford	Conduite intérieure (cf. référence 240)	*Sedan (refer to 240 release)*	1940	—	—
2249	Ford	Club coupé	*Club coupé*	1949	1967	1/25
2251	Ford	Coupé (série Cruisin USA)	*Coupé (Cruisin USA series)*	1940	1980	1/25
2252	Mercury	Coupé (série Cruisin USA)	*Coupé (Cruisin USA series)*	1949	1980	1/25
2253	Studebaker	Commander hardtop	*Commander hardtop*	1953	1967	1/25
2253	Chevrolet	Bel Air décapotable (série Cruisin USA)	*Bel Air convertible (Cruisin USA series)*	1951	1980	1/25
2254	Ford	Mustang hardtop (série Cruisin USA)	*Mustang hardtop (Cruisin USA series)*	1966	1980	1/25
2255	Ford	Club coupé (série Cruisin USA)	*Club coupé (Cruisin USA series)*	1949	1980	1/25
2256	Ford	Décapotable (série Cruisin USA)	*Convertible (Cruisin USA series)*	1950	1980	1/25
2257	Ford	Thunderbird (maquette Styline)	*Thunderbird (Styline kit)*	1957	1962	1/25
2257	Ford	Camionnette (série Cruisin USA)	*Pickup (Cruisin USA series)*	1953	1980	1/25
2258	Chevrolet	Corvette coupé (série Cruisin USA)	*Corvette coupé (Cruisin USA series)*	1963	1980	1/25
2261	Pontiac	Grand Prix hardtop (série Cruisin USA)	*Grand Prix hardtop (Cruisin USA series)*	1965	1980	1/25
2262	Buick	Riviera hardtop (série Cruisin USA)	*Riviera hardtop (Cruisin USA series)*	1965	1980	1/25
2263	Ford	Galaxie 500 XL hardtop (série Cruisin USA)	*Galaxie 500 XL hardtop (Cruisin USA series)*	1965	1980	1/25
2264	Chevrolet	Impala hardtop (série Cruisin USA)	*Impala hardtop (Cruisin USA series)*	1970	1980	1/25
2303	Ford	Décapotable	*Convertible*	1950	1978	1/25
2304	Mercedes-Benz	300 SL coupé	*300 SL coupé*	1954	1978	1/25
2305	Pontiac	Custom Turbo Firebird hardtop (snap kit)	*Custom Turbo Firebird hardtop (snap kit)*	1981	1981	1/25
2306	Chevrolet	Cheverra Z-28 (Camaro carrosserie spéciale de Cars & Concepts, Inc.) (snap kit)	*Cheverra Z-28 (custom Camaro by Cars & Concepts, Inc.) (snap kit)*	1981	1981	1/25

Référence du fabricant *Manufacturer's Reference*	Désignation *Designation*	Type	*Type*	Date de la voiture *Date of car*	Date du modèle *Date of model*	Echelle *Scale*
2308	Chevrolet	Camaro Z-28 hardtop (snap kit)	*Camaro Z-28 hardtop (snap kit)*	1981	1981	1/25
2332	Ford	Sports roadster (cf. référence 332)	*Sports roadster (refer to 332 release) . . . .*	1932	—	—
2332	Willys/Ford	Coupé/carrosserie spéciale conduite intérieure.	*Coupé/custom sedan . . . . .*	1932/40	1967	1/25
2333	Willys	Coupé dragster	*Coupé dragster . . . .*	1933	1967	1/25
2334	Ford	Camionnette	*Pickup. . . . .*	1934	1966	1/25
2336	Ford	Coupé/roadster	*Coupé/roadster . . . .*	1936	1967	1/25
2340	Ford	Coupé.	*Coupé. . . . .*	1940	1966	1/25
2342	Ford	Victoria	*Victoria . . . .*	1932	1967	1/25
2345	Chevrolet	Chevelle El Camino camionnette	*Chevelle El Camino pickup . . .*	1965	1967	1/25
2349	Mercury	Coupé (aussi comme 02-349). .	*Coupé (also as 02-349) . . . .*	1949	1963	1/25
2350	Ford	Décapotable «Showboat» . . .	*Convertible "Showboat" . . . .*	1950	1967	1/25
2353	Ford	Camionnette «Wildcat».	*Pickup "Wildcat" . . . .*	1953	1967	1/25
2356	Ford	Victoria	*Victoria . . . .*	1956	1967	1/25
2357	Ford	Thunderbird	*Thunderbird . . . .*	1957	1966	1/25
2358	Chevrolet	Impala hardtop	*Impala hardtop . . . .*	1957	1966	1/25
2359	Chevrolet	El Camino camionnette.	*El Camino pickup . . . .*	1959	1967	1/25
2361	—	Fiat double dragster	*Fiat double dragster . . . . . .*	—	1967	1/25
2362	Bill Cushenbery	Silhouette (avec remorque) . . .	*Silhouette (with trailer). . . . .*	—	1967	1/25
2364	Studebaker	Avanti coupé	*Avanti coupé . . . .*	1963	1967	1/25
2370	Ford	Cobra roadster	*Cobra roadster . . . .*	1964	1967	1/25
2400	Ford	Coupé.	*Coupé. . . . .*	1940	1980	1/25
2401	Ford	Modèle T fourgonnette de livraison (Budweiser)	*Model T delivery van (Budweiser) . . . .*	1923	1978	1/25
2402	Willys	Coupé (hotrod)	*Coupé (street rod). . . . . . .*	1933	1980	1/25
2403	Ford	Conduite intérieure	*Sedan . . . .*	1939/40	1980	1/25
2432	Ford	Victoria	*Victoria . . . .*	1932	1964	1/25
2440	Ford	Conduite intérieure	*Sedan . . . .*	1939/40	1967	1/25
2449	Mercury	Coupé.	*Coupé. . . . .*	1949	1967	1/25
2457	Chevrolet	Bel Air hardtop	*Bel Air hardtop . . . .*	1957	1967	1/25
2461	Ford	Sunliner décapotable	*Sunliner convertible . . . . . .*	1961	1967	1/25
2463	—	Hull Raiser (bateau de course avec remorque)	*Hull Raiser (dragboat with trailer) . . . .*	—	1967	1/25
2465	Chevrolet	Chevelle station-wagon	*Chevelle station wagon. . . . .*	1965	1967	1/25
2501	Chevrolet	Fourgon Chevrolet 30 «Kiss Van»	*Chevyvan 30 "Kiss Van" . . . .*	1973	1978	1/25
2502	Ford	Fourgon Econoline 150 «6 Wheel Van»	*Econoline 150 van "6 Wheel Van" . . . .*	1977	1978	1/25
2504	Ford	Fourgon Econoline 150 «Matilda» (fourgon vedette film).	*Econoline 150 van "Matilda" (movie van) . . . .*	1977	1978	1/25
2512	Toyota	4×4 camionnette «Fire Chief» (snap kit) pompiers	*4×4 pickup "Fire Chief" (snap kit) . . . .*	1981	1981	1/25
2513	Toyota	4×4 camionnette (snap kit) . . .	*4×4 pickup (snap kit) . . . . .*	1981	1981	1/25
2527	Ford	Modèle T touring	*Model T touring. . . . .*	1927	1967	1/25
2532	Willys/Ford	Coupé/conduite intérieure carrosserie spéciale	*Coupé/custom sedan . . . . .*	1932/40	1964	1/25
2557	Ford	Fairlane 500 hardtop.	*Fairlane 500 hardtop. . . . . .*	1957	1967	1/25
2600	Pontiac	GTO hartop/décapotable	*GTO hardtop/convertible . . . .*	1965	1965	1/25
2632	Ford	Modèle B sports roadster	*Model B sports roadster . . . .*	1932	1965	1/25
2637	Chevrolet	Coupé.	*Coupé. . . . .*	1937	1967	1/25
2701	Ford	Courier «Minivan» camionnette	*Courier "Minivan" pickup. . . .*	1978	1978	1/25
2702	Ford	Courier «Firestone» camionnette	*"Firestone" Courier pickup . . .*	1978	1978	1/25
2703	Chevrolet	El Camino camionnette (Chevelle)	*El Camino pickup (Chevelle) . .*	1965	1978	1/25
2704	Ford	Camionnette «Highstepper». . .	*Pickup "Highstepper" . . . . .*	1953	1978	1/25
2706	Ford	Courier 4×4 camionnette «Bush Baby»	*Courier 4×4 pickup "Bush Baby"*	1978	1979	1/25
2707	Ford	Ranger XLT camionnette «Macho Machine».	*Rancher XLT pickup "Macho Machine" . . . .*	1978	1978	1/25
2708	Ford	Bronco «Wild Hoss»	*Bronco "Wild Hoss" . . . . . .*	1978	1979	1/25
2709	Subaru	Brat camionnette	*Brat pickup. . . . .*	1979	1979	1/25
2711	AMC	Jeep CJ-7 (snap kit).	*Jeep CJ-7 (snap kit). . . . . .*	1980	1980	1/25
2715	—	AMT-Top (Jeep CJ-7 carrosserie spéciale) (snap kit)	*AMT-Top (custom Jeep CJ-7) (snap kit) . . . .*	1980	1980	1/25
2755	Chevrolet	Nomad station-wagon	*Nomad wagon . . . .*	1955	1965	1/25
2757	Chevrolet	Bel Air hardtop (cf. référence T-757)	*Bel Air hardtop (refer to T-757 release) . . . .*	1957	—	—
2758	Chevrolet	Bel Air hardtop	*Bel Air hardtop . . . .*	1958	1964	1/25
2759	Chevrolet	El Camino camionnette.	*El Camino pickup . . . .*	1959	1965	1/25

Référence du fabricant *Manufacturer's Reference*	Désignation *Designation*	Type	*Type*	Date de la voiture *Date of car*	Date du modèle *Date of model*	Echelle *Scale*
2801	Chevrolet	Monza 2+2 «Peanut 1» fantaisie	*Monza 2+2 "Peanut 1" funny car*	—	1977	1/25
2802	Ford	Mustang II «Budweiser» fantaisie	*Mustang II "Budweiser" funny car*	—	1977	1/25
2803	Ford	Pinto «Schlitz» fantaisie	*Pinto "Schlitz" funny car*	—	1977	1/25
2804	Pontiac	Astre «Pabst» fantaisie	*Astre "Pabst" funny car*	—	1977	1/25
2805	Chevrolet	Monza 2+2 «Miller» fantaisie	*Monza 2+2 "Miller" funny car.*	—	1977	1/25

Maquettes série Collectors / *Collectors series kits*

Référence du fabricant	Désignation	Type	*Type*	Date de la voiture	Date du modèle	Echelle
2829	Ford	Modèle A roadster	*Model A roadster*	1929	1967	1/25
2830	Ford	Coupé 5 glaces	*Five window coupé*	1932	1967	1/25
2831	Ford	Victoria	*Victoria*	1932	1967	1/25
2832	Ford	Roadster	*Roadster*	1932	1967	1/25
2833	Ford	Roadster	*Roadster*	1936	1967	1/25
2834	Ford	Coupé	*Coupé*	1940	1967	1/25
2835	Chevrolet	Coupé	*Coupé*	1937	1967	1/25
2836	Ford	Conduite intérieure	*Sedan*	1939	1967	1/25

Maquettes série Trophy / *Trophy series kits*

Référence du fabricant	Désignation	Type	*Type*	Date de la voiture	Date du modèle	Echelle
2901	Ford	Mustang fastback «Macho Mustang»	*Mustang fastback "Macho Mustang"*	1973	1978	1/25
2902	Plymouth	Coupé «Rocker» hotrod	*Coupé "Rocker" hotrod*	1941	1978	1/25
2903	Ford	Modèle A roadster «A-Venger»	*Model A roadster "A-Venger"*	1929	1979	1/25
2905	Ford	Victoria	*Victoria*	1932	1979	1/25
2953	Ford	Cobra Race Team (Cobra roadster/Ford camionnette)	*Cobra Race Team (Cobra roadster/Ford pickup)*	1953/64	1967	1/25
2965	Chevrolet	Indy Offy Roadster Team (El Camino camionnette/ Agajanian's Willard Battery voiture de course Indianapolis)	*Indy Offy Roadster Team (El Camino pickup/Agajanian's Willard Battery Indy racer)*	1963/65	1967	1/25
3000	Penske	PC6 Cam 2 voiture de course Indianapolis «Rick Mears»	*PC6 Cam 2 Indy racer "Rick Mears"*	—	1979	1/25
3001	Penske	PC6 Gould Charge voiture de course Indianapolis «Mario Andretti»	*PC6 Gould Charge Indy racer "Mario Andretti"*	—	1979	1/25
3002	Penske	PC6 Norton Spirit voiture de course Indianapolis «Bobby Unser»	*PC6 Norton Spirit Indy racer "Bobby Unser"*	—	1979	1/25
3005	Chevrolet	Coupé «Salt Shaker» Bonneville voiture de course	*Coupé "Salt Shaker" Bonneville racer*	1937	1978	1/25
3006	Studebaker	Commander hardtop «Salty Dog» Bonneville voiture de course	*Commander hardtop "Salty Dog" Bonneville racer*	1953	1978	1/25
3007	Penske	PC6 vainqueur Indianapolis 1979 «Rick Mears»	*PC6 1979 Indy Winner "Rick Mears"*	—	1980	1/25
3011	—	«Sand Dragon» (dragster)	*"Sand Dragon" (rail dragster)*	—	1980	1/25
3030	AMC	Matador «Bobby Allison» Sportsman voiture de course	*Matador "Bobby Allison" Sportsman racer*	1977	1980	1/25
3101	Chevrolet	Corvette coupé «Farrah's Foxy Vette»	*Corvette coupé "Farrah's Foxy Vette"*	1977	1978	1/25
3102	Chevrolet	Corvette «Eckler» version carrosserie spéciale	*Corvette "Eckler" custom version*	1977	1978	1/25
3105	Ford	Thunderbird «Vagas» (série TV)	*Thunderbird "Vagas" (TV show car)*	1957	1979	1/25

Maquettes série Elegance Trophy / *Elegance Trophy series kits*

Référence du fabricant	Désignation	Type	*Type*	Date de la voiture	Date du modèle	Echelle
3204	Ford	Camionnette	*Pickup*	1934	1967	1/25
3205	Pontiac	GTO hardtop	*GTO hardtop*	1965	1967	1/25
3207	Ford	Thunderbird	*Thunderbird*	1957	1967	1/25
3212	Ford	Victoria	*Victoria*	1932	1967	1/25
3215	Chevrolet	Nomad station-wagon	*Noman wagon*	1955	1967	1/25
3217	Chevrolet	Bel Air hardtop	*Bel Air hardtop*	1957	1967	1/25

Référence du fabricant / *Manufacturer's Reference*	Désignation / *Designation*	Type	*Type*	Date de la voiture / *Date of car*	Date du modèle / *Date of model*	Echelle / *Scale*
Maquettes série Trophy / *Trophy series kits*						
4020	Chaparral	II Can Am voiture de course . . .	*II Can Am racer . . . .*	1965	1967	1/25
4021	Lola	70 Can Am voiture de course . .	*70 Can Am racer . . . .*	1964	1967	1/25
4022	McLaren	Elva Can Am voiture de course. .	*Elva Can Am racer. . . . . . .*	1965	1967	1/25
4023	Hussein	Can Am voiture de course. . . .	*Can Am racer. . . . .*	1964	1967	1/25
4165	Datsun	280ZX Turbo coupé	*280 ZX Turbo coupé . . . . . .*	1981	1981	1/25
4166	Chevrolet	Camaro Z-28 hardtop (Street Machine)	*Camaro Z-28 hardtop (Street Machine) . . . .*	1968	1981	1/25
4167	Ford	Mustang fastback (Street Machine)	*Mustang fastback (Street Machine) . . . .*	1973	1981	1/25
4168	Chevrolet	Nova «Super Nova» conduite intérieure (Street Machine) . .	*Nova "Super Nova" sedan (Street Machine) . . . . . .*	1976	1981	1/25
4169	Mercury	Cougar XR-7 hardtop (Street Machine)	*Cougar XR-7 hardtop (Street Machine) . . . .*	1969	1981	1/25
4173	Chevrolet	Camaro Z-28 hardtop	*Camaro Z-28 hardtop . . . . .*	1968	1981	1/25
4180	Ford	Modèle B roadster (série Reggie Jackson).	*Model B roadster (Reggie Jackson series) . . . .*	1932	1981	1/25
4181	Studebaker	Avanti coupé (série Reggie Jackson).	*Avanti coupé (Reggie Jackson series) . . . .*	1963	1981	1/25
4182	Ford	Cobra roadster (série Reggie Jackson).	*Cobra roadster (Reggie Jackson series) . . . .*	1964	1981	1/25
4183	Chevrolet	Corvette décapotable (série Reggie Jackson) (en fait un modèle de 1960)	*Corvette convertible (Reggie Jackson series) (really a 1960)*	1959	1981	1/25
4611	Ford	Ranger F-350 camionnette . . .	*Ranger F-350 pickup . . . . .*	1977	1981	1/25
5565	Ford	Fairlane GT hardtop (série Color Me)	*Fairlane GT hardtop (Color Me series) . . . .*	1967	1967	1/25
5567	Chevrolet	Corvette coupé (série Color Me)	*Corvette coupé (Color Me series)*	1967	1967	1/25
5662	Chevrolet	Corvette décapotable	*Corvette convertible . . . .*	1962	1967	1/25
6501	Ford	«Budweiser Race Team» LN 8000 transporteur + Mustang II fantaisie	*"Budweiser Race Team" LN 8000 transporter + Mustang II funny car. . . . . .*	—	1978	1/25
6750	Chevrolet	Chevelle hardtop «Time Machine» fantaisie.	*Chevelle hardtop "Time Machine" funny car . . . . .*	1965	1967	1/25
6751	Chevrolet	Fourgon II Nova hardtop «Twister» fantaisie.	*Chevy II Nova hardtop "Twister" funny car. . . . .*	1965	1967	1/25
6752	Plymouth	Barracuda fastback «Hemi Hustler» fantaisie	*Barracuda fastback "Hemi Hustler" funny car. . . . . .*	1966	1967	1/25
6753	Ford	Mustang fastback «Mustang 427» fantaisie.	*Mustang fastback "Mustang 427" funny car . . . .*	1966	1967	1/25
6758	Edsel	Pacer hardtop fantaisie	*Pacer hardtop funny car . . . .*	1958	1967	1/25
6763	Pontiac	Tempest hardtop «Farmer» fantaisie	*Tempest hardtop "Farmer" funny car . . . .*	1963	1967	1/25
6764	Oldsmobile	F/85 décapotable «Streaker» fantaisie	*F/85 convertible "Streaker" funny car. . . . .*	1964	1967	1/25
6765	Ford	Falcon hardtop fantaisie	*Falcon hardtop funny car . . . .*	1965	1967	1/25
6766	Mercury	Cyclone hardtop fantaisie. . . .	*Cyclone hardtop funny car . . .*	1967	1967	1/25
6773	Studebaker	Commander hardtop fantaisie . .	*Commander hardtop funny car. .*	1953	1967	1/25
6777	Chevrolet	Corvette coupé fantaisie	*Corvette coupé funny car . . . .*	1967	1967	1/25
6867	Chevrolet	Camaro décapotable (Pace car Indianapolis 1967)	*Camaro convertible (1967 Indy Pace Car) . . . .*	1967	1967	1/25
Maquettes série All Stars / *All Stars series kits*						
R751	Ford	Mustang fastback (cf. référence 7111)	*Mustang fastback (refer to 7111 release) . . . .*	1965	—	—
R752	Ford	Thunderbird hardtop (cf. référence 7113)	*Thunderbird hardtop (refer to 7113 release) . . . .*	1960	—	—
R753	Studebaker	Avanti coupé (cf. référence 7114)	*Avanti coupé (refer to 7114 release) . . . .*	1963	—	—
R754	Chevrolet	Corvette Sting Ray coupé (cf. référence 7973)	*Corvette Sting Ray coupé (refer to 7973 release) . . . .*	1963	—	—
7101	Ford	Mustang fastback	*Mustang fastback . . . .*	1965	1965	1/32
7102	Ford	Ranchero camionnette	*Ranchero pickup . . . .*	1961	1965	1/32
7103	Ford	Thunderbird hardtop	*Thunderbird hardtop . . . . . .*	1960	1965	1/32
7104	Studebaker	Avanti coupé	*Avanti coupé . . . .*	1963	1965	1/32
7111	Ford	Mustang fastback	*Mustang fastback . . . .*	1965	1967	1/32
7113	Ford	Thunderbird hardtop	*Thunderbird hardtop . . . . . .*	1960	1967	1/32

Référence du fabricant *Manufacturer's Reference*	Désignation *Designation*	Type	*Type*	Date de la voiture *Date of car*	Date du modèle *Date of model*	Echelle *Scale*
7114	Studebaker	Avanti coupé	*Avanti coupé*	1963	1967	1/32
7190	Agajanian	Indy Offy roadster	*Indy Offy roadster*	1963	1965	1/32
7232	Ford	Coupé trois glaces	*Three window coupé*	1932	1965	1/32
7240	Ford	Conduite intérieure	*Sedan*	1940	1965	1/32
7963	Chevrolet	Corvette Sting Ray coupé	*Corvette Sting Ray coupé*	1963	1965	1/32
7973	Chevrolet	Corvette Sting Ray coupé	*Corvette Sting Ray coupé*	1963	1967	1/32

Maquettes série Mini Collectors / *Mini Collectors series kits*

Référence du fabricant *Manufacturer's Reference*	Désignation *Designation*	Type	*Type*	Date de la voiture *Date of car*	Date du modèle *Date of model*	Echelle *Scale*
T103	Chevrolet	Corvette coupé (carrosserie spéciale)	*Corvette coupé (custom)*	1967	1974	1/43
T104	Plymouth	Barracuda fastback (carrosserie spéciale)	*Barracuda fastback (custom)*	1967	1974	1/43
T105	Chevrolet	Bel Air hardtop	*Bel Air hardtop*	1957	1974	1/43
T106	Jaguar	XK-E coupé	*XK-E coupé*	—	1974	1/43
T107	Ford	Mustang fastback	*Mustang fastback*	1969	1974	1/43
T108	AMC	AMX sports coupé	*AMX sports coupé*	1969	1974	1/43
T109	Ford	Coupé	*Coupé*	1936	1975	1/43
T110	Ford	Coupé	*Coupé*	1948	1975	1/43
T111	Chevrolet	Chevelle hardtop	*Chevelle hardtop*	1969	1975	1/43
M760	Volkswagen	Conduite intérieure (Coccinelle)	*Sedan (Beetle)*	—	1969	1/43
M762	Ford	Coupé	*Coupé*	1948	1969	1/43
M763	Chevrolet	Bel Air hardtop	*Bel Air hardtop*	1957	1969	1/43
M764	Ford	Coupé	*Coupé*	1936	1969	1/43
M774	Ford	Thunderbird hardtop	*Thunderbird hardtop*	1969	1969	1/43
M776	Chevrolet	Corvette Sting Ray coupé	*Corvette Sting Ray coupé*	1969	1969	1/43
M780	Ford	Mustang fastback	*Mustang fastback*	1969	1969	1/43
M781	Chevrolet	Camaro hardtop	*Camaro hardtop*	1969	1969	1/43
M782	Ford	Torino fastback	*Torino fastback*	1969	1969	1/43
M783	Mercury	Cougar hardtop	*Cougar hardtop*	1969	1969	1/43
M784	Chevrolet	Chevelle hardtop	*Chevelle hardtop*	1969	1969	1/43
M785	AMC	AMX coupé	*AMX coupé*	1969	1969	1/43
M786	Chevrolet	Corvette Sting Ray coupé	*Corvette Sting Ray coupé*	1968	1968	1/43
M787	Ford	Mark II voiture de course	*Mark II racer*	—	1968	1/43
M788	Pontiac	Firebird hardtop	*Firebird hardtop*	1968	1968	1/43
M789	Jaguar	XK-E coupé	*XK-E coupé*	—	1968	1/43
M791	Chevrolet	Corvette coupé (carrosserie spéciale – cf. référence 3506)	*Corvette coupé (custom – refer to 3506 release)*	—	1967	—
M792	Chevrolet	Camaro hardtop (carrosserie spéciale – cf. référence 3507)	*Camaro hardtop (custom – refer to 3507 release)*	—	1967	—
M793	Ford	Mustang fastback (carrosserie spéciale – cf. référence 3508)	*Mustang fastback (custom – refer to 3508 release)*	—	1967	—
M794	Mercury	Cougar hardtop (carrosserie spéciale – cf. référence 3509)	*Cougar hardtop (custom – refer to 3509 release)*	—	1967	—
M795	Pontiac	GTO hardtop (carrosserie spéciale – cf. référence 3510)	*GTO hardtop (custom – refer to 3510 release)*	—	1967	—
M796	Plymouth	Barracuda fastback (carrosserie spéciale – cf. référence 3511)	*Barracuda fastback (custom – refer to 3511 release)*	—	1967	—
M797	Ford	Mustang fastback (cf. référence 3517)	*Mustang fastback (refer to 3517 release)*	—	1968	—
M798	Ford	Thunderbird hardtop (cf. référence 3518)	*Thunderbird hardtop (refer to 3518 release)*	—	1968	—
2101	Chevrolet	Corvette Sting Ray coupé (carrosserie spéciale)	*Corvette Sting Ray coupé (custom)*	1967	1981	1/43
2102	Chevrolet	Bel Air hardtop	*Bel Air hardtop*	1957	1981	1/43
2103	Ford	Mustang fastback	*Mustang fastback*	1969	1981	1/43
2104	Chevrolet	Camaro SS hardtop	*Camaro SS hardtop*	1969	1981	1/43
2105	Pontiac	Firebird 400 hardtop	*Firebird 400 hardtop*	1968	1981	1/43
2106	Chevrolet	Chevelle SS hardtop	*Chevelle SS hardtop*	1969	1981	1/43
2107	Ford	Torino fastback	*Torino fastback*	1969	1981	1/43
2108	Chevrolet	Camaro hardtop (carrosserie spéciale)	*Camaro hardtop (custom)*	1967	1981	1/43
2109	Plymouth	Barracuda ('Cuda) fastback carrosserie spéciale	*Barracuda ('Cuda) fastback custom*	1967	1981	1/43
2110	AMC	AMX coupé	*AMX coupé*	1969	1981	1/43
3506	Chevrolet	Corvette Sting Ray (carrosserie spéciale) coupé	*Corvette Sting Ray (custom) coupé*	1967	1967	1/43
3507	Chevrolet	Camaro hardtop (carrosserie spéciale)	*Camaro hardtop (custom)*	1967	1967	1/43

Référence du fabricant / *Manufacturer's Reference*	Désignation / *Designation*	Type	*Type*	Date de la voiture / *Date of car*	Date du modèle / *Date of model*	Echelle / *Scale*
3508	Ford	Mustang fastback (carrosserie spéciale)	*Mustang fastback (custom)*	1967	1967	1/43
3509	Mercury	Cougar hardtop (carrosserie spéciale)	*Cougar hardtop (custom)*	1967	1967	1/43
3510	Pontiac	GTO hardtop (carrosserie spéciale)	*GTO hardtop (custom)*	1967	1967	1/43
3511	Plymouth	Barracuda fastback (carrosserie spéciale)	*Barracuda fastback (custom)*	1967	1967	1/43
3517	Ford	Mustang fastback	*Mustang fastback*	1968	1968	1/43
3518	Ford	Thunderbird hardtop	*Thunderbird hardtop*	1968	1968	1/43

Maquettes à grande échelle / *Large scale model kits*

Référence du fabricant / *Manufacturer's Reference*	Désignation / *Designation*	Type	*Type*	Date de la voiture / *Date of car*	Date du modèle / *Date of model*	Echelle / *Scale*
370	Cord	812 Sportsman décapotable	*812 Sportsman convertible*	1937	1965	1/12
T841	Chevrolet	Bel Air hardtop	*Bel Air hardtop*	1957	1976	1/16
T842	Chevrolet	Nomad station-wagon	*Nomad wagon*	1955	1977	1/16
T843	Chevrolet	Nomad station-wagon	*Nomad wagon*	1957	1977	1/16
T845	Chevrolet	Bel Air décapotable	*Bel Air convertible*	1957	1977	1/16
T846	Chevrolet	Bel Air décapotable	*Bel Air convertible*	1955	1977	1/16
2424	Cord	812 Sportsman décapotable	*812 Sportsman convertible*	1937	1980	1/12
4801	Ford	Thunderbird (avec hardtop)	*Thunderbird (with hardtop)*	1957	1979	1/16
4802	Ford	Thunderbird (avec hardtop)	*Thunderbird (with hardtop)*	1955	1978	1/16
4803	Chevrolet	Bel Air hardtop	*Bel Air hardtop*	1955	1977	1/16
4804	Ford	Mustang hardtop	*Mustang hardtop*	1964	1979	1/16

Camions série Big Rig / *Big Rig trucks*

Référence du fabricant / *Manufacturer's Reference*	Désignation / *Designation*	Type	*Type*	Date de la voiture / *Date of car*	Date du modèle / *Date of model*	Echelle / *Scale*
T351	—	North American Van Lines (NAVL) (cf. référence 2020)	*North American Van Lines (NAVL) (refer to 2020 release)*	—	—	—
T352	—	Dirt Hauler (cf. référence 2021)	*Dirt Hauler (refer to 2021 release)*	—	—	—
T447	Ford	C-900 tracteur/Haulaway remorque (Thrill Show)	*C-900 tractor/Haulaway trailer (Thrill Show)*	—	1973	1/25
T448	Ford	LN-8000 transporteur + T405 Pinto fantaisie	*LN-8000 transporter + T405 Pinto funny car*	—	1973	1/25
T500	Peterbilt	359 Conventional «California Hauler»	*359 Conventional "California Hauler"*	—	1969	1/25
T501	Peterbilt	359 Conventional (nouveau moule)	*359 Conventional (new tool)*	—	1976	1/25
T502	Peterbilt	352 «Pacemaker» Cabover	*352 "Pacemaker" Cabover*	—	1970	1/25
T503	Ford	LNT-8000 camion-benne	*LNT-8000 dump truck*	—	1971	1/25
T504	Ford	LN-8000 T Conventional	*LN-8000 T Conventional*	—	1970	1/25
T505	Ford	«Louisville Lugger» transporteur voiture de course (LN-8000)	*"Louisville Lugger" Race Car Hauler (LN-8000)*	—	1970	1/25
T506	Fruehauf	Remorque citerne	*Tanker trailer*	—	1970	1/25
T507	Fruehauf	Remorque container	*40' box van trailer*	—	1970	1/25
T508	Loadcraft	Remorque surbaissée	*Lowboy trailer*	—	1971	1/25
T508	Loadcraft	Remorque surbaissée (avec chargement)	*Lowboy trailer (with load)*	—	1977	1/25
T509	Chevrolet	Titan 90 Cabover	*Titan 90 Cabover*	—	1971	1/25
T510	GMC	Astro 95 Cabover	*Astro 95 Cabover*	—	1971	1/25
T510	GMC	Astro 95 Cabover	*Astro 95 Cabover*	—	1976	1/25
T511	American La France	Série 1000 grande échelle pompiers	*1000 series Ladder Chief*	—	1971	1/25
T511	Kenworth	«Alaska Hauler» Conventional	*"Alaska Hauler" Conventional*	—	1977	1/25
T512	Fruehauf	Remorque citerne	*Plated tanker trailer*	—	1971	1/25
T513	American La France	Série 1000 fourgon pompe à incendie	*1000 series Pumper*	—	1971	1/25
T514	American La France	Série 1000 modèle Aero Chief grande échelle	*1000 series Aero Chief*	—	1971	1/25
T514	Trailmobile	Fourgon déménagement (inscriptions Mayflower)	*Moving van (Mayflower decals)*	—	1977	1/25
T515	Ford	«Short Hauler» fourgon (inscriptions Ryder)	*"Short Hauler" Trailmobile van (Ryder decals)*	—	1971	1/25
T515	Ford	"Short Hauler" fourgon	*"Short Hauler" Trailmobile van*	—	1977	1/25
T519	Kenworth	W-925 Conventional	*W-925 Conventional*	—	1971	1/25
T520	Kenworth	K-123 Cabover	*K-123 Cabover*	—	1971	1/25

Référence du fabricant / *Manufacturer's Reference*	Désignation / *Designation*	Type	*Type*	Date de la voiture / *Date of car*	Date du modèle / *Date of model*	Echelle / *Scale*
T521	Trailmobile	Double fourgon (2 remorques 8 m)	*Double vans (two 27' trailers)*	—	1971	1/25
T521	Trailmobile	Double fourgon (2 remorques 8 m)	*Double vans (two 27' trailers)*	—	1977	1/25
T522	Peterbilt	Dépanneuse	*Wrecker*	—	1972	1/25
T523	—	Remorque Haulaway (transporteur d'autos)	*Haulaway trailer (auto carrier)*	—	1971	1/25
T523	—	Remorque Haulaway (transporteur d'autos)	*Haulaway trailer (auto carrier)*	—	1976	1/25
T524	Fruehauf	Fourgon postal 12 m	*40' Exterior Post van*	—	1972	1/25
T525	Trailmobile	Fourgon 8 m	*27' van*	—	1971	1/25
T526	Autocar	A64B Conventional	*A64B Conventional*	—	1972	1/25
T527	White	Road Boss Conventional	*Road Boss Conventional*	—	1974	1/25
T528	Peerless	Transport de bois (remorque)	*Log/beam trailer (with load)*	—	1976	1/25
T529	Chevrolet	Titan 90 Cabover	*Titan 90 Cabover*	—	1976	1/25
T530	White	Freightliner SD Cabover	*Freightliner SD Cabover*	—	1972	1/25
T531	—	Remorque citerne Union 76	*Union 76 tanker trailer*	—	1975	1/25
T532	Fruehauf	Fourgon postal 12 m	*40' Exterior Post van*	—	1975	1/25
T533	Peterbilt	Dépanneuse	*Wrecker*	—	1977	1/25
T535	Mack	Série R Conventional	*R-series Conventional*	—	1976	1/25
T536	Mack	Cruisliner Cabover	*Cruisliner Cabover*	—	1977	1/25
T537	Diamond Rio	C-11664 DFL Conventional	*C-11664 DFL Conventional*	—	1972	1/25
T540	White	Freightliner – Dual Drive Cabover	*Freightliner – Dual Drive Cabover*	—	1977	1/25
T541	White	Western Star Conventional	*Western Star Conventional*	—	1977	1/25
T542	White	Road Boss Conventional	*Road Boss Conventional*	—	1977	1/25
T545	Fruehauf	Remorque 12 m pont plat	*40' flatbed platform trailer*	—	1976	1/25
T546	White	Western Star Conventional	*Western Star Conventional*	—	1973	1/25
T548	Ford	C-600 camion livraison urbaine (inscriptions Hertz)	*C-600 City Delivery truck (Hertz decals)*	—	1972	1/25
T548	Ford	C-600 camion livraison urbaine (inscriptions NAPA)	*C-600 City Delivery truck (NAPA decals)*	—	1977	1/25
T549	Ford	C-900 Cabover + remorque (inscriptions US Mail)	*C-900 Cabover + trailer (US Mail decals)*	—	1977	1/25
T551	Peterbilt	352 Pacemaker Cabover (inscriptions Budweiser)	*352 Pacemaker Cabover (Budweiser decals)*	—	1977	1/25
T552	Fruehauf	Fourgon (inscriptions Budweiser)	*Van (Budweiser decals)*	—	1977	1/25
T553	Mack	Cruisliner Cabover (inscriptions Schlitz)	*Cruisliner Cabover (Schlitz decals)*	—	1978	1/25
T554	Fruehauf	Fourgon (inscriptions Schlitz)	*Van (Schlitz decals)*	—	1978	1/25
T555	White	Freightliner Cabover (inscriptions Pabst)	*Freightliner Cabover (Pabst decals)*	—	1978	1/25
T556	Fruehauf	Fourgon (inscriptions Pabst)	*Van (Pabst decals)*	—	1978	1/25
T558	Caterpillar	D8H bulldozer + remorque surbaissée	*D8H bulldozer + lowboy trailer*	—	1972	1/25
T558	GMC	Astro 95 Cabover (inscriptions Miller)	*Astro 95 Cabover (Miller decals)*	—	1978	1/25
T559	Kenworth	Challenge porte-malaxeur ciment	*Challenge cement mixer*	—	1971	1/25
T559	Fruehauf	Fourgon (inscriptions Miller)	*Van (Miller decals)*	—	1978	1/25
T560	Kenworth	Conventional «Movin' On» (série TV)	*Conventional "Movin' On" (TV show model)*	—	1975	1/25
T564	Trailmobile	Déménageuse (inscription Allied)	*Moving van (Allied decals)*	—	1972	1/25
T567	Ford	C-900 Cabover	*C-900 Cabover*	—	1972	1/25
T568	White	Freightliner Dual Drive Cabover	*Freightliner Dual Drive Cabover*	—	1973	1/23
T569	Ford	LN8000 Transporteur + Dart de Petty (T229)	*LN8000 Transporter + T229 Petty Dart*	—	1977	1/25
T594	Wilson	Bétaillère	*Livestock van*	—	1973	1/25
T596	Ford	C-600 camion pont à pieux	*C-600 stake truck*	—	1972	1/25
T598	American La France	Série 1000 grande échelle pompiers	*1000 series Ladder Chief*	—	1975	1/25
T599	American La France	Série 1000 fourgon pompe à incendie	*1000 series Pumper*	—	1975	1/25
T635	Ford	Louisville chasse-neige (LNT-8000)	*Louisville snow plow (LNT-8000)*	—	1973	1/25
T635	Ford	Louisville chasse-neige (LN-8000)	*Louisville snow plow (LN-8000)*	—	1974	1/25
T700	Peterbilt	359 Conventional	*359 Conventional*	—	1973	1/43
T701	Fruehauf	Fourgon frigorifique	*Reefer van*	—	1973	1/43
T702	Kenworth	K-123 Cabover	*K-123 Cabover*	—	1973	1/43

Référence du fabricant / *Manufacturer's Reference*	Désignation / *Designation*	Type	*Type*	Date de la voiture / *Date of car*	Date du modèle / *Date of model*	Echelle / *Scale*
T704	Fruehauf	Fourgon postal	*Exterior Post van*	—	1973	1/43
T705	Peterbilt	359 Conventional dépanneuse (double grue Holmes 750)	*359 Conventional wrecker (Holmes 750 twin booms)*	—	1974	1/43
T781	Peterbilt	359 Conventional + Fruehauf fourgon 12 m (inscriptions 7-Up	*359 Conventional + Fruehauf 40' van (7-Up decals)*	—	1977	1/43
T782	Kenworth	K-123 Cabover + fourgon 12 m Fruehauf (inscriptions Goodyear)	*K-123 Cabover + 40' Fruehauf van (Goodyear decals)*	—	1977	1/43
T783	Kenworth	K-123 Cabover + fourgon 12 m Fruehauf (inscriptions Pepsi)	*K-123 Cabover + 40' Fruehauf van (Pepsi decals)*	—	1977	1/43
T784	Peterbilt	359 Conventional + fourgon frigorifique 12 m Fruehauf (inscriptions Dannon)	*359 Conventional + 40' Fruehauf reefer van (Dannon decals)*	—	1977	1/43
T785	Peterbuilt	359 Conventional + dépanneuse (2 modèles)	*359 Conventional + wrecker (two models)*	—	1977	1/43
T817	Autocar	Camion-benne	*Dump truck*	—	1972	1/25
T817	Autocar	Camion-benne	*Dump truck*	—	1977	1/25
T818	Caterpillar	D8H bulldozer	*D8H bulldozer*	—	1972	1/25
2020		North American Van Lines (NAVL) camion	*North American Van Lines (NAVL) truck*	—	1967	1/25
2021		Dumper	*Dirt Hauler dump truck*	—	1967	1/25
5001	GMC	General Conventional	*General Conventional*	—	1978	1/25
5002	Chevrolet	Bison Conventional	*Bison Conventional*	—	1979	1/25
5003	Kenworth	«Super Boss» camion dragster de Tyrone Malone	*"Super Boss" Tyrone Malone dragster*	—	1978	1/25
5004	Kenworth	Aerodyne transporteur «Papa Truck» du camion «Super Boss» de Tyrone Malone	*Aerodyne "Papa Truck" Super Boss transporter truck (Tyrone Malone)*	—	1981	1/25
5006	Peterbuilt	«Turnpiker» Cabover	*"Turnpiker" Cabover*	—	1979	1/25
5007	Kenworth	«Bandag Bandit» dragster de Tyrone Malone	*"Bandag Bandit" Tyrone Malone dragster*	—	1980	1/25
5008	Kenworth	Aerodyne transporteur «Hide Out Truck» du «Bandag Bandit» de Tyrone Malone	*Aerodyne "Hide Out Truck" Bandag Bandit transporter truck (Tyrone Malone)*	—	1981	1/25
5014	Kenworth	K-123 Cabover (inscriptions Coors)	*K-123 Cabover (Coors decals)*	—	1980	1/25
5018	Kenworth	Aerodyne Cabover	*Aerodyne Cabover*	—	1980	1/25
5020	Mack	Série R Conventional	*R-Series Conventional*	—	1980	1/25
5021	Kenworth	Aerodyne Cabover (série BJ and the Bear à la TV)	*Aerodyne Cabover (BJ and the Bear decals) (TV)*	—	1980	1/25
5025	Kenworth	Aerodyne Cabover (inscriptions BJ and the Bear) (série TV) (snap kit)	*Aerodyne Cabover (BJ and the Bear decals) TV show model (snap kit)*	—	1980	1/32
5026	Kenworth	Aerodyne Conventional (snap kit)	*Aerodyne Conventional (snap kit)*	—	1980	1/32
5105	White	Freightliner Cabover (inscriptions Coors)	*Freightliner Cabover (Coors decals)*	—	1979	1/25
5201	Trailmoblie	Fourgon déménagement (inscriptions North American Van Lines)	*Moving van (North American Van Lines decals)*	—	1978	1/25
5203	Fruehauf	Fourgon frigorifique (inscriptions Coors)	*Reefer van (Coors decals)*	—	1979	1/25
6121	American La France	Série 1000 grande échelle pompiers	*1000 series Ladder Chief*	—	1981	1/25
6122	American La France	Série 1000 fourgon pompe à incendie	*1000 series Pumper*	—	1981	1/25
6133	GMC	Astro 95 Cabover	*Astro 95 Cabover*	—	1981	1/25
6501	Ford	LN 8000 transporteur avec Mustang II fantaisie «Budweiser Race Team»	*LN 8000 transporter + Mustang II funny car "Budweiser Race Team"*	—	1978	1/25
6605	Peerless	Transporteur de bois (avec chargement)	*Logging trailer (with logs)*	—	1981	1/25
6803	Mack	Dépanneuse double grue Holmes (snap kit)	*Wrecker (Holmes Twin Boom) (snap kit)*	—	1981	1/32
6804	Mack	Superliner Conventional (snap kit)	*Superliner Conventional (snap kit)*	—	1981	1/32
6901	—	Fourgon (inscriptions Suzuki) (snap kit)	*Box van (Suzuki decals) (snap kit)*	—	1981	1/32

Référence du fabricant / *Manufacturer's Reference*	Désignation / *Designation*	Type	*Type*	Date de la voiture / *Date of car*	Date du modèle / *Date of model*	Echelle / *Scale*
6902	—	Remorque frigorifique (inscriptions Tropicana) (snap kit)	*Reefer trailer (Tropicana decals) (snap kit)*	—	1981	1/32
8403	Autocar	Camion-benne	*Dump truck*	—	1981	1/25

Coffrets cadeaux camions série Big Rig / *Big Rig truck gift sets*

Référence du fabricant / *Manufacturer's Reference*	Désignation / *Designation*	Type	*Type*	Date de la voiture / *Date of car*	Date du modèle / *Date of model*	Echelle / *Scale*
G431	—	T500+T507	*T500+T507*	—	1970	1/25
G432	—	T502+T506	*T502+T506*	—	1970	1/25
G434	—	T519+T521	*T519+T521*	—	1971	1/25
G435	—	T504+T523	*T504+T523*	—	1971	1/25
G436	—	T526+T521	*T526+T521*	—	1972	1/25
G437	—	T504+T525	*T504+T525*	—	1972	1/25
G449	—	T510+T524	*T510+T524*	—	1972	1/25
G464	—	T530+T564	*T530+T564*	—	1972	1/25
G819	—	T519+T507 (Kenworth Big Rig Set)	*T519+T507 (Kenworth Big Rig Set)*	—	1976	1/25
G820	—	T535+T528 (Mack Big Rig Set)	*T535+T528 (Mack Big Rig Set)*	—	1976	1/25
G824	Schlitz	Big Rig Set (Mack Cruisliner + Fruehauf remorque 12 m)	*Big Rig Set (Mack Cruisliner + Fruehauf 40' trailer)*	—	1977	1/25
G825	Pabst	Big Rig Set (GMC Astro 95 + Fruehauf frigorifique)	*Big Rig Set (GMC Astro 95 + Fruehauf reefer)*	—	1977	1/25
G826	Miller	Big Rig Set (White Freightliner + Fruehauf fourgon 12 m)	*Big Rig Set (White Freightliner + Fruehauf 40' van)*	—	1977	1/25
7705	BJ/Bear	Big Rig Set (5025 + remorque frigorifique (snap kit)	*Big Rig Set (5025 + reefer trailer) (snap kit)*	—	1981	1/32
8767	Coors	Big Rig Set (White Freightliner + Fruehauf fourgon frigorifique)	*Big Rig Set (White Freightliner + Fruehauf reefer van)*	—	1978	1/25
8768	Budweiser	Big Rig Set (Peterbilt 352 + Fruehauf fourgon 12 m)	*Big Rig Set (Peterbilt 352 + Fruehauf 40' van)*	—	1979	1/25
8775	Coors	Big Rig Set (Kenworth K-123 + Fruehauf fourgon 12 m)	*Big Rig Set (Kenworth K-123 + Fruehauf 40' van)*	—	1980	1/25

ANBRICOS □ GB

Matière / *Material:* *White metal*

Référence du fabricant / *Manufacturer's Reference*	Désignation / *Designation*	Type	*Type*	Date de la voiture / *Date of car*	Date du modèle / *Date of model*	Echelle / *Scale*
1	Alexander	«Y» 36 bus DP 49 F	*"Y" 36 coach DP 49 F*	1936	—	4 mm
2	Leyland	PLSC3 Lion B 35 F	*PLSC3 Lion B 35 F*	1927	—	4 mm
3	Bristol	RELL 36 ECW B 51 F Série 2	*RELL 36 ECW B 51 F Series 2*	1936	—	4 mm
4	Bristol	RELL 36 ECW B 41 D Série 2	*RELL 36 ECW B 41 D Series 2*	1936	—	4 mm
5	Leyland	TD 1, ouvert à l'arrière, Leyland L 27/24 R	*TD 1, open staircase, Leyland L 27/24 R*	1929	—	4 mm
6	Leyland	TD 1, fermé à l'arrière, Leyland L 27/24 R	*TD 1, enclosed staircase, Leyland L 27/24 R*	1929	—	4 mm
7	Leyland	PD 2, Leyland H 32/26 R	*PD 2, Leyland H 32/26 R*	1951	—	4 mm
8	Leyland	PD 2, Leyland L 27/26 R	*PD 2, Leyland L 27/26 R*	1951	—	4 mm
9	Plaxton	Panorama 1 C 49 F	*Panorama 1 C 49 F*	1936	—	4 mm
10A	Atlantean	PDR 33' Roe H 45/33 D	*PDR 33' Roe H 45/33 D*	1933	—	4 mm
10F	Daimler	Fleetline Roe H 45/33 D	*Fleetline Roe H 45/33 D*	—	—	4 mm
11	Bedford	OB Duple Vista C 29 F	*OB Duple Vista C 29 F*	1946	—	4 mm
12	Bristol	FLF Lodekka ECW H 38/32 F	*FLF Lodekka ECW H 38/32 F*	—	—	4 mm
13	AEC	Rt. III/Roe H 33/25 R	*Rt. III/Roe H 33/25 R*	1952	—	4 mm
14	Burlingham	Seagull C 41 C	*Seagull C 41 C*	—	—	4 mm
15	Crossley	DD 42/7 Cross. H 56 R	*DD 42/7 Cross. H 56 R*	1947	—	4 mm
16	Leyland	TS 8 Roe B 34 F	*TS 8 Roe B 34 F*	1938	—	4 mm
17	Alexander	«Y» 36' bus B 53 F	*"Y" 36' bus B 53 F*	—	—	4 mm
18	Daimler	Weymann H 28/26 R	*Weymann H 28/26 R*	1934	—	4 mm
18A	AEC	Rt. Weymann H 28/26 R	*Rt. Weymann H 28/26 R*	1934	—	4 mm
19	AEC	Rt. III Weymann L 27/26 R, Lt. RLH Classe	*Rt. III Weymann L 27/26 R, Lt. RLH Class*	1952	—	4 mm
20	Leyland	PLS C3 Lion B 35 R	*PLS C3 Lion B 35 R*	1927	—	4 mm
21	Bristol	SC 4 LK-ECW B 35 F	*SC 4 LK-ECW B 35 F*	1955	—	4 mm
22	AEC	Regal III Burlingham C 35 F	*Regal III Burlingham C 35 F*	1948	—	4 mm
23	Atlantean	AN 68-Park Royal Roe	*AN 68-Park Royal Roe*	—	—	4 mm
24	Bedford	SB Duple Super Vega	*SB Duple Super Vega*	1955	—	4 mm
—	Sheffield	«Roberts» tram	*"Roberts" tram*	—	—	4 mm
—	Dennis	2 tonnes, camion	*2-ton normal control lorry*	1934	—	4 mm
—	Bedford	5 tonnes, camion	*5-ton normal control lorry*	1946	—	4 mm

Référence du fabricant / *Manufacturer's Reference*	Désignation / *Designation*	Type	*Type*	Date de la voiture / *Date of car*	Date du modèle / *Date of model*	Echelle / *Scale*

ANGUPLAS — E

Matière / *Material:* Plastique / *Plastic*

Série Mini-cars / *Mini-cars series*

1	Pegaso	Sport Z 103	*Sport Z 103*	1957	1958	1/86
2	Seat	1400 berline	*1400 saloon*	1957	1958	1/86
3	Seat	1400 2 couleurs	*1400 2 colours*	1957	1958	1/86
4	Seat	600	*600*	1958	1958	1/86
5	Renault	4 CV	*4 CV*	1947	1958	1/86
6	Pegaso	Benne basse	*Low tipping truck*	1957	1958	1/86
7	Pegaso	Benne haute	*High tipping truck*	1957	1958	1/86
8	DKW	Camionnette bâchée	*Tarpaulin-covered van*	1957	1958	1/86
9	Seat	1400 taxi.	*1400 taxi.*	1957	1958	1/86
10	DKW	Pickup.	*Pickup.*	1958	1959	1/86
11	Pegaso	Camion laitier	*Milk truck*	1958	1959	1/86
12	Pegaso	Essence «Campsa»	*"Campsa" fuel*	1958	1959	1/86
12bis	Pegaso	Gas Oil «Campsa»	*"Campsa" gas oil*	1958	1959	1/86
13	Pegaso	Transport pour 5 autos	*Car carrier for 5 cars*	1958	1959	1/86
13bis	Pegaso	Transport vide	*Empty car carrier*	1958	1959	1/86
14	Ford	Edsel	*Edsel*	1958	1959	1/86
15	Ebro	«Pepsi-Cola»	*"Pepsi-Cola"*	1958	1959	1/86
16	Voisin	Biscuter, capotée	*Biscuter, with hood*	1957	1959	1/86
17	Voisin	Biscuter, ouvert	*Biscuter, without hood*	1957	1959	1/86
18	Ford	Edsel décapotable	*Edsel convertible*	1958	1959	1/86
19	Ebro	Camion-benne	*Tipping truck*	1959	1959	1/86
20	Renault	Dauphine	*Dauphine*	1956	1959	1/86
21	Citroën	2 CV	*2 CV*	1949	1959	1/86
22	Chausson	Autobus	*Bus*	1959	1959	1/86
23	Ebro	Tonneaux «Damm»	*"Damm" drums*	1959	1959	1/86
24	Elcano Armax	Elévateur	*Elevator*	1958	1959	1/86
25	Lanz	Bulldog, tracteur	*Bulldog tractor*	1959	1959	1/86
26	Land Rover	Pickup Jeep	*Pickup Jeep*	1959	1959	1/86
27	Land Rover	Jeep bâchée	*Jeep with hood*	1959	1959	1/86
28	DKW	Kombi II	*Kombi II*	1959	1959	1/86
29	DKW	Ambulance	*Ambulance*	1959	1959	1/86
30	Ebro	«Coca-Cola»	*"Coca-Cola"*	1959	1959	1/86
31	Nelson	Grue	*Crane*	1959	1959	1/86
32	Pegaso	Semi-remorque «Fruehauf»	*"Fruehauf" trailer*	1959	1959	1/86
33	Seat	1400 break	*1400 break*	1959	1959	1/86
34	Seat	1400 «Coca-Cola»	*1400 "Coca-Cola"*	1959	1959	1/86
35	Seat	1400 berline	*1400 saloon*	1959	1960	1/86
36	Mercedes-Benz	W 196	*W 196*	1954	1960	1/86
37	Orix	Fiacre de Berlin	*Berlin cab*	1907	1960	1/86
38	Volkswagen	Berline.	*Saloon*	1959	1960	1/86
39	Renault	Etoile Filante	*Etoile Filante*	1956	1960	1/86
40	Hispano-Suiza	Torpédo	*Torpedo*	1910	1960	1/86
41	Willys	Jeep	*Jeep*	1942	1960	1/86
42	Jaguar	D Le Mans	*D Le Mans*	1956	1960	1/86
43	Le Zèbre	2 places	*2-seater*	1910	1960	1/86
44	Ferrari	Formule 1	*Formula 1*	1956	1960	1/86
45	Alfa Romeo	Giuletta Sprint	*Giuletta Sprint*	1959	1960	1/86
46	Seat	600 Multipla	*600 Multipla*	1959	1960	1/86
47	Studebaker	Lark	*Lark*	1959	1960	1/86
48	Barreiros	Diesel TT 90 22	*Diesel TT 90 22*	1959	1960	1/86
49	Seat	Serra sport	*Serra sport*	1959	1960	1/86
50	Citroën	5 CV	*5 CV*	1922	1960	1/86
51	Mercedes-Benz	Minibus	*Minibus*	1960	1961	1/86
52	Studebaker	Big Six	*Big Six*	1916	1961	1/86
53	Citroën	2 CV fourgonnette	*2 CV van*	1960	1961	1/86
54	Seat	Serra Sport	*Serra Sport*	1959	1961	1/86
55	Land Rover	Station-wagon	*Station wagon*	1960	1961	1/86
56	Ford	Falcon berline	*Falcon saloon.*	1960	1961	1/86
57	Willys	Jeep FC 150	*Jeep FC 150*	1960	1961	1/86
58	Mercedes-Benz	220 S berline	*220 S saloon*	1960	1961	1/86
59	Pegaso	Autobus	*Bus*	1960	1961	1/86
60	Pegaso	Semi-remorque citerne Fruehauf	*Fruehauf tanker trailer*	1959	1961	1/86
61	Willys	Jeep station-wagon	*Jeep station wagon*	1960	1961	1/86
62	MG	A	*A*	1957	1961	1/86
63	Rolls-Royce	Silver Cloud	*Silver Cloud*	1959	1961	1/86
64	Ford	Galaxie	*Galaxie*	1960	1961	1/86

Référence du fabricant *Manufacturer's Reference*	Désignation *Designation*	Type	*Type*	Date de la voiture *Date of car*	Date du modèle *Date of model*	Echelle *Scale*
65	Austin	Mini Seven	*Seven Mini*	1961	1962	1/86
66	Sava	Camion livraison «Butane»	*"Butane" delivery truck*	1961	1962	1/86
67	Borgward	Isabella berline	*Isabella saloon*	1956	1962	1/86
68	Ford	Modèle T	*Model T*	1910	1962	1/86
69	Citroën	ID 19 break	*ID 19 estate car*	1957	1962	1/86
71	Thornycroft	Transporteur de char	*Tank transporter*	1955	1962	1/86
72	Pegaso	Grande échelle	*Fire escape*	1961	1962	1/86
73	Land Rover	Voiture de pompiers	*Fire engine*	1961	1962	1/86
74	Pegaso	Voiture de pompiers	*Fire engine*	1961	1962	1/86
75	Ford	Taunus 17 M	*Taunus 17 M*	1961	1962	1/86
76	Jaguar	Mk IX berline	*Mk IX saloon*	1958	1962	1/86
77	Rover	3 l. berline	*3 l. saloon*	1961	1962	1/86
78		Voiture amphibie militaire	*Military amphibious truck*	1962	1963	1/86
79	Ford	Anglia	*Anglia*	1961	1963	1/86
80	Pegaso	Semi-remorque avec containers de ciment	*Cement container trailer*	1961	1963	1/86
81	Jaguar	XK E	*XK E*	1961	1963	1/86
82	Leyland	Autobus à impériale	*Doubledecker bus*	1961	1963	1/86
83	Volkswagen	Karmann-Ghia	*Karmann-Ghia*	1961	1963	1/86
84	Sava	Benne à ordures	*Refuse truck*	1960	1963	1/86
85	Rolls-Royce	Phantom I sport	*Phantom I sport*	1927	1963	1/86
86	Cadillac	Fleetwood	*Fleetwood*	1962	1963	1/86
87	Unic	Bétonnière	*Cement mixer*	1962	1963	1/86
88	Pegaso	Benne	*Tipper truck*	1962	1963	1/86
89	Ford	Comet	*Comet*	1962	1963	1/86
90	Volkswagen	1500 berline	*1500 saloon*	1963	1964	1/86
91	Ford	Thames plateau	*Thames flat truck*	1963	1964	1/86
92	Studebaker	Hawk	*Hawk*	1962	1964	1/86
93	Fiat	Ballila	*Ballila*	1935	1964	1/86
94	Ford	Consul 315	*Consul 315*	1961	1964	1/86
95		Autobus à impériale	*Doubledecker bus*	1920	1964	1/86
97	Fiat	1500 berline	*1500 saloon*	1962	1964	1/86
98	Hanomag-Barreiros	Tracteur agricole	*Farm tractor*	1962	1964	1/86
99	Volvo	P 1800 sport	*P 1800 sport*	1962	1965	1/86
100	Seat	1400 familiale	*1400 estate car*	1963	1965	1/86
101		Pelleteuse	*Shoveller*	1963	1965	1/86
102	Unic	Semi-remorque avec chaudière	*Trailer with boiler*	1963	1965	1/86
103	Skoda	Octavia berline	*Octavia saloon*	1959	1965	1/86
104	Berlier	Benne-carrière	*Quarry truck*	1964	1965	1/86
105	Citroën	11 CV Légère	*11 CV Legere*	1936	1965	1/86
106	Barreiros	Camion bâché avec remorque	*Tarpaulin-covered truck with trailer*	1964	1965	1/86
107	Saab	96 berline	*96 saloon*	1963	1965	1/86
108	Austin-Sava	Camionnette 1,5 t	*1.5 t van*	1964	1965	1/86
109	BMW	700 coupé	*700 coupé*	1964	1965	1/86
110	Bugatti	57 C	*57 C*	1937	1965	1/86
111	Daf	Daffodil berline	*Daffodil saloon*	1963	1965	1/86
112	Lancia	Aprilia berline	*Aprilia saloon*	1937	1965	1/86
113	Land Rover	«Shell»	*"Shell"*	1964	1965	1/86
114	Studebaker	Avanti	*Avanti*	1962	1965	1/86
115		Pelle excavatrice	*Shovel*	1963	1965	1/86
116	Willys	Jeep d'aéroport	*Airport Jeep*	1963	1965	1/86
117 NA	Citroën	Camionnette 1200 kg	*1200 kg van*	1956	1966	1/86
118 NB	Renault	Floride	*Floride*	1959	1966	1/86
119 NC	Panhard	Dyna	*Dyna*	1950	1966	1/86
120 ND	Unic	Semi-remorque transport de ciment	*Cement trailer*	1965	1966	1/86
121 NE	Citroën	DS 19	*DS 19*	1956	1966	1/86
122 NF	Unic	Benne Marrel	*Marrel tipper truck*	1963	1966	1/86
123 NG	Simca	Ariane	*Ariane*	1957	1966	1/86
124	Opel	Kadett	*Kadett*	1963	1966	1/86
125	Ford	Zephyr	*Zephyr*	1963	1966	1/86

Série Super Mini-cars / *Super Mini-cars series*

1	Seat	1400 familiale	*1400 estate car*	1961	1962	1/43
2	Fiat	Ballila berline	*Ballila saloon*	1935	1962	1/43
3	Ford	Galaxie berline	*Galaxie saloon*	1960	1962	1/43
4	Le Zèbre	Voiturette 2 places	*Two-seater baby car*	1910	1962	1/43

Référence du fabricant / *Manufacturer's Reference*	Désignation / *Designation*	Type	*Type*	Date de la voiture / *Date of car*	Date du modèle / *Date of model*	Echelle / *Scale*
5	Cadillac	Fleetwood berline	*Fleetwood saloon . . . .*	1961	1962	1/43
6	Ford	T Torpedo	*T Torpedo . . . .*	1915	1962	1/43
7	Orix	Fiacre de Berlin	*Berlin cab . . . .*	1907	1964	1/43

ANTOINE ☐ I

Matière / *Material:* Résine / *Resin*

1	Fiat	Voiture de pompiers, type 635 . .	*Fire engine, type 635. . . . . .*	—	1981	1/43
2	Fiat	Voiture de pompiers, type 15ter .	*Fire engine, type 15ter . . . . .*	—	1982	1/43

AOSHIMA ☐ J

Cette liste est sans doute incomplète. En l'absence d'informations fournies par le fabricant, elle a été établie sur la base du dernier catalogue et d'une publication japonaise recensant les maquettes en plastique disponibles en 1982.
In the absence of information from the manufacturer direct, this list may not be complete: it was compiled from Aoshima catalogues and the Japanese Plastic Model Catalogue 1982 (a list of items available).

Matière / *Material:* Plastique / *Plastic*

Série voitures de tourisme modifiées / *Tuning Car Series*

1	Nissan	Laurel HT 2000 SGX.	*Laurel HT 2000 SGX. . . . . . .*	—	—	1/24
2	Nissan	Skyline HT 2000 GT Turbo 2 portes	*Skyline HT 2000 GT Turbo 2-door. . . . .*	—	—	1/24
3	Nissan	Cedric HT 2000 SGL-E 4 portes	*Cedric HT 2000 SGL-E 4-door .*	—	—	1/24
4	Nissan	Skyline 2000 GT-X 4 portes. . .	*Skyline 2000 GT-X 4-door . . .*	—	—	1/24
—	Nissan	Cedric HT 2000 GX 2 portes	*Cedric HT 2000 GX 2-door . . .*	—	—	1/24
—	Nissan	Skyline 2000 GTX-E 4 portes . .	*Skyline 2000 GTX-E 4-door. . .*	—	—	1/24
—	Nissan	Skyline 2000 GT Turbo 4 portes	*Skyline 2000 GT Turbo 4-door. . . . .*	—	—	1/24
—	Nissan	Gloria HT 2000 SGL-E 4 portes	*Gloria HT 2000 SGL-E 4-door. .*	—	—	1/24

Série 4 roues motrices (la plupart motorisées) / *4 WD Jeeps (most of these are battery-powered)*

1	Mitsubishi	Jeep H-J58	*Jeep H-J58 . . . .*	—	—	1/20
2	Toyota	Land Cruiser BJ 40	*Land Cruiser BJ 40 . . . .*	—	—	1/20
3	Mitsubishi	Jeep, bâchée	*Jeep, canvas top . . . .*	—	—	1/20
4	Toyota	Land Cruiser hardtop.	*Land Cruiser hardtop. . . . . .*	—	—	1/20
5	Mitsubishi	Jeep «California» hors série . . .	*"California" Jeep (customized)*	—	—	1/20
6	Toyota	Land Cruiser «California»	*"California" Land Cruiser (customized) . . . .*	—	—	1/20
7	Custom Jeep	Base Mitsubishi	*Mitsubishi-based . . . .*	—	—	1/20
8	Custom Land Cruiser	Base Toyota	*Toyota-based. . . . .*	—	—	1/20
9	Mitsubishi	Jeep, bâchée, carrosserie en métal	*Jeep, canvas top, metallic body*	—	—	1/20
10	Toyota	Land Cruiser hardtop, carrosserie en métal	*Land Cruiser hardtop, metallic body . . . .*	—	—	1/20

Série tout-terrain avec treuil et phares fonctionnant / *4 WD Winch Truck Series (with working headlights)*

1	Toyota	Hi-Lux.	*Hi-Lux. . . . .*	—	—	1/24
2	Datsun	Pickup.	*Pickup. . . . .*	—	—	1/24
3	Toyota	Hi-Lux fourgonnette	*Hi-Lux tank top van . . . . . .*	—	—	1/24
4	Datsun	Fourgonnette	*Tank top van . . . .*	—	—	1/24
5	Toyota	Hi-Lux, pneus ballon.	*Hi-Lux with balloon tyres. . . .*	—	—	1/24
6	Datsun	avec pneus ballon	*with balloon tyres . . . .*	—	—	1/24
7	Toyota	Hi-Lux sports.	*Hi-Lux sports. . . . .*	—	—	1/24
8	Datsun	Pickup sports	*Sports pickup. . . . .*	—	—	1/24

Série Jeep avec treuil (motorisées) / *Winch Jeeps (motorizable) series*

1	Mitsubishi	Jeep J-J58.	*Jeep J-J58. . . . .*	—	—	1/20
2	Toyota	Land Cruiser BJ 40	*Land Cruiser BJ 40 . . . .*	—	—	1/20
3	Mitsubishi	Jeep, bâchée	*Jeep canvas top. . . . .*	—	—	1/20

Référence du fabricant / *Manufacturer's Reference*	Désignation / *Designation*	Type	*Type*	Date de la voiture / *Date of car*	Date du modèle / *Date of model*	Echelle / *Scale*
4	Toyota	Land Cruiser hardtop	*Land Cruiser hardtop*	—	—	1/20
5	Mitsubishi	Jeep, version compétition	*Jeep (racing)*	—	—	1/20
6	Toyota	Land Cruiser, version compétition	*Land Cruiser (racing)*	—	—	1/20

Série fourgonnettes Honda, motorisées et avec accessoires / *Honda Van Series (motorizable), all slightly custom, with accessories such as surfboards, rollerskates, etc.)*

Référence du fabricant / *Manufacturer's Reference*	Désignation / *Designation*	Type	*Type*	Date de la voiture / *Date of car*	Date du modèle / *Date of model*	Echelle / *Scale*
1	Honda	Step Van fourgon «We love Step Van»	*Step Van "We love Step Van"*	—	—	1/20
2	Honda	Step Van fourgon «Come on Sportsman»	*Step Van "Come on Sportsman"*	—	—	1/20
3	Honda	Step Van «European Knight»	*Step Van "European Knight"*	—	—	1/20
4	Honda	Step Van «Discover American Sports»	*Step Van "Discover American Sports"*	—	—	1/20

Série «Les meilleures voitures» / *Best Car Series*

Référence du fabricant / *Manufacturer's Reference*	Désignation / *Designation*	Type	*Type*	Date de la voiture / *Date of car*	Date du modèle / *Date of model*	Echelle / *Scale*
1	Lamborghini	Countach LP 400	*Countach LP 400*	—	—	1/20
2	Ferrari	512 BB	*BB 512*	—	—	1/20
3	Lamborghini	Countach LP 500 S	*Countach LP 500 S*	—	—	1/20
4	Lamborghini	Jota	*Jota*	—	—	1/20
5	Lamborghini	Miura	*Miura*	—	—	1/20
6	Ferrari	Dino 246 GT	*Dino 246 GT*	—	—	1/20
7	De Tomaso	Pantera GTS.S	*Pantera GTS.S*	—	—	1/20
8	Maserati	Boomerang (prototype)	*Boomerang (prototype)*	—	—	1/20
—	Mitsubishi	Galant Lambda 2000 GSR	*Galant Lambda 2000 GSR*	—	—	1/20
—	Toyota	Celica LB 2000 GT	*Celica LB 2000 GT*	—	—	1/20
—	Mazda	RX-7	*RX-7*	—	—	1/20
1	Lancia	Stratos Turbo (compétition)	*Stratos Turbo (racing)*	—	—	1/20
2	Mitsubishi	Galant Lambda 2000 GSR Turbo (compétition)	*Galant Lambda 2000 GSR Turbo (racing)*	—	—	1/20
3	Toyota	Celica LB 2000 GTV Turbo (compétition)	*Celica LB 2000 GTV Turbo (racing)*	—	—	1/20
4	Mazda	RX-7 silhouette compétition	*RX-7 Silhouette racing*	—	—	1/20

Série «modèles de précision» / *Precision Models Big Car Series*

Référence du fabricant / *Manufacturer's Reference*	Désignation / *Designation*	Type	*Type*	Date de la voiture / *Date of car*	Date du modèle / *Date of model*	Echelle / *Scale*
1	Lamborghini	Countach LP 500 (avec moteur)	*Countach LP 500 (motor included)*	—	—	1/16
2	Lamborghini	Countach LP 400 (avec moteur)	*Countach LP 400 (motor included)*	—	—	1/16
3	Lancia	Stratos Turbo (avec moteur)	*Stratos Turbo (motor included)*	—	—	1/16
4	Maserati	Boomerang (prototype, avec moteur)	*Boomerang (prototype, motor included)*	—	—	1/16

Série «voitures de course» / *Speed Race Car Series*

Référence du fabricant / *Manufacturer's Reference*	Désignation / *Designation*	Type	*Type*	Date de la voiture / *Date of car*	Date du modèle / *Date of model*	Echelle / *Scale*
1	Lamborghini	Countach LP 500 S	*Countach LP 500 S*	—	—	1/24
2	Maserati	Boomerang (prototype)	*Boomerang (prototype)*	—	—	1/24
3	Porsche	935-77 Turbo	*935-77 Turbo*	—	—	1/24
4	Lancia	Stratos Turbo	*Stratos Turbo*	—	—	1/24
5	Toyota	Celica Turbo	*Celica Turbo*	—	—	1/24
6	Datsun	260 Z Turbo	*Fairlady 260 Z Turbo*	—	—	1/24
7	Ferrari	512 BB Turbo	*BB 512 Turbo*	—	—	1/24
8	Mazda	RX-7 compétition	*RX-7 Rotary Racing*	—	—	1/24
9	Porsche	935/78 double turbo	*935/78 twin turbo*	—	—	1/24
10	BMW	M1 double turbo	*M1 twin turbo*	—	—	1/24
11	Porsche	936/78 double turbo	*936/78 twin turbo*	—	—	1/24
12	Nissan	280 Z compétition	*New Fairlady 280 Z racing*	—	—	1/24
13	Toyota	2000 GT Turbo	*2000 GT Turbo*	—	—	1/24
14	March 75/S	A moteur rotatif Mazda	*Mazda rotary engine*	—	—	1/24

Référence du fabricant *Manufacturer's Reference*	Désignation *Designation*	Type	*Type*	Date de la voiture *Date of car*	Date du modèle *Date of model*	Echelle *Scale*

Série «voitures pour spécialistes» / *Speciality Car Series*

1	Toyota	Soarer 2800 GT Extra	*Soarer 2800 GT Extra*	—	—	1/24
2	Isuzu	Piazza	*Piazza*	—	—	1/24
—	Toyota	Soarer Turbo	*Soarer Turbo*	—	—	1/24
—	Toyota	Celica XX	*Celica XX*	—	—	1/24

Série «voitures de luxe» / *Luxury Car Series*

—	Nissan	Laurel HT 2000 SGX (série)	*Laurel HT 2000 SGX (normal)*	—	—	1/24
—	Nissan	Skyline HT 2000 GT Turbo (série)	*Skyline HT 2000 GT Turbo (normal)*	—	—	1/24

Série motos / *Motorbike Series*

1	Honda	Hawk III CB 400 N	*Hawk III CB 400 N*	—	—	1/12
2	Honda	Hawk III CB 400 N Touring	*Hawk III CB 400 N Touring*	—	—	1/12
3	BMW	R-100 S	*R-100 S*	—	—	1/12
4	BMW	R-100 RT	*R-100 RT*	—	—	1/12
5	Suzuki	GS 400 E	*GS 400 E*	—	—	1/12
6	Suzuki	GS 400 L	*GS 400 L*	—	—	1/12
7	Suzuki	GS 400 E Touring	*GS 400 E Touring*	—	—	1/12
8	Honda	Hawk CB 250 N.	*Hawk CB 250 N.*	—	—	1/12
9	Kawasaki	Z 400 FX.	*Z 400 FX.*	—	—	1/12
10	Kawasaki	Z 400 FX Special	*Z 400 FX Special*	—	—	1/12
11	Suzuki	GSX 400 E	*GSX 400 E*	—	—	1/12
12	Suzuki	GSX 250 E	*GSX 250 E*	—	—	1/12
13	Yamaha	XJ 400	*XJ 400*	—	—	1/12
14	Honda	Hawk III CB 400 N Special	*Hawk III CB 400 N Special*	—	—	1/12
15	Suzuki	GS 400 E Special	*GS 400 E Special*	—	—	1/12
16	Kawasaki	Z 400 FX Special DX	*Z 400 FX Special DX*	—	—	1/12
17	Yamaha	XJ 400 Special	*XJ 400 Special*	—	—	1/12
18	Kawasaki	Z 550 FX.	*Z 550 FX.*	—	—	1/12
19	Suzuki	GSX 400 F	*GSX 400 F*	—	—	1/12
—	Suzuki	GSX 400 F Special	*GSX 400 F Special*	—	—	1/12

Série «mon scooter», modèles disponibles en versions standard ou spéciales / *My Scooter Series (models available as normal or special)*

1	Yamaha	Beluga 80	*Beluga 80*	—	—	1/12
2	Suzuki	Gemma	*Gemma*	—	—	1/12
3	Honda	Tact	*Tact*	—	—	1/12

Série «collection classique» / *Classic Collection Series*

1	Harley-Davidson	—	—	1918	—	1/16
2	Henderson	—	—	1912	—	1/16
3	Militaire	—	—	1914	—	1/16
4	Ace	—	—	1924	—	1/16
5	Bianchi	(voiture)	*(car)*	1907	—	1/32

AR — F

Matière / *Material:* Plomb et tôle emboutie / *Lead and tin plate*

—	Renault	Char d'assaut FT 17	*FT 17 light tank*	1917	1920	1/60
—	—	Tracteur agricole (avec volant)	*Farm tractor (flywheel)*	—	1925	1/60
—	—	Tracteur agricole	*Farm tractor*	—	—	1/60
—	Caterpillar	Tracteur à chenilles	*Tractor on tracks*	—	—	1/65
—	—	Remorque brise-motte	*Disc harrow trailer*	—	—	1/60
—	—	Remorque charrue	*Three furrows plough trailer*	—	—	1/60
—	—	Auto de course 8 cylindres	*8 cylinder racing car*	1930	1930	1/50
—	Yellow Cab	Taxi	*Taxi*	1920	1920	1/50
—	Yellow Cab	Taxi (sans montants pare-brise)	*Taxi (no windscreen pillars)*	1920	1920	1/50
—	—	Rouleau compresseur	*Steam road roller*	1920	—	1/50
—	Latil	Camion laitier 11 pots	*Milk truck with 11 churns*	1925	1925	1/60
—	Latil	Echelle pompiers	*Fire engine with ladder*	1925	—	1/60

Référence du fabricant / *Manufacturer's Reference*	Désignation / *Designation*	Type	*Type*	Date de la voiture / *Date of car*	Date du modèle / *Date of model*	Echelle / *Scale*
—	Latil	Camion benne bâchée	*Covered lorry*	1925	—	1/60
—	Latil	Fardier 3 grumes	*Flat bed truck with 3 logs*	1925	—	1/60
—	Latil	Camion benne basculante	*Tipping truck*	1925	—	1/60
—	Latil	Camion benne basculante (cab. découverte	*Tipping truck (open cab)*	1925	—	1/60
—	Latil	Camion-citerne	*Tanker*	1925	—	1/60
—	Latil	Camion plateau avec tonneaux	*Flat bed truck with barrels*	1925	—	1/60
—	Latil	Camion DCA	*AA gun on flat bed truck*	1925	—	1/60
—	Latil	Camion maraîcher	*Market gardeners truck*	1925	—	1/60
—	Peugeot 301	Laitier 11 pots	*Milk truck with 11 churns*	1935	1935	1/50
—	Peugeot 301	Laitier plateau 5 pots	*Flat bed milk truck (5 churns)*	1935	—	1/50
—	Peugeot 301	Laitier ridelles 4 pots	*Milk truck (4 churns)*	1935	—	1/50
—	Peugeot 301	Laitier ridelles 6 pots	*Milk truck (6 churns)*	1935	—	1/50
—	Peugeot 301	Porte câble	*Cable drum truck*	1935	—	1/50
—	Peugeot 301	Camion maraîcher bâché	*Covered market gardeners truck*	1935	—	1/50
—	Peugeot 301	Camion miroitier	*Glass transporter*	1935	—	1/50
—	Peugeot 301	Ambulance bâché	*Ambulance with top up*	1935	—	1/50
—	Peugeot 301	Monte-charge	*Conveyor*	1935	—	1/50
—	Peugeot 301	Fourgon postes	*Mail van*	1935	—	1/50
—	Peugeot 301	Echelle pompiers	*Fire engine with ladder*	1935	—	1/50
—	Peugeot 301	Fourgon ambulance civile	*Ambulance van (civilian)*	1935	—	1/50
—	Peugeot 301	Fourgon ambulance militaire	*Military ambulance van*	1935	—	1/50
—	Peugeot 301	Benne à ridelles	*Wagon*	1935	—	1/50
—	Peugeot 301	Camion-citerne	*Tanker*	1935	—	1/50
—	Peugeot 301	Camion bâché	*Covered wagon*	1935	—	1/50
—	Peugeot 301	Camion plateau 3 grumes	*Flat bed truck with 3 logs*	1935	—	1/50
—	Peugeot 301	Camion plateau avec foudre	*Flat bed truck with vat*	1935	—	1/50
—	Peugeot 301	Bâché postes	*Covered mail van*	1935	—	1/50
—	Peugeot 301	Canon DCA	*AA gun*	1935	—	1/50
—	Peugeot 301	Dépanneuse	*Wrecker*	1935	—	1/50
—	Peugeot 301	Camion plateau avec 3 tonneaux	*Flat bed truck with 3 barrels*	1935	—	1/50
—	Peugeot 301	Camion benne basculante	*Tipping truck*	1935	—	1/50
—	Peugeot 301	Projecteur	*Searchlight lorry*	1935	—	1/50
—	Renault Nerva	Camion plateau	*Flat bed truck*	1938	1946	1/50
—	Renault Nerva	Maraîcher	*Market garderners truck*	1938	1946	1/50
—	Renault Nerva	Camion-citerne	*Tanker*	1938	1946	1/50
—	Renault Nerva	Dépanneuse	*Wrecker*	1938	1946	1/50
—	Peugeot 201	Cabriolet 2 places	*2 seater convertible*	1928	1930	1/45
—	Peugeot 301	Berline avec compas	*Saloon with irons*	1930	1930	1/42
—	Peugeot 301	Berline 2e type (toit gravé)	*Saloon 2nd type (embossed roof)*	1930	1931	1/42
—	Peugeot 301	Berline 2e type (toit lisse)	*Saloon 2nd type (plain roof)*	—	—	—
—	Peugeot 301	Berline 3e type (gros coffre)	*Saloon 3rd type (big trunk)*	1930	1931	1/42
—	Peugeot 301	Berline 3e type (toit gravé)	*Saloon 3rd type (embossed roof)*	1930	1931	1/42
—	Peugeot 301	Coupé surbaissé	*Streamlined coupé*	1930	1931	1/42
—	Peugeot 301	Coupé	*Coupé*	1930	1931	1/42
—	Peugeot 302	Berline aérodynamique	*Airflow saloon*	1935	1936	1/43
—	Peugeot 402	Coupé Andreau	*Andreau coupé*	1937	1937	1/43
—	Peugeot 402	Berline Andreau	*Andreau saloon*	1938	1938	1/43
—	Peugeot 402	Fuseau Sochaux	*Fuseau Sochaux coupé*	1937	1937	1/43
—	Peugeot 402	Fuseau Sochaux (roues avant couvertes)	*Fuseau Sochaux coupé (covered front wheel arches)*	1937	—	1/43
—	Peugeot 402	Cabriolet Darl'Mat	*Darl'Mat convertible*	1937	1937	1/43
—	Peugeot 601	Coupé 2 portes	*2 door coupé*	1935	1937	1/43
—	Napier Campbell	Blue Bird (avec mécanisme)	*Blue Bird (clockwork)*	1934	1935	1/43
—	Napier Campbell	Blue Bird (sans mécanisme)	*Blue Bird (not clockwork)*	1934	1938	—
—	Renault TN4	Bus parisien	*Paris bus*	1928	1930	1/86
—	Renault TN4	Bus parisien (toit tôle)	*Paris bus (tin plate roof)*	1928	1930	1/86

Ces deux modèles ne sont pas gravés AR-France et pourraient être des copies produites par un concurrent:
These two models are not embossed AR-France and could be copies produced by a competitor:

Référence du fabricant / *Manufacturer's Reference*	Désignation / *Designation*	Type	*Type*	Date de la voiture / *Date of car*	Date du modèle / *Date of model*	Echelle / *Scale*
—	Peugeot 201	Coupé	*Coupé*	1928	1930	1/45
—	Peugeot 301	Roadster 2 places	*2 seater roadster*	1930	1930	1/42

Référence du fabricant / *Manufacturer's Reference*	Désignation / *Designation*	Type	*Type*	Date de la voiture / *Date of car*	Date du modèle / *Date of model*	Echelle / *Scale*

ARBUR — GB

Matière / *Material:* Zamac / *Diecast*

—	Sunbeam	Berline	*Saloon*	1950	1950-52	1/43
—	—	Voiture de pompiers	*Fire engine*	1948	1948-52	1/50
—	—	Semi-remorque plateau	*Artic. flat bed*	1950	1950-52	1/50
—	—	Semi-remorque benne	*Artic. tipping truck*	1950	1950-52	1/50
—	—	Semi-remorque fourgon	*Tractor with van trailer*	1950	1950-52	1/50

ARCADE TOYS — USA

Matière: Métal / *Material: Metal*

	Hudson	Spider	*Spider*	1934	—	1/40
	Studebaker	Spider	*Spider*	1934	—	1/40
	Hupmobile	Spider	*Spider*	1934	—	1/40
	Ford	Spider	*Spider*	1934	—	1/40
	Pontiac	Dépanneuse	*Break-down truck*	1934	—	1/40
	Dodge	Pickup à ridelles	*Pickup with racks*	1934	—	1/40
	Lincoln	Zephyr	*Zephyr*	1934	—	1/40
	Pierce-Arrow	Silver	*Silver*	1934	—	1/40
	Rep	Pompiers	*Fire engine*	1934	—	1/40
	Seagrave	Pompe à vapeur	*Steam pump*	1934	—	1/40
		Voiture de course aérodynamique	*Streamlined racing car*	1934	—	1/40
	GMC	Bus «Greyhound»	*"Greyhound" bus*	1934	—	1/40
	Reo	Autobus semi-remorque	*Semi-trailer bus*	1934	—	1/40
		Benne aérodynamique	*Streamlined tipper*	1934	—	1/40

ARII □ J

Cette liste est sans doute incomplète. En l'absence d'informations fournies par le fabricant, elle a été établie sur la base du plus récent catalogue de la marque.

In the absence of information from the manufacturer direct, this list may not be complete: it was compiled from the latest Arii catalogue.

Matière / *Material:* Plastique / *Plastic*

Série voitures Hotrod / *Hotrod Machines Series*

—	Mercury	Cougar Hotrod	*Cougar Hotrod*	—	—	1/20
—	Ford	Mustang Mach 1 Hotrod	*Mustang Mach 1 Hotrod*	—	—	1/20
—	Toyota	Celica LB 2000 GT Hotrod	*Celica LB 2000 GT Hotrod*	—	—	1/20
—	Mazda	RX-3 Hotrod	*RX-3 Hotrod*	—	—	1/20
—	Nissan	Bluebird U SSS-E Hotrod	*Bluebird U SSS-E Hotrod*	—	—	1/20
—	Mazda	Cosmo AP rotatif Hotrod	*Cosmo AP Rotary Hotrod*	—	—	1/20

Série «voitures pour spécialistes» / *Speciality Car Series*

AR 122A	Datsun	280 Z-T 2 places	*280 Z-T 2-seater*	—	—	1/24
AR 122B	Nissan	Skyline 2000 GT	*Skyline 2000 GT*	—	—	1/24
AR 122C	Mazda	RX-7 Limited	*RX-7 Limited*	—	—	1/24
AR 122D	Mitsubishi	Galant Lambda Eterna 2000	*Galant Lambda Eterna 2000*	—	—	1/24

Série «Nowi» / *"Nowi" Series*

AR 101A	Nissan	Skyline Turbo 2000 GT-ES	*Skyline Turbo 2000 GT-ES*	—	—	1/24
AR 101B	Toyota	Celica LB 2000 GT	*Celica LB 2000 GT*	—	—	1/24
AR 101C	Nissan	Skyline 2000 GT-X	*Skyline 2000 GT-X*	—	—	1/24
AR 101D	Toyota	Celica LB 2000 GT	*Celica LB 2000 GT*	—	—	1/24

Série véhicules 4 roues motrices / *4 WD Off Road Series*

AR 106A-H	Toyota	Hi-Lux	*Hi-Lux*	—	—	1/24
—	Nissan	Safari	*Safari*	—	—	1/24
—	Toyota	Hi-Lux Custom (style US)	*Hi-Lux Custom (American style)*	—	—	1/24

Référence du fabricant / *Manufacturer's Reference*	Désignation / *Designation*	Type	*Type*	Date de la voiture / *Date of car*	Date du modèle / *Date of model*	1/Echelle / *1/Scale*
—	Nissan	Safari Custom (style US)	*Safari Custom (American style)*	—	—	1/24
—	Toyota	Hi-Lux hardtop	*Hi-Lux hardtop*	—	—	1/24
—	Nissan	Safari hardtop	*Safari hardtop*	—	—	1/24
—	Toyota	Hi-Lux hors série	*Hi-Lux (high roof)*	—	—	1/24
—	Nissan	Safari hors série	*Safari (high roof)*	—	—	1/24
—	Toyota	Hi-Lux hors série	*Hi-Lux (roof type)*	—	—	1/24
—	Nissan	Safari hors série	*Safari (roof type)*	—	—	1/24
Série voitures japonaises / *Japanese Car Series*						
AR 123A	Nissan	Fairlady Z	*Fairlady Z*	—	—	1/24
AR 123B	Mitsubishi	Galant Lambda	*Galant Lambda*	—	—	1/24
AR 123C	Nissan	Skyline	*Skyline*	—	—	1/24
AR 123D	Mazda	RX-7	*RX-7*	—	—	1/24
Série voitures japonaises au 1/28 / *1:28 Japanese Car Series*						
AR 203A	Toyota	2000 GT	*2000 GT*	—	—	1/28
AR 203B	Mazda	Cosmo AP	*Cosmo AP*	—	—	1/28
AR 203C	Nissan	Fairlady 280	*Fairlady 280*	—	—	1/28
AR 203D	Nissan	Sylvia SE-X	*Sylvia SE-X*	—	—	1/28
Série voitures à moteur à ressort / *Automatic Action Series (with spring)*						
AR 102-1	Nissan	Skyline 2000 GT-EX	*Skyline 2000 GT-EX*	—	—	1/32
AR 102-2	Mazda	Cosmo AP Limited (toit landau)	*Cosmo AP Limited (Landau top)*	—	—	1/32
AR 102-3	Mitsubishi	Galant Lambda 2000 GSL	*Galant Lambda 2000 GSL*	—	—	1/32
AR 102-4	Toyota	Celica LB 2000 GT-V	*Celica LB 2000 GT-V*	—	—	1/32
AR 102-5	Lamborghini	Countach LP 400	*Countach LP 400*	—	—	1/32
AR 102-6	De Tomaso	Pantera GT-S	*Pantera GT-S*	—	—	1/32
AR 102-7	Lamborghini	Jota	*Jota*	—	—	1/32
AR 102-8	Ferrari	BB 512 GT	*512 GT BB*	—	—	1/32
Série buggy tout-terrain / *WD Buggy Series*						
—	Sand Buggy	—	—	—	—	1/32
—	Volkswagen	Buggy	*Buggy*	—	—	1/32
—	Red Buggy	—	—	—	—	1/32
—	Fellow Buggy	—	—	—	—	1/32
—	Mitsubishi	Jeep	*Jeep*	—	—	1/32
—	Suzuki	Jimmy	*Jimmy*	—	—	1/32
Série autobus HO / *HO Bus Series*						
AR 16 A	autobus	Japan Air Lines	*Japan Air Lines*	—	—	1/HO
AR 16 B	autobus	Hato	*Hato*	—	—	1/HO
AR 16 C	autobus	Express	*Express*	—	—	1/HO
AR 16 D	autobus	Tour de ville	*Sightseeing*	—	—	1/HO

ARISTON — I

Matière / *Material:* Résine / *Resin*

Référence du fabricant / *Manufacturer's Reference*	Désignation / *Designation*	Type	*Type*	Date de la voiture / *Date of car*	Date du modèle / *Date of model*	1/Echelle / *1/Scale*
1	BMW	«328» spider «Mille Miglia»	*"328" spider "Mille Miglia"*	1938	1975	1/43
2	Fiat	«A» 1400	*"A" 1400 cc*	1950	1975	1/43
3	Fiat	600 Abarth 1000 TC, gr. 2	*600 Abarth 1000 TC, Gr. 2*	1970	1976	1/43
4	Mercedes	300 SC	*300 SC*	1955	1975	1/43
5	Mercedes	170 CV spider	*170 CV spider*	1935	1975	1/43

Référence du fabricant *Manufacturer's Reference*	Désignation *Designation*	Type	*Type*	Date de la voiture *Date of car*	Date du modèle *Date of model*	Echelle *Scale*

ARTIGIANA □ I

Matière / *Material:* Résine / *Resin*

1	Ferrari	125 sport, Piacenza	*125 sport, Piacenza*	1947	1981	1/43
2	Ferrari	815 AAC sport	*815 AAC sport*	1940	1981	1/43
5	Ferrari	212 Inter, Pininfarina	*212 Inter, Pininfarina*	1952	1981	1/43

ASAHI TOY CO. — J

Matière / *Material:* Zamac / *Die cast*

1	Toyota	Crown berline	*Crown saloon*	1959	1959	1/43
2	Toyota	Masterline break	*Masterline station wagon*	1960	1960	1/43
2s	Toyota	Masterline break	*Masterline station wagon*	1960	1962	1/43
2sa	Toyota	Masterline ambulance	*Masterline ambulance*	1960	1963	1/43
3	Subaru	360	*360*	1959	1960	1/43
4	Toyota	Land Cruiser	*Land Cruiser*	1959	1960	1/43
5	Datsun	Bluebird berline	*Bluebird saloon*	1960	1960	1/43
6	Prince	Slyline berline	*Skyline saloon*	1960	1960	1/43
6g	Prince	Skyline berline	*Skyline saloon*	1960	1961	1/43
7	Toyota	Corona berline	*Corona saloon*	1960	1960	1/43
7s	Toyota	Corona berline	*Corona saloon*	1960	1962	1/43
8	Nissan	Austin A55 berline	*Austin A55 saloon*	1959	1960	1/43
9	Hillman	Minx berline	*Minx saloon*	1961	1961	1/43
9s	Hillman	Minx berline	*Minx saloon*	1961	1962	1/43
10	Nissan	Cedric berline	*Cedric saloon*	1960	1961	1/43
10s	Nissan	Cedric berline	*Cedric saloon*	1960	1962	1/43
10st	Nissan	Cedric berline taxi Tokyo	*Cedric saloon Tokyo taxi*	1960	1963	1/43
11	Toyota	Corona break	*Corona station wagon*	1960	1961	1/43
11s	Toyota	Corona break	*Corona station wagon*	1960	1962	1/43
12	Toyota	Crown berline	*Crown saloon*	1961	1961	1/43
12s	Toyota	Crown berline police	*Crown saloon police car*	1961	1963	1/43
13	Mazda	R 360 coupé	*R 360 coupé*	1960	1961	1/43
14	Toyota	Publica berline	*Publica sedan*	1960	1961	1/43
15	Prince	Skyline Sport cabriolet	*Skyline Sports convertible*	1960	1961	1/43
16	Prince	Skyline Sport coupé	*Skyline Sports coupé*	1961	1961	1/43
17	Datsun	Bluebird berline	*Bluebird saloon*	1962	1962	1/43
18	Isuzu	Bellel berline	*Bellel saloon*	1963	1963	1/43
19	Toyota	Coupé sport	*Sports coupé*	1962	1962	1/43
20	Toyota	Crown berline	*Crown sedan*	1963	1963	1/43
21	Toyota	Masterline break	*Masterline station wagon*	1963	1964	1/25
21a	Toyota	Masterline ambulance	*Masterline ambulance*	1963	1964	1/43
22	Prince	Gloria berline	*Gloria sedan*	1964	1964	1/43
22t	Prince	Gloria berline taxi	*Gloria sedan taxi*	1964	1965	1/43
23	Toyota	Land Cruiser bâché	*Land Cruiser covered*	1963	1963	1/43
24	Mitsubishi	Colt 1000 berline	*Colt 1000 sedan*	1964	1965	1/43
25	Datsun	Bluebird berline	*Bluebird sedan*	1966	1966	1/43
26	Hino	Contessa 1300 berline	*Contessa 1300 sedan*	1965	1965	1/43
27	Toyota	Corona berline	*Corona sedan*	1965	1965	1/43
29	Hino	Contessa 1300 berline	*Contessa 1300 sedan*	1965	1965	1/43
30	Mazda	Familia berline	*Familia sedan*	1964	1965	1/43
31	Toyota	Coupé Sport 800	*Sports coupé 800*	1964	1965	1/43
32	Nissan	Silvia coupé	*Silvia coupé*	1965	1966	1/43
33	Nissan	Cedric berline	*Cedric sedan*	1965	1966	1/43
34	Honda	S 800 cabriolet	*S 800 convertible*	1966	1967	1/43
35	Honda	S 800 coupé	*S 800 coupé*	1966	1967	1/43
36	Toyota	2000 GT coupé	*2000 GT coupé*	1967	1967	1/43
37	Honda	N360	*N360*	1967	1967	1/43
38	Toyota	Crown Super berline	*Crown Super sedan*	1968	1970	1/43
39	Toyota	Crown coupé	*Crown coupé*	1971	1971	1/43
40	Mitsubishi	Galant GTO	*Galant GTO*	—	1972	1/43
41	Toyota	Crown coupé police	*Crown coupé police car*	1971	1972	1/43
43	Honda	Moto RC 162	*RC 162 motorcycle*	—	1972	—
44	Suzuki	Moto 750 GT	*750 GT motorcycle*	—	1972	—
45	Nissan	Skyline 2000 GT coupé	*Skyline 2000 GT coupé*	1972	1972	1/43
46	Yamaha	Moto 650 XS Sport	*650 XS Sport motorcycle*	—	1972	—
47	Datsun	Sunny Coupé Excellent 1400	*Sunny Coupé Excellent 1400*	1972	1972	1/43
48	Honda	Moto 750	*750 motorcycle*	—	1972	—
50	Honda	Moto 750 police	*750 police motorcycle*	—	1972	—

Référence du fabricant / *Manufacturer's Reference*	Désignation / *Designation*	Type	*Type*	Date de la voiture / *Date of car*	Date du modèle / *Date of model*	Echelle / *Scale*
51	Toyota	Corona Mk II 2000 G SS	*Corona Mk II 2000 G SS . . . .*	1972	1972	1/43
52	Datsun	Bluebird U HT SSS	*Bluebird U HT SSS . . . . . .*	1972	1973	1/43
54	Nissan	Cedric 2600 GX berline.	*Cedric 2600 GX sedan . . . . .*	1973	1973	1/43
55	Toyota	Crown coupé taxi	*Crown coupé taxi . . . .*	1971	1973	1/43
56	Toyota	Crown coupé pompiers.	*Crown coupé fire chief . . . . .*	1971	1973	1/43
57	Toyota	Crown coupé ambulance	*Crown coupé ambulance . . . .*	1971	1973	1/43
58	Mitsubishi	Galant GTO rallye	*Galant GTO rally version . . . .*	—	1973	1/43
59	Nissan	Skyline 2000 GT coupé rallye . .	*Skyline 2000 GT coupé rally . .*	1972	1973	1/43
60	Yamaha	Moto side-car police	*Police sidecar motorcycle . . . .*	—	1972	—
61	Yamaha	Moto police	*Police motorcycle . . . .*	—	1972	—
62	Yamaha	Moto side-car.	*Sidecar motorcycle . . . . . .*	—	1972	—
101	Toyota	Toyace	*Toyace . . . .*	1960	1960	1/43
102	Toyota	Toyace	*Toyace . . . .*	1962	1962	1/43
103	Toyota	Toyace bâché.	*Toyace covered . . . .*	1962	1962	1/43

Série Sigma 143 / *Sigma 143 series*

1	Lotus	Esprit	*Esprit . . . .*	1978	1978	1/43
2	Rolls-Royce	Camargue	*Camargue . . . .*	1978	1978	1/43
3	Volkswagen	Coccinelle	*Beetle . . . .*	1979	1979	1/43

Série Sigma 500 / *Sigma 500 series*

1	Maserati	Boomerang.	*Boomerang. . . . .*	1978	1978	1/50
2	Lancia	Stratos Turbo Alitalia.	*Stratos Turbo Alitalia. . . . . .*	1978	1978	1/50
3	De Tomaso	Pantera	*Pantera . . . .*	1978	1978	1/50
4	Ferrari	BB 512	*BB 512 . . . .*	1979	1979	1/50
5	Toyota	Celica Turbo	*Celica Turco . . . .*	1979	1979	1/50
6	Porsche	935	*935 . . . .*	1977	1979	1/50

ATKINSON / AKORN □ GB

Matière / *Material:* Plastique thermo-formé / *Vacuum-formed plastic*

	Chaparral	2F	*2F . . . .*	1967	1/43	1/43
	Porsche	908, longue queue.	*908, long tail . . . .*	1968	1/43	1/43
	Ford	3 l, Alan Mann, prototype. . . .	*3 l., Alan Mann, prototype . . .*	1968	—	1/43
	ERA	GP	*Grand Prix . . . .*	1936	—	1/43
	Brabham	Ford BT 33, Formule 1	*Ford BT 33, Formula 1 . . . . .*	—	—	1/43
	Morgan	+4, hardtop, Le Mans (existe en tourisme)	*+4 hardtop, Le Mans (also street version) . . . .*	1962	—	1/43
	Lotus	Elite, Le Mans	*Elite, Le Mans . . . .*	1952	—	1/43
	Morgan	3 roues	*Three-wheeler . . . .*	—	—	1/43
	Lotus	«Wedge», Formule Ford	*"Wedge", Formula Ford . . . .*	1970	—	1/43
	Ferrari	P5 Pininfarina	*P5 Pininfarina . . . .*	—	—	1/43
	Chaparral	2G	*2G . . . .*	—	—	1/43
	Chaparral	2H	*2H . . . .*	—	—	1/43
	Porsche	917, queue courte	*917, short tail. . . . .*	1969	—	1/43

AURORA □ USA

Matière / *Material:* Plastique / *Plastic*

151	Rambler	Modèle E touring	*Model E touring. . . . .*	1903	1975	1/16
152	Oldsmobile	Curved Dash runabout	*Curved Dash runabout . . . . .*	1904	1975	1/16
153	Buick	Modèle 14 roadster	*Model 14 roadster. . . . . . .*	1911	1975	1/16
154	Stanley Steamer	Modèle E2 runabout	*Model E2 runabout . . . . . .*	1909	1975	1/16
155	Mercer	35J raceabout	*35J raceabout . . . .*	1913	1975	1/16
156	Stutz	Bearcat	*Bearcat . . . .*	1914	1975	1/16
486		Batmobile (vedette série TV) . .	*Batmobile (TV show car) . . . .*	1966	1966	1/32
489	Green Hornet	Black Beauty (vedette série TV)	*Black Beauty (TV show car). . .*	1966	1967	1/32
506	Chevrolet	Corvair Monza GT (prototype Chevrolet)	*Corvair Monza GT (Chevrolet prototype) . . . .*	1964	1965	1/32
507	Ford	Modèle T roadster «Sad Sack». .	*Model T roadster "Sad Sack" . .*	1927	1963	1/32
508	Ford	Modèle A camionnette «Wolf Wagon»	*Model A pickup "Wolf Wagon"*	1929	1963	1/32

Référence du fabricant *Manufacturer's Reference*	Désignation *Designation*	Type	*Type*	Date de la voiture *Date of car*	Date du modèle *Date of model*	Echelle *Scale*
509	Ford	Coupé 3 glaces «Hot Ram Rod»	*Three window coupé "Hot Ram Rod"*	1932	1963	1/32
510	Alfa Romeo	2600	*2600*	1963	1963	1/32
511	MG	TD	*TD*	1951	1959	1/32
512	Jaguar	XK-120	*XK-120*	1953	1959	1/32
513	Ferrari	342 America	*342 America*	1949	1959	1/32
514	Ferrari	Sportster	*Sportster*	1949	1959	1/32
515	Cunningham	Sportster	*Sportster*	1950	1959	1/32
516	Austin-Healey	A 100 Six	*A 100 Six*	1958	1960	1/32
517	Mercedes-Benz	300 SL roadster	*300 SL roadster*	1956	1960	1/32
518	Triumph	TR 3 A	*TR 3 A*	1958	1960	1/32
519	Chevrolet	Corvette	*Corvette*	1961	1963	1/32
520	Ford	Thunderbird	*Thunderbird*	1960	1963	1/32
521	Monroe Special	Indianapolis Special	*Indianapolis Special*	1920	1959	1/30
522	Murphy Special	Indianapolis Special	*Indianapolis Special*	1922	1959	1/30
523	Miller	Bowes Seal Fast Special (voiture de course Indianapolis)	*Bowes Seal Fast Special (Indy racer)*	1932	1959	1/30
524	Gilmore Special	Indianapolis Special	*Indianapolis Special*	1935	1959	1/30
525	Maserati	Voiture de course Indianapolis	*Indianapolis racer*	1940	1959	1/30
526		«Fuel injection» voiture de course Indianapolis	*Fuel injection Indianapolis racer*	1953	1959	1/30
527	Ford	Modèle T coupé «T for Two»	*Model T coupé "T for Two"*	1927	1963	1/32
528	Ford	Modèle T roadster camionnette «Shiftin Drifter»	*Model T roadster pickup "Shiftin Drifter"*	1927	1963	1/32
529	Ford	Modèle A camionnette «Beatnik Box»	*Model A pickup "Beatnik Box"*	1929	1963	1/32
530		«Hot Rod» remorque show	*"Hot Rod" show trailer*	—	1963	1/32
531	Pontiac	«Fireball» décapotable, moteur électrique	*"Fireball" convertible, electric drive*	1959	1961	1/25
532	Ford	Roadster «Hot Rod», moteur électrique	*Roadster "Hot Rod", electric drive*	1932	1962	1/25
533	Jaguar	XK-E coupé	*XK-E coupé*	1961	1963	1/32
534	Ford	Roadster Rolls «Scat Cat» (calandre Rolls-Royce)	*Roadster Rolls "Scat Cat" (Rolls grille)*	1932	1964	1/32
535	Ford	Modèle T roadster «Spyder» dragster	*Model T roadster "Spyder" dragster*	1925	1964	1/32
536	Ford	Modèle T camionnette «The Charger»	*Model T C cab pickup "The Charger"*	1925	1964	1/32
537	Chevrolet	Roadster «Moody Monster»	*Roadster "Moody Monster"*	1928	1964	1/32
538	Triumph	Spitfire	*Spitfire*	1963	1964	1/32
539	Porsche	1200 Carrera	*1200 Carrera*	1958	1964	1/32
540	Ford	Mustang décapotable	*Mustang convertible*	1964	1965	1/32
541	MG	TD «Bullet Custom»	*TD "Bullet Custom"*	1951	1961	1/32
542	Jaguar	XK120 «Hellcat Custom»	*XK120 "Hellcat Custom"*	1953	1961	1/32
543	Ferrari	Sportster «Tiger Shark Custom»	*Sportster "Tiger Shark Custom"*	1949	1961	1/32
544	Cunningham	Sportster «Phantom Custom»	*Sportster "Phantom Custom"*	1950	1961	1/32
545	Mercedes-Benz	300 SL roadster «Lightning Custom»	*300 SL roadster "Lighting Custom"*	1956	1963	1/32
546	Triumph	TR 3 A «Wildcat Custom»	*TR 3 A "Wildcat Custom"*	1958	1963	1/32
547	Chevrolet	Corvette «Astrovette Custom»	*Corvette "Astrovette Custom"*	1961	1963	1/32
548	Ford	Thunderbird décapotable «Thunderhawk Custom»	*Thunderbird convertible "Thunderhawk Custom"*	1960	1963	1/32
549	Alfa Romeo	2600 «Ramjet Custom»	*2600 "Ramjet Custom"*	1963	1964	1/32
550	Austin-Healey	A 100 Six «Sonic I Custom»	*A 100 Six "Sonic I Custom"*	1958	1964	1/32
551	Ford	Modèle A touring «Hot Rod Touring Car»	*Model A touring "Hot Rod Touring Car"*	1929	1965	1/32
552	Ford	Modèle A camionnette «Surf Buggy»	*Model A roadster pickup "Surf Buggy"*	1930	1965	1/32
553	La Salle	Corbillard «Hearse With A Curse»	*Hearse "Hearse With A Curse"*	1938	1965	1/32
554	Ford	Conduite intérieure «32 Skid Doo»	*Sedan "32 Skid Doo"*	1932	1964	1/32
555	Chevrolet	Camionnette «Draggin Wagon»	*Pickup "Draggin Wagon"*	1963	1964	1/32
556	Buick	Touring «Get A Way»	*Touring "Get A Way"*	1924	1964	1/32
557	Ford	Conduite intérieure «Hi-Stepper»	*Sedan "Hi-Stepper"*	1922	1965	1/32
558	Ford	«Woodin Wagon»	*"Woodin Wagon"*	1930	1965	1/32
559	Ford	GT	*GT*	1964	1965	1/32
560	Studebaker	Avanti coupé	*Avanti coupé*	1963	1964	1/25
561	Porsche	904 GT coupé	*904 GT coupé*	1965	1966	1/25
562	Aston Martin	DB 4 coupé	*DB 4 coupé*	1964	1965	1/25
563	Ferrari	GTO Berlinetta coupé	*GTO Berlinetta coupé*	1962	1964	1/25

Référence du fabricant / *Manufacturer's Reference*	Désignation / *Designation*	Type	*Type*	Date de la voiture / *Date of car*	Date du modèle / *Date of model*	Echelle / *Scale*
564	Maserati	3500 GT coupé	*3500 GT coupé*	1963	1964	1/25
565	Pontiac	Décapotable «Fireball»	*Convertible "Fireball"*	1959	1961	1/25
566	Jaguar	XK-E coupé	*XK-E coupé*	1961	1962	1/25
567	Jaguar	XK-E décapotable (avec hardtop)	*XK-E convertible (with hardtop)*	1961	1963	1/25
568	Ford	Roadster + dragster	*Roadster + dragster*	1922	1963	1/25
569	Ford	Coupé + coupé Hot Rod	*Coupé + coupé Hot Rod*	1934	1963	1/25
570	Carl Casper	Undertaker dragster	*Undertaker rail dragster.*	—	1963	1/25
570	Carl Casper	Undertaker dragster	*Undertaker rail dragster.*	—	1971	1/25
571	Stutz	Bearcat	*Bearcat*	1914	1961	1/16
572	Mercer	35J raceabout	*35J raceabout*	1913	1961	1/16
573	Stanley Steamer	Modèle E2 runabout	*Model E2 runabout*	1909	1961	1/16
574	Buick	Modèle 14 roadster (Bug)	*Model 14 roadster (Bug)*	1911	1963	1/16
575	Rambler	Modèle E touring	*Model E touring.*	1903	1963	1/16
576	Oldsmobile	Curved Dash runabout	*Curved Dash runabout*	1904	1963	1/16
577	Jaguar	XK-E coupé «Spitfire» (série Battle Aces)	*XK-E coupé "Spitfire" (Battle Aces series)*	1961	1971	1/25
578	Porsche	904 GT coupé «Messerschmidt» (série Battle Aces)	*904 GT coupé "Messerschmidt" (Battle Aces series)*	1965	1971	1/25
579	Ferrari	GTO Berlinetta «Scorpion» (série Battle Aces)	*GTO Berlinetta "Scorpion" (Battle Aces series)*	1962	1971	1/25
580	Ford	GT «Flying Tiger» (série Battle Aces)	*GT "Flying Tiger" (Battle Aces series)*	1965	1971	1/25
581	Chaparral	II «Lightning» (série Battle Aces)	*II "Lightning" (Battle Aces series)*	1964	1971	1/25
582		Archie's Car (personnage bande dessinée)	*Archie's Car (cartoon character)*	—	1969	1/25
583	Mercury	Station-wagon «Mod Squad» (vedette série TV)	*Woody wagon "Mod Squad" (TV show car)*	1949	1970	1/25
584	Chaparral	II	*II*	1964	1966	1/25
585	Aston Martin	DB 5 «James Bond» (vedette film)	*DB 5 "James Bond" (movie car)*	1964	1966	1/25
591	Ford	Modèle T conduite intérieure «Dropout Bus»	*Model T sedan "Dropout Bus"*	1927	1970	1/32
592	Ford	Conduite intérieure «Peppermint Fuzz»	*Sedan "Peppermint Fuzz"*	1932	1970	1/32
593	Ford	Station-wagon «Boob Tube»	*Woody wagon "Boob Tube"*	1930	1970	1/32
594	Ford	Modéle A phaéton «Blackbeards Tub»	*Model A phaeton "Blackbeards Tub"*	1929	1970	1/32
595		Voiture blindée «Butterfly Chaser»	*Armored car "Butterly Chaser".*	—	1971	1/32
596	Ford	Modèle A camionnette «The Wurst».	*Model A pickup "The Wurst"*	1930	1970	1/32
597	Ford	Modèle T camionnette «Tepee T»	*Model T C cab pickup "Tepee T"*	1925	1970	1/32
599	American La France	Voiture de pompiers	*Fire engine*	—	1964	1/32
599	American La France	Voiture de pompiers	*Fire engine*	—	1971	1/32
601	Sunbeam	Tiger	*Tiger*	1964	1965	1/32
602	Chevrolet	Corvair Monza SS décapotable (prototype de la GM)	*Corvair Monza SS convertible (GM prototype)*	1964	1965	1/32
603	Ford	Modèle T coupé «Snap Dragin»	*Model T coupé "Snap Dragin"*	1927	1966	1/32
620		Buggy (ancien Baja Boot)	*Dune buggy (old Baja Boot)*	—	1976	1/32
621	Ford	Conduite intérieure (hors série)	*Sedan (custom).*	1932	1976	1/32
622	Ford	Modèle T conduite intérieure (hors série)	*Model T sedan (custom)*	1922	1976	1/32
623	Ford	Modèle T dragster	*Model T dragster*	—	1976	1/32
624	Buick	Touring	*Touring*	1924	1976	1/32
625	Ford	Camionnette (hors série)	*Pickup roadster (custom).*	1932	1976	1/32
626	Ford	Modèle T coupé (hors série)	*Model T coupé (custom)*	1921	1977	1/32
627	Chevrolet	Roadster (hors série).	*Roadster (custom)*	1928	1977	1/32
628	Ford	Modèle A Woody (hors série)	*Model A Woody (custom)*	1929	1977	1/32
629	Ford	Modèle T camionnette (hors série)	*Model T C cab pickup (custom)*	1925	1977	1/32
662	Packard	Ambulance «Meat Wagon»	*Ambulance "Meat Wagon"*	1937	1965	1/32
663		Voiture blindée	*Armored car*	—	1965	1/32
664	Pontiac	GTO hardtop...	*GTO hardtop...*	1965	1965	1/32
665	Ford	Mustang fastback	*Mustang fastback*	1965	1965	1/32
666	Chevrolet	Corvair Corsa hardtop	*Corvair Corsa hardtop*	1965	1967	1/32
667	Plymouth	Barracuda fastback	*Barracuda fastback*	1966	1967	1/32
668	Chaparral	II	*II*	1964	1966	1/32
669	Cobra	GT coupé (Daytona).	*GT coupé (Daytona).*	1964	1966	1/32
670	Mercury	Comet hardtop «Exterminator»	*Comet hardtop "Exterminator".*	1966	1967	1/32

Référence du fabricant *Manufacturer's Reference*	Désignation *Designation*	Type	*Type*	Date de la voiture *Date of car*	Date du modèle *Date of model*	Echelle *Scale*
671	Lola-Ford	Zerex spécial	*Zerex special*	1964	1966	1/32
672	BRM	Rover coupé	*Rover coupé*	—	1968	1/32
673	Ford	«Demolition Derby»	*"Demolition Derby"*	1956	1966	1/32
674	Fiat-Abarth	1000 décapotable	*1000 convertible*	1965	1966	1/32
675	Chevrolet	Monza SS décapotable (prototype de la GM)	*Monza SS convertible (GM prototype)*	1965	1967	1/32
677	Chevrolet	Mako Shark (prototype de la GM)	*Mako Shark (GM prototype)*	—	1968	1/32
680	Plymouth	Barracuda fastback «Hemi Under Glass»	*Barracuda fastback "Hemi Under Glass"*	1966	1967	1/32
681	Hurst	Baja Boot buggy	*Baja Boot dune buggy*	—	1970	1/32
681		Citerne lait 22 000 litres (1950)	*5000 gallon milk tanker (1950s)*	—	—	—
682		Citerne 22 000 litres (1950)	*5000 gallon road tanker (1950s)*	—	—	—
683		Semi-remorque avec pelle mécanique (1950)	*Semi-trailer with mechanical shovel (1950s)*	—	—	—
684		Fourgon semi-remorque (1950)	*Semi-trailer van (1950s)*	—	—	—
828		Chitty Chitty Bang Bang (voiture vedette de film)	*Chitty Chitty Bang Bang (movie car)*	—	1969	1/25
832L		The Banana Splits Banana buggy (série TV)	*The Banana Splits Banana buggy (TV show)*	—	—	1/25

Maquettes série Racing Scenes / *Racing Scenes kits*

Référence du fabricant	Désignation	Type	*Type*	Date de la voiture	Date du modèle	Echelle
841		Pilotes voitures fantaisie (2)	*Funny car drivers (two figures)*	—	1974	1/16
842		Mécaniciens, outils, caisse à outils	*Mechanic & tools & tool box*	—	1974	1/16
843	Donovan	Moteur suralimenté de 6,8 l	*417 blown engine*	—	1974	1/16
844	Chrysler	«392» moteur à injection	*"392" fuel injected engine*	—	1974	1/16
845	Chevrolet	Carrosserie Vega fantaisie	*Vega funny car body*	—	1974	1/16
846	Ford	Carrosserie Pinto fantaisie	*Pinto funny car body*	—	1974	1/16
847		Châssis voiture fantaisie	*Funny car chassis*	—	1974	1/16
848		Garage	*Garage*	—	1974	1/16
851	Chevrolet	Vega fantaisie (moteur Donovan)	*Vega funny car (Donovan engine)*	—	1975	1/16
852	Ford	Pinto fantaisie (moteur Donovan)	*Pinto funny car (Donovan engine)*	—	1975	1/16

Modèles série Cigarbox (boîte à cigares) / *Cigarbox models series*
Avec châssis en métal injecté / *With diecast metal chassis*

Référence du fabricant	Désignation	Type	*Type*	Date de la voiture	Date du modèle	Echelle
6101	Chevrolet	Corvette Sting Ray coupé	*Corvette Sting Ray coupé*	1963	1968	HO
6102	Ferrari	Berlinetta GTO	*Berlinetta GTO*	1962	1968	HO
6103	Chevrolet	Mako Shark (voiture de rêve)	*Mako Shark (prototype show car)*	—	1968	HO
6104	Ford	«J»	*"J" car*	1965	1968	HO
6105	Ford	GT voiture de course	*GT racer*	—	1968	HO
6106	Lola	GT voiture de course	*GT racer*	—	1968	HO
6107	Ford	XL500	*XL500*	—	1968	HO
6108	Oldsmobile	Toronado	*Toronado*	—	1968	HO
6109	Buick	Riviera	*Riviera*	1963	1968	HO
6110	Ford	Thunderbird	*Thunderbird*	—	1968	HO
6111	Ferrari	Dino	*Dino*	—	1968	HO
6112	Porsche	904	*904*	—	1968	HO
6113	Ford	Cobra coupé (Daytona)	*Cobra coupé (Daytona)*	—	1968	HO
6114	Chaparral	II	*II*	—	1968	HO
6115	Chevrolet	Camaro	*Camaro*	1968	1968	HO
6116	Mercury	Cougar	*Cougar*	1968	1968	HO
6117	McLaren	Elva	*Elva*	—	1968	HO
6118	Ford	Mustang décapotable	*Mustang convertible*	—	1968	HO
6119		Buggy (Type Manx)	*Dune buggy (Manx type)*	—	1968	HO
6120	De Tomaso	Mangusta	*Mangusta*	—	1968	HO
6121	Ford	Voiture de course Lola Formule 1	*Lola Formula I racer*	—	1968	HO
6122	Ferrari	Voiture de course Formule 1	*Formula I racer*	—	1968	HO
6123	Cooper	Maserati Formule 1	*Maserati Formula I racer*	—	1968	HO
6124	Ford	Lotus Formule 1	*Lotus Formula I racer*	—	1968	HO
6125	Honda	Formule 1	*Formula I racer*	—	1968	HO
6126	BRM	Formula 1	*Formula I racer*	—	1968	HO
6127	Jaguar	XK-E coupé	*XK-E coupé*	—	1968	HO

Référence du fabricant *Manufacturer's Reference*	Désignation *Designation*	Type	*Type*	Date de la voiture *Date of car*	Date du modèle *Date of model*	Echelle *Scale*
6128	Ford	Mustang hardtop	*Mustang hardtop*	—	1968	HO
6129	Ford	Cobra roadster	*Cobra roadster*	1963	1968	HO
6130	Pontiac	Firebird	*Firebird*	—	1968	HO
6131	Willys	«Gasser» coupé	*"Gasser" coupé*	—	1968	HO
6137		Jeep	*Jeep*	—	1968	HO
6138		Bus	*Bus*	—	1968	HO
6143		Fourgonnette	*Panel truck*	—	1968	HO
6144	GMC	Tracteur	*Tractor.*	—	1968	HO
6145		Remorque fourgon	*Van trailer*	—	1968	HO
6146		Semi-remorque citerne	*Tank trailer*	—	1968	HO
6147		Semi-remorque pont plat	*Flatbed trailer*	—	1968	HO
6148		Camion-citerne	*Oil truck*	—	1968	HO
6149		Déménageuse	*Moving van*	—	1968	HO
6150	Ford	Camion pont à pieux	*Stake truck*	—	1968	HO
6153	Volkswagen	Conduite intérieure (Coccinelle)	*Sedan (Beetle)*	—	1968	HO

En 1968, Aurora lance sa série Speedline pour concurrencer celle de Mattel intitulée Hot Wheels. Des modèles de la série Cigarbox antérieure, dont certains ont été annoncés mais sans doute jamais commercialisés, sont désormais vendus comme modèles Speedline. Leur numéro de référence est composé des deux derniers chiffres du numéro des modèles Cigarbox précédés du chiffre 68.
In 1968, Aurora introduced the Speedline Series to counter the Mattel "Hot Wheels". Previous Cigarbox models (some of which had been announced but not released) were now released as Speedline Models, for which Aurora retained the last two digits of the Cigarbox model code, but prefaced it with a 68, as follows.

Référence du fabricant	Désignation	Type	*Type*	Date de la voiture	Date du modèle	Echelle
6801	Corvette	Sting Ray	*Sting Ray*	—	1968	HO
6802	Ferrari	Berlinetta	*Berlinetta*	—	1968	HO
6803	Chevrolet	Mako Shark	*Mako Shark*	—	1968	HO
6804	Ford	«J»	*"J" car*	—	1968	HO
6805	Ford	GT	*GT*	—	1968	HO
6806	Lola	GT	*GT*	—	1968	HO
6807	Ford	XL-500	*XL-500*	—	1968	HO
6810	Ford	Thunderbird	*Thunderbird*	—	1968	HO
6811	Ferrari	Dino	*Dino*	—	1968	HO
6812	Porsche	904	*904*	—	1968	HO
6813	Ford	Cobra Daytona coupé	*Cobra Daytona coupé*	—	1968	HO
6815	Chevrolet	Camaro	*Camaro*	—	1968	HO
6816	Mercury	Cougar	*Cougar*	—	1968	HO
6818	Ford	Mustang décapotable	*Mustang convertible*	—	1968	HO
6820	De Tomaso	Mangusta	*Mangusta*	—	1968	HO
6821	Lola Ford	Formule 1	*Formula I racer*	—	1969	HO
6822	Ferrari	Formule 1	*Formula I racer*	—	1969	HO
6823	Cooper	Maserati Formule 1	*Maserati Formula I racer*	—	1969	HO
6824	Lotus Ford	Formule 1	*Formula I racer*	—	1969	HO
6825	Honda	Formule 1	*Formula I racer*	—	1969	HO
6826	BRM	Formule 1	*Formula I racer*	—	1969	HO
6827	Jaguar	XK-E	*XK-E*	—	1968	HO
6828	Ford	Mustang hardtop	*Mustang hardtop*	—	1968	HO
6829	Ford	Cobra roadster	*Cobra roadster*	—	1968	HO
6830	Pontiac	Firebird	*Firebird*	—	1968	HO
6831	Willys	«Gasser»	*"Gasser"*	—	1968	HO
6833	Cheetah	Coupé	*Coupé*	—	1968	HO
6853	Volkswagen	Conduite intérieure	*Sedan*	—	1968	HO

Les modèles suivants constituent de véritables nouveautés dans la gamme Speedline. Les références 6857, 6858 et 6861 à 6865 ont été annoncées, mais jamais mises en vente.
The following releases were unique to Speedline Models. Numbers 6857, 6858 and 6861-6865 were announced but never released.

Référence du fabricant	Désignation	Type	*Type*	Date de la voiture	Date du modèle	Echelle
6835		Cheeta	*Cheeta.*	—	1969	HO
6854	Dodge	Charger	*Charger*	—	1969	HO
6855	Ford	Torino fastback	*Torino fastback*	—	1969	HO
6856	Alfa Romeo	Voiture de course	*Racer*	—	1969	HO

Les modèles des séries Cigarbox et Speedline ne sont pas exactement à l'échelle HO étant donné qu'ils dérivent des modèles de slot produits par Aurora dans la gamme Aurora Model Motoring.
Cigarbox and Speedline Models were not exact HO scale as most were based on the Aurora Model Motoring electric slot cars.

Référence du fabricant / *Manufacturer's Reference*	Désignation / *Designation*	Type	*Type*	Date de la voiture / *Date of car*	Date du modèle / *Date of model*	Echelle / *Scale*

Maquettes à construire en plastique Snap-A-Roos / *Snap-A-Roos, plastic kits*

Les Snap-A-Roos sont des modèles à assembler sans colle moulés en Australie et provenant de RL.
Snap-A-Roos are Australian-molded snap-together models from RL.

Réf.	Désignation	Type	*Type*	Date voiture	Date modèle	Echelle
9257	Série Old Time Cars / *Old Time Cars*					
	Bugatti	Grand Prix	*Grand Prix*	1926	1975	1/67
	Ford	Modèle T touring	*Model T touring*	1915	1975	1/81
	Morris	Oxford	*Oxford*	1913	1975	1/78
	Mercedes	Voiture de course	*Racer*	1904	1975	1/78
9258	Série Old Timers / *"Old Timers"*					
	Bentley			1927	1975	1/78
	Packard			1912	1975	1/108
	Sunbeam			1913	1975	1/56
	Oldsmobile	Curved dash	*Curved dash*	1901	1975	1/56
9259	Série Grand Prix Racers / *"Grand Prix Racers"*					
	Ferrari	Voiture de course	*Racer*	—	—	1/64
	Honda	Voiture de course	*Racer*	—	—	1/64
	BRM	Voiture de course	*Racer*	—	—	1/64
	Brabham	Voiture de course	*Racer*	—	—	1/64
9260	Série Heavy Movers (travaux publics) / *"Heavy Movers"*					
		Camion à pont plat	*Flat bed truck*	—	—	1/230
		Elévateur	*Fork lift*	—	—	1/72
		Transport de bois	*Timber transporter*	—	—	1/130
9261	Série Big Hooks / *"Big Hooks"*					
		Dépanneuse	*Tow truck*	—	—	1/87
	Jaguar	XK-E	*XK-E*	—	—	1/87
		Grue	*Construction crane*	—	—	1/150

AURORE MODELS — CH

Matière / *Material:* Résine / *Resin*

Désignation	Type	*Type*	Date voiture	Date modèle	Echelle
Porsche	Projet de Formule 1	*Formula 1 prototype*	1977	1977	1/43
BMW	3.20 Junior team	*3.20 Junior team*	1977	1977	1/43
Bugatti	57G tank, GP France	*57G tank, French GP*	1936	1977	1/43
Bugatti	T 50 Drophead coupé	*T 50 Drophead coupé*	1931	1978	1/43
Bugatti	T 57 S-TS torpédo sport	*T 57 S-TS torpedo sports*	1935	1978	1/43
Bugatti	T 57 Stelvio	*T 57 Stelvio*	1935	1978	1/43
Bugatti	T 41, 111 Royale «Binder»	*T 41, 111 Royale "Binder"*	1938	1979	1/43
Bugatti	T 41, 111 Royale «Esders»	*T 41, 111 Royale "Esders"*	1932	1979	1/43
Bugatti	T 41, 131 Royale «Park-Ward»	*T 41, 131 Royale "Park-Ward"*	1933	1979	1/43
Bugatti	T 41, 141 Royale «Kellner»	*T 41, 141 Royale "Kellner"*	1933	1978	1/43
Bugatti	T 57 Aérolithe Coupé Sport	*T 57 Aérolithe sports coupé*	1935	1979	1/43
Bugatti	T 59 Sport 4,7 l «50 B»	*T 59 sports, 4.7 l., "50 B"*	1938	1979	1/43
Bugatti	T 64, prototype	*T 64, prototype*	1939	1979	1/43
Bugatti	T 68 Coupé	*T 68, coupé*	1942	1979	1/43
Bugatti	T 73 A, prototype	*T 73 A, prototype*	1947	1979	1/43
Bugatti	T 59 sport, Roi des Belges	*T 59 sports, "Roi des Belges"*	1938	1980	1/43
Bugatti	T 30 Aéroprofilée	*T 30, Aeroprofilee*	1925	1980	1/43
Bugatti	T 52 «Baby» (en laiton)	*T 52 "Baby" (model in brass)*	1931	1980	1/43
Bugatti	T 57 S James Young	*T 57 S, James Young*	1936	1980	1/43
Bugatti	T 57 Ventaux, Gangloff	*T 57, Ventaux, Gangloff*	1937	1980	1/43
Bugatti	T 57 Gd Sport, «A. Derain»	*T 57 Gd sports, "A. Derain"*	1936	1980	1/43
Bugatti	T 59 3,8 l Gd Sport	*T 59 3.8 l. Gd sports*	1938	1981	1/43
Bugatti	T 57 Aravis cab. Gangloff	*T 57 Aravis cab. Gangloff*	1935	1981	1/43
Bugatti	T 57 S roadster Gangloff	*T 57 S roadster Gangloff*	1935	1981	1/43
Bugatti	T 35 C «E. Junek»	*T 35 C "E. Junek"*	1935	1981	1/43
Dodge	Cabriolet Langenthal	*Convertible, Langenthal*	1936	1981	1/43
Mercedes	200 Jaray	*200 Jaray*	1934	1978	1/43
Alfa Romeo	T 2900 B Coupé Pininfarina	*T 2900 B Pininfarina coupé*	1937	1979	1/43
Cadillac	Séville promotionnelle	*Seville, promotional*	1980	1980	1/43
Porsche	907, Sebring	*907, Sebring*	1968	1981	1/43
Du Pont	Dual Cowl Roadster	*Dual cowl roadster*	1931	1981	1/43
Phantom	Corsair	*Corsair*	1938	1981	1/43

Référence du fabricant / *Manufacturer's Reference*	Désignation / *Designation*	Type	*Type*	Date de la voiture / *Date of car*	Date du modèle / *Date of model*	Echelle / *Scale*

AUSTIN CRAFT □ USA

Matière / *Material:* Bois / *Wood*

	Jeep	US Army	*US Army*	—	—	—
		Remorque (pour Jeep)	*Trailer (for Jeep)*	—	—	—
		Camion US Army 1½ tonne	*US Army truck 1½ ton*	—	—	—
		Camion US Army 2½ tonnes	*US Army truck 2½ ton*	—	—	—

Les modèles ci-dessus sont de 1945 ou même antérieurs à cette date.
The above models are 1945 or older releases.

AUTHENTIC — USA

Matière / *Material:* Zamac / *Die cast*

101	Chevrolet	Camionnette	*Pickup truck*	—	—	1/64
102	Chevrolet	Camionnette camper	*Camper*	—	—	1/64
103	Chevrolet	Benne basculante	*Dump truck*	—	—	1/64
105	Chevrolet	Services industriels	*Utility truck*	—	—	1/64
107	Chevrolet	Camionnette avec caravane	*Custom camper*	—	—	1/64
108	Chevrolet	Fourgonnette	*Box van*	—	—	1/64

AUTO BUFF — USA

Matière / *Material:* *White metal*

AB 1	Ford	Camionnette pickup	*Pickup truck*	1953	1980	1/43
AB 2	Ford	Camionnette fermée	*Panel truck*	1953	1980	1/43
AB 3	Ford	Coupé	*Coupé*	1948	1980	1/43
AB 4	Ford	Décapotable, avec capote	*Convertible, top up*	1948	1980	1/43
AB 5	Ford	Décapotable, sans capote	*Convertible, top down*	1948	1980	1/43
AB 6	Ford	Camionnette pickup	*Pickup truck*	1940	1980	1/43
AB 7	Ford	Camionnette fermée de livraison	*Panel delivery truck*	1940	1980	1/43
AB 8	Ford	Coupé	*Coupé*	1940	1980	1/43
AB 9	Ford	Décapotable, sans capote	*Convertible, top down*	1940	1980	1/43
AB 10	Ford	Décapotable, avec capote	*Convertible, top up*	1940	1980	1/43
AB 11	Ford	2 portes	*Two-door sedan*	1940	1980	1/43
AB 12	Ford	Modèle A, coupé	*Model A, coupé*	1928	1980	1/43
AB 13	Ford	Modèle A, pickup roadster, sans capote	*Model A, pickup roadster, top down*	1928	1980	1/43
AB 14	Ford	Modèle A, pickup roadster, avec capote	*Model A, pickup roadster, top up*	1928	1980	1/43
AB 15	Ford	Modèle A, roadster, avec capote	*Model A, roadster, top up*	1928	1981	1/43
AB 16	Ford	Modèle A, de livraison, toit ouvert	*Model A, town panel delivery, open roof*	1928	1981	1/43
AB 17	Ford	Modèle A, camionnette à plateau	*Model A, stake bed truck*	1928	1981	1/43
AB 18	Ford	Camionnette à plateau	*Stake bed truck*	1953	1981	1/43
AB 19	Ford	Coupé	*Coupé*	1934	1981	1/43
AB 20	Ford	Roadster, sans capote	*Roadster, top down*	1934	1981	1/43
AB 21	Ford	Roadster, avec capote	*Roadster, top up*	1934	1981	1/43
AB 22	Ford	Coupé	*Coupé*	1936	1981	1/43
AB 23	Ford	Décapotable, sans capote	*Convertible, top down*	1936	1981	1/43
AB 24	Ford	Décapotable, avec capote	*Convertible, top up*	1936	1981	1/43
AB 25	Ford	Modèle A, «Auto Buff», camion	*Model A, "Auto Buff", hauler*	—	1981	1/43
AB 26	Ford	Camionnette pickup	*Pickup truck*	1947	1981	1/43
AB 27	Ford	Camionnette à plateau	*Stake truck*	1947	1981	1/43
AB 28	Ford	Crestliner	*Crestliner*	1950	1981	1/43
AB 29	Ford	Crestliner décapotable, sans capote	*Crestliner convertible, top down*	1950	1981	1/43
AB 30	Ford	Crestliner décapotable, avec capote	*Crestliner convertible, top up*	1950	1981	1/43
AB 31	Ford	Starliner	*Starliner*	1954	1981	1/43
AB 32	Ford	Starliner décapotable, sans capote	*Starliner convertible, top down*	1954	1981	1/43
AB 33	Ford	Starliner, décapotable, avec capote	*Starliner convertible, top up*	1954	1981	1/43
AB 34	Ford	Jeep de l'armée	*Army Jeep*	1942	1981	1/43
AB 35	Ford	Jeep de la Navy	*Navy Jeep*	1942	1981	1/43

Référence du fabricant / *Manufacturer's Reference*	Désignation / *Designation*	Type	*Type*	Date de la voiture / *Date of car*	Date du modèle / *Date of model*	Echelle / *Scale*

AUTODIN □ F

Matière / *Material:* Résine / *Resin*

	Matra	Simca 680 «Gitanes» Le Mans. .	*Simca 680 "Gitanes" Le Mans.* .	1974	1977	1/43

AUTO MINIS — GB

Matière / *Material:* *White metal*

1	Bentley	Type R, Continental	*R type, Continental*	1952	1981	1/43
2	Mercedes	450 SLC	*450 SLC*	1979	—	1/43

AUTO-REPLICAS □ GB

Matière / *Material:* *White metal*

1	ERA	Grand Prix	*Grand Prix*	1936	1972	1/43
2	Maserati	Grand Prix «8 C»	*"8 C" Grand Prix*	1934	1973	1/43
3	AC	Cobra 4,7 l	*Cobra 4.7 l*	1960	1973	1/43
4	Bugatti	Brescia	*Brescia*	1923	1973	1/43
5	Healey	Silverstone	*Silverstone*	1949/50	1973	1/43
6	MG	K3 Magnette	*K3 Magnette*	1934	1974	1/43
7	Morgan	Plus 8 roadster	*Plus 8 roadster*	1973/74	1974	1/43
8	Porsche	356 speedster.	*356 speedster.*	1955	1974	1/43
9	Tatra	«77 A», limousine	*"77 A", limousine*	1936	1974	1/43
10	Amilcar	. . . .	. . . .	1925	1974	1/43
11	Morgan	4+4.	*4+4*.	1974	1975	1/43
12	Amilcar	Châssis uniquement	*Frame only*	1925	1975	1/43
13	Ferrari	166 MM berlinette.	*166 MM berlinetta.*	1951	1975	1/43
14	Triumph	TR6	*TR6*	—	1975	1/43
15	Fiat	Abarth 850	*Abarth 850*	—	1975	1/43
16	Packard	12 cyl. roadster	*12 cyl. roadster*	1938	1976	1/43
17	Fergusson	F1 «P 99», quatre roues motrices	*F1 "P 99", four-wheel drive* . . .	—	1976	1/43
18	Lotus	Super Seven	*Super Seven*	—	1976	1/43
19	Fiat	124 Abarth spider	*124 Abarth spider*	—	1976	1/43
20	Bugatti	Type 23	*Type 23*	1926	1976	1/43
21	Renault	40 CV, voiture de record . . .	*40 CV, record car*	1926	1977	1/43
22	Allard	P1, berline	*P1, saloon*	—	1977	1/43
23	Bentley	Tourer.	*Tourer*.	1937	1977	1/43
24	Packard	Sedan	*Sedan*	1938	1978	1/43
25	Morgan	+4 coupé	*+4 coupé*	1950	1978	1/43
26	Bugatti	Type 23 Town Carriage.	*Type 23 Town Carriage.*	—	1978	1/43
27	Maserati	8 CM	*8 CM*	1933	1979	1/43
28	Citroën	GS break.	*GS break*.	—	1979	1/43
29	Alfa Romeo	8 C, Le Mans	*8 C, Le Mans*	1932	1979	1/43
30	Bugatti	Sport type 13 (LWB)	*Sport type 13 (LWB)*	1926	1980	1/43
31	Aston Martin	DB 2/4 coupé	*DB 2/4 coupé*	1954	1980	1/43
32a	Jaguar	Type C, Le Mans	*C type, Le Mans.*	195?	1980	1/43
32b	Jaguar	Type C, Le Mans	*C type, Le Mans.*	1953	1980	1/43
33a	Chevrolet	«Bel Air», ouverte	*"Bel Air", open*	1955	1981	1/43
33b	Chevrolet	«Bel Air», coupé	*"Bel Air", coupé.*	1955	1981	1/43
35	Alfa Romeo	8 C Castagna	*8 C Castagna*	1932	1981	1/43
1001	Bugatti	Type 34	*Type 34*	—	1978	1/24
1002	Frazer-Nash	TT Replica	*TT Replica*	1933	1978	1/24

AUTOSTYLE □ I

Matière / *Material:* *White metal*

1	Ferrari	Dino	*Dino*	—	1975	1/43
2a	Ferrari	«512» NART	*"512" NART*	—	1976	1/43
2b	Ferrari	«512» Francorchamps (jaune). .	*"512" Francorchamps (yellow)*	—	1976	1/43
2uff	Ferrari	«512» officielle	*"512" works car.*	—	1976	1/43
3	Ferrari	California	*California*	—	1975	1/43
4	Alfa Romeo	Disco Volante.	*Disco Volante.*	—	1976	1/43
5	Maserati	Eldorado, Indianapolis	*Eldorado, Indianapolis*	—	1977	1/43
5a	Maserati	Eldorado, Monza	*Eldorado, Monza*	—	1977	1/43
6	Fiat	509 SM	*509 SM*	—	1978	1/43
7	Lancia	Astura, compétition	*Astura, racing car*	—	1979	1/43
7a	Lancia	Astura, civile	*Astura, road car*	—	1979	1/43

Photographic acknowledgements

9: Horst Neuffer □ 11: Grand Prix Models, Horst Neuffer □ 12: Horst Neuffer □ 13: Eric de Ville □ 14: Revell Inc. □ 15: J.-C. Piffret, CAR □ 16: Horst Neuffer □ 17: Horst Neuffer □ 18: Testor □ 19: MPC □ 20: Kojima □ 21: Horst Neuffer □ 22: Ertl, MPC, Revell Inc., Revell Inc. □ 23: Scale Racing Cars, F. Hronik, J.-C. Piffret, J.-C. Piffret □ 24: Monogram □ 25: Monogram, Monogram, Revell Inc. □ 26: Ertl, Monogram □ 27: Newcon, Western Models □ 28: Italeri, Revell Inc., AMT, Monogram □ 29: J. Hiramatsu □ 30-31: Horst Neuffer □ 32: FDS, Tron □ 33: Horst Neuffer, Somerville, Horst Neuffer □ 34: Eric de Ville, J.-C. Piffret, J.-C. Piffret □ 35: Horst Neuffer, Michele Conti □ 36: Brooklin Models, Monogram □ 37: Tamiya, Monogram, Revell Inc., Revell Inc., Revell Inc. □ 38: Horst Neuffer □ 39: Record, Aurore Models □ 40: Horst Neuffer □ 41: Horst Neuffer □ 42: Grand Prix Models, Eric de Ville, Eric de Ville, Eric de Ville □ 43: Italeri, Horst Neuffer □ 44: Eric de Ville, Horst Neuffer, Eric de Ville □ 45: Eric de Ville □ 46: FDS, AMT □ 48: Tomy □ 49: Yonezawa □ 50: Eric de Ville □ 51: Precision Miniatures, Eric de Ville, Eric de Ville □ 52: Horst Neuffer □ 53: Eric de Ville □ 54: J.-C. Piffret, Nichimo, Nichimo, Nichimo □ 55: Tamiya □ 56: Revell Inc. □ 58: Tamiya, Revell Inc., Tamiya □ 59: Nichimo □ 60: Fujimi, Horst Neuffer □ 61: Tamiya □ 62: Tsukuda □ 63: Horst Neuffer □ 64: Tamiya □ 65: Tamiya, Horst Neuffer □ 66: Revell Inc., Horst Neuffer □ 67: Horst Neuffer □ 68: Horst Neuffer □ 85-94: Centro Storico Fiat □ 96: Dennis Doty □ 97: Dennis Doty □ 98: Dennis Doty □ 99:Dennis Doty □ 100: Eric de Ville □ (102: Eric de Ville) □ 103: Dennis Doty, Eric de Ville, Eric de Ville, Eric de Ville □ 104: Eric de Ville □ 105: Eric de Ville □ 106: J.-M. Roulet □ 107: Eric de Ville □ 108: Eric de Ville □ 109: Eric de Ville □ 110: Eric de Ville □ 111: Eric de Ville □ 112: Eric de Ville □ 113: Eric de Ville □ 114: Eric de Ville □ 115: Eric de Ville, Eric de Ville, J.-M. Roulet □ 117: Audi □ 118-119: Horst Neuffer □ 120: Audi □ 121: Nitto □ 122-123: Horst Neuffer □ 124: Nitto □ 125: Don Shenk □ 126-127: Don Shenk □ 128: Don Shenk □ 129: François Verlinden □ 130: François Verlinden □ 131: François Verlinden, Daimler-Benz □ 132: Daimler-Benz □ 133-140: Adriano Heitmann □ 142: Eric de Ville □ 143: Eric de Ville, Paasche, Eric de Ville □ 144: Eric de Ville □ 145: Eric de Ville □ 146: Eric de Ville.

Published by Edita SA, Lausanne, Switzerland
Photolithography by Actual, Biel, Switzerland
Printed by Imprimeries Réunies SA, Lausanne, Switzerland
Bound by Maurice Busenhart SA, Lausanne, Switzerland

Printed in Switzerland